Refiguring American Film Genres

Refiguring American Film Genres

History and Theory

Nick Browne, Editor

UNIVERSITY OF CALIFORNIA PRESS

Berkeley / Los Angeles / London

University of California Press
Berkeley and Los Angeles, California

University of California Press, Ltd.
London, England

© 1998 by
The Regents of the University of California

Library of Congress Cataloging-in-Publication Data

Refiguring American film genres : history and theory / Nick Browne,
    editor
        p. cm.
    Includes bibliographical references and index.
    ISBN 0-520-20730-0 (alk. paper). — ISBN 0-520-20731-9 (alk.
paper)
        I. Film genres—United States.   I. Browne, Nick.
PN1993.5.U6R443   1998   97-42091
791.43′6—dc21   CIP

Printed in the United States of America
9 8 7 6 5 4 3 2 1

The paper used in this publication meets the minimum requirements of
American National Standard for Information Sciences—Permanence of
Paper for Printed Library Materials, ANSI Z39.48–1984.

Contents

Illustrations

Acknowledgments

This book grew out of discussions among contributors at a residential seminar entitled "American Film Genres" convened by Nick Browne, sponsored by the University of California Humanities Research Institute, and held at the Irvine campus in the fall of 1992. The graciousness of Professor Mark Rose, director, and the effective support of the Institute staff made this event singular and memorable. The current director Pat O'Brian provided funds for typing, indexing, and photographs. William Murphy oversaw the process at the Press. Kristin Hatch of UCLA facilitated the completion of the manuscript. We regret that it was not possible to include Nita Rollins's lengthy and remarkable contribution, "Cinaesthetic Wonderings," in this volume.

Preface

Nick Browne

Reflection on film genres has generally assumed the possibility of a "system" of genres through a critical gesture that sought to identify the classical Hollywood cinema with a set of discrete, self-evident, and constellated categories. Within the complex network of aesthetic and thematic resemblances evident in any large body of films, this approach typically identified a clear dominant across time and studio by asserting or assuming an internal, genetic finality. The structuralist project of the 1970s carried forward and defined this tendency by identifying genres with distinctive patterns of narrative order and visual iconography. Regulation (by establishing norms), classification (by constructing typologies), and explanation (by providing formal description) were the hallmarks of this era.

The essays presented here show that the approach today toward the theory and criticism of film genre is the reverse field of the formalist and structuralist undertaking. The implicit, ideal order of the structuralist system of genre has dissolved. This volume marks a range of distinctive styles of cultural and historical interpretation of the form and meaning of film genres. Genres, here, are understood to gravitate toward specific assemblages of local coherencies—discrete, heterotopic instances of a complex cultural politics. The operations of particular genres are pictured as working through the history of cinema at different levels and angles to other genres and other social institutions—public entertainments and arts, of course, but also nonaesthetic social sectors including religion, law, war, civil rights, medicine, and diplomacy. We can observe in the work presented here an adjustment of the theory and interpretation of film genre to a broader and more dynamic understanding of the function of popular culture in American society. Notwithstanding what appears as the displacement of the traditional topics of the poetics of genre, the reader may find across these essays three principal preoccupations.

First, these essays revise the critical foundations of genre theory by examining and reformulating the presuppositions by which genres are thought to be designated, constructed, and employed. These displacements occur variously by means of mode (Williams), theme (Braudy), and chronotope (Sobchack). Linda Williams's assertion of the foundational status of melodrama amounts to a statement of a new ontology of cinematic form and signification by marking out an absolute reference point prior to "realism" for the consideration of any genre treatment. Likewise, Leo Braudy's formulation of the place of nature as a periodically reinstated transgeneric theme informing and mobilized by a wide range of generic preoccupations is posed as a ritualistic understanding of generic order. Vivian Sobchack presents an alternative to a traditional critical analysis of genre conventions through the identification and interpretation of the chronotope, the historically specific discursive form that condenses the major affective features of an era with its imaginative representation. The contrast between, on the one hand, the mode and the theme as repetitive transhistorical and transgeneric instances of the order of genre with, on the other, the contingent historical valences associated with the chronotope opens a new space for an understanding of the historicity of genre formations.

Second, these essays develop new perspectives on the history and historicity of film genres. This inquiry takes place in three principal ways: analyses of the constitution of particular film genres; analyses of the alteration or mutation of received genre forms by incorporation of specific historical materials made necessary by novel historical situations; and analyses of the industrial life cycle of a genre though commodification and of the changing cultural politics of genre criticism.

Do genres terminate? Are new ones recognizable? The "trial movie," with its inherent theatricality and conventions of narrative focalization and address to the audience, is presented by Carol J. Clover as a living, open-ended cultural form whose subject matter—the ambiguities of the administration of justice—displays the democratic foundations of genre appeal that date back to the first days of cinema. In contrast, the cycle of World War II combat films is a special case of adaptation of stars and conventions of existing genres to historical imperatives and their abrupt termination. Thomas Schatz shows how in the space of a few years war themes were first integrated into peacetime forms, progressively rethought in terms of style and tone, and then rapidly demobilized with the end of the circumstances that gave them form. He presents an unusually compressed instance of the adaptation of topics of historical urgency to long-standing fictional formats. Michael Rogin shows how and in the name of what interests the "New Deal genre," the blackface musical, amalgamated with the "social problem film" in the period from the 1930s to the 1950s. Rogin argues that the evolution of the social problem film was embedded in the effort to recognize, stage, and mask the performative qualities of American identity. Interests in cultural assimilation linked Jewish Americans and African Americans cinematically and informed the specific historical moment of generic synthesis. For George Lipsitz, genres and their supporting stereotypes are a codification and dissemination of a racial ideology and, under particular historical circumstances, are distressed by cultural anxieties. Thus Lipsitz reads the reinscription of an African American presence across a range of genres in the 1970s as both undercutting and revising genre presuppositions, a reinscription that was used to justify retrenchment and repression of emergent civil interests. Generic disfiguration of racial imagery reflects the transitional cultural politics associated with the nation's effort to adjust to the economic reality of widespread deindustrialization.

The third nodal point in the crisscrossing of preoccupations evident in these essays is the reformulation of the question of the logic of internal relations among genres. Here, genre is, tacitly, a loose assemblage of cultural forms shaped by social conflict and historical vicissitude. In this regard, the book's understanding of genre as cultural pattern belongs more to Wittgenstein than to Kant. Generic change in several of these essays is figured as a process in which constituencies seek, assert, control, or oppose popular representation. Genrification of social interests means emergent social dramas and traditional generic configurations are bound to clash.

The cultural logic of generic exchange, reference, and contestation is thoroughly historical and includes a range of strategic operations. In these essays, melodrama seeks to drive out realism; noir inverts and excludes melodrama; the social problem film borrows from the musical; the trial film calls on melodrama; the horror film supplies a range of adaptable social references; and comedy, melodrama, and documentary draw upon the transgeneric themes of war and nature. As the product of an industrial and cultural process, genre offers a range of opportunities for historical transvaluation. David Russell argues that the horror genre is best characterized by the cultural instability of the ontology of

its central figure. Rick Altman's essay presents a fundamental, new perspective on the processes of commodification of genre forms. In his
analysis of the dynamics of genre change, melodrama moved from an
action designation to a sentimental mode and through the cultural politics of gender to a self-assertive vehicle for film feminism. The result of
these multiple contestations is that new genre theory has challenged
"natural selection" as its model and gravitated, implicitly, toward the
model of maps with temporary and contested borders. Like the forms
of the films themselves, the assignment of genre names and the mobile
relations among them can be understood as historically contingent, culturally overdetermined outcomes.

By traversing the history of American film, these essays in cultural criticism indicate both the local contours and general circumstances associated with the historicization of film genres as cultural forms. Film genres
appear here as repetitive, contested sites for stagings of a distinctive
form of cultural capital, "the movies," that in networks with other social
institutions reproduce, revise, and redistribute broadly held views of
American life.

Reusable Packaging

Generic Products and the Recycling Process

RICK ALTMAN

Prior to the mid-twentieth century, discussions of genre almost always invoked historical precedents. Indeed, the late-Renaissance rise of generic consciousness was specifically predicated on a revival of the genres of classical Greece and Rome: comedy, tragedy, satire, ode, epic, and the like. Even the anti-genre romantics could not escape the tyranny of genre history as they sought to destroy generic specificity and with it the weight of the past. When science provided a model of apparently stable biological species permanently separated by reproductive incompatibility, the concept of biological evolution—immediately adapted to social and literary categories—quickly reestablished the traditional link between generic thinking and historical observation. In a turn-of-the-century world dominated by Ferdinand Brunetière's *Evolution of Genres*, there could be no question of genres existing outside of history.

Half a century later, however, under the influence of Jungian psychology and structural anthropology, genres found themselves in new company. Instead of being read in the context of Horace and Boileau, they found themselves surrounded by pagan rituals, native ceremonies, undated traditional texts, and descriptions of human nature. No longer was attention concentrated on the appearance, transformation, combination, and disappearance of genres, and thus on new, modified, or vanishing genres, but on generic permanence and in particular on genres that might justify the claim that genres are in fact permanent. With Northrop Frye identifying genres as embodiments of myth and Sheldon Sacks connecting genres to stable characteristics of the human mind, it is hardly surprising that a generation of film critics should have considered film genres as nothing more than the latest incarnation of broader, older, more permanent generic structures. Although, following John Cawelti and his culture-specific notion of formula fiction, critics have seen Hollywood genres as specifically American, they nevertheless happily attribute to film genres a distinguished ancestry including Greek comedies, western novels, stage melodramas, and Viennese operettas.

Not surprisingly, the myth-oriented rediscovery of genre criticism during the third quarter of this century has seriously jeopardized our ability to think of genres as anything other than the stable manifestations of more or less permanent fundamental human (or American) concerns. In one sense, this is only reasonable, because the prestige associated with the term *genre* over the past few decades derives from our belief that the notion of genre, like Alice's rabbit hole, provides a magic connector between this fallen world and the more satisfying, more permanent realm of archetype and myth. Once filled by prayer, the role of mediating between humankind and the eternal has now fallen to genre. In short, we must see genres as stable if they are to do the work we require of them. In laying so much emphasis on generic fixity—necessary for access to the benefits of archetypal criticism—two generations of genre critics have done violence to the historical dimensions of genre. Stressing the apparently representative straight stretches of the mighty genre river rather than its tortuous tributaries, its riverbed-defying floods, or its tidewater-dominated estuary, recent genre theory has devoted too little attention to the logic and mechanisms whereby genres become recognizable as such. This essay offers a corrective to that tendency.

In the recent past, all genre study began with the questions of permanence and coherence: What do these texts have in common? What shared structures permit them to make more meaning as a genre than the sum of their meanings as individual texts? What forces explain, and what patterns reveal, generic longevity? Here, however, I look instead at problems of transience and dissemination: How is it that some structures fail to achieve generic recognition? What changes are required for others to be constituted as genres? If genres are the temporal reflection of transhistorical values, what explains the regular conflicts regarding their definition, extent, and function? Traditionally, by stressing coincident structures and concerns, genre criticism has labored mightily to conceal or conquer difference and disagreement; the principle observed here instead foregrounds discrepancies in order to explain what makes difference possible. Only when we know how difference is spawned in the apparently universal generic context will we be in a position to arbitrate the many border disputes growing out of genre's role as a representative of permanence in a world of change.

Adjectives and Nouns

Stressing discrepancy rather than coincidence, we cannot help but notice that generic terminology sometimes involves nouns, sometimes adjectives. Indeed, the very same word sometimes appears as both parts of speech: *musical comedies* or just plain *musicals, western romances* or merely *westerns, documentary films* or *film documentaries*. Interestingly, there would seem to be historical consistency in these generic doublets.[1] Earlier uses of the term are invariably adjectival in nature, describing and delimiting a broader established category. Not just *poetry*, but *lyric poetry* or *epic poetry*. Later uses involve stand-alone substantival treatment, with a corresponding change in the status of the new category. Lyric poetry is a type of poetry; the more types of poetry we name, the more we reinforce the existence of poetry as an independent category, with each type corresponding to a different potential aspect of poetry. When we drop the noun and promote the adjective to substantival status—a *lyric*—we have done quite a bit more than pass from a general type—poetry—to a specific case—a lyric poem. By giving the adjective the status of a noun, we imply that *lyric* exists as a category independent of *poetry*, the noun that it originally modified. When a descriptive adjective becomes a categorical noun, it is thus loosened from the tyranny of that noun. *Epic poetry* calls to mind Homer, Virgil, or Milton, poets all. But what mental images does the stand-alone substantive *an epic* call forth? *The Song of Roland? War and Peace? Alexander Nevsky? Lonesome Dove?* No longer is our imagination bound to poetic form; instead it seeks out similar texts across media. Before, epic was one of the possible qualities of the primary category *poetry;* now film is one of the possible manifestations of the primary category *epic.*

The number of generic terms that have gone through this substantifying process is surprising. *Narrative poetry:* the nature of *narrative*. *Scenic photography:* a *scenic* (one of the staples of silent-film exhibition). *Serial publication:* a *serial. Commercial message:* a *commercial. Roman noir, film noir*: just plain *noir*. In some cases a neologism is required in order to incorporate the adjective into a noun. A *biographical picture* becomes a *biopic*. *Musical drama* turns into *melodrama*. On the same model, a documentary drama can be termed a *docudrama*. Science fiction stories are *sci-fi*. Often, the exigencies of journalism even generate clones of these substantified terms: musicals are *singies*, westerns are *oaters*, melodramas are *mellers, tearjerkers,* or *weepies*.

In each case the development of the stand-alone noun signals the liberation of the former adjective from its noun and the formation of a new category with its own independent status. Consider the history of comedy. Over the centuries comedy has been characterized in a variety of ways, according to its source, tone, costuming, exhibition, and the like. Now we have a series of categories that have become more or less loosened from the parent genre: burlesque, farce, masque, screwball, slapstick, and so on. This progression recalls the fact that *comedy* itself did not start as a noun but as one of a set of adjectives designating the possible types of theater or song; the word *comedy* comes from one type of singing (the kind associated with reveling), whereas *tragedy* comes from another (the type associated with goats, or satyrs). In other words, even such apparently basic terms as *comedy* and *tragedy*, like *epic* and *lyric*, had to earn substantival status. What initially were descriptive adjectives had to commandeer entire texts and demonstrate a clear ability to pilot them independently. In the same way, (*burlesque*) *comedy*, originally characterized by travesty, caricature, and nonsense jokes (the original meaning of the adjective *burlesque*), had to take on consistent special characteristics in order to become first *burlesque* (*comedy*), with the adjective outweighing the noun, then *"burlesque,"* with the slight discomfort that accompanies neologisms, and eventually just plain *burlesque*, standing alone on the generic stage, stripped of any necessary connection with comedy.

The constant sliding of generic terms from adjective to noun offers important insight into film genres and their development. Before the western became a separate genre and a household word virtually around the world, there were such things as western chase films, western scenics, western melodramas, western romances, western adventure films, and even western comedies, western dramas, and western epics. That is, each of these already existing genres could be and was produced with settings, plots, characters, and props corresponding to current notions of the West. In 1907 the West was a drawing card, and thus even familiar melodramas could be given new life if they were staged with western trappings (just as the recent popularity of high-tech sports shoes gave rise to such unexpected phenomena as a commercial employing sports shoes to advertise rental cars). In a similar manner, the musical was preceded by musical comedy, musical drama, musical romance, musical farce, and even the doubly redundant all-talking, all-singing, all-dancing musical melodrama. Just as turn-of-the-century America was fascinated by anything western, the sliced bread of the late twenties was sound film; in 1929, a film seemed incomplete unless music was added to its existing generic framework.

As long as western trappings or music were just add-ons, however, neither the western nor the musical could exist as a genre. Three changes had to occur before full genrification could take place:

1. Abandoning the add-on approach ("Let's just add music to this comedy"), studios had to shift attention away from preexisting substantive genres toward transgeneric adjectival material. Musical *melodrama* and musical *comedy* have little in common, but *musical* melodrama and *musical* comedy reveal protogeneric relationships. The primary vehicle of this change is standardization and automatization of the reading formation through which previous successes are evaluated and imitated.

2. Films had to reveal shared attributes stretching beyond the genre's eponymous material (music, Wild West, and so on) but nevertheless sufficiently connected to that material to justify using the name for that material as a generic label. In the western, this began when western material was combined with melodramatic plots and characters (villain, endangered woman, law-abiding young man). In the musical, it had to await the use of music as both catalyst and expression of heterosexual romance.

3. The public, whether self-consciously or not, had to become sufficiently aware of the structures binding disparate films into a single category that the process of viewing would always be filtered through the generic concept. That is, the expectations that come with generic identification (character types and relations, plot outcome, production style, and the like) must become part and parcel of the process whereby meaning is attributed to films.

Conceptually aiding these three parallel processes, and like them taking place not all at once but over a period of time, the substantification of the generic label signals the beginning of a privileged period for film genre that we appropriately celebrate by use of the term *genre film*. All too often in the past, *genre film* has been used interchangeably with the more general designator *film genre* or simply to designate a film with obvious connections to a widely recognized genre. A more precise use is in order. Genre films are the films produced after general identification and consecration of a genre through substantification, during the limited period when shared textual material and structures lead audiences to interpret films not as separate entities but according to generic expectations and against generic norms. If one of the attractions of the very notion of genre is its ability to celebrate connections among the various players in the film game, then any short span of genre film production and reception is the ideal object of film genre theory, because it is there that the various forces are most clearly aligned and the overall power of generic terms apparently at its height. Indeed, so seductive is this alignment that many genre studies never stray outside its bounds.

Genre as Process

Attention to coincidence having been banned from this project, another discrepancy now offers itself for analysis. Too often, attempts to understand origins have led to careful description of situations favoring change, enumeration of devices vehicling change, and evaluation of factors motivating change, only to limit deployment of the resultant model to a single moment, that of origin. But what if the model thus constructed were applicable to other moments as well? What if genre were not the permanent *product* of a singular origin but the *temporary by-product* of an ongoing *process*?

Let us begin with two discrepancies. The first we have already noted. The genres formed when adjectives become nouns in the process of genrification (for example, *comedy, melodrama*, and *epic*) are themselves subject to replacement when they are in turn modified by other terms that then graduate from adjective to substantive (for example, *burlesque, musical*, and *western*). Yet even the latter terms never achieve security, because they too can be displaced according to the same process that brought them to the fore. Thus at any given time, we find an unselfconscious mixture of terminology. With no way to distinguish among the terms, we regularly intermingle current and former genres, either in an adjectival or a substantival state. Lumped in the same sentence are films made under a genre-film regime and films subsequently assimilated to that genre; genres that once existed, that now exist, and that have not yet fully begun to exist; genres recently substantified and others still adjectival in nature; genres currently boasting genre-film audiences and others that long ago lost those audiences.

A second discrepancy is more surprising in nature because it in fact contradicts everything that has ever been said about the value of genre terms to the production process. Received wisdom suggests that genres provide models for development of studio projects, simplify communication among studio personnel, and ensure long-term economic benefits. So far, so good; all of these functions are surely fulfilled by genres. The role played by generic concepts in production, it is claimed, is then reflected in studio film publicity, where generic concepts are prominently displayed. Never having looked closely at film publicity campaigns with this problem in mind, I too for a long time believed that Hollywood regularly overtly exploits the generic identities of its genre films. Surprisingly, when I took a genre-sensitive look at advertisements and press books, I found something quite different.

Whereas film reviews almost always include generic vocabulary as a convenient and widely understood shorthand, film publicity seldom employs generic terms as such. Indirect references to genre are of course regularly used, but they almost always evoke not a single genre but multiple genres. A widely distributed poster for *Only Angels Have Wings* (1939) is typical in this regard. The topmost prose promises "Everything the Screen can give you . . . all in one MAGNIFICENT picture. . !" A box on the lower left adds specificity to this general statement:

EACH DAY
a Rendezvous
with Peril!
EACH NIGHT
a Meeting
with Romance!
Set against the
mighty tapestry of the
FOG-SHROUDED ANDES!

The graphic design of the poster reinforces this tripartite guarantee, with photographic close-ups of three different couples separated by sketches of a crashing plane and of a tropical port dominated by an enormous peak. The only specifically generic vocabulary is located front and

Only Angels Have Wings, Howard Hawks. © Columbia, 1939.

center but in small type overwhelmed by the size of the names of the stars, Cary Grant and Jean Arthur, "TOGETHER FOR THE FIRST TIME . . . IN AN EXCITING ROMANTIC ADVENTURE!" Hollywood has no interest, as this poster clearly suggests, in explicitly identifying a film with a single genre. On the contrary, the industry's publicity purposes are much better served by implying that a film offers "Everything the Screen can give you." This usually means offering something for the men ("EACH DAY a Rendezvous with Peril!"), something for the women ("EACH NIGHT a Meeting with Romance!"), and an added something for that tertium quid audience that prefers travel to adventure or romance ("the mighty tapestry of the FOG-SHROUDED ANDES").

Again and again in Hollywood publicity materials we find the same combination. DeMille's *Northwest Mounted Police* (1940) is "the Mightiest Adventure Romance of All Time!!! . . . two surging love stories woven into an unforgettable drama of human emotions . . . told against the blazing beauty of the northern forests." With Gable and Harlow, *Saratoga* (1937) is "as exciting as the Sport of Kings it dramatizes . . . and is the romance of a daring gambler and a girl who thought she wanted to ruin him." *A Damsel in Distress* (1937) has Fred Astaire and "Mad adventure! Daring deeds! White hot love with music!" Publicity for Warner's *The Singing Marine* (1937) reduces the formula to just a few words, promising "the crowning martial musical." At every turn, we find that Hollywood labors to identify its pictures with multiple genres, in order to benefit from the increased interest that this strategy inspires in diverse demographic groups. When specific genre terms are used, they are invariably offered in adjective-noun pairs, one term intended to guarantee appeal to each sex: western romance, romantic adventure, epic drama, and the like. Whenever possible, still other generic affiliations are implied, especially when comedy is involved. The key words in ads for the Ritz Brothers' version of *The Three Musketeers* (1939), for example, are "CLASHING BLADES AND LOVABLE MAIDS! RINGING TUNES AND BALMY BUFFOONS!" Thus guaranteed adventure, romance, music, and comedy, how can we possibly resist?

We now regularly identify *The Story of Louis Pasteur* (1936) and *Dr. Ehrlich's Magic Bullet* (1940) as biopics. Although Warners almost certainly did not think of the former as a continuation of the politically oriented tradition of *Disraeli* (1929), *Alexander Hamilton* (1931), and *Voltaire* (1933), they clearly considered the latter film as furthering the sequence begun by films depicting the life stories of Pasteur and Zola.

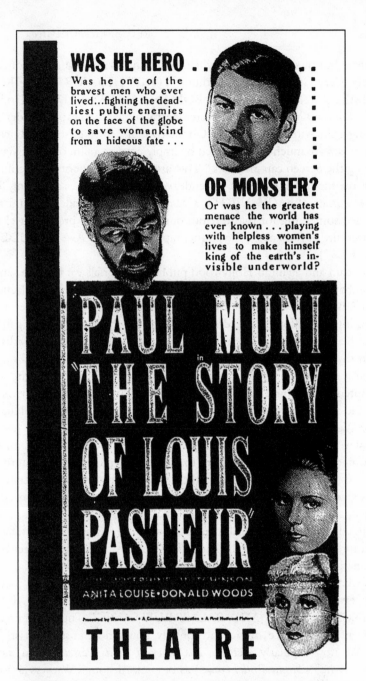

The Story of Louis Pasteur, William Dieterle. © Warner Bros., 1936.

Whereas Pasteur's story comes at the beginning of a cycle, Ehrlich's comes near the end. Nevertheless, aspects of the publicity for the two films are handled in similar fashion. *Pasteur*'s posters feature two radically different vignettes of Paul Muni; seen from eye level, he is a good-looking, well-shaven ladies' man, but in high angle he is a bearded, back-lit, heavily shaded, horror-film star. The caption reads, "WAS HE HERO . . . OR MONSTER?" Posters for *Dr. Ehrlich's Magic Bullet* of course never reveal what the magic bullet really is (a cure for syphilis). Instead, they reinforce the title's composite offer (a doctor for the ladies, a bullet for the men, magic for the tertium quid) with three scenes illustrating "A CHILD'S LAUGHTER ... A WOMAN'S LOVE ... 1000 MEN'S HOPE." Rarely has there been a better example of Hollywood's strategy: tell them nothing about the film, but make sure that everyone can imagine something that will bring them to the theater.

Whether through sparsely used specific generic terms or the more common strategy of broad generic implication, Hollywood's stock-in-trade is the romantic combination of genres, not the classical practice of generic purity. In one sense, this is hardly surprising: by definition, genres are broad public categories shared across the entire industry, and Hollywood studios have little interest in anything that must be shared with other studios. On the contrary, they are primarily concerned to create cycles of films that will be identified with only a single studio. After his 1929 success in *Disraeli*, for example, Warners moved George Arliss through a series of films, each time retaining one or more apparent money-making features from a previous success, but never falling into a fully imitable pattern. Searching for something it alone can sell, Warners stressed its actor, its style, its cycles. When the time came to advertise *Dr. Ehrlich's Magic Bullet*, therefore, reference was made to Pasteur and Zola not because all three are biopics, but in order to tie *Ehrlich* in with an ongoing cycle of Warners hits. Once the biopic bandwagon got moving, of course, any studio could hop on and take advantage of its momentum. Having no cycle of its own to sell, Twentieth Century Fox thus advertised *The Story of Alexander Graham Bell* (1939) in the context of the larger biographical genre, but this was a strategy used only after a genre has been fully formed by industrywide adherence.

Once they are fully formed, as these examples suggest, genres may continue to play an exhibition or reception role as convenient labels or reading formations, but they actually work against studio economic

Dr. Ehrlich's Magic Bullet, William Dieterle. © Warner Bros., 1940.

interests. This unexpected observation helps us to bring together the two discrepancies mentioned earlier. Both adjectives and nouns, we first noted, can be used to designate genres. Although heavily used by critics, such terminology is generally avoided by studio publicity, which prefers to imply generic affiliation indirectly, with at least two generic

Dr. Ehrlich's Magic Bullet, William Dieterle.
© Warner Bros., 1940.

The Story of Alexander Graham Bell, Irving Cummings. © Twentieth Century Fox, 1939.

connections invariably involved. Putting these two observations together with the recognition that studios prefer to establish cycles (which are proprietary) rather than genres (which are sharable), we may make a number of unexpected hypotheses that serve as a preliminary foundation for a new model of generic process.

1. By assaying and imitating the money-making qualities of their own most lucrative films, studios seek to initiate film cycles that will provide successful, easily exploitable models associated with a single studio. Stressing studio-specific resources (contract actors, proprietary characters, recognizable styles), these cycles always also include common features that can be imitated by other studios (subject matter, character types, plot patterns).

2. New cycles are usually produced by associating a new type of material or approach with already existing genres. *The Great Train Robbery* (1903) and its immediate successors associated crime films, railway films, and scenics with the "Wild West." *The Singing Fool* (1928) and its imitators were musical melodramas, musical comedies, or musical romances. Early biopics applied the biographical model to historical romances, adventure films, and melodramas.

3. When conditions are favorable, single-studio cycles can be built into industrywide genres. Conditions are more likely to be favorable when the cycle is defined by elements that can be shared by other studios (common plots and settings rather than proprietary characters or contract players) and easily perceived by audiences.

4. When cycles become genres, adjectival genre labels are substantified. Just as Kleenex tissues were soon referred to simply as *Kleenex* and eventually reduced to the "generic" term *kleenex,* so *musical comedy* became *the musical.* The difference of course lies in the fact that product names may be registered and protected, whereas genre terminology is shared by all. Knowing that their competitors may not use them, manufacturers strive for generalized application of their trademarks (Linoleum, Kleenex, Kodak, Hoover, Insinkerator, and so on), whereas a film studio has little to gain from genrification.

5. Once a genre is recognized and practiced throughout the industry, individual studios have no further economic interest in practicing it as such; instead, they seek to create a new cycle by associating a new type of material or approach with the existing

genre, thus initiating a new round of genrification. Without the ability to ensure a significant measure of product differentiation, studios cannot expect a substantial economic return on their investment. When a genre reaches the saturation point, studios must either abandon it or handle it in a new way. Though this does not necessarily guarantee the creation of a new genre, it always recreates the circumstances out of which new genres are generated. At this point, then, the entire process has the potential to begin again.

The progression described here is by no means specific to film genre. As compared to literature and its approach to genre, however, cinema foregrounds and accelerates the product differentiation aspects of the process.

Genrification as Process

Over the past few millennia, every extant general term has been subjected to a version of the process described above. Discourse as a whole has been divided into poetry, painting, and history. Poetry, in turn, has been characterized as epic, lyric, or dramatic. Moving down yet another step, dramatic poetry—or theater, as it came to be called—may be considered as comic or tragic (and eventually even tragicomic). Note that the category-producing substantification process in these classic cases appears extremely measured and sensible. New types are produced not one by one but by an apparently scientific subdivision process. In other words, the terminology involved seems to represent the permanent and stable result of synchronic categorization. We commonly image such relationships through a branching diagram such as those that are used to locate a given species in a Linnaean configuration. Thus tigers are configured (in simplified form) as shown in figure 1. In order to establish such a chart, we must imagine the charted animals as existing in a timeless, unchanging museum (like the natural history museums erected around the world during the nineteenth century). In addition, we must imagine ourselves, as authors or users of the chart, as objective observers, radically separated from the animals that the chart classifies.

Generic terminology is commonly based on a classificatory model of

Figure 1

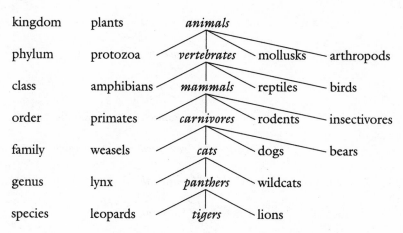

this type—the classical origins, extended life, and seeming permanence of the terms and the overall structure that contains them apparently justifying neglect of history and of our own place within it. Consider the not-so-famous case of *mirthful martial musical romantic comic dramatic poetic discourse*. When we try to make sense of Warners's series of annual musicals built around the service academies and related military motifs—including *Flirtation Walk* (1934), *Shipmates Forever* (1935), *Sons O' Guns* (1936), and *The Singing Marine*—we understand the contemporary label *martial musical* as part of the overall classification simplified in figure 2. The more recent categories are treated with the classificatory neatness of their classical predecessors, even when their status, title, characteristics, and durability remain uncertain. Yet the accelerated genrification process characteristic of the last century's fully commodified genres follows not a librarian's deliberate Dewey-decimal desires, but the entrepreneurial spirit and its heightened adrenaline levels.

This is not the place to decide whether or not genrification was ever merely a scientific categorizing process, free from commercial or political interests. What we can surely affirm at this point, however, is that the constitution of film cycles and genres is a never-ceasing process, closely tied to the twin capitalist needs of product differentiation and readily identifiable commodities. The "martial" musical is at first neither a genre nor a species in the permanent sense that we borrow from Linnaeus. Instead, it is a Warners cycle, an attempt to produce a well-

Figure 2

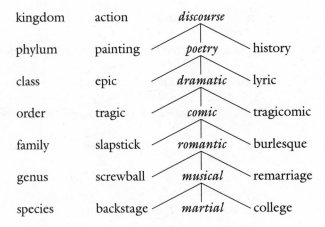

kingdom	action		*discourse*	
phylum	painting		*poetry*	history
class	epic		*dramatic*	lyric
order	tragic		*comic*	tragicomic
family	slapstick		*romantic*	burlesque
genus	screwball		*musical*	remarriage
species	backstage		*martial*	college

differentiated product that will return a good profit to the studio's backers. As such, it has the wherewithal to become (depending on the actual level of studio investment and audience reaction) what I have termed an "adjectival" genre. But as an adjectival genre, the martial musical gains the opportunity eventually to become a broadly practiced substantival genre. Just as musical comedy spawned the musical, so martial musicals might (but will not necessarily) give rise to the "martial" genre.

But why stop there? Posters for *Sons O' Guns* identified it as a "*mirthful* martial musical." If romantic comedy can become the spawning ground for a new genre, eventually being displaced by the slow invasion of music and the values, situations, and relations it vehicles, then why can't the process continue from the musical to the *martial or even eventually the *mirthful.[2] Through this process-oriented logic we discover to our surprise that the number of levels is in no way fixed. Just as geology places us only on the latest level, not on the fundamental or final level, so a process-oriented understanding of genrification keeps us from thinking of the kingdom-phylum-order-class-family-genus-species sequence as complete or closed.

Genres are not just post facto categories, then, but part of the constant category-splitting and category-creating dialectic that constitutes the history of types and terminology. Instead of imaging this process in terms of static classification, we might want to see it as a regular alternation between an expansive principle—the creation of a new cycle—and a principle of contraction—the consolidation of a genre (see figure 3).

Sons O' Guns, Lloyd Bacon. © Warner Bros., 1936.

But this formulation fails to take account of the special relationship studied in the preceding section, namely the connection between adjective and noun genres. The proposed model must therefore be revised as suggested in figure 4. That is, a fresh cycle may be initiated by attaching a new adjective to an existing noun genre, with the adjective standing for some recognizable location, plot type, or other differentiation factor. Under certain conditions, so much attention may be attracted to the tacked-

Figure 3

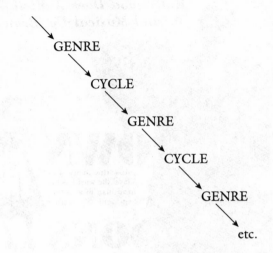

Figure 4

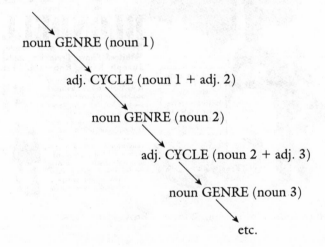

on adjective that it changes parts of speech and inaugurates its own noun genre, only to remain constantly subject to eventual regenrification through the constitution of yet another adjectival cycle. And so forth.

A process-oriented representation of our not-so-famous *mirthful martial musical romantic comic dramatic poetic discourse* would thus look something like figure 5. Yet even this model is too rigid, too linear, in its attempt to avoid stability at all costs. The musical, for example,

Figure 5

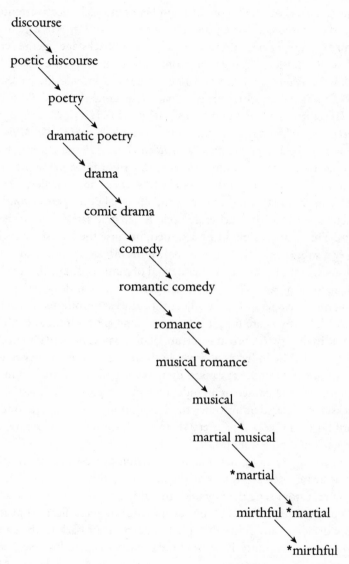

discourse

poetic discourse

poetry

dramatic poetry

drama

comic drama

comedy

romantic comedy

romance

musical romance

musical

martial musical

*martial

mirthful *martial

*mirthful

achieves cycle status not just by modifying the silent romance genre with the new musical technology; on the contrary, early musical forays involve modification of every genre in sight, drawn from every level of the historical genrification process. Indeed, promotion from adjective to noun genre is strongly favored by the ability of adjectival material to be applied to multiple noun genres. Thus the ability of music to be attached to drama and comedy as well as to romance enhances the likelihood that a noun genre will be created out of a number of musical adjective genres.

As the asterisks in figure 5 suggest, not every cycle spawns a genre. In the 1929–1930 period, for example, adjectival "backstage" genres compete with "musical" genres for promotion to noun-genre status. According to *Photoplay*, *Close Harmony* (1929) is a "vaudeville backstage hit," *Broadway Hoofer* (1930) is a "backstage comedy," and *Puttin' on the Ritz* (1930) is a "backstage story," while *Variety* styles *Glorifying the American Girl* (1929) as a "backstage formula," *Behind the Make-Up* (1929) as a "backstage picture," and *It's a Great Life* (1930) as a "backstage yarn." In 1930, the time was certainly right for some wag to coin the term *backstager, on the model of "soaper" and "meller," yet no such term was forthcoming. Just as the *martial never gets beyond the adjectival level, so the backstage cycle never graduates to noun-genre status. This is not, as might be assumed, because the backstage cycle is simply a subgenre of the musical. *Behind the Make-Up* and many other backstage formula films are either devoid of music or shunt the music to a single location and a few short passages, as film noir does with its sultry nightclub singers. If some adjectival cycles are promoted to generic status while others are not, it is because some are both more easily applicable in theory to a broad spectrum of film types and actually adopted in practice by the industry as a whole. Ironically, it was the general demise of musical films that caused them, rather than backstage films, to be perceived and named as an independent genre. As the *martial and *backstager cases demonstrate, there is nothing automatic about the genrification process. For every dozen cycles, only a few genres ever emerge, and even fewer endure.

In passing, we note that the cycle-creation process may at any point in time be initiated at any level of the generic past. Like the earth around us, genre history is marked by folds that bring previous generic levels to the surface, where they can once again enter the genrification process. Think of how many times the epic has been thrust back to the surface by the energy of enterprising producers. Western epics, historical epics, biblical epics, wartime epics, science fiction epics, and many others testify to the epic's permanent youth. Certainly, the ability of classical nouns to serve as host for modern adjectives lies at the heart of genre theory's many difficulties. The geological metaphor helps to explain the simultaneous presence of phenomena of radically different ages. The term *epic* dates from the first ice age, and *romance* from the second, whereas *western* and *musical* are creations of the current era, yet all are simultaneously visible on the surface of the current generic lexicon.

That the nonlinearity of this situation should create confusion is hardly surprising, especially since producers have tended to stress adjectives and cycle creation, whereas critics have paid attention instead to nouns and genre formation. When we understand the process whereby cycles and genres are created, we at least understand the source of our confusion and thus take the all-important first step toward dissipating it.

Are Genres Subject to Redefinition?

Unlike new worlds discovered by early modern explorers, which were drawn on the other side of the globe, newly created genres must be drawn on the same mental sketch pad that holds the previous map. Instead of conveniently locating Florida or the Indies somewhere across the western sea, we usually represent slapstick, romantic, and burlesque comedy on the same map, within the very same space that holds, say, epic, lyric, and dramatic poetry and tragic, tragicomic, and comic theater. Even though the musical was not recognized as a separate genre until late 1930, and was not defined consistently with current usage until at least 1933, in today's criticism the term *musical* nevertheless shares space with generic terms like *backstage, western, romantic,* and *slapstick*—none of which is in Aristotle, but all of which have specific historical origins that set them on a different hierarchical level from the musical. With genres, it is as if terms designating phylum, class, order, family, genus, and species were all folded together willy-nilly, providing little clarity to would-be generic spectators.

Just as our knowledge of the changing borders of France underlies any current use of the term *France*, so categories such as *poetry, drama,* and *comedy* coexist with *the musical.* Imagine the chaos that would result if we were regularly to alternate among the various maps to which the term *France* has been attached at differing points in time. It would be nearly impossible to communicate effectively without first specifying which map serves as point of reference. Yet this is precisely what we do when we use generic terminology. The word *drama* no longer means the same thing it meant before *musical drama* was drained away from the definition of just plain *drama* by creation of the term *melodrama.* The map looked one way when musical comedy was a cycle within the genre of comedy, and another way when the musical was established as a stand-alone genre. We would surely benefit from careful description of successive generic maps, yet most critics remain unaware that generic cartography involves multiple superimposed maps of differing ages and extents. The familiar questions of generic terminology (Should the term *genre* be reserved for comedy and tragedy or may it be applied as well to epic, lyric, and drama? Or are the latter modes rather than genres? Is film noir a style or a genre?) reveal the extent to which critics believe they are dealing with a stable set of terms, fixed once and forever inert.

Working simultaneously with overlapping generic maps is the price we must pay for recognizing the continuous, process-based nature of generic creation. Zoologists working in the Linnaean tradition may succeed in convincing themselves that they are dealing with a fixed grid, but we have seen the process of genrification at work too clearly to return to a rigid, immutable model. According to the Darwinian approach to evolution, the specificity of a new genus is guaranteed by its inviolability. That is, no genus is interfertile with another genus. Besides the lack of fertility between genera, the purity and thus the identity of the species is also guaranteed by the fact that previous life forms, once extinct, disappear from the world forever. Only in the multi-era imaginary world of a Jurassic Park do the categories of a previous evolutionary state continue to exist.

In the genre world, however, every day is Jurassic Park day. Not only are all genres interfertile, they may at any time be crossed with any genre that ever existed. The "evolution" of genres is thus far broader in scope than the evolution of species. Unencumbered by the limitations of the flesh, the process of genre creation offers us not a single synchronic chart but an always incomplete series of superimposed generic maps. Every time our eyes concentrate on the map, we find that a new map, currently in the process of being drafted, is just coming into view. Never is the map completed, because it is the record not of the past, but of a living geography, of an ongoing process.

Postmortem for a Phantom Genre

Recent writing about melodrama offers an interesting test case for this process-oriented approach to genre. The term *melodrama* has had a surprisingly lively existence since Rousseau borrowed it in 1770 from an Italian synonym for opera to describe his play *Pygmalion*. Certainly, the longevity of the term derives at least in part from critics' willingness to imagine genres as similar to human bodies. Not a single molecule of my body today was present in my body even ten years ago, yet current notions of personhood make it easy for me to image myself as a continuous being, regardless of changes in my physical makeup. There have of course been societies where such individualism was unknown, where continuity was located in the universe as a whole rather than in any individual body seen as the temple of a specific personality. In the post-romantic world, however, continuity is mapped through bodies and the names attached to them. In this century, personal continuity is thus available to serve as a model for generic continuity. To be sure, melodrama changes, but so does each of us; like individual humans, it is claimed, melodrama maintains a core of continuity in spite of its evolving corpus.

One of the main strategies devised to ensure generic continuity involves treatment of a genre not as an evolving category or even as a corpus of films, but as a universal tendency. Thus Lucien Goldmann speaks of a "tragic vision," Gerald Mast imagines a "comic mind," and Peter Brooks assumes a "melodramatic imagination." The titles of books and articles on literary and film genre regularly include terms that style the genre as the expression of a universal human tendency: *attitude, experience, imagination, inspiration, mystique, situation, spirit, vision*, and the like. The reason for holding on to generic terms so tightly, we must conclude, is that they enjoy a level of prestige that cannot easily be matched by other concepts or terms. Note that this statement applies not to film producers, who find too little product differentiation in unmodified genre terms, but to critics. We critics are the ones who have a vested interest in reusing generic terminology, which serves to anchor our analyses in universal or culturally sanctioned contexts, thus justifying our all too subjective, tendentious, and self-serving positions. We are thus the ones who see to it that generic vocabulary remains available for use. Whereas producers are actively destroying genres by creating new cycles, some of which will eventually be genrified, critics are regularly trying to fold the cyclical differences into the genre, thus authorizing continued use of a familiar, universalizing, sanctioned, and therefore powerful term.

Recently, critics have analyzed the inconsistent way in which the term *melodrama* has been used over the years. Starting with Russell Merritt in 1983, there has been persistent questioning of the critical tendency to define and understand melodrama through the excesses of forties "weepies" and the fifties films of Douglas Sirk. Seen from a distance, this questioning fits into a broader current in film studies. As film history has progressed from poor cousin of the Parisian semiotic patriarch to full-fledged New World head of family, a number of earlier generic analyses have been criticized for their tendency to reduce a broad and durable genre to a particularly successful cycle of films or to a limited period. Thus Tag Gallagher has castigated Tom Schatz for limiting the western to the films of John Ford and the post-1939 period. In the same manner, I myself have pointed out the tendency of Delamater, Schatz, and Feuer to privilege MGM's Freed unit in their construction and analysis of the musical. A similar case might be made regarding Elsaesser's treatment of William Dieterle's Warner Bros. films as representative of the biopic. Others overemphasize the role of early Universal films in the history of the horror film.

But does the problem involve nothing more than stressing one group of films at the expense of others? Russell Merritt suggests that something else is at stake. Under the intriguing title "Melodrama: Postmortem for a Phantom Genre," he points out that film critics have regularly written about melodrama as if the term were "self-evidently clear and coherent" (26). For Merritt, however, melodrama is a slippery and evolving category. Citing examples from the first two decades of this century, Ben Singer provides still greater historical specificity in support of a similar argument. He points out that although most recent critics have treated melodrama as an introspective, psychological, women's genre, in the early years of cinema melodrama was specifically associated with action, adventure, and working-class men. Carefully attending to the critical practice of the silent period, Merritt and Singer successfully question current usage of the term *melodrama*. Indeed, a rapid glance at any standard treatment of silent-film genres reveals the extent to which current definitions of melodrama fail to reflect earlier understanding of the term. In his treatment of the western, family, society, rural, crime, and military subgenres of silent-feature melodrama, Richard Koszarski emphasizes the villain-hero-heroine triangle, true-to-type characters, and visually powerful dramatic confrontations rather than the self-sacrificing psychology of downtrodden women usually stressed in recent definitions of the genre.

The first scholar to directly tackle the disparity between recent and traditional definitions of film melodrama is Steve Neale, who has exhaustively studied the use of melodrama and related terms (*meller, melodramatic*) in the trade journal *Variety* from 1938 to 1959, with extension for selected films to the 1925–1938 period. What Neale discovers is that, during this key period, the term *melodrama* "continued precisely to mean what it did in the teens and twenties": "The mark of these films is not pathos, romance, and domesticity," he points out, "but action, adventure, and thrills; not 'feminine' genres and the woman's films but war films, adventure films, horror films, and thrillers, genres traditionally thought of as, if anything, 'male'" ("Melo Talk" 69).

In other words, Neale claims that critics have been mistaken in their use of the term. Employing trade press usage of the term *melodrama* to exemplify his earlier claim that genres are established once and for all by the industry at the time of production ("Questions" 48–52), Neale points out that films featuring women or clearly aimed at female audiences are rarely designated as melodrama, meller, or melodramatic, "because these films usually lack the elements that conventionally define these terms from the trade's point of view" ("Melo Talk" 74). In passing it is worth noting the extent to which Neale conflates the trades of film criticism and film production as two sides of the same industry. We have already seen how the interests and practices of these two separate parts of the film industry may diverge. Later, we will have cause to recognize the important effects of this divergence.

For the time being, Neale's methods are less important than his purpose and his results. Though he never states specific conclusions, it seems clear that a major goal of the article is to demonstrate that scholars have misused the term *melodrama* and its derivatives in describing what are now often called "woman's films." As Neale shows, in the forties and fifties, *melodrama* meant something else; thus, recent critics make improper use of the term when they apply it to the weepies. Yet a generation of feminist critics has systematically used the term *melodrama* in reference to the female-oriented films of the forties and fifties. Their analyses have taken for granted—and thus reinforced—the existence and nature of this genre and its corpus. How are we to understand this discrepancy? Are current definitions of the melodrama just plain wrong, as Merritt, Singer, and Neale imply? Or is another principle at work here? In order to come to terms with this problem, it is necessary to trace the history of the constitution of the woman's film as a genre, along with its connections to melodrama.

Rebirth of a Phantom Genre

For Molly Haskell, in 1974 the first of the recent critics to draw attention to the genre, a woman's film is a film that has a woman at the center of its universe. Just as initial generic recognition of the western and the musical was facilitated by negative—and thus category-strengthening—evaluations, so Haskell acknowledges from the start the deprecatory connotations of the term *woman's film* as it had been intermittently employed by two generations of critics:

Among the Anglo-American critical brotherhood (and a few of their sisters as well), the term "woman's film" is used disparagingly to conjure up the image of the pinched-virgin or little-old-lady writer, spilling out her secret longings in wish fulfillment or glorious martyrdom, and transmitting these fantasies to the frustrated housewife. . . . As a term of critical opprobrium, "woman's film" carries the implication that women, and therefore women's emotional problems, are of minor significance. . . . At the lowest level, as soap opera, the "woman's film" fills a masturbatory need, it is soft-core emotional porn for the frustrated housewife. The weepies are founded on a mock-Aristotelian and politically conservative aesthetic whereby women spectators are moved, not by pity and fear but by self-pity and tears, to accept, rather than reject, their lot. That there should be a need and an audience for such an opiate suggests an unholy amount of real misery. And that a term like "woman's film" can be summarily used to dismiss certain films, with no further need on the part of the critic to make distinctions and explore the genre, suggests some of the reasons for this misery. (154–55)

Strong terms these, and extraordinarily revelatory of the purpose of feminist investment in the revitalization of *woman's film* as a term and a genre. Citing well-known literary victims like Anna Karenina and Emma Bovary as generic models, along with examples drawn from films previously thought of as dramas, melodramas, films noirs, or screwball comedies, Haskell delineates four subgenres of what she calls the "woman's film," identifiable according to the type of activity engaged in by the heroine: sacrifice, affliction, choice, or competition.

We recognize in Haskell's analysis a familiar technique of cycle and genre formation, though this time the critic rather than the producer appears to be the initiator of the process. By attaching the term *woman's* to a succession of different, already existing genres, Haskell succeeds in building an adjectival genre that was not fully constituted during the period of the films' production, or at least in expanding it considerably in a direction of her choice. We have already noted the extent to which the building of genres is often a critical, rather than a production-based, concern, so the only thing surprising about Haskell's attempt to rehabilitate the woman's film by broadening and strengthening its definition is the delay between the production of the films in question and the moment of critical intervention.

Indeed, Haskell's purpose is furthered by the many critics who have taken up her call. For Mary Ann Doane, "the 'woman's film' is not a 'pure' genre—a fact which may partially determine the male critic's derogatory dismissal of such films. It is crossed and informed by a number of other genres or types—melodrama, film noir, the gothic or horror film—and finds its point of unification ultimately in the fact of its address" ("The Woman's Film" 68). We note that this is precisely the type of statement that might have been made in 1910 regarding the western or in 1930 describing the musical. When they are still styled as cycles—whether by producers or critics—nascent genres never appear to be pure. Because the new generic content is expressed as an adjective modifying multiple different nouns, its very existence seems dependent on and derivative of those nouns. The preceding quote clearly images *woman's film* as a convenient term to describe a number of separate subgenres of diverse genres: woman's gothic, woman's horror, woman's film noir, and woman's melodrama. The application of the term *woman's* to each of these genres brings the four subgenres together, but the adjectival nature of its use precludes the woman's film from being seen as a fully independent genre.

In order to understand the process by which the woman's film eventually evolved into a full-fledged genre, it is necessary at this point to subject certain aspects of mid-eighties feminist criticism to such microscopic methodological and orthographic scrutiny that the original purpose of the essays analyzed will be provisionally lost to view. In the long run, however, this close inspection will bring the essays' broader goals and functions into focus. We first note that for Doane in 1984, as for Haskell in 1974, the term *woman's film* still had to be set off by quotation marks. A decade ago, woman's film had a kind of starred existence, like a suspected but never actually witnessed ancient Indo-European root word. The quotation marks are there not only for Haskell in 1974 and Doane in 1984, but also for many other mid-eighties publications, including influential 1984 articles by Judith Mayne and Linda Williams. In fact, when in 1984 Doane mentions her book in progress, she refers to the book as "The 'Woman's Film': Possession and Address" (though she uses the same title—without quotation marks—for her article). "The book focuses," she says, "on 'women's films' of the 1940s" ("The Woman's Film" 81). In 1984, the quotation marks still seemed required.

When the book was published in 1987, however, it was instead entitled *The Desire to Desire: The Woman's Film of the 1940s*. Following a practice begun in England by Claire Johnston, Annette Kuhn, and Pam Cook, already adopted in this country by Tania Modleski and soon to be followed by virtually the entire critical community (with the exception of a few male critics like Robert Lang and David Cook), Doane strips the term *woman's film* of its quotation marks, thereby abandoning any remnant of doubt regarding the category's right to independent existence. Hesitation remains, however, regarding the generic status of the newly enfranchised category. In explaining the topic of her book, Doane regularly refers to the woman's film as a genre. Just two pages in, she says that "the cinema in general, outside of the genre of the woman's picture, constructs its spectator as the generic 'he' of language. . . . The woman's film is therefore in many ways a privileged site for the analysis of the given terms of female spectatorship and the inscription of subjectivity precisely because its address to a female viewer is particularly strongly marked" (*The Desire* 3). Only a few pages later, Doane further specifies her purpose in *The Desire to Desire*. "The aim of this study," she says, "is to outline the terms in which a female spectator is conceptualized—that is, the terms in which she is simultaneously projected and assumed as an image . . . by the genre of the woman's film" (9). Still within the opening methodological chapter, Doane explains that "the conditions of possibility of the woman's film as a genre are closely linked to the commodity form" (27). This is why, she contends, "The woman's film as a genre, together with the massive extracinematic discursive apparatus, insure that what the woman is sold is a certain image of femininity. There is a sense in which the woman's film is not much to look at—the nonstyle or zero-degree style of films of the genre has frequently been noted" (30). Doane's removal of the quotation marks from the expression *"woman's film"* is apparently justified by her acceptance of the woman's film as a full-fledged genre.

Yet in the final section of the first chapter we unexpectedly read the following:

The woman's film undoubtedly does not constitute a genre in the technical sense of the term, insofar as the unity of a genre is generally attributed to consistent patterns in thematic content, iconography, and narrative structure. The heterogeneity of the woman's film as a category is exemplified by the disparity between gothic films such as *Undercurrent* (1946) or *Dragonwyck* (1946), influenced by film noir and the conventions of the thriller, and a love story such as *Back Street* (1941) or a maternal melodrama such as *To Each His Own* (1946). But the group does have a coherence and that coherence is grounded in its address to a female spectator. The woman's film, quite simply, attempts to engage female subjectivity. (34)

Initially, it may seem that Doane contradicts herself by first stressing and then contesting the generic nature of the woman's film. In retrospect, however, an entirely different attitude seems justified: Doane hesitates about the generic status of the woman's film precisely because she is in the process of changing that status. Now, I do not mean to suggest that Doane was by herself capable of turning a motley assortment of old films into a widely recognized genre, yet I would suggest that a major purpose of *The Desire to Desire* is to establish the woman's film as a genre. One of the founding arguments for genrifying the woman's film is plain to see in the preceding quote: according to Doane, the coherence, and thus the generic status, of the woman's film "is grounded in its address to a female spectator."

The other telling argument involves the assimilation of the woman's film to an already established genre, capable of lending to the woman's film some of its long-standing genericity. Sliding conveniently from one category to another, Doane points out that "the melodramatic mode is often analyzed in terms which situate it as a 'feminine' form, linking it intimately with the woman's film in its address to a female audience" (*The Desire* 72–73). And a paragraph later: "Because it foregrounds sacrifice and suffering, incarnating the 'weepie' aspect of the genre, the maternal melodrama is usually seen as the paradigmatic type of the woman's film" (73). In arguing for a privileged connection between the woman's film and melodrama, Doane is following a line initiated in print by Laura Mulvey and Tania Modleski and widely circulated at conferences and colloquia from the early eighties on. Though both Mulvey and Modleski end up at the same place—establishing virtual identity between melodrama and the woman's film—their strategies are quite different. Identifying realism with Hollywood's address to men, Mulvey claims that in contrast "the woman's film was identified with melodrama" and that "there appears to be no absolute line of demarcation between melodrama and the woman's film" ("Melodrama" 21, 36). Following Geoffrey Nowell-Smith's insights regarding the connections between melodrama and hysteria, Modleski takes a different tack. Pointing out the origin of the term *hysteria* in female anatomy, Modleski finds in the hysterical nature of melodrama "a clue as to why for a large period of film history melodrama and the 'woman's film' have been virtually synonymous terms" ("Time and Desire" 20–21).

Promotion of the woman's film as a genre has at the same time been abetted by massive borrowings from Thomas Elsaesser's 1972 article entitled "Tales of Sound and Fury: Observations on the Family Melodrama." Though Elsaesser's topic is ostensibly a particular kind of melodrama dealing with family matters, most of his conclusions are broadly stated and have regularly been taken to apply to melodrama as a whole, whence the tendency over the past decade to assume that family melodrama is synonymous with melodrama as such. Robert Lang summarizes the standard position by claiming that "if the notion of family is conceived of flexibly, the family can be said to represent melodrama's true subject, making the family melodrama a genre, where all other films are only to a greater or lesser degree melodramatic, but do not belong to the genre we call the melodrama" (49). All of this apropos of a term (*family melodrama*) that Neale never found once in his exhaustive study of the terminology applied to Hollywood woman's films and melodramas.

Despite the fact that the notion of woman's film was originally cobbled out of female-oriented cycles within a variety of genres, woman's melodrama was promoted by critics during the eighties to the role of synecdoche for all of the others. In the same manner, family melodrama, once a peripheral melodramatic subgenre, was saddled with the responsibility of representing all other types of melodrama. All that remained, in order to guarantee the generic status of woman's film and a redefinition of melodrama as family melodrama, was to link the two through their common feature of being primarily addressed to women. Only when this junction took place—in conferences on both sides of the Atlantic as well as in passages like the ones quoted from Doane—would the woman's film abandon its quotation marks in favor of full generic status. Since the late eighties, the generic status of the category has never been in doubt (see, for example, the work of Caryl Flinn, Jane Gaines, and Maureen Turim). Indeed, a new generation of introductory texts has begun to treat the woman's film as fully the equal of established genres (Dick 104–7; Sklar 116–17, 210–11; Maltby 133–36), and the quotation marks are now a thing of the past.

Only a few short years ago, the very existence of a stand-alone woman's film category was in doubt, and during the heyday of the woman's film, the term *family melodrama* was not even used by the trade press. Yet during the eighties, critics regularly conflated the two categories, eventually styling the woman's film and family melodrama as the very core of melodrama as a genre. Introducing the term *woman's film* into serious critical discourse, Molly Haskell evinces a desire to use a new level of respect for the term itself as a weapon in the ongoing struggle to empower women. If we want to understand some of the reasons for women's misery, Haskell insists, we have but to look at the fact "that a term like 'woman's film' can be summarily used to dismiss certain films, with no further need on the part of the critic to make distinctions and explore the genre" (155).

One of the major tasks of feminist film criticism over the past twenty years has been to rehabilitate the term *woman's film* and thereby restore value to women's activities. In fact, not only has woman's film been rehabilitated, but the entire genre of melodrama has now been redefined through the woman's film (to the point of raising the hackles of historical critics aware that neither category—woman's film or family melodrama—had the contemporary existence that is attributed to it today). Like the parallel move made by *western* and *musical* from adjective to substantive, the slide from *"woman's film"* to *woman's film* carries far more than simple grammatical ramifications. Once it could be divorced from specific films and preexisting genres, the woman's film was free to take on a life of its own, drawing to its corpus virtually any film apparently addressed to women. But not just films. Tania Modleski (*Loving*) and Jane Feuer ("Melodrama") stress the importance of gothic romances and television soap operas for any study of woman's film. Starting with Annette Kuhn's 1982 *Women's Pictures: Feminism and Cinema* and E. Ann Kaplan's 1983 *Women and Film: Both Sides of the Camera*, the corpus was expanded to include not only classic Hollywood films, popular novels, and television programs, but also recent films and videos produced by women. Increasingly, the term *woman's film* has been used as a broad-based banner, flown at academic conferences and film festivals alike, under which a variety of women's activities may march arm in arm.

Principles of Generic Recycling

Where does this leave us in our attempt to understand the process of genre constitution and transformation? It permits us to formulate new hypotheses regarding the genrification process, complementing those offered earlier.

1. The genre constitution process is not limited to a cycle's or genre's first appearance. It would be convenient indeed if all generic categories, once constituted, could be counted on to remain forever stationary. The benefits of such a stable system shine so brightly that a number of critics have declared undying allegiance to original industry-spawned definitions. Yet it must be manifest that industry interests in novelty guarantee a constantly shifting generic map. Neither melodrama as a category nor melodramatic texts have stayed the same since Pixérécourt, Belasco, and Griffith any more than comedy has remained stable since the Greeks. It would indeed be convenient if genre stability were guaranteed,

but it is decidedly not so, and our genre theories must be established accordingly.

2. Taking one version of the genre as representative of the genre as a whole is not only a common practice, it is a normal step in the regenrification process. Rhetorically, the most effective method of redefining a genre is not to do so overtly, but rather to promote a subset of the genre to a representative position. When Northrop Frye needed to define *comedy* in a particular manner, in order to fit conveniently into his overall pattern of mythoi, he simply appointed New Comedy as the only worthy bearer of comedy's flag. Recognizing the importance to the Greeks of both Aristophanes' Old Comedy tradition and of Menander's New Comedy strain, Frye nevertheless claims that "today, when we speak of comedy, we normally think of something that derives from the Menandrine tradition" ("The Argument" 58). Stretching the notion of comedy beyond its original theatrical meaning to cover all media, Frye effectively redefined comedy for a generation of critics. A similar logic governs the common attempt, initiated by Jerome Delamater, to build an "integrated musical" genre around films produced by Arthur Freed for MGM during the forties and fifties.

3. Most generic labels carry sufficient prestige that they are retained for the designation of newly formed genres, even when they are only partially appropriate. Frye could have chosen to label one of his mythoi simply as *New Comedy*, but such a designation sounds limited and neologistic as compared to the traditional and powerful simplicity of just plain *comedy*. Delamater might well have treated the "integrated musical" as one of many subgenres of the musical. Instead, the integrated approach to the musical is termed the genre's "Platonic ideal" and attention to the MGM musical is justified accordingly: "Choosing to concentrate on the MGM musical is based on more than judgmental whim, however. The MGM musical seems to contain every element which characterizes the musical as a genre. The concepts of the star vehicle, studio style, the producer's touch, and the Platonic ideal of the integrated musical come together at MGM and become manifest in many of that studio's films from the late-1930s to the mid-1950s" (130). In passing, we may note that Delamater uses the term *MGM* inaccurately, if purposefully. During the period in question, three units produced musicals concurrently at MGM, led by producers Jack Cummings, Arthur Freed, and Joe Pasternak.

Only Freed, however, systematically turned out integrated musicals. When Delamater identifies the integrated musical with "the MGM musical," he thereby raises the Freed unit to representative status for all of MGM. In the same way, the association of the woman's film with family melodrama retains the power of the more general term, while applying that term to a corpus of films many of which do not fit the original action-oriented meaning of the term *melodrama*.

4. Any group of films may at any time be generically redefined by contemporary critics. One of the founding principles of genre study is the importance of reading texts in the context of other similar texts. We have seen how studios may provide those very texts. Immediately following the success of *Disraeli*, Warners failed to produce films that would ensure a biopic-oriented reading of *Disraeli*. After the unexpected success of *The Story of Louis Pasteur*, however, Warners produced a series of films guaranteeing that *Pasteur* would be understood through a particular tradition, that of the newly identified biopic. But producers are not the only ones who can establish a context of films within which a given film will be read. Just as Frye ensured that Molière would be read within a New Comedy context, rather than against the Old Comedy–related slapstick tradition, the romance-oriented comedy-ballet mode, or the tragic dark comedy strain (each of which many of Molière's plays fit just as well as New Comedy), so Elsaesser and the rehabilitators of the woman's film have ensured that, say, Sirk's *Tarnished Angels* (1957) would be read in the unexpected context of *Stella Dallas* (1937) and *Rebecca* (1940), films that another era would have placed in entirely different genres. Placing films that include a great deal of male action, like most of Sirk's later work, in the context of films built around female performers and domestic plots, has the effect of concentrating critical attention on Sirk's women, thus transferring his films effectively from one genre to another.

5. In the regenrification process, critics regularly take on the cycle-formation function previously associated only with film production. To some recent genre theorists, for whom traditional genre definitions remain sacrosanct, the process of generic redefinition may seem unauthorized, interventionist, and thus undesirable. Yet as treated here, critics' recourse to regenrification as part of their critical and rhetorical arsenal is entirely expected, reason-

able, and in any case not preventable. Feminist critics are thus not wrong to redefine the woman's film and family melodrama, they are simply going about their business. Though we often like to think of ourselves as objective and distanced from our objects of study, we too have objectives and needs, we too must differentiate our products from those of rival critics. In other words, today's critics find themselves in the same position vis-à-vis yesterday's films as yesterday's producers vis-à-vis day-before-yesterday's films. Just as producers would assay a successful film, replicating certain aspects in order to initiate a successful cycle, so critics in all periods assess recent criticism, replicating certain aspects of successful publications in order to initiate a successful critical cycle. But those same critics also assay groups of films, creating new cycles in support of their own interests. The redefinition and rehabilitation of the woman's film and family melodrama provide a particularly clear example of this process.

6. Studio-initiated cycles become genres only through industrywide adoption of their basic characteristics. This rule governs both studio-produced and critic-initiated cycles: until a cycle is consecrated as a genre by industrywide recognition, it remains a cycle. Thus family melodrama, first constituted as a cycle by Thomas Elsaesser, became a genre virtually replacing melodrama when first Tom Schatz and then the feminist critics previously cited reiterated in their analyses Elsaesser's implied corpus, context, and reading formation. The woman's film in turn remained no more than a cycle, slightly redefined from contemporary critical usage, until its quotation marks were removed and its affinities with the newly redefined family melodrama were discovered. Once it gained generic independence, the redefined and regenrified woman's film garnered the freedom to associate with an entirely new class of texts: popular novels, radio programs, television shows, and films made by women.

Opposition, Poaching, Remapping, Bricolage

In recent years, critics have offered descriptions of the reading process following the model either of Stuart Hall or Michel de Certeau. In an important article entitled "Encoding/Decoding," Hall describes readers as either accepting, negotiating, or opposing an intended reading. For de Certeau, "readers are travelers; they move across lands belonging to someone else, like nomads poaching their way across fields they did not write, despoiling the wealth of Egypt to enjoy it themselves" (174). The "poaching nomad" metaphor proves strikingly revelatory of Hall's and de Certeau's fundamental conservatism. According to de Certeau's account, there once was a great nation named Egypt, now despoiled by a tribe of nomads. Nothing before, nothing after. But how did Egypt get to be a great nation and what happened to the nomads? De Certeau's "snapshot" historiography occludes discussion of these questions.

Instead of describing the overall process of reading and its relationship to institutions, both Hall and de Certeau are content to enlarge a single moment of that process. How did intended readings become identifiable as such? Indeed, how did some people achieve the right to encode meanings, while others are reduced to decoding? As Hall and his followers model the situation, even the most oppositional reading is still just an act of decoding, ultimately dependent on a prior act of encoding. Though the connections between encoding and decoding are carefully traced, no path leads from decoding to subsequent encodings, from opposing to intending, from the margins of a current society to the center of a reconfigured society. Similarly, de Certeau assumes that the map has already been drawn by others and that no nomadic activity can ever alter it. Readers are not even squatters, who might claim their rights and thus settle the land; they are poachers on land owned by someone else, who established claim to the land in some mythic past. But who first mapped Egypt and just what did happen to Joseph, Moses, and their tribe of nomads?

Over the past two decades, reception studies have become a growth industry. Surprisingly, however, reception-oriented theorists have failed to draw the radical conclusions of their insights. Stressing localized reception (in time as well as space) of texts produced by someone outside the reception sphere, critics have never taken seriously the ability of audiences to generate their own texts and thus to become encoders, mapmakers, and owners in their own right. Only when we voluntarily restrict our vision to a narrow slice of history do the players appear to be Egypt and the nomads. When we take a wider view, we easily recognize that civilizations have a more complex relation to poachers and nomads. In fact, every civilization was, in an important sense, produced by the settling of nomads. But once they have settled and drawn a new map, every former band of nomads is nothing more than another Egypt now subject to the poaching of a new band of nomads. With each cycle, the nomadic poachers become property owners, thereby establishing the capital that attracts still others' poaching activity.

Tales of marauding tribes on the upper reaches of the Nile may seem entirely unrelated to film genre, yet the system is the same. In order to create new film cycles, producers must attach new adjectives to existing substantival genres. In so doing, producers are "poaching" on established genre territory. Yet, as we have seen, this unauthorized, product-differentiating activity often congeals into a new genre immediately subject to further nomadic raiding. Cycles and genres, nomads and civilizations, raids and institutions, poachers and owners—all are part of the ongoing remapping process that alternately energizes and fixes human perception. When cycles settle into genres, their fixity makes them perfect targets for raids by new cycles. When their wandering in the wilderness is done, nomads spawn civilizations only to be robbed and plundered by yet another wandering tribe. After their raid on existing film vocabulary, feminist film critics formed a series of successful institutions that for now protect their acquisitions but must eventually succumb to yet other raiders. Successful poachers eventually retire with their spoils to a New World, where they will in turn be despoiled by a new generation of poachers. Those who poached on *drama* by adding to it a nomadic *melo-* need not be surprised when a new group of nomads kidnaps the resultant *melodrama* and mates it with a wandering *family*.

When Steve Neale demonstrates that recent critics' genre terms are inconsistent with the generic terminology originally used to describe those films, he appears to be saying that recent critics are using the wrong generic terms. This article has offered another way of looking at the problem. Instead of seeing some critics as right and others as wrong, we must interpret both approaches as attempts to capture jurisdiction over the right to redefine the texts in question. Rather than assume that generic labels have—or should have—a stable existence, we must heed the examples of the woman's film and family melodrama, recognizing the permanent availability of all cultural products to serve as signifiers in the cultural bricolage that is our life.

Notes

1. The following account differs considerably from the approach taken by Alastair Fowler, the only English-language critic who has dealt seriously with the

difference between adjective-based and noun-based generic nomenclature. In chapter 7 of *Kinds of Literature: An Introduction to the Theory of Genres and Modes*, Fowler identifies noun-based terms with genres (for example, comedy) and adjectival terminology with what he calls modes (for example, the comic novel). In Fowler's account, the latter are always derivative of the former; a careful study of film genre terminology leads to the quite different conclusions presented here. See also the work of Jean-Louis Leutrat and Suzanne Liandrat-Guigues (95, 105–7), who describe the differences between the term *western* as noun and adjective.

    2. The asterisks used here according to the conventions of linguistics designate hypothetical categories never actually observed in the field.

Works Cited

Altman, Rick. *The American Film Musical.* Bloomington: Indiana UP, 1987.

Brooks, Peter. *The Melodramatic Imagination: Balzac, Henry James, Melodrama, and the Mode of Excess.* New Haven: Yale UP, 1976.

Brunetière, Ferdinand. *L'Evolution des genres dans l'histoire de la littérature.* Paris: Hachette, 1890–1894.

Cook, David. *A History of Narrative Film.* 2nd ed. New York: Norton, 1990.

Cook, Pam. "Melodrama and the Women's Picture." *Gainsborough Melodrama.* Ed. Sue Aspinall and Sue Harper. London: British Film Institute Dossier 18, 1983.

de Certeau, Michel. *The Practice of Everyday Life.* Tr. Stephen F. Rendall. Berkeley: U of California P, 1984.

Delamater, Jerome. "Performing Arts: The Musical." *American Film Genres.* Ed. Stuart Kaminsky. Dayton: Pflaum, 1974.

Dick, Bernard F. *Anatomy of Film.* 2nd ed. New York: St. Martin's, 1990.

Doane, Mary Ann. *The Desire to Desire: The Woman's Film of the 1940s.* Bloomington: Indiana UP, 1987.

———. "The Woman's Film: Possession and Address." *Re-Vision: Essays in Feminist Film Criticism.* Ed. Mary Ann Doane, Patricia Mellencamp, Linda Williams. Frederick, Md.: American Film Institute/University Publications of America, 1984. 67–82.

Elsaesser, Thomas. "Film History as Social History: The Dieterle/Warner Brothers Bio-pic." *Wide Angle* 8.2 (1986): 15–31.

———. "Tales of Sound and Fury: Observations on the Family Melodrama." *Film Genre Reader.* Ed. Barry Keith Grant. Austin: U of Texas P, 1986. 278–308.

Feuer, Jane. *The Hollywood Musical.* 2nd ed. Bloomington: Indiana UP, 1993.

———. "Melodrama, Serial Form, and Television Today." *Screen* 25.1 (Jan. 1984): 4–16.

Flinn, Caryl. *Strains of Utopia: Gender, Nostalgia, and Hollywood Film Music.* Princeton: Princeton UP, 1992.

Fowler, Alastair. *Kinds of Literature: An Introduction to the Theory of Genres and Modes.* Cambridge: Harvard UP, 1982.

Frye, Northrop. *Anatomy of Criticism.* Princeton: Princeton UP, 1957.

———. "The Argument of Comedy." *English Institute Essays.* New York: Columbia UP, 1949.

Gaines, Jane. "Costume and Narrative: How Dress Tells the Woman's Story." *Fabrications: Costume and the Female Body.* Ed. Jane Gaines and Charlotte Herzog. New York: Routledge, 1990. 180–211.

Gallagher, Tag. "Shoot-Out at the Genre Corral: Problems in the 'Evolution' of the Western." *Film Genre Reader.* Ed. Barry Keith Grant. Austin: U of Texas P, 1986. 202–16.

Goldmann, Lucien. *Le Dieu caché: Etude sur la vision tragique dans les Pensées de Pascal et dans le théâtre de Racine.* Paris: Gallimard, 1959.

Hall, Stuart. "Encoding/Decoding." *Culture, Media, Language.* Ed. Stuart Hall, Dorothy Hobson, Andrew Lowe, and Paul Willis. London: Hutchinson, 1980.

Haskell, Molly. *From Reverence to Rape: The Treatment of Women in the Movies.* New York: Penguin, 1974.

Johnston, Claire. "Women's Cinema as Counter-Cinema." *Notes on Women's Cinema.* London: Society for Education in Film and Television, 1973. 24–31.

Kaplan, E. Ann. *Women and Film: Both Sides of the Camera.* New York: Methuen, 1983.

Koszarski, Richard. *An Evening's Entertainment: The Age of the Silent Feature Picture, 1915–1928.* New York: Scribner's, 1990.

Kuhn, Annette. *Women's Pictures: Feminism and Cinema.* London: Routledge and Kegan Paul, 1982.

Lang, Robert. *American Film Melodrama: Griffith, Vidor, Minnelli.* Princeton: Princeton UP, 1989.

Leutrat, Jean-Louis, and Suzanne Liandrat-Guigues. *Les Cartes de l'Ouest. Un genre cinématographique: le western.* Paris: Armand Colin, 1990.

Maltby, Richard, and Ian Craven. *Hollywood Cinema: An Introduction.* Oxford: Blackwell, 1995.

Mast, Gerald. *The Comic Mind: Comedy and the Movies.* Indianapolis: Bobbs-Merrill, 1973.

Mayne, Judith. "The Woman at the Keyhole: Women's Cinema and Feminist Criticism." *Re-Vision: Essays in Feminist Film Criticism.* Ed. Mary Ann Doane, Patricia Mellencamp, Linda Williams. Frederick, Md.: American Film Institute/University Publications of America, 1984. 49–66.

Merritt, Russell. "Melodrama: Post-Mortem for a Phantom Genre." *Wide Angle* 5.3 (1983): 24–31.

Modleski, Tania. *Loving with a Vengeance: Mass-Produced Fantasies for Women.* Hamden, Conn.: Archon Books, 1982.

———. "Time and Desire in the Woman's Film." *Cinema Journal* 23.3 (1984): 19–30.

Mulvey, Laura. "Melodrama In and Out of the Home." *High Theory/Low Culture: Analyzing Popular Television and Film.* Ed. Colin McCabe. Manchester: Manchester UP, 1986.

———. "Notes on Sirk and Melodrama." *Movie* 25 (winter 1977–1978): 53–56. Reprinted in *Home Is Where the Heart Is.* Ed. Christine Gledhill. London: British Film Institute, 1987.

Neale, Stephen. "Melo Talk: On the Meaning and Use of the Term 'Melodrama' in the American Trade Press." *Velvet Light Trap* 32 (fall 1993): 66–89.

———. "Questions of Genre." *Screen* 31.1 (1990): 45–66.

Nowell-Smith, Geoffrey. "Minnelli and Melodrama." *Screen* 18.2 (1977): 113–18.

Sacks, Sheldon. "The Psychological Implications of Generic Distinctions." *Genre* 1.2 (1968): 106–15, 120–23.

Schatz, Thomas. *Hollywood Genre: Formulas, Filmmaking, and the Studio System.* New York: Random House, 1981.

Singer, Ben. "Female Power in the Serial-Queen Melodrama: The Etiology of an Anomaly." *camera obscura* 22 (Jan. 1990): 90–129.

Sklar, Robert. *Film: An International History of the Medium.* New York: Prentice Hall and Harry N. Abrams, 1993.

Turim, Maureen. *Flashbacks in Film: Memory and History.* New York: Routledge, 1989.

Williams, Linda. "'Something Else Besides a Mother': *Stella Dallas* and the Maternal Melodrama." *Cinema Journal* 24.1 (1984): 2–27.

Melodrama Revised

LINDA WILLIAMS

Melodrama is the fundamental mode of popular American moving pictures. It is not a specific genre like the western or horror film; it is not a "deviation" of the classical realist narrative; it cannot be located primarily in woman's films, "weepies," or family melodramas—though it includes them. Rather, melodrama is a peculiarly democratic and American form that seeks dramatic revelation of moral and emotional truths through a dialectic of pathos and action. It is the foundation of the classical Hollywood movie.

American melodrama originates in the well-known theatrics and spectacles of the nineteenth-century stage, which many critics and historians have viewed as antithetical to cinematic realism. I will argue, however, that supposedly realist cinematic *effects*—whether of setting, action, acting or narrative motivation—most often operate in the service of melodramatic *affects*. We should not be fooled, then, by the superficial realism of popular American movies, by the use of real city streets for chases, or by the introduction of more complex psychological motivations for victims and villains. If emotional and moral registers are sounded, if a work invites us to feel sympathy for the virtues of beset victims, if the narrative trajectory is ultimately more concerned with a retrieval and staging of innocence than with the psychological causes of motives and action, then the operative mode is melodrama. In cinema the mode of melodrama defines a broad category of moving pictures that move us to pathos for protagonists beset by forces more powerful than they and who are perceived as victims. Since the rise of American melodrama on the mid-nineteenth-century stage, a relatively feminized victimhood has been identified with virtue and innocence. At least since Uncle Tom and Little Eva, the suffering victims of popular American stage and screen have been the protagonists endowed with the most moral authority.

In the present essay I set out the terms of a revised theory of a melo-dramatic mode—rather than the more familiar notion of the melodra-matic genre—that seems crucial to any further consideration of popular American moving pictures. An initial survey of the status and place of melodrama in film studies serves as an explanation for the neglect of this basic mode.

The Place of Melodrama in Film Studies

In her insightful introduction to a volume of essays on melodrama, *Home Is Where the Heart Is: Studies in Melodrama and the Woman's Film*, Christine Gledhill tells us that film studies has conceived melodrama in "predominately pejorative terms."[1] From the turn of the century to the sixties, melodrama was the "anti-value for a critical field in which tragedy and realism became cornerstones of 'high' cultural value, needing protection from mass, 'melodramatic' entertainment" (5). Popular cinema was validated only as it seemed to diverge from melodramatic origins in works of humanist realism.

Gledhill notes that the rise of genre criticism in the sixties did little to recover the reputation of melodrama, partly because genre criticism was marked by defensiveness and partly because it focused on discrete genres whose iconography was recognizable at a glance. In the few places where melodrama was seen to have a visible generic existence— in the family melodrama and the woman's film—melodrama could offer neither the thematic and evolutionary coherence exhibited by, say, the western, nor sufficient cultural prestige to appeal to the cognoscenti— condemned as it was by association with a mass and, above all, "female audience" (6).

The two major strikes against melodrama were thus the related "ex-cesses" of emotional manipulativeness and association with feminin-ity. These qualities only began to be taken seriously when excess could be deemed ironic and thus subversive of the coherence of mainstream cinema. Thus, as Gledhill notes, melodrama was "redeemed" as a genre in film studies in the early seventies through a reading of the ironic melodramatic excesses located especially in the work of Douglas Sirk. "Through discovery of Sirk, a genre came into view" (7).

Sirk's gloriously overblown melodramas of the fifties—*Magnificent Obsession* (1954), *All That Heaven Allows* (1956), *Written on the Wind* (1957), *Imitation of Life* (1959)—were enthusiastically defended by seventies film critics and theorists, along with a range of other films by Nicholas Ray, Vincente Minnelli, and Elia Kazan, as scathing critiques of the family and of a repressed and perverse fifties normalcy. In 1972 Thomas Elsaesser's essay "Tales of Sound and Fury" made important links between Hollywood cinema and the heritage of European melodramatic forms. As Gledhill notes, the essay transcended its own formalist approach, suggesting that American cinema begins and rests within a melodramatic tradition.[2]

Unfortunately, however, the issue of the formative influence of melodrama was not pursued by Elsaesser or others. Gledhill insightfully points out that "to have pursued Elsaesser's line of investigation would have meant rethinking, rather than dismissing, the 'great tradition' of humanist realism. . . . In particular it would have meant rethinking both realism and the nineteenth-century novel in their relationship with melodrama" (8).

Film studies established a rigid polarity: on the one hand, a bourgeois, classical realist, acritical "norm," and on the other hand, an antirealist, melodramatic, critical "excess." In this way melodrama could never be investigated as a basic element of popular cinema, but only as an oppositional excess. More importantly, this so-excessive-as-to-be-ironic model rendered taboo the most crucial element of the study of melodrama: its capacity to generate emotion in audiences.

Critics of fifties family melodrama delighted in the way the repressed emotions of characters seemed to be "siphoned off" onto the vivid colors and mute gestures and general hysteria of the mise-en-scène, but they were strangely silent about the emotional reactions of audiences to all this hysteria induced by the mise-en-scène. It was almost as if there were a "bad" melodrama of manipulated, naively felt, feminine emotions and a "good" melodrama of ironical hysterical excess thought to be immune to the more pathetic emotions.[3]

As a way of surveying feminist film critics' approach-avoidance to affective response in the study of the melodramatic woman's film, I would like to summarize a debate that took place originally between E. Ann Kaplan and myself over a hypothetical female viewer's response to the melodramatic woman's film, *Stella Dallas* (King Vidor, 1937). My concern here is not to reanimate old arguments, but rather to restate what, in a veiled and coded way, this debate now seems to have really been about: women's attraction-repulsion to the pathos of virtuous suffering.

King Vidor's *Stella Dallas*, starring Barbara Stanwyck as the ambitious working-class woman whose daughter becomes her life, is an excruciatingly pathetic maternal melodrama of mother-daughter possession and loss. In 1984 I published an article entitled "'Something Else Besides a Mother': *Stella Dallas* and the Maternal Melodrama" in *Cinema Journal*.[4] Uncomfortable with the "gaze is male" formulation of much feminist film theory of the time, which saw all mainstream cinema structured by male desire and a masculine subject position,[5] as well as with the exceptional, ironic status of what was then valued in Sirkian melodrama, I was interested in the construction of feminine viewing positions in more straightforwardly sentimental woman's films. In particular, I disagreed with E. Ann Kaplan's previously published reading of the film, which saw a female viewer who identified with Stella, the film's suffering mother protagonist, as acceding to the necessity for her sacrifice. Kaplan argued that the female spectator was rendered as passive and pathetic as Stella herself by the end of the film.[6]

Without abandoning the basic paradigm of a centered and unifying, distanced cinematic "gaze," I nevertheless borrowed concepts from Peter Brooks's study of late-eighteenth- and nineteenth-century stage melodrama to argue that *Stella Dallas* belonged to a melodramatic mode distinct from classical realism in its emphasis on the domestic sphere of powerless women and children protagonists whose only possible agency derives from the virtue of their suffering. "What happens," I asked, "when a mother and daughter, who are so closely identified that the usual distinctions between subject and object do not apply, take one another as their primary objects of desire?" And "what happens when the significant viewer of such a drama is also a woman?"[7]

My answer ran counter to Kaplan's and borrowed from an earlier essay by Christine Gledhill in which she noted that "there are spaces in which women, out of their socially constructed differences as women, can and do resist."[8] Maternal melodramas, I argued, not only address female audiences about issues of primary concern to women, but these melodramas have inscribed in them "reading positions" based upon the different ways women take on their identities under patriarchy—reading positions that result from the social fact of female mothering.[9]

At the pathos-filled end of the film, the viewer sees Stella looking through a picture window at her daughter, who is marrying into an upper-class milieu to which Stella herself will never belong. Outside the window in the rain, self-exiled from the ideal world within, Stella, the mother who gives up the one thing in the world dear to her, is nevertheless triumphant in her tears. Is the female viewer so identified with Stella's triumphant tears, I asked, that she has no ability to criticize or resist the patriarchal value system that makes her presence in her daughter's newly acquired social milieu excessive?

Because the end of the film so insistently frames the issue of female spectatorship—placing Stella like a movie spectator outside the window gazing at the daughter who is now lost to her—*Stella Dallas* seemed a crucial film. Kaplan argued that a female viewer was positioned by the film, like Stella herself, as powerless witness of a scene that excluded her. I argued that although this final scene functions to efface Stella, the female spectator does not necessarily acquiesce in the necessity of this sacrifice, nor does she identify solely with the effaced Stella at this final moment.

I argued, in other words, that there was room for some negotiation in a female viewing position that was animated by the contradiction of identifying both as a woman and a mother.[10] The crux of my argument, however, rested upon a fairly complex reinterpretation of psychoanalytic concepts of fetishistic disavowal. I claimed that the female spectator is as capable of experiencing the contradiction between knowledge and belief in an image as any healthily neurotic male viewer. However, in arguing that women spectators could be voyeurs and fetishists too, though with a difference, I unfortunately recuperated the monolithic gaze paradigm of spectatorship that I had wanted to escape. What seemed to be at issue was the question of spectatorial unity: could a female spectator be divided in her reactions to a work that was not ironically parodying the powerful maternal emotions of pride in the success of the child and, simultaneously, sorrow in loss? I answered, against Kaplan, that such division was possible, but the way I cast the division, as Brechtian distanciation and critique, avoided the more crucial and obvious question of spectatorial emotion in melodrama.

The quintessentially feminine emotion of pathos was viewed as a key agent of women's oppression by feminists in the early and mid-eighties. Anger was viewed by feminism as a liberating emotion, pathos as enslaving.[11] Viewer identification with pathetic suffering seemed only to invoke the dangerous specter of masochism, which seemed antithetical to a woman's quest to break out of patriarchal power and control. The entirely negative specter of masochism loomed large in Mary Ann

Doane's brilliant 1987 study of the woman's film, *The Desire to Desire*. To Doane the excessive pathos of the woman's film always threatened to overwhelm the female spectator in a dangerously close masochistic "over-identification" with the victimized woman.[12] With the marked exception of Gledhill, none of the feminist critics to join directly or indirectly in this debate could conceive of a female spectator moved by the wedding spectacle on the other side of the window as anything but manipulated.[13] The only way I could retrieve what I sensed to be the importance of melodrama was to argue that such moving images also made us angry, that women were not their dupes; we were critical too. I wrote: "It is a terrible underestimation of the female viewer to presume that she is wholly seduced by a naive belief in these masochistic images. . . . For unlike tragedy, melodrama does not reconcile its audience to an inevitable suffering. Rather than raging against a fate that the audience has learned to accept, the female hero often accepts a fate that the audience at least partially questions."[14]

Though I still agree with this today, I am struck by the unwillingness to recognize the importance of melodramatic pathos—of being moved by a moving picture. Both drawn to and repelled by the spectacle of virtuous and pathetic suffering, feminist critics were torn: we wanted to properly condemn the abjection of suffering womanhood, yet in the almost loving detail of our growing analyses of melodramatic subgenres—medical discourse, gothic melodrama, romance melodrama, maternal melodrama—it was clear that something more than condemnation was taking place. An opposition to female suffering was certainly an important goal of feminism, but in the process of distinguishing our "properly" feminist distance from melodrama's emotions, we failed to confront the importance of pathos itself and the fact that a surprising power lay in identifying with victimhood.[15]

It was not simply that feminist critics who offered analyses of woman's films were divided over the effects of pathos on audiences; we were convinced that pathos was, in itself, an excess of feeling that threatened to overwhelm the emerging liberated woman. With the great advantage of hindsight, I would say that the entire *Stella Dallas* debate was over what it meant for a woman viewer to cry at the end of the film. Did the emotion swallow us up, or did we have room within it to think? Could we, in other words, think both with and through our bodies in our spectating capacities as witnesses to abjection? And wasn't this whole debate carried out as if men never cried at the movies?[16] The persistent error in all this early work on melodramatic woman's films was the idea that these were exceptional texts, both as melodramas and as melodramas with a specific address to women viewers. Strong emotions that can move audiences to tears are not the special province of women, but of a melodramatic "feminization" that, as Ann Douglas long ago noted, has been a persistent feature of American popular culture at least since the mid-nineteenth century.[17] If the sad-ending maternal melodrama with its pathos centered on the lost connection to the mother seemed the quintessential example of all melodrama, then the thing to do would be to explore this pathos in relation to a range of other popular films rather than to bracket it as melodramatic excess. Instead, we perpetuated the notion that melodrama was a minority genre in which the excessive and archaic nineteenth-century emotions of women anachronistically flourished.

Once again it was Christine Gledhill who saw that the real problem in our thinking about the exceptional nature of melodrama was inextricable from prevalent theories of the classical realist text. Melodrama needs to be understood, Gledhill argued, as an aesthetic and epistemological mode distinct from (if related to) realism, having different purposes, and deploying different strategies, modes of address, forms of engagement and identification.[18] Borrowing from Peter Brooks's study of the nineteenth-century novel's inheritance from the melodramatic stage, Gledhill argued that melodrama emerged as a response to an implicit gap in bourgeois epistemology.[19] Where realism ignores these contradictions in its confidence in the causal explanations of the human sciences, modernism seeks obsessively to expose them. Melodrama, however, takes a different approach: "it both insists on the realities of life in bourgeois democracy—the material parameters of lived experience, individual personality, the fundamental psychic relations of family life—and, in an implicit recognition of the limitations of the conventions of representation . . . proceeds to insist on, force into an aesthetic presence, desires for identity, value, and fullness of signification beyond the powers of language to supply."[20] As a result, melodrama is structured upon the "dual recognition" of how things are and how they should be. In melodrama there is a moral, wish-fulfilling impulse towards the achievement of justice that gives American popular culture its strength and appeal as the powerless yet virtuous seek to return to the "innocence" of their origins.

In thus turning to melodrama—not as a genre exceptional to a classical realist norm, but as a more pervasive mode with its own rhetoric and aesthetic—Gledhill embraces melodrama's central feature of pathos and "solves" the problem of its apparent monopathy. She argues that if a melodramatic character appeals to our sympathy, it is because pathos involves us in assessing suffering in terms of our privileged knowledge of its nature and causes. Pathos is thus "intensified by the misrecognition of a sympathetic protagonist because the audience has privileged knowledge of the 'true' situation."[21] Gledhill shows, for example, how scene after scene of *Stella Dallas* permits the viewer to see a character misconstruing the meaning of an act or gesture. These scenes work, she argues, because the audience is outside a particular point of view but participating in it with a privileged knowledge of the total constellation. Pathos in the spectator is thus never merely a matter of losing oneself in "over-identification." It is never a matter of simply mimicking the emotion of the protagonist, but, rather, a complex negotiation between emotions and between emotion and thought.

The understanding of melodrama has been impeded by the failure to acknowledge the complex tensions between different emotions as well as the relation of thought to emotion. The overly simplistic notion of the "monopathy" of melodramatic characters—the idea that each character in melodrama sounds a single emotional note that is in turn simply mimicked by the viewer—has impeded the serious study of how complexly we can be "moved." Certainly Stella, smiling through her tears, is the very embodiment of internally conflicted and complex emotions. If pathos is crucial to melodrama, it is always in tension with other emotions and, as I hope to show in the following, is in a constant dynamic relation with that other primary staple of American popular movies: action—the spectacular rescues, chases, and fights that augment, prolong, and conclude pathos.

The question to put to *Stella Dallas*, and by extension to the "subgenre" of the woman's film, and finally to the pervasive melodramatic mode of American cinema, is thus not whether it is complicit with or resistant to dominant, patriarchal ideology.[22] All American melodrama is produced, and operates within, dominant patriarchal, western, capitalist discourses and ideologies. However, these discourses and ideologies are frequently contradictory and constantly in flux. Popular American movies have been popular because of their ability to seem to resolve basic contradictions at a mythic level—whether conflicts between garden and civilization typical of the western, or between love and ambition typical of the biopic, the family melodrama, and the gangster film.[23]

The most fruitful approach to melodrama would thus not be to argue over the progressive or regressive nature of particular texts for particular viewers—whether women, gays, lesbians, African Americans, Native Americans, Italian Americans, Jewish Americans, and so on. Rather, we should do as Gledhill suggests and has magnificently begun to do herself: pick up the threads of a general study of melodrama as a broadly important cultural form inherited from the nineteenth-century stage, in tension with and transformed by realism and the more realistic techniques of cinema, yet best understood *as melodrama*, not failed tragedy or inadequate realism.

Melodrama should be viewed, then, not as an excess or an aberration but in many ways as the typical form of American popular narrative in literature, stage, film, and television. It is the best example of American culture's (often hypocritical) notion of itself as the locus of innocence and virtue. If we want to confront the centrality of melodrama to American moving-image culture, we must first turn to the most basic forms of melodrama, and not only to a subghetto of woman's films, to seek out the dominant features of an American melodramatic mode. For if melodrama was misclassified as a sentimental genre for women, it is partly because other melodramatic genres such as the western and gangster films, which received early legitimacy in film study, had already been constructed, as Christine Gledhill notes, in relation to supposedly masculine cultural values.[24]

Because this pat division between a presumably realist sphere of masculine action and a presumably melodramatic sphere of feminine emotion was not challenged, narrative cinema as a whole has been theorized as a realist, inherently masculine, medium whose "classical" features are supposedly anathema to its melodramatic infancy and childhood.[25] Whereas silent cinema has always been recognized as melodrama at some level, the "essential" art and language of cinema has not. Rather, melodrama has been viewed either as that which cinema has grown up out of or that to which it sometimes regresses.

However, as both Steve Neale and Christine Gledhill note, exhibition categories continued to assert the melodramatic base of most genres well into the sound era. The names of these categories are themselves revealing: western melodrama, crime melodrama, sex melodrama, backwoods melodrama, romantic melodrama, and so on.[26] A glance through the *AFI Catalog of Features, 1921–1930*, reveals an even more remarkable proliferation of categories of melodrama: stunt melodrama, society melodrama, mystery melodrama, rural melodrama, action melodrama, crook melodrama, underworld melodrama, and even comedy-melodrama, as well as just plain melodrama. Though one might attribute this proliferation of types of melodrama to the predominance of the silent era in this period, a look at a more recent AFI volume—that covering 1961–1970—shows that many of these categories have persisted at least in the eyes of archivists and catalogists. In fact, in addition to nine of the preceding categories, this period even lists a new one, science fiction melodrama.[27] What is striking in these examples is the way the noun *melodrama* functions as a basic mode of storytelling. The term indicates a form of exciting, sensational, and, above all, moving story that can be further differentiated by specifications of setting or milieu (such as *society melodrama*) or genre (such as *western melodrama*). It is this basic sense of melodrama as a modality of narrative with a high quotient of pathos and action to which we need to attend if we are to confront the most fundamental appeal of movies.

The Melodramatic Mode: Excess or Norm?

Perhaps the most important single work contributing to the rehabilitation of the term *melodrama* as a cultural form has been Peter Brooks's *The Melodramatic Imagination: Balzac, Henry James, Melodrama, and the Mode of Excess*. Brooks offers a valuable appreciation of the historical origins of the nineteenth-century melodramatic project. This appreciation is still the best grounding for an understanding of its carryover into twentieth-century mass culture. Brooks's real project was not to study melodrama per se but to understand the melodramatic elements informing the fiction of Honoré de Balzac and Henry James. In the process, however, he sought out the roots of the melodramatic imagination in the French popular theater and offered important reasons for its rise and persistence.

Brooks's greatest advantage in this project may have been his ignorance of film theory and criticism. Unlike film critics who have seen melodrama as an anachronism to be overcome or subverted, Brooks takes it seriously as a quintessentially modern (though not modernist) form arising out of a particular historical conjuncture: the postrevolutionary, post-Enlightenment, postsacred world where traditional imperatives of truth and morality had been violently questioned and yet in which there was still a need to forge some semblance of truth and morality.[28]

Brooks's central thesis is that, in the absence of a moral and social order linked to the sacred, and in the presence of a reduced private and domestic sphere that has increasingly become the entire realm of personal significance, a theatrical form of sensation developed that carried the burden of expressing what Brooks calls the "'moral occult,' the domain of operative spiritual values which is both indicated within and masked by the surface of reality" (5). This quest for a hidden moral legibility is crucial to all melodrama.

The theatrical function of melodrama's big sensation scenes was to be able to put forth a moral truth in gesture and to picture what could not be fully spoken in words. Brooks shows that the rise of melodrama was linked to the ban on speech in unlicensed French theaters. Usually, the unspeakable truth revealed in the sensation scene is the revelation of who is the true villain, who the innocent victim. The revelation occurs as a spectacular, moving sensation—that is, it is felt as sensation and not simply registered as ratiocination in the cause-effect logic of narrative—because it shifts to a different register of signification, often bypassing language altogether. Music, gesture, pantomime, and, I would add, most forms of sustained physical action performed without dialogue, are the most familiar elements of these sensational effects.

Brooks points to Guilbert de Pixérécourt's 1818 melodrama *La Fille de l'exilé*, in which a sixteen-year-old Siberian girl travels to Moscow to seek pardon from the czar for her exiled father. On the way she falls into the hands of Ivan, her father's persecutor, himself now threatened by ferocious Tartars. The girl saves Ivan in a big sensation scene by holding the cross of her virtuous dead mother over his head. The Tartars shrink back under the power of this holy sign. But the sensation does not end there. Ivan tells the Tartars that the poor girl who protects him is actually the devoted daughter of the man he once persecuted: "Ah! such generosity overwhelms me! I lack the words to express. . . . All I can do is admire you and bow my head before you." In a "spontaneous movement" the Tartars form a semicircle around the girl and fall on their knees, astonished at her goodness. The sensation so grandiosely orchestrated here is that of the recognition of virtue by the less virtuous (24–25). Melodramatic denouement is typically some version of this public or private recognition of virtue prolonged in the frozen tableau whose picture speaks more powerfully than words. Each play is not only the drama of a moral dilemma but also the drama of a moral sentiment—usually of a wronged innocence—seeking to say its name but unable, in a postsacred universe, to speak directly (43). Despite the fact that Brooks's study works hard to give melodrama its due rather than to treat it as failed tragedy or as realism manqué, his subtitle, *The Mode of Excess*, indicates that he too views melodrama as a mode in excess of a more classical norm. Instead of tracing the importance of theatrical melodrama in popular culture where it has most powerfully moved audiences, Brooks traces its influence on the "higher art" bourgeois novel, first in Honoré de Balzac, then in the subtle, unspoken revelations of guilt and innocence so crucial to the novels of Henry James. His real interest is thus in how melodrama is subtly embedded in the canon of the nineteenth-century realist novel.

We have already seen how Christine Gledhill solves the problem of Brooks's opposition between realism and melodrama by arguing that melodrama is always grounded in what, for its day, is a strong element of realism: "Taking its stand in the material world of everyday reality and lived experience, and acknowledging the limitations of the conventions of language and representation, it proceeds to force into aesthetic presence identity, value and plenitude of meaning." [29] In other words, Gledhill shows that melodrama is grounded in the conflicts and troubles of everyday, contemporary reality. It seizes upon the social problems of this reality—problems such as illegitimacy, slavery, racism, labor struggles, class division, disease, nuclear annihilation, even the Holocaust. All the afflictions and injustices of the modern, post-Enlightenment world are dramatized in melodrama. Part of the excitement of the form is the genuine turmoil and timeliness of the issues it takes up and the popular debate it can generate when it dramatizes a new controversy or issue. Such was the case when the controversy surrounding the humanity of slaves arrived on the scene in popular melodrama in 1852. Such was the case more recently as homophobia, persecution of the Irish by the British, and persecution of the Jews by the Germans came on the scene in three of the most noted films in the competition for the 1993 Academy Awards: *Philadelphia* (Jonathan Demme), *In the Name of the Father* (Jim Sheridan), and *Schindler's List* (Steven Spielberg).

Where melodrama differs from realism is in its will to force the status quo to yield signs of moral legibility within the limits of the "ideologically permissible." [30] Anyone who has ever taught Greek tragedy to college students knows the difficulty of explaining the concept of tragic fate to them. Try as one might to explain that Oedipus or Agamemnon are not actually punished for wrongdoing when they meet their fates, American students imbued with the popular values of melodrama cannot help but see these fates as punishment for antidemocratic, "overweening" pride. Thus Americans read Greek tragedy melodramatically.

The British, to some extent, and the French, to a greater extent, have long traditions of classical tragedy that lead them to believe that the "norms" of literature and theater are antithetical to melodrama. Americans, however, have a different set of norms. Whether we look at the novelistic romances of Hawthorne, Stowe, or Twain, the popular theater of Belasco, Aiken, Daly, or Boucicault, the silent films of Griffith, DeMille, or Borzage, or the sound films of Ford, Coppola, or Spielberg, the most common thread running among them is not merely a lack of realism or an "excess" of sentiment, but the combined function of realism, sentiment, spectacle, and action in effecting the recognition of a hidden or misunderstood virtue. Hawthorne's Hester Prynne, Stowe's Uncle Tom, Twain's Jim and Huck, Ford's searcher, and Spielberg's E.T., Elliot, and Schindler all share the common function of revealing moral good in a world where virtue has become hard to read.

Let us consider for a moment two highly melodramatic scenes in two of the Oscar-winning films mentioned previously: the moment in *Philadelphia* when Andrew Becket (Tom Hanks) bares his torso to the jury to reveal the marks of skin lesions on his AIDS-stricken body, and the moment toward the end of *Schindler's List* when Schindler (Liam Neeson) emotionally breaks down to reveal his regret at not having rescued more Jews. Both moments are pathetic; both reveal their heroes in instants of weakness and vulnerability that become emblematic of their moral goodness, and both are moments when other people recognize and bear witness to a goodness that is inextricably linked to suffering. The fragile, disease-wracked body of the gay man "on trial," the powerful body of Schindler cowed and speechless in this singular moment of weakness before the Jews he has rescued, share the mute pathos inherent to melodrama.

Both scenes can also easily be criticized as false to a realist representation of the characters. Hanks is portrayed, against gay stereotype, as far too untheatrical a character to find emotional satisfaction in revealing his body in this way; Schindler is portrayed as a man who would never stop to reflect upon the moral good or bad of what he has done—this, indeed, is the genius of Thomas Keneally's novel, based on highly distanced, factual reportage. There is no such moment of moral self-reflection and recognition in Keneally's novel. Yet the theatrical displays of virtue constitute the key emotional highlights of both films and, though false to realism, are melodramatically viable.

Much of the derision of melodrama in American popular culture derives from the sense that such emotional displays of virtue necessarily cheapen a more pure and absolute (and also sternly masculine) morality. Ann Douglas's study of nineteenth-century American culture traces the long process by which a rigorous Calvinist morality was supplanted by what she views as a cheaply sentimental "feminization" of American culture carried out by ministers and lady novelists. Using Little Eva's death in Harriet Beecher Stowe's *Uncle Tom's Cabin* as her own melo-dramatic point of departure, Douglas argues that a wholesale debase-ment of American culture took place in the idealization of feminine qualities of piety, virtue, and passive suffering.

Douglas opposes a popular literature of "excessive" feminine sen-timentalism to a high canonical literature—Melville, Thoreau, Whit-man—which was masculine and active but never popular. Her study of the feminization of nineteenth-century American culture is an ex-planation of how a masculine "high" culture was supplanted by a femi-nine "low" culture. Douglas blames the increased anti-intellectualism and consumerism of American culture, as well as the ensuing back-lash of popular culture masculinization, on a facile cultural feminism.[31] Rather than blame the excesses of feminization, however, we need to investigate the reasons for its popularity: the search for moral legibility in an American context in which the old Calvinist moral certainty was waning. Mass culture melodrama in novels, plays, and later in film and television has been the most important cultural form to fill that void. The end of Calvinist morality thus functions much like the end of the sacred in Brooks's model. In a country with a much less established tra-dition of high art and letters than Europe, it is not surprising that melo-drama filled this void so thoroughly. Another way of putting this would be to say that whereas England had Dickens, and France had Hugo—both popular melodramatists who were also in a sense "great" writers—America had Stowe and later a host of melodramatic filmmakers: Grif-fith, Ford, Vidor, Coppola, Demme, Spielberg, and so on.

We are diverted, therefore, from the significance of melodrama if we pay too much attention to what has been condemned as its excessive emotionality and theatricality. Theatrical acting and Manichaean po-larities are not the essence of this form. They are the means to some-thing more important: the achievement of a felt good, the merger—perhaps even the compromise—of morality and feeling.

Recent critics have attempted to recuperate emotionality and sensa-tionalism from the status of excess. Tom Gunning has rehabilitated the term *attraction* in order to address the emotional and sensational side of cinema spectatorship. Gunning borrows the term from Sergei Eisenstein's celebration of spectacles with particularly strong "sensual or psychological impact" and the ability to aggressively grab and move spectators.[32] The acknowledgment of the existence of a "cinema of attractions" different from the linear narrative of the "classical" realist text has fruitfully called attention to the spectacle side of cinematic visual pleasures in early cinema.

However, when the term simply posits the existence of an ideological "other"—whether spectacle or spectator—who "escapes" the dominant ideology of the classical, it remains implicated in the putative dominance of the "classical." Janet Staiger argues convincingly that the notion of a war between working class attraction or sensation on the one hand and bourgeois cause-effect narrative with a bourgeois constituency on the other is an over-simplification. Staiger deftly negotiates between those historians who have placed too large a claim on the otherness of cinematic attractions vis-à-vis the classical narrative and those who, like her former collaborators David Bordwell and Kristen Thompson, have argued that "narrative continuity and clarity are the only means of pleasure [audiences] seek during an evening at the theater or movies."[33] Demolishing claims that even the quite primitive 1903 Edwin S. Porter version of *Uncle Tom's Cabin* was a pure spectacle of unreadable cause-effect—since all classes of audience knew the story that lay behind the tableau and since even the tableaux were arranged in a cross-cut manner—Staiger claims that the film "interlaces spectacle with a tight crisscrossing of two subplots for a final, *if melodramatic*, climax. Narrativity and visual spectacle existed as available sites of affective response for all spectators of various classes" (emphasis mine).[34] Staiger offers an important corrective to the concept of a purely linear cause-effect narrative, noting that narrativity and visual spectacle work together to produce affective response. However, as with Brooks and Gunning, the notion of excess still lurks in the telling "if melodramatic" in the preceding quotation, as if *Uncle Tom's Cabin* could ever not be melodramatic. We must study melodrama as melodrama, not as a form that wants to be something else.

Another critic to address the vexed question of the classic versus the melodramatic is Rick Altman. Against Bordwell, Thompson, and Staiger's notion of the dominance of the classical Hollywood cinema, Altman argues that melodrama is more deeply "embedded" within even our most hallowed notion of the classic text than has been realized.[35] For example, he argues that the notion of the "classic" in the "classical Hollywood cinema" is a linear chain of psychologically based causes leading from an initial question or problem to a final, well-motivated solution. According to Bordwell, Thompson, and Staiger, this classical paradigm of narrative logic in which events are subordinated to personal causes of psychologically defined individual characters became the standardized mode of production for the feature film.[36]

Ephemeral spectacle, showmanship, and moments of "artistic motivation," in which audiences admire the show rather than get caught up in the cause-effect linear progress toward narrative resolution, are treated as exceptional moments of what Russian formalist critics call "laying bare the device." Such moments of "flagrant" display are for Bordwell, Thompson, and Staiger of *The Classical Hollywood Cinema* exceptional, and regressive, throwbacks to vaudeville, melodrama, and other spectacle-centered entertainments, though sometimes they are quasi-legitimized by genre.[37] For Bordwell et al. it is the nineteenth-century well-made play that is the major theatrical influence on classical narrative.

The notion that the classical Hollywood narrative subordinates spectacle, emotion, and attraction to the logic of personal causality and cause and effect assumes that the "action" privileged by the form is not spectacular. However, we have only to look at what's playing at the local multiplex to realize that the familiar Hollywood feature of prolonged climactic action is, and I would argue has always been, a melodramatic spectacle (and Gunning's notion of attraction) no matter how goal-driven or embedded within narrative it may be.

Nothing is more sensational in American cinema than the infinite varieties of rescues, accidents, chases, and fights. These "masculine" action-centered multiple climaxes may be scrupulously motivated or wildly implausible depending on the film. However, though usually faithful to the laws of motion and gravity, this realism of action should not fool us into thinking that the dominant mode of such films is realism. Nor should the virility of action itself fool us into thinking that it is not melodramatic.

Altman argues that film scholars have not attended to the popular theater as the original source of these spectacles. He rightly chides film historians and scholars for skipping over such works in their rush to link the emerging film to the realist novel. He also points out that this repression of popular theater has the effect of denying Hollywood cinema its fundamental connection to popular melodramatic tradition. "Unmotivated events, rhythmic montage, highlighted parallelism, overlong spectacles—these are the excesses in the classical narrative system that alert us to the existence of a competing logic, a second voice."[38] To Altman, these excesses give evidence of an "embedded melodramatic mode that subtends classical narrative from *Clarissa* to *Casablanca*." He warns that we should recognize the possibility that such excesses may themselves be organized as a system.[39] I would argue further that if we are to understand melodrama as a system, then we would do well to eliminate the term *excess* from attempts to describe this systematicity. For like Brooks, Altman too easily cedes to the dominance of the classical, realist model with melodrama as its excess. In this model, melodrama remains an archaic throwback rather than, as in Gledhill's model, a fully developed third alternative to both realist and modernist narrative.

Film study needs an even bolder statement: not that melodrama is a submerged, or embedded, tendency within realist narrative—which it certainly can be—but that it has more often itself been the dominant form of popular moving-image narrative. The supposed excess is much more often the mainstream, though it is often not acknowledged as such because melodrama consistently decks itself out in the trappings of realism and the modern (and now, the postmodern). What Altman refers to as the dialectic of the melodramatic mode of narrative in American popular culture is nothing less than the process whereby melodrama sheds its old-fashioned values, acting styles, and ideologies to gain what Gledhill calls the "imprimateur of 'realism'" while it still delivers the melodramatic experience.[40]

Thus the basic vernacular of American moving pictures consists of a story that generates sympathy for a hero who is also a victim and that leads to a climax that permits the audience, and usually other characters, to recognize that character's moral value. This climax revealing the moral good of the victim can tend in one of two directions: either it can consist of a paroxysm of pathos (as in the woman's film or family melodrama variants) or it can take that paroxysm and channel it into the more virile and action-centered variants of rescue, chase, and fight (as in the western and all the action genres).

Much more often melodrama combines pathos and action. *Philadelphia* and *Schindler's List* combine both through the device of splitting the more active hero function (in the person of Schindler and the black, originally homophobic, lawyer played by Denzel Washington) from that of the more passive, suffering victims (Andrew Becket and the none-too-individualized Jews). The important point, however, is that action-centered melodrama is never without pathos, and pathos-centered melodrama is never without at least some action.

But virtuous sufferer and active hero can also be combined in the same person. Stella Dallas throws herself quite actively into the self-sacrificial task of alienating her daughter's affections. She also physically pushes through the crowd in order to effect the ultimate sacrifice of seeing but not participating in her daughter's wedding. Rambo—to cite a stereotypically masculine, action-oriented example—suffers multiple indignities and pathetically suffers in ways that elicit audience empathy before he begins his prolonged rescue-revenge.

Big "sensation" scenes, whether of prolonged "feminine" pathos or prolonged "masculine" action, or mixtures of both, do not interrupt the logical cause-effect progress of a narrative toward conclusion. More often, it is these spectacles of pathos and action that are served by the narrative. As American melodrama developed from stage to screen, and from silence to sound, it frequently instituted more realistic causations and techniques for the display of both pathos and action, but it never ceased to serve the primary ends of displaying both.

To study the relation between pathos and action is to see that there is no pure isolation of pathos in woman's films nor of action in the male action genres. If, as Peter Brooks argues, melodrama is most centrally about moral legibility and the assigning of guilt and innocence in a post-sacred, post-Enlightenment world where moral and religious certainties have been erased, then pathos and action are the two most important means to the achievement of moral legibility.

An early model in silent cinema for this pathos, self-sacrificing side of melodrama is Griffith's *Broken Blossoms* (1919), where the Chinese victim-hero proves his virtue by not taking sexual advantage of the waif he befriends. His attempt to save her from the clutches of her brutal father comes too late, however, and in the pathos-filled ending, in which a virtuous heroine in need of rescue does not get saved in the nick of time, he can only lay out her body and join her in death. This pathos side of melodrama continues in a range of sad-ending melodramas: in most woman's films, in many family melodramas, in sad musicals in which song and dance do not save the day—*Applause* (1929), *Hallelujah* (1929), *A Star is Born* (1954, 1976)—and in "social problem" films without optimistic endings, such as *I Am a Fugitive from a Chain Gang* (1932) or *You Only Live Once* (1937). It also continues in biopics such as *Silkwood* (1983) or *Malcolm X* (1992). In these films, victim-heroes, following in the footsteps of the nineteenth-century melodrama's Uncle Tom and Little Eva, achieve recognition of their virtue through the more passive "deeds" of suffering or self-sacrifice.

The action side of the melodramatic mode finds its silent cinema prototype in Griffith's *The Birth of a Nation* (1915) and *Way Down East* (1920). It is continued in most of the male action genres—westerns, gangster films, war films, cop films, and Clint Eastwood films—as well as happy musicals and social problem films in which more active hero-victims either solve problems through action, as in *Salt of the Earth* (1953) and *Norma Rae* (1979), or are themselves rescued from some fix. In these films the suffering of the victim-hero is important for the establishment of moral legitimacy, but suffering is less extended and ultimately gives way to action. Similarly the recognition of virtue is at least partially achieved through the performance of deeds. Here pathos mixes with other emotions: suspense, fear, anxiety, anger, laughter, and so on, experienced in the rescues, chases, gunfights, fistfights, and spaceship fights of the various action genres.

Obviously there is also a powerful gender and racial component to these two poles of melodrama: the "Yellow man" in *Broken Blossoms,* like his prototype Uncle Tom, is highly feminized and relegated to passive forms of action. Women and minorities traditionally suffer the most and act the least in melodrama. Yet there are notable exceptions. Eliza, the mulatta slave who, unlike Tom in *Uncle Tom's Cabin*, escapes across the ice floes of the Ohio river, is masculinized via action just as Tom is feminized through passive suffering.

Critics and historians of moving images have often been blind to the forest of melodrama because of their attention to the trees of genre. For example, the *Rambo* films were very quickly assimilated into the specific genre of the Vietnam films but have not been much considered as the male action melodramas they so clearly are.[41] Yet a quick look at the first two films in the series, *First Blood* (1982) and *Rambo: First Blood Part II* (1985), can help us to see the much more important influence of the mode of melodrama as a means of "solving" problems of moral legitimacy.

In the first film John Rambo (Sylvester Stallone), a traumatized Vietnam vet, goes on a rampage in a small northwestern town where he has come to find a buddy from the war. The film ends on a spectacular display of pathos as Rambo breaks down and cries in the arms of his former commander. Weeping over a multitude of losses—the loss of the war, the loss of buddies, the loss of innocence—Rambo is presented entirely as a victim of a government that would not let him win. *Rambo: First Blood Part II*, the more wildly popular sequel to this film, rechannels this pathos into action as Rambo is given his chance to "win this time." But even the virile action-orientation of the sequel is premised upon our continued perception of Rambo as a virtuous victim whose only motive is a melodramatic desire to return to the innocence of an unproblematic love of country and the simple demand for that love's return: "for our country to love us as much as we love it."

Thus even the sequel works hard to establish the pathos of Rambo's victim status; it begins with Rambo suffering silently on a chain gang. *Rambo* has been justly derided as representing the height of American bad conscience—even false consciousness—about the Vietnam War. But if we want to criticize *Rambo*, or for that matter the rash of films from *The Green Berets* and *The Deer Hunter* to *Platoon* and *Casualties of War* lined up on both sides of the Vietnam fiasco, we do well to see that what makes them tick is precisely their ability to address the moral dilemma of bad conscience, to reconfigure victims and villains. What makes them tick is thus not simply their action-adventure exploits but the activation of such exploits within a melodramatic mode struggling to "solve" the overwhelming moral burden of having been the "bad guys" in a lost war. The greater the historical burden of guilt, the more pathetically and the more actively the melodrama works to recognize and regain a lost innocence.

In its own way, *Schindler's List* represents a more respectable and serious but no less melodramatic example of the impulse to regain a lost innocence vis-à-vis the guilt of the Holocaust. The venal Schindler ultimately relieves the rest of us—Americans and Germans alike—of the historical burden of guilt, not because he was the exceptional man who acted when others did not, but because he was so much the ordinary, materialistic businessman. Schindler's rescue of over a thousand Jews also rescues the potential moral good of all ordinary people who played along with the Nazis.

This may sound as if I am equating melodrama with the most egregious false consciousness. In one sense I am. Melodrama is by definition the retrieval of an absolute innocence and good in which most thinking people do not put much faith. However, what we think and what we feel at the "movies" are often two very different things. We go to the movies not to think but to be moved. In a postsacred world, melodrama represents one of the most significant, and deeply symptomatic, ways we negotiate moral feeling.

Steven Spielberg and George Cosmatos (*Rambo*'s director) make us "feel good" about the Holocaust and Vietnam by rewriting the primary scenario of destruction and devastation with the historically quite fanciful (even if one of them is true) rescues of helpless victims (Jews in *Schindler's List;* MIAs in *Rambo*). But even if no rescue is possible, as in the case of Spike Lee's *Malcolm X*, which strictly observes the facts of Malcolm's assassination, the film is recognizably melodramatic in its recognition of innocence. What counts in melodrama is the feeling of righteousness, achieved through the sufferings of the innocent. This, ultimately, is why the movie's Schindler must finally break character and suffer for the insufficiencies of his actions. Suffering gives him the moral recognition that melodrama—not realism—requires. Without it, Schindler is merely heroic.

Westerns, war films, and Holocaust films, no less than woman's films, family melodramas, and biopics, participate, along with any drama whose outcome is the recognition of virtue, in the melodramatic mode of American film. Film criticism may do well to shift from the often myopic approach to the superficial coherence of given genres and toward the deeper coherence of melodrama.

The Case of D. W. Griffith

One natural starting point for reconsidering the melodramatic origins of American cinema is the work of D. W. Griffith. Critics have been quick to acknowledge the importance of melodrama in the work of Griffith, yet oddly enough this acknowledgment is usually cursory. Almost all of the major studies of Griffith give the melodramatic components of his art short shrift, preferring to emphasize the ways in which the first author and "father" of American cinema transcended melodrama rather than how he reinvented stage melodrama for the cinema.[42] One reason for the lack of interest in Griffith's melodrama is that his art and technique, often equated with the art and technique of "the movies" themselves, were thoroughly established by an influential first generation of film historians and scholars as that which not only grew out of, but also outgrew, the more "infantile" and "primitive" form of stage melodrama.[43]

The story of Griffith, the failed dramatist and genuinely bad playwright who began to direct melodramatic potboilers of little girls kidnapped by gypsies and who then outgrew those potboilers and developed complexly "woven" narratives, more subtle acting, and realistic, even epic, action is well known.[44] However, rather than see Griffith as nourished by melodrama, critics have preferred the story of the bold innovator who severed cinema's slavish relation to the melodramatic stage by envisioning a more realistic, novelistically inspired epic narrative.

For example, in the famous story of Griffith's defense of the invention of parallel montage in the 1908 *After Many Years*, Griffith's much quoted literary defense of his art—"Doesn't Dickens write that way?"—has been interpreted by many subsequent critics as a defense of novelistic realism and the literary technique of alternating scenes from two different spaces and story lines.[45] It seems more likely, however, as Rick Altman has noted, that Griffith's supposed invocation of the model of Dickens, especially as a precedent for parallel montage, was modeled upon Dickens's own adoption of elements of the melodramatic stage and its episodic narratives. The fact that Dickens was himself an enthusiastic novelistic melodramatist, whose works were frequently adapted to the stage, is usually ignored in this anecdote.[46]

Indeed, the entire critical reception of D. W. Griffith has been predicated upon the notion that what is aesthetically good, modern, innovative, and culturally redeemable in his work is epic, realistic, novelistic, or "purely" cinematic, whereas what is aesthetically bad, old-fashioned, time-bound, and embarrassingly racist in his work is Victorian, theatrical, and melodramatic. With some recent notable exceptions, this evaluation has been predicated upon a splitting of the good and the bad in his work that is itself melodramatic.[47]

In what follows I try briefly to articulate what is typical, and typically melodramatic, about one of Griffith's most popular and least controversial films. I choose *Way Down East* (1920) because of its status as a well-loved, enduringly popular, locus classicus of the American silent cinema, and because it has obvious roots in the American melodramatic stage. When Griffith made this film he was laughed at for reviving a "horse and buggy melodrama" considered past resuscitation.[48] He surprised everyone with the viability of the hoary material in what was to be his last truly popular film. Yet despite the obvious melodramatic form of this work, its critical status, like the critical status of most of Griffith's films, has seemed to reside in the way it transcends its melodramatic material. My goal is thus the somewhat obvious, but oddly neglected, task of situating *Way Down East* as a melodrama.

Another reason for examining this particular film is that, unlike some of Griffith's earlier, more controversial, racially based melodramas— most significantly *The Birth of a Nation* (1915) and *Broken Blossoms* (1919), but also many of the early Biograph films—*Way Down East* allows an investigation into some of the primary, and enduring, features of melodrama without the added complication of racist stereotyping.[49]

Way Down East is a 1920 film adaptation of Lottie Blair Parker and Joseph Grismer's popular stage melodrama first performed in 1898 under that title. This play was itself an adaptation of Parker's play of 1896 called *Annie Laurie*. All versions tell the story of a poor country girl who goes to the city to claim help from rich relations for her ailing mother. While she is there, an aristocratic cad tricks her into a mock marriage and leaves her pregnant. The baby dies soon after birth, and a destitute Anna finds work on the Bartletts' New England farm where she and Squire Bartlett's young son, David (Richard Barthelmess), become enamored.

However, when the stern squire learns that Anna has had a child out of wedlock, he expels her from his house in the middle of a blizzard. David then rescues her from the storm. Both versions of the play begin with Anna arriving at the Bartlett farm, a woman with a secret. The story of her earlier pregnancy and the death of the child only comes out when the villain, Sanderson, encounters Anna at the farm.

Griffith altered the play by telling the story of Anna (Lillian Gish) from the beginning. He shows her domestic life with her mother; her country-bumpkin trip to the decadent city where she is ridiculed by female cousins, elegantly decked out by an eccentric aunt, and seduced into a fake marriage by the suave villain. One of the most moving scenes in the film is also a Griffith "invention"—though actually one borrowed from Thomas Hardy's 1891 novel *Tess of the d'Urbervilles:* Anna's baptism of her dying baby.

Sarah Kozloff has argued that Hardy's novel and an 1887 stage play, later made into a film by Edwin S. Porter in 1913, formed a part of the material Griffith adapted when he made his film in 1920. Kozloff makes the point that Griffith stole the Hardy material, finding evidence in Griffith's personal papers of a typed extract of the baptism scene from the novel.[50] However, if we recall Rick Altman's argument regarding the influence of popular theatrical melodrama on silent cinema, we can see that such "stealing" is hardly exceptional. Even if Griffith did mark the passage in Hardy's novel, his knowledge of it was most likely through its various dramatizations, which included this scene. Besides, as Altman argues, popular melodrama consists precisely of such borrowings and, more precisely, of borrowings from increasingly realistic sources even as it forged them, as Spielberg formed *Schindler's List*, into more melodramatic forms.

What, then, are the melodramatic qualities of this film? I will isolate five features, each of which was significantly modernized by Griffith from the stage melodrama, each of which seems central to the melodramatic mode, with occasional reference to more recent films.

1. Melodrama begins, and wants to end, in a space of innocence. Peter Brooks notes that classic stage melodrama usually begins by offering a moment of virtue taking pleasure in itself. Gardens and rural homes are the stereotypical locuses of such innocence. The narrative proper usually begins when the villain intrudes upon the idyll.[51] The narrative ends happily if the protagonists can, in some way, return to this space of innocence, unhappily if they do not. Often the ideal space of innocence is posited in American stage melodrama as the rural "Old Kentucky" home—the maternal place of origin. This quest, not for the new but for the old space of innocence, is the fundamental reason for melodrama's profound conservatism. The most classic forms of the mode are often suffused with nostalgia for rural and maternal origins that are forever lost yet—hope against hope—refound, reestablished, or, if permanently lost, sorrowfully lamented.

The beginning of *Way Down East* is emblematic: Anna sews with her mother; in Gish's girlish performance, she is the perfect example of what Brooks calls innocence "taking pleasure in itself."[52] Expelled from this place of maternal goodness, she goes to the city to find rich relations. There she encounters the feminine antithesis of the space of innocence: the decadent city where New Women with bobbed hair slink about in low-cut dresses. Decked out similarly by an eccentric aunt, Anna catches the eye of Sanderson (Lowell Sherman), a stereotypical cad, who proceeds to seduce and abandon her. Later, her mother dead, the "helpless and unfriended" Anna gives birth alone. When the baby dies after her impromptu baptism, she wanders alone until she finds work at the farm of Squire Bartlett. Here she finds a second rural haven and a second mother in Mrs. Bartlett. The melodramatic climax of her rescue finally restores Anna to this substitute space of innocence.

Way Down East is thus a happy-ending melodrama in that it regains the space of innocence with which the film began. The film ends in a three-way marriage between all the eligible couples and in a final kiss that is significantly not between any of the heterosexual couples but instead between the two mothers—Anna and Mrs. Bartlett—who represent a restoration of the original innocence of the mother-daughter "space of innocence" of the film's beginning.

Nostalgia for a lost innocence associated with the maternal suffuses this film. Pathos arises, most fundamentally, from the audience's awareness of this loss. In nineteenth-century American melodrama, the Civil War frequently functioned as the dividing line between an idealized past and a present suffused with its loss. Griffith's *The Birth of a Nation* (1915) is the classic twentieth-century film example of this quest to regain a lost innocence associated with the "mothering heart" of maternity.[53]

2. Melodrama focuses on victim-heroes and the recognition of their virtue. Thomas Elsaesser argues that a characteristic feature of melodrama is its concentration on "the point of view of the victim."[54] One of the reasons Elsaesser privileges fifties family melodrama as the genre's quintessential form is the tendency for these films to "present *all* the characters convincingly as victims."[55] Elsaesser argues that melodrama is a special case from the usual kinetic dynamism of American cinema in which pressure builds upon a victim who then finds an outlet in action. I would suggest, however, that if the focus on victims is central to a melodramatic mode, that it is in no way a special case of a "closed" melodramatic world crushing helpless protagonists in opposition to the "openness" of the action genres. Rather the victim-hero of melodrama gains an empathy that is equated with moral virtue through a suffering that can either continue in the ways Elsaesser so well describes for family melodrama or the ways that other critics have described for the woman's film, or this victim-hero can turn his or her virtuous suffering into action. Melodrama can go either way.

In other words, melodrama does not reside specifically in either the happy-ending success of the victim-hero or the sad-ending failure of the same. Though an initial victimization is constant, the key function of victimization is to orchestrate the moral legibility crucial to the mode. For example, the happy-ending dramatic outcome that is often derided as the most unrealistic element of the mode—the reward of virtue—is only a secondary manifestation of the more important recognition of virtue. Virtue can be recognized in a variety of ways: through suffering alone or through suffering followed by deeds. In classic stage melodrama Brooks calls the mechanism of this recognition of virtue an "aesthetics of astonishment."[56]

We saw, for example, how the theatrical form of this astonishment was stage managed in Brooks's example from *La Fille de l'exilé*. In stage melodrama, the moment of recognition is often the classic theatrical tableau used at the ends of scenes to offer a concentrated summing up of and punctuation for the tensions of the whole act. In the stage tableau, the actors would move into a held "picture," sometimes self-consciously imitating existing paintings or engravings, sometimes striking conventional poses of grief, anger, threat, and so on.[57] The tableau was used theatrically as a silent, bodily expression of what words could not fully say. It was also a way of crystallizing the dramatic tensions within a scene and of musically prolonging their emotional effects. The sustained closeup of a character's prolonged reaction to dramatic news before the cut to commercial in soap opera is the contemporary inheritor of this tradition adapted to the needs of commercial interruption.

In *Way Down East* the equivalent moment of theatrical astonishment is the moment Squire Bartlett "names" Anna as an unwed mother just as a large group is about to sit down to dinner at the Bartlett farm. The reaction of general astonishment on the part of the guests is punctuated by Anna's sorrow and shame, David's rising anger toward his father, and his mother's empathic concern for all. But this astonishment is only the negative setup for a much more complex process by which Anna's virtue will ultimately be recognized. Named as unvirtuous in the presence of the very man who had dishonored her, Anna then "names" this man the author of her unjust fate. Just as Bartlett pointed the melodramatic finger at Anna, so she now points that same finger at Sanderson to even greater general astonishment.

Astonishment does not, however, resolve the conflict over where virtue and vice truly lie. It simply enhances the tension over the seemingly unsolvable problem. For Anna *is* the unwed mother named by Squire Bartlett. This nomination thus sets up the need for the melodramatic climax in action. This climax occurs in the stage play in the off-stage blizzard from which David saves Anna. It occurs in the film in the much more prolonged, and more melodramatic, climax of Anna's rescue not only from a blizzard but from plunging over a waterfall on a broken floe of ice.

3. Melodrama appears modern by borrowing from realism, but realism serves the melodramatic passion and action. To understand just how the climax of *Way Down East* achieves the happy-ending issue-in-action of the classic melodramatic rescue, we need to understand that what really victimizes Anna is not merely the personal villain Sanderson, but the patriarchal double standard that permits men to sow wild oats and then punishes women for the consequences. One of Griffith's inimitable, socially preachy titles states the problem: "Today's woman brought up from childhood to expect ONE CONSTANT MATE possibly suffers more than at any moment in the history of mankind, because not yet has the man-animal reached this high standard, except perhaps in theory." As Virginia Wright Wexman has noted, in the same year in which American women won suffrage, *Way Down East* realisti-

cally posed the problem of a woman with no rights, with no proper place in the public sphere, a woman who is sexually deceived by a powerful, aristocratic man and then condemned by the stern patriarchy that does not grant her equal rights.[58] Griffith graphically portrayed this victimization in several ways: in the highly realistic scene of Anna's seduction; in another scene showing—unprecedentedly in discrete long shot—the travail of childbirth; in the wrenching scene mentioned above of the baby's death; and finally in the last-minute rescue from the breaking ice of an unmistakably real river and waterfall. None of these scenes appeared in the stage melodrama. All are usually cited as examples of Griffith's realism "transcending" melodrama.

Richard Schickel praises the realistic qualities in the film while he derides the

classic casting-out scene, inspiration since of a thousand cartoons and parodies. . . . It is the ability to show real sleigh rides and spacious barn dances, to place Gish and Barthelmess in a real blizzard, and on a real river as the winter ice breaks, that gives the film an insuperable advantage over the stage. Whatever reservations one entertains about the motives and psychology of these characters, whatever strain has been placed on credibility by the coincidences on which the story so heavily depends, they are (almost literally) blown away by the storm sequence, so powerfully is it presented.[59]

However, a more accurate account of D. W. Griffith's version of *Way Down East* would see these changes as a way of modernizing stage melodrama into a popular cinematic form compatible with changing standards of realism rather than the triumph of realism over melodrama. John Cawelti has noted that "social melodrama"—the kind of melodrama that encompasses serious social problems—evolves in the direction of an increased plausibility even as it continues to obey the basic formula of the nineteenth century: the virtuous but humble maiden pursued by the more powerful villain and defended by the humble hero.[60]

Christine Gledhill notes that the mode of realism pushes toward renewed truth and stylistic innovation, whereas melodrama's search for something lost, inadmissible, or repressed ties it to the past.[61] Such is certainly the case with *Way Down East*. Though the film is undeniably more realistic than the stage version, its solution to the problem of out-of-wedlock maternity is fundamentally melodramatic. That is, the problem is not addressed as a social problem. Instead, the narrative works to retrieve Anna's personal innocence so that she can return to the rural happiness of her original bond with her mother rather than confront the more deep-seated problem that causes her suffering.

The film thus "solves" the problem of the persisting double standard by avoiding its source in a flawed patriarchal law.[62] Rather than argue that Griffith took a melodramatic stage play and made it realistic by confronting the harsh realities of Anna Moore's victimization, we can say that having brought up the pressing social problem of out-of-wedlock motherhood, and having presented the dilemma of the stern patriarch who condemns the woman for crimes for which she is not responsible, the narrative then entirely evades this problem by retrieving Anna's innocence through a climax of pathos and action.

4. Melodrama involves a dialectic of pathos and action—a give and take of "too late" and "in the nick of time." We have seen how Christine Gledhill dispelled the specter of a feminine "over-identification" with suffering victims by showing that spectators—even female ones—do not simply lavish pity on suffering objects. Rather, the audience knows more than the victim and identifies among various perspectives. We have also seen that pathos is not the only emotional note sounded by melodrama. However, pathos is crucial, and even in happy-ending melodramas where the emphasis is on action, there is tension between the paroxysm of pathos and the exhilaration of action.

What is the pleasure of pathos and how does it work with action? Franco Moretti's fascinating essay "Kindergarten" is one of few works to analyze the phenomenon of crying in response to "moving literature." Moretti writes not about melodrama but about what might be called a particularly melodramatic form of Italian boy's fiction. Perhaps because it is about boy's literature, the essay does not spend too much time worrying about the excess femininity of tears. Instead, Moretti notes the vast literature on what makes for the somatic response of laughter and the paucity of literature on the response of tears. Setting out to be a kind of Bergson of tears, Moretti ventures an explanation connected, like Bergson's, to temporality: we cry when something is lost and it cannot be regained. Time is the ultimate object of loss; we cry at the irreversibility of time. We cry at funerals, for example, because it is then that we know, finally and forever, that it is too late.[63]

Moretti borrows the rhetorical term *agnition*—the resolution of a clash between two mutually opposed points of view—as the key "moving" device in the stories he discusses.[64] He argues that the precise trigger to crying occurs at the moment when agnition reduces the tension between desire and reality: it is too late for the father to make amends to his dying son. The tension ends, according to Moretti, because desire is finally shown to be futile. When we let go of this desire, the sadness that results is also a kind of relief. Tears can thus be interpreted, Moretti argues, as both an homage to the desire for happiness and the recognition that it is lost.[65] Hence tears are always a kind of false consciousness, released, hypocritically as it were, when it is already too late. But, Moretti also notes, at least tears acknowledge that in this sad reconciliation with the world, something important has been lost.

It is this feeling that something important has been lost that is crucial to crying's relation to melodrama. A melodrama does not have to contain multiple scenes of pathetic death to function melodramatically. What counts is the feeling of loss suffused throughout the form. Audiences may weep or not weep, but the sense of a loss that implicates readers or audiences is central. And with this feeling of "too late," which Peter Brooks has explained as the longing for a fullness of being of an earlier, still-sacred universe, time and timing become all important. In an adaptation of Moretti's thesis to film melodrama, Steve Neale suggests that we don't cry just when it *is* too late, we cry even in happy-ending melodrama out of the desire that it *not* be too late. Happy-ending melodramas can move us to tears, Neale explains, when—hope against hope—desire is fulfilled and time is defeated. He cites *The Big Parade* (1925), *Only Yesterday* (1933) and *Yanks* (1979) as examples; I would cite *Way Down East*, *Rambo*, and *Schindler's List*. In such cases, as Neale argues, we cry because we fulfill an infantile fantasy that on some level we know is infantile and fantastic.[66]

Neale thus explains psychoanalytically the pleasurable tears of the happy-ending melodrama: crying is a demand for satisfaction that can never be satisfied; yet tears sustain the fantasy that it can. However, if the pathos of tears derives from the knowledge of loss, and if what is lost is time—the past and our connection to the lost time of innocence—then we need to examine the timing of the relation between the pathos of lost time and the action that sometimes regains it.

Moretti argues that a key element of "moving literature" occurs when what one character knows is reconciled with what another knows, but "too late." In death scenes, for example, tears unite us not to the victim who dies but to the survivors who recognize the irreversibility of time.[67] In the pathetic scene of the death of Anna's baby, we see an example of Moretti's agnition played out when Anna's desire to believe that her baby is only cold comes into conflict with her suspicion, and the doctor's certainty, that her baby is dead. When Anna hears this news, so Moretti would say, the discrepancy between her and the doc-

Anna Moore (Lillian Gish), David Bartlett (Richard Barthelmess). *Way Down East*, D. W. Griffith. © United Artists, 1920.

tor's point of view is reconciled; tension is released, and at this point only, Anna, and we, can cry. Both Moretti and Neale note that tears are a product of powerlessness. It seems to me, however, that because tears are an acknowledgment of hope that desire will be fulfilled, they are also a source of future power; indeed they are almost an investment in that power. Mute pathos entitles action. Let us see how this works in *Way Down East* by turning again to the climactic scene of astonishment that precedes the famous rescue from the ice.

Wronged by the upper-class villain Sanderson but silenced by his power throughout the bulk of the film, Anna is forced to serve Sanderson as a guest in the home of the family that has taken her in. But she cannot speak of his wrong to her because of the double standard that would shame her more than him. It is only when a busybody gossip reveals what all believe to be her sexual taint that she is forced into action—to name Sanderson as the man who was the father of that baby.

This naming of the villain, which occurs in both the stage play and the film, is Anna's big moment of action. It is well earned by her many earlier moments of silent pathos, which the audience, but none of the other characters, has been able to appreciate. Our tension mounts as we await this long-wished-for and equally long-delayed "nomination" of the guilty villain. But nomination is only a first step; it is not yet an achieved public recognition of where true guilt and innocence lie. For this recognition to really work, the film must move from pathos to action and from the tears that pay homage to "too late" to a rescue that is "in the nick of time."

We are so familiar with the in-the-nick-of-time rescue of the happy-ending melodrama that we take its seemingly facile effects for granted. This is not to say that there is a shortage of analyses of Griffith's editing of this, and many other, last-minute rescues. As V. I. Pudovkin has noted in a famous appreciation of Griffith's film, Anna's ordeal is in three stages:

First the snowstorm, then the foaming, swirling river in thaw, packed with ice blocks that rage yet wilder than the storm, and finally the mighty waterfall, conveying the impression of death itself. In this sequence of events is repeated, on large scale as it were, the same line of the increasing despair—despair striving to make an end, for death, that has irresistibly gripped the chief character. This harmony—the storm in the human heart and the storm in the frenzy of nature—is one of the most powerful achievements of the American genius.[68]

Each of these stages of Anna's ordeal, intercut with David's painfully delayed pursuit, increases our sense of her helplessness and our hope-against-hope for her rescue. David's last-minute capture of Anna's body at the very last moment before she and he plummet over the falls has been seen as an unrealistic heroic exploit saved by the beauty and power of the natural elements that form its context as well as by the device of parallel montage. Because some of the best appreciations of Griffith's editing come from Soviet directors, American critics have often seen Griffith's melodrama through the lens of what it might have become had Griffith been able to transcend, as Eisenstein wished, the "Dickensian [read melodramatic] limits" of his montage. Eisenstein cites this rescue to fault the lack of unity between the race of the ice break and the race of David to the rescue, accusing the film of not becoming the human flood that Pudovkin's *Mother* becomes.[69] In effect both Eisenstein and Pudovkin laud the technique of parallel montage but fault the rescue itself as an intrinsically hokey outcome, a product of dualistic thinking in which "reconciliation" is hypothetical wish fulfillment. If rescue as unrealistic reconciliation is ideologically flawed, especially from a Soviet perspective, this same Soviet perspective calls attention to temporal, rhythmic elements that make Griffith, and American melodrama on the whole, work with audiences. Audiences never fail to respond with pleasure and excitement at this incredibly prolonged rescue from the ice.

It seems to me, therefore, that there is a need for a better understanding of these temporal and rhythmic elements on their own, melodramatic, terms. To watch a last-minute rescue—whether of Anna from the ice, or of American POWs from the Vietnamese prison in *Rambo*, or of the women prisoners from Auschwitz in *Schindler's List*—is to feel time in two contradictory ways: although a rapid succession of shots specifying the physical danger gives the effect of speed, of events happening extremely fast, the parallel cutting between the breaking ice, David's pursuit, Anna's unconscious body, and the churning falls prolongs time beyond all possible belief. Actions feel fast, and yet the duration of the event is slowed down.[70] We are moved in both directions at once in a contradictory hurry-up and slowdown.[71]

Perhaps the best way to understand what we feel is to draw an analogy to music. The sustained play with hurry-up and slowdown is much like the approach to the end of a romantic symphony. Romantic music is the musical form that was adopted by what film historians have called the classical but I am calling the melodramatic cinema. Nineteenth-century symphonic music begins in an original key area, a home base (or tonic) out of which the variations and digressions into new keys and rhythms occur. It then returns in the final movement, with much fanfare, and sometimes considerable delay, to the tonic. Melodramatic narrative does much the same. Primed by the beginning tonic of the original theme— the register of the original space of innocence—the narrative wants to return to this point of origin and teases us throughout all subsequent development with the haunting threat of its loss.[72]

If and when a film moves to the fast-paced register of suspenseful action, we experience enormous relief from the constant repetition of loss. Exhilarated, we are caught up in the physical logic, one might even say the physics, of time and space. But, as Thomas Elsaesser noted, this exhilaration does not progress linearly. Whether in stage melodrama's episodic "cutting" back and forth between endangered heroine and pursuing hero, or the film melodrama's cross-cut editing, we encounter an intensely rhythmic tease: will we ever get back to the time before it was too late? Only the teasing prolongation of the outcome, constantly threatening that it must by now certainly be too late, permits the accomplishment—the viewers' felt acceptance—of the fantasy that it is not.

This teasing delay of the forward moving march of time has not been sufficiently appreciated as key to the melodramatic effect. Nor has it been appreciated as an effect that cinema realized more powerfully than stage or literary melodrama. It needs to be linked with melodrama's larger impulse to reverse time, to return to the time of origins and the space of innocence that can musically be felt in terms of patterns of anticipation and return. The original patterns—whether of melody, key, rhythm, or of physical space and time—thus take on a visceral sort of ethics. They are *felt* as good. The "main thrust" of melodramatic narrative, for all its flurry of apparent linear action, is to get back to the beginning.

Melodrama offers the hope that it may not be too late, that there may still be an archaic sort of virtue, and that virtue and truth can be achieved in private individuals and individual heroic acts rather than, as Eisenstein wanted, in revolution and change. For these reasons the prolonged play with time and timing so important to the last-minute rescue should not be attributed to the linear cause-effect outcome of classical realism or the naturalism of scenery, sets, or acting. The rescue, chase, or fight that defies time and that occupies so much time in the narrative is the desired mirror reversal of the defeat by time in the pathos of "too late."

The physical "realism" of this climax, so devoted to convincing viewers of the reality of the forces that combine to make the victim-hero suffer, is thus part and parcel of its melodrama. At its deepest level melodrama is an expression of feeling toward a time that passes too fast. This may be why the spectacular essence of melodrama seems to rest in those moments of temporal prolongation when "in the nick of time" defies "too late."

There is another way in which this particular last-minute rescue works to restore the beginning rather than to move toward a new end. We have seen that just before she runs out into the storm, Anna nominates Sanderson as the villain. This nomination produces astonishment, but it does not produce the public recognition of Anna's virtue. In the eyes of a patriarchal law that the film cannot directly confront, her guilt remains. Yet somehow the snowstorm of the play, the ordeal on the ice in the film, eradicate this guilt and make possible the final denouement that recognizes, and thus restores, Anna's innocence.

Why is this recognition only possible after the rescue on the ice? How does the nick-of-time rescue function to solve the problem of Anna's sexual guilt in the eyes of the patriarch? To answer we need to realize that what is at stake in the rescue is much more than Anna and David's lives. At stake is the viability of the patriarchal law that has more harshly blamed the unwed mother than the man for sexual misconduct and that is therefore, at least technically, allied with the villain. Indeed, if any film of Griffith's deserved to be called *The Mother and the Law*—the actual title of the modern sequence of *Intolerance*—it is this one. When David saves Anna from the icy river and waterfall, he also saves the system that has so harshly expelled her. He tempers his father's law with his mother's love, saving the patriarchal family from casting out the maternal figure of love capable of tempering its stern law.

He is able to do so, however, precisely because at this moment it is no longer the villain, nor even his father, who endangers Anna, but instead the icy river. We have seen how Griffith's use of these elements has been praised as both transcending melodrama and falling back into it. I argue, however, for the need to recognize such moments as quintessentially melodramatic. One of the key features of melodrama is its compulsion to "reconcile the irreconcilable"—that is, its tendency to find solutions to problems that cannot really be solved without challenging the older ideologies of moral certainty to which melodrama wishes to return. By posing the problem of injustice to the unwed mother, Griffith set himself the impossible task of reconciling the double standard with a culture and an ideology that did not, in fact, grant equality to women.

When the good-hearted but stern patriarch, Squire Bartlett, learns that Anna has been an unwed mother, he feels his moral duty is to expel Anna from his home. Though he has grown to love Anna, "the law is the law." The film is not simply about a "good" woman victimized by a "bad" man, but about what happens when a "good" man condemns, according to his code of ethics, a "good" woman. The happy-ending resolution of this conflict must reconcile a maternal empathy that feels for Anna with the stern, paternal law that cannot, within the limits of conventional ideology, be fundamentally challenged.

In a similar way, *Rambo* sets itself the problem of reconciling democratic ideology with the historical injustice of America's intervention in and wholesale destruction of Vietnam, and *Schindler's List* sets itself the problem of reconciling a common humanity with the historical injustice of the Holocaust and the fact that most people and countries did nothing to save the Jews. In each case an official law runs up against resis-

Squire Bartlett (Burr McIntosh), Anna Moore (Lillian Gish), and David Bartlett (Richard Barthelmess). *Way Down East*, D. W. Griffith. © United Artists,
1920.

tance. But this resistance does not directly address the actual wrong—
whether double standard, intervention in Vietnam, or genocide. Instead, it addresses an effect of that wrong: Anna on the ice, American
MIAs, one train of Jews diverted from Auschwitz.

In *Way Down East*, when David rescues Anna from the river, the fight
that properly should be with his father is displaced onto the river. At this
point in the film the natural elements take on the role of the villain.
What, then, does the perilous ice accomplish that the personal villain
does not? I believe it affords a covert satisfaction of the same punishing
law that unjustly accuses Anna. Ice, icy water, and snow are frigid elements that counter the sexual fires that produced the illegitimate child
that still haunts her. In effect they wash Anna metaphorically clean of
the crimes she technically did commit and which the patriarchal double
standard still believes stain her.

The "moving picture" of the frozen heroine—enshrined in extratextual legend in the stories of Lillian Gish's very real suffering from

frostbite during the shooting of the film—suggests that in this case rescue from icy death doubled as punishment for a sexual heat that still haunted the heroine's reputation. In Thomas Hardy's more realistic and modernist version of a similar story, Tess commits suicide. Anna's flight into the storm is a similarly suicidal, self-punishing gesture. But Anna is melodramatically saved *by* the icy river. Griffith, operating here in a more optimistic and mainstream vein of American melodrama, wanted, as in the stage play on which his film was based, to save his victim-heroine, but like Hardy and like the plays derived from Hardy, he wanted realistically to show her sexual victimization. Griffith therefore had to devise a rescue that could save Anna from the more vivid sins he had, unlike the stage play, realistically insisted on showing. He needed a better resolution of Anna's sexual "guilt" than had been offered by the brief, offstage mechanical snowstorm of the original play. In other words, he needed a more realistic melodrama.[73]

5. Melodrama presents characters who embody primary psychic roles organized in Manichaean conflicts between good and evil.[74] This is melodrama's simplistic moral stereotyping of character: Anna is the good daughter, David is the good son, the squire is the stern father. The drama operates to reveal true moral identities. This is melodrama's much derided quality of "monopathy": characters lack the complex mixes of feelings and the psychological depth of realism.[75]

It is easy to view the primary psychic and Manichaean characters of melodrama as archaic features of crude theatricalism lacking the depth and social texture of more realistic and psychologically nuanced characters. However, such a view perpetuates the antagonism between melodrama and realism, casting realism as the modern and melodrama as the archaic form of characterization.

When Peter Brooks writes that evil is a "swarthy cape-enveloped man with a deep voice," he notes that moral forces are viewed in melodrama as expressions of personality embodied in physical being and gesture.[76] However, the features of the villain are not fixed; one era's swarthy cape-enveloped villain is another era's smiling villain. Evil, like innocence, can be differently embodied and differently revealed. It is the constant goal of melodrama to reveal the moral occult through acts and gestures that are felt by audiences as the emotional truths of personality. What is truly modern about melodrama is its reliance on personality—and on the revelation of personality through body and gesture—as the key to both emotional and moral truth.

Christine Gledhill argues that the entire Hollywood star system, including the tradition of method acting, is a more sophisticated development of the traditions of melodramatic character and performance.[77] Adapting Peter Brooks's notion that amid the collapse of the sacred as the standard of value, the individual ego became "the measure of all things," Gledhill argues that this reduction of morality to an individual embodiment of ethical forces prepared the way for the psychologization of character and the performance orientation of twentieth-century popular culture.[78] Faced with the familiar dilemmas of modernity—the decentered self, the failure of language to say what is meant—melodrama responded with a heightened personalization and expression of the self. The cult of the star fed into this personalization. The contemporary phenomenon of the commodified star whose task is not so much to act as it is to embody a "truthful" "presence"—an authentic performance of his or her "self"—is merely another example of the melodramatic attempt to articulate what Brooks calls "full states of being."[79] The method acting popularized by Lee Strasberg on the American stage and in film in the fifties became known as a means of increasing performative realism, but Gledhill convincingly shows that it actually drew realism toward melodramatic concerns by dissolving the boundaries between acting and psychotherapy and by providing the melodramatic imagination with a new form of the articulation of the moral occult: now it is the very existence of an individual self that is at stake. The pathos of melodrama becomes the pathos of the assertion of self in the face of encroaching meaninglessness and nonentity.[80] In a very real sense, then, melodrama has evolved in the direction of expressing ever more primary psychic roles, not just in the silent cinema's typage—of the father, mother, son, daughter, and so on—but in the primary psychic resources drawn upon by actors to express the very pathos of their being.

In the early nineteenth-century melodramas cited by Brooks, the villain would thus indeed be the swarthy cape-enveloped man with a deep voice, and the victim-hero would be a young man or woman whose goodness was equally visible in manifest bodily signs. On the mid-nineteenth-century American stage, a remarkable reversal of this latter stereotype occurred in the forging of a new type of victim-hero in the swarthy complexion of Uncle Tom, whose blackness flew in the face of previous conventions of good and evil. The quintessential villain of this longest-playing nineteenth-century American melodrama was Simon Legree, known by his slave driver's whip, long mustaches, and Yankee speech.

Lennox Sanderson (Lowell Sherman) and Anna Moore (Lillian Gish). *Way Down East*, D. W. Griffith. © United Artists, 1920.

By the 1920s and the advent of an advanced silent cinema typified by *Way Down East*, victim-heroes became part of a cinematic star system that not only codified goodness in blond innocence (for Gish) or earnest handsomeness (for Barthelmess) but also through closeups that isolated and privileged these features as part of the discourse of the star. The villain was here a sophisticated variation of the by now too easily deciphered swarthy, cape-enveloped man. Lennox Sanderson is a suave man of the world who hesitates before committing his villainous seduction and abandonment and who even apologizes for his wrongdoing afterwards.

One reason that family melodrama of the 1950s has been taken as such a memorable example of the melodramatic mode could be that it exemplifies that moment in American moving pictures when popular psychology and method acting became the reigning form of the assertion of personality, when morality became explainable by Oedipus. At this point the eruption of symptoms and unconscious gestures began to substitute for the more straightforward bodily expression of good

Anna Moore (Lillian Gish). *Way Down East*, D. W. Griffith. © United Artists, 1920.

and evil. Thus Robert Stack's swallowed voice, squeezed frame, and hunched way of holding a martini in *Written on the Wind* was typical of a whole generation of Oedipally beset protagonists.

It is perfectly true that black and white Manichaean polarities simplify and twist the real social and historical complexities of the problems addressed by melodrama. It is also true that the melodramatic solution to the real issues raised by the form can only occur through a perverse process of victimization. Virtuous suffering is a pathetic weapon against injustice, but we need to recognize how frequently it has been the melodramatic weapon of choice of American popular culture.

Conclusion

Melodrama is neither dead nor dying. It has long been the alchemy whereby we turn our deepest sense of guilt into a testament of our virtue. The intrinsic theatricality of melodrama's primary psychic roles and Manichaean divisions between good and evil needs to be understood as a form of public testimony to an elusive virtue. The perceived excesses of the mode may in fact be a function of a particularly American insistence on innocence and good, as if American national identity required a constant assertion of innocence in a way that, say, French national identity does not.

Carol J. Clover's essay about the genre of courtroom drama (in this volume) describes a feature that might be usefully generalized to American melodrama. Noting that the courtroom genre positions the audience as a jury who judges the guilt or innocence of adversaries according to a dramatically performed contest of plots, Clover argues that the genre is rooted in the Anglo-American tradition of common law and its system of trial by jury (90 percent of the world's jury trials are American). In contrast to the inquisitorial, written presentation of juryless civil law descended from the Romans, American common law relies upon adversarial, oral argumentation before a jury.

In this adversarial, dual focus, oral—as opposed to written—system of justice, the jury adjudicates between two sets of facts, two stories pointing either to innocence or to guilt. This quest for a democratic, plain-speaking recognition of innocence and guilt, a guilt or innocence that can be spoken out loud and seen by all, is inherently melodramatic. Audiences of melodrama are positioned like juries of common law trials. Guilt or innocence is determined by orchestrated recognitions of truth that are inextricably tied to how audiences, who are essentially juries of peers, feel toward the accused.

Though *Way Down East* is hardly a courtroom drama, we can see that its most clichéd melodramatic element—the scene of the revelation of Anna's guilt before a group of assembled peers, followed by her counteraccusation to the man who wronged her—contains the essence of a trial that then shifts into a register of action in Anna's flight and rescue. In Anna's case the ordeal of trial becomes trial by ordeal in which bodily exhibition of suffering is a paradoxical means of exculpation. The audience's ability to adjudicate between guilt and innocence rests ultimately, in action melodrama, upon just such forms of physical ordeal and trial as suffered by Anna in the blizzard and on the ice.

Michel Foucault writes in *Discipline and Punish* that classical torture offers the "regulated mechanism of an ordeal: a physical challenge that must define the truth."[81] In the search for innocence or guilt, investigation and punishment are now mixed. The location of the proof of innocence in the survival of a ritual ordeal partakes of an archaic system of physical test and trial. Yet we have seen also that melodrama partakes of the more democratic trial by a jury of peers. It may be just such a paradoxical mix of the archaic and the democratic, the old-fashioned and the new, the humane and the brutal, that constitutes the key element of melodrama.

In this essay I have tried to reorient film study to the typicality, rather than the exceptionality, of film melodrama. Melodrama is much more than an embarrassing heritage of Victorian drama. It has always mattered and continues to matter in American culture and in American film. In the past when melodramas have succeeded in moving viewers, there has been an unfortunate tendency to attribute the convulsion to epic, realistic, or quintessentially "cinematic" causes. I would argue, however, that the sexual, racial, and gender problems of American history have found their most powerful expression in melodrama.

We can rail at the simplification and obfuscation of the solution to these problems; we can regret the absence of moral ambiguity in the resolution of persistent and deeply rooted problems—most insistently of race, class, gender, and ethnicity—that melodrama addresses; we can regret the perverse location of moral power in the role of victims; but even as we rail at the limitations of the form we need to recognize that melodrama is the persistent, dominant, and popular form of address to these problems. It is thus in ever modernizing forms of melodrama, not epic, not "classical realism," that American democratic culture has most powerfully articulated the moral structure of feeling that animates its goals of justice.

Notes

1. Christine Gledhill, "The Melodramatic Field: An Investigation," in *Home Is Where the Heart Is: Studies in Melodrama and the Woman's Film*, ed. Gledhill (London: BFI, 1987), 5.

2. Thomas Elsaesser, "Tales of Sound and Fury: Observations on the Family Melodrama," *Monogram* 4 (1975): 1–15. Reprinted in Gledhill, *Home*, and in Marcia Landy, ed. *Imitations of Life: A Reader on Film and Television Melodrama* (Detroit: Wayne State University Press, 1991).

3. See, for example, Geoffrey Nowell-Smith, "Minnelli and Melodrama," *Screen* 18, no. 2 (summer 1977): 113–18. Reprinted in Gledhill, *Home*, and in Landy, *Imitations*. Christine Gledhill comments on this division by noting the effective creation of two audiences of melodrama, "one which is implicated, identifies and weeps, and one which, seeing through such involvement, distances itself. The fact that . . . the first is likely to be female and the other male was not remarked on" (Gledhill, "The Melodramatic Field," 12).

4. Linda Williams, "'Something Else Besides a Mother': *Stella Dallas* and the Maternal Melodrama," *Cinema Journal* 24, no. 1 (fall 1984): 2–27. Reprinted in Gledhill, *Home*, and in Landy, *Imitations*.

5. See Laura Mulvey, "Visual Pleasure and Narrative Cinema," *Screen* 16, no. 2 (autumn 1975): 6–18. Reprinted in Mulvey, *Visual and Other Pleasures* (Bloomington: Indiana University Press, 1989). See also Mary Ann Doane, *The Desire to Desire: The Woman's Film of the 1940s* (Bloomington: Indiana University Press, 1987); E. Ann Kaplan, *Woman and Film: Both Sides of the Camera* (New York: Methuen, 1983).

6. Williams, "Something Else," 5.

7. Ibid.

8. Gledhill, "Recent Developments in Feminist Film Criticism," *Quarterly Review of Film Studies* 3, no. 4 (1978). Revised and reprinted in Mary Ann Doane, Patricia Mellencamp, and Linda Williams, eds., *Re-Vision: Essays in Feminist Film Criticism* (Frederick, Md.: University Publications of America, 1984), 42.

9. Williams, "Something Else," 5.

10. Christine Gledhill has fruitfully used the term *negotiation* to describe the way audiences do not conform to the supposedly rigidly prescribed viewing positions described in feminist "gaze theory." "Pleasurable Negotiations," in *Female Spectators*, ed. E. Deidre Pribram (New York: Verso, 1988).

11. Later, the investigation of masochistic pleasures in looking would prove a fertile, if perhaps overly reactive, alternative to the lock-step of the sadistic-voyeuristic male-gaze paradigm. See Gaylin Studlar, *In the Realm of Pleasure: Von Sternberg, Dietrich and the Masochistic Aesthetic* (Urbana: University of Illinois Press, 1988); see also Kaja Silverman, ed., *Male Subjectivity at the Margins* (New York: Routledge, 1992) and Carol J. Clover, *Men, Women, and Chainsaws* (Princeton: Princeton University Press, 1992).

12. Doane, *The Desire to Desire*.

13. Those who joined the debate include Patrice Petro and Caryl Flinn, "Dialogue," *Cinema Journal* 25, no. 1 (fall 1985); Jackie Byers, *All That Hollywood Allows: Re-Reading Gender in 1950s Melodrama* (Chapel Hill: University of North Carolina Press, 1991), 166–209.

14. Williams, "Something Else," 22.

15. This paradoxical power of the victim seems one of the great unexamined moral forces of American culture and one that is inextricable from our highly litigious legal system. To suffer innocently, to be the victim of an abusive power, is to gain moral authority, to become a kind of hero, no matter how pathetic, from Uncle Tom to Rodney King, from the helpless and unfriended victim of the nineteenth-century melodrama to Erik and Lyle Menendez.

16. This assumption that men don't cry, and are not even invited to cry by contemporary melodrama, seems particularly specious given the increasing number of film and television narratives focused on male victim-heroes. Even when these victim-heroes are encased in fantastically muscular "hard bodies," even when the narrative empowers them to fight and win (as in the *Rambo* and *Die Hard* series), the bulk of these films pivot upon melodramatic moments of masculine pathos usually ignored by critics who emphasize the action and violence. And when the victim-hero doesn't win, the pathos of his suffering seems per-

fectly capable of engendering what Thomas Schatz (in private conversation) has termed a good "guy cry." See, for example, films as diverse as *A River Runs through It* (Robert Redford, 1992) and *Philadelphia* (Jonathan Demme, 1993).

17. See Ann Douglas, *The Feminization of American Culture* (New York: Avon, 1977).

18. Christine Gledhill, "Dialogue," *Cinema Journal* 25, no. 4 (summer 1986): 44–48.

19. Peter Brooks, *The Melodramatic Imagination: Balzac, Henry James, Melodrama, and the Mode of Excess* (New Haven: Yale University Press, 1976).

20. Gledhill, "The Melodramatic Field," 45.

21. Ibid., 45–46.

22. This is the question E. Ann Kaplan has subsequently put to the form of the maternal melodrama. Kaplan argues that there are two basic kinds of maternal melodramas: those that are "complicit" and those that are "resistant" to dominant patriarchal capitalist ideology. *Motherhood and Representation: The Mother in Popular Culture and Melodrama* (London: Routledge, 1992), 12–16, 76–179. I argue that such typologies are beside the point because so many ideologies are in conflict and flux within the general parameters of a dominant patriarchal culture.

23. Robert Ray, for example, has noted this mythic dimension of the "classic Hollywood cinema," citing it as one of the important elements of what Truffaut once called "a certain tendency of the Hollywood cinema" and relating it to the tradition of American exceptionalism. However, Ray may too quickly subsume this mythic-resolution-seeking nature of popular films to the subordination of style to story, of affects and effects to narrative, typical of the model of the bourgeois realist text derived from the novel. I am arguing that the "certain tendency of the Hollywood cinema" is at least as importantly melodramatic as it is realistic. *A Certain Tendency of the Hollywood Cinema* (New Jersey: Princeton University Press, 1985), 32–33, 56–57.

24. Gledhill writes, "In Hollywood, realism came to be associated with the masculine sphere of action and violence." "The Melodramatic Field," 35.

25. This pat division between melodrama and realism has been especially the case in "gaze theory"—the theory that dominant cinema is organized for the power and pleasure of a masculine spectator-subject—but it has also been evident in formalist and cognitivist paradigms as well.

26. Gledhill, "The Melodramatic Field," 35. Steve Neale, "Melo Talk: On the Meaning and Use of the Term 'Melodrama' in the American Trade Press," *Velvet Light Trap* (fall 1993): 66–89.

27. My colleague Rhona Berenstein, citing publicity from *Mad Love* (1935) and *Trader Horn* (1931), adds the categories horror melodrama and jungle melodrama respectively.

28. Brooks, *The Melodramatic Imagination*, 15.

29. Gledhill, "The Melodramatic Field," 38.

30. Ibid., 38.

31. Douglas, *The Feminization*.

32. See Sergei Eisenstein, "Montage of Attractions," trans. Daniel Gerould, *The Drama Review* 18 (March 1974): 78–79. And see Tom Gunning, "The Cinema of Attraction," *Wide Angle* 8, no. 3/4 (1986); Gunning, "An Aesthetics

of Astonishment: Early Film and the (In)Credulous Spectator," *Art and Text* 34 (spring 1989): 114–133, reprinted in Williams, ed., *Viewing Positions: Ways of Seeing Film* (New Brunswick, N.J.: Rutgers University Press, 1994).

33. Janet Staiger, *Interpreting Films: Studies in the Historical Reception of American Cinema* (Princeton: Princeton University Press, 1992), 118.

34. Ibid., 118.

35. Rick Altman, "Dickens, Griffith, and Film Theory Today," *South Atlantic Quarterly* 88, no. 2 (1989): 331. Reprinted in Jane Gaines, ed. *Classical Hollywood Narrative* (Durham: Duke University Press, 1992), 331.

36. David Bordwell, Janet Staiger, Kristen Thompson, *The Classical Hollywood Cinema: Film Style and Mode of Production to 1960* (New York: Columbia University Press, 1985).

37. Ibid., 21–22.

38. Altman, "Dickens, Griffith, and Film Theory Today," 346.

39. Ibid., 347.

40. Christine Gledhill, "Between Melodrama and Realism," 137.

41. Susan Jeffords, *The Remasculinization of America: Gender and the Vietnam War* (Bloomington: Indiana University Press, 1989), 128. See also Jeffords's *Hard Bodies: Hollywood Masculinity in the Reagan Era* (New Brunswick: Rutgers University Press, 1994).

42. See, for example, Richard Schickel's biography, *D. W. Griffith: An American Life* (New York: Simon and Schuster, 1984). See also, for the typical organization of genres, Tom Schatz, *Hollywood Genres: Formulas, Filmmaking, and the Studio System* (New York: Random House, 1981). Schatz organizes genres into western, gangster, hard-boiled detective, screwball comedy, musical, and family melodrama. In the final section he refers to Griffith and acknowledges, as almost all critics do in passing, that on some level all film is melodrama. However, Schatz, like most critics, immediately drops the point to proceed with the more conventional containment of melodrama as a genre that came of age in the 1950s and then languished there. In a similar way, Robert Lang, who discusses Griffith at some length in his book, *American Film Melodrama: Griffith, Vidor, Minnelli* (Princeton: Princeton University Press, 1989), assimilates Griffith, somewhat awkwardly, to a psychoanalytic model of fifties family melodrama and its hysterical, subversive excesses. More recently, however, Lang's interesting introduction to the screenplay, along with many critical sources, sees the more conventional attributes of melodrama in Griffith's films. *The Birth of a Nation: D. W. Griffith, Director* (New Brunswick, N.J.: Rutgers University Press, 1994).

43. An interesting case in point is Nicholas Vardac's *From Stage to Screen: Theatrical Origins of Early Film: David Garrick to D. W. Griffith* (Cambridge: Harvard University Press, 1949). Vardac's pioneering book is a crucial document of the connection between nineteenth-century stage spectacle and the early films of Porter and Griffith, showing how the development of editing in Porter and Griffith continued a tradition of episodic, melodramatic, stage pictorialism. Though Vardac sees the rise of cinema as a transcendence of the "old melodrama" arriving at a new cinematic realism, he nevertheless gives the best and earliest account of the strong and enduring relations between the two traditions.

44. See, for example, David Cook's chapter on Griffith in *A History of Nar-*

rative Film (New York: W. W. Norton, 1981). See also Schickel, *D. W. Griffith*; Tom Gunning, *D. W. Griffith and the Origins of American Narrative Film* (Urbana: University of Illinois Press, 1991); Michael Rogin, "'The Sword Became a Flashing Vision': D. W. Griffith's *Birth of a Nation*," *Representations* 6 (spring 1984): 190–221.

45. Cited by Linda Arvidson, *When the Movies Were Young* (1925; reprint, New York: Dover Publications, 1969). See also Sergei Eisenstein, "Dickens, Griffith, and the Film Today," in *Film Form: Essays in Film Theory*, ed. and trans. Jay Leyda (New York: Harcourt, Brace, and World, 1949), 201.

46. Rick Altman points this out in order to emphasize the dual status of Dickens as realist novelist and melodramatist. "Dickens, Griffith, and Film Theory Today," 17–19.

47. See, for example, James Agee, *Agee on Film* (New York: Grosset and Dunlap, 1969), 313–18; David Cook, Richard Schickel, and Stan Brakhage, *Film Biographies* (Berkeley: Turtle Island, 1977)—all of whom participate in this splitting; and see also Rogin, "The Sword," for a brilliant reversal of this division, which invites us to see Griffith's racism as inextricably linked to a melodramatic vision of villainous racial "others." In contrast, Gunning's *D. W. Griffith and the Origins of American Narrative Film* avoids the melodramatic dichotomy by concentrating on a careful tracing of cinematic narrative technique from the "cinema of attractions" to a cinema of narrative integration that subordinates film form to the development of stories and characters in the 1908–1909 period only. Yet Gunning's splendid study, devoted as it is to what was specifically cinematic in Griffith's "narrator systems" of storytelling, does not draw the connection between this system of narration and the heritage of stage and literary melodrama.

48. See Lillian Gish, *The Movies, Mr. Griffith, and Me* (New York: Avon, 1969), 229.

49. I should note that my ultimate goal is not to avoid the role of race in American film melodrama or in Griffith. Indeed, I am currently engaged in an extended study of racial melodrama. In the current study, however, I hope to establish parameters for a deeper investigation of the intersections of race and gender by looking first at a less controversial, well-loved melodrama in which gender alone figures prominently in the construction of a "moral occult."

50. See Sarah Kozloff, "Where Wessex Meets New England: Griffith's *Way Down East* and Hardy's *Tess of the d'Urbervilles*," *Literature/Film Quarterly* 13, no. 1 (1985): 35–41.

51. Brooks, *The Melodramatic Imagination*, 29.

52. Ibid.

53. The fact that the space of innocence posited by this film is also the place of slavery considerably complicates the nature of this innocence, but this longing for a home that was probably never quite so wonderful as remembered is a typical feature of all melodrama, whether it is Tom in *Uncle Tom's Cabin* lamenting his old home, Rock Hudson lamenting "how far we have come from the river" in *Written on the Wind* (1956), or, more recently, the lost and regained innocence of the couple in *Indecent Proposal* (Adrian Lyne, 1993).

54. Elsaesser, "Tales of Sound and Fury," 86.

55. Ibid.

56. Brooks, *The Melodramatic Imagination*, 25–27.

57. Martin Miesel, "Speaking Pictures," in *Melodrama*, ed. Daniel Gerould (New York: New York Literary Forum, 1980), 58–59.

58. For an excellent discussion of the relation of suffrage to the suffering heroine and masculine rescue in this film, see Virginia Wright Wexman, *Creating the Couple: Love, Marriage, and Hollywood Performance* (Princeton: Princeton University Press, 1993), 43–63.

59. Schickel, "Tales of Sound and Fury," 431.

60. Cawelti, "The Evolution of Social Melodrama," in Landy, 33–34.

61. Gledhill, "The Melodramatic Field," 31–32.

62. Martha Vicinus aptly names this wish-fulfilling tendency to bogus solution in nineteenth-century domestic melodrama the "reconciliation of the irreconcilable." We can see, however, that the mechanism persists throughout the form. "Helpless and Unfriended: Nineteenth-Century Domestic Melodrama," *New Literary History*, 13, no. 1 (autumn 1981): 132.

63. Franco Moretti, "Kindergarten," in *Signs Taken for Wonders: Essays in the Sociology of Literary Forms* (London: Verso, 1983), 159–62.

64. Ibid., 160–61.

65. Ibid., 180.

66. Steve Neale, "Melodrama and Tears," *Screen* 27, no. 6 (November-December 1986), 8.

67. Moretti, "Kindergarten," 179.

68. V. I. Pudovkin, *Film Technique and Film Acting* (New York: Grove Press, 1970), 129.

69. Eisenstein, "Dickens, Griffith, and the Film Today," 235.

70. This is the same logic that would later justify the use of slow motion at the climax of such actions.

71. However, if we invest too much time in suspenseful delays required by "the nick of time" rescue, the film cannot revert to the "too late" ending. Too late must come relatively quickly; in the nick of time must be slow, although time in this ending is experienced as fast.

72. I am indebted to a seminar by Susan McClary for this description of romantic music as giving the effect of a return to origins. For a discussion of the ways nineteenth-century romantic music patterns were adopted by Hollywood, see Claudia Gorbaman, *Unheard Melodies: Narrative Film Music* (Bloomington: Indiana University Press, 1987) and Caryl Flinn, *Strains of Utopia: Gender, Nostalgia, and Hollywood Film Music* (Princeton: Princeton University Press, 1992). Flinn notes that it is music that connects listeners to an "idealized past, offering them the promise of a retrieval of lost utopian coherence" (50). This is to say that music often carries the burden of making the viewer-listener feel the longing for plenitude that is so important to the melodramatic mode.

73. This better resolution was, in effect, to prolong what had been a brief, offstage rescue into an on-scene ordeal that was itself a form of punishment. Not unlike the ancient system of trial by ordeal for women accused of adultery, Griffith had his heroine thrown in a river. In Mesopotamia, if a woman survived the ordeal she was presumed to be judged innocent by the river gods. Yet obviously the ordeal itself was a form of punishment. See Gerda Lerner, *The Creation of Patriarchy* (New York: Oxford University Press, 1986), 115.

74. Brooks, *The Melodramatic Imagination*, 2–4.

75. Monopathy was first named by Robert Heilman, *Tragedy and Melodrama: Versions of Experience* (Seattle: University of Washington Press, 1968), 85. It was linked to Manichaeanism by Brooks (*The Melodramatic Imagination*, 36) and discussed by Elsaesser in relation to the "non-psychological" conception of character ("Tales of Sound and Fury").

76. Brooks, *The Melodramatic Imagination*, 160.

77. Christine Gledhill, "Signs of Melodrama," in *Stardom: Industry of Desire*, ed. Gledhill (London: Routledge, 1991), 208.

78. Brooks, *The Melodramatic Imagination*, 16; Gledhill, "Signs of Melodrama," 209.

79. Gledhill, "Signs of Melodrama," 216–18.

80. Ibid., 221, 225.

81. Michel Foucault, *Discipline and Punish: The Birth of the Prison*, trans. Alan Sheridan (New York: Random House, 1979).

World War II and the Hollywood "War Film"

THOMAS SCHATZ

Introduction

In terms of film genre, World War II stands out as a remarkably complex and distinctive period. The war era was perhaps the most overtly genre-driven period in American film history, with "war themes" permeating a range of established movie genres as the "war film" steadily coalesced into a single dominant cycle: the World War II combat film. This "conversion to war production" remains utterly unique in Hollywood's history. Never before or since have the interests of the nation and the movie industry been so closely aligned, and never has Hollywood's status as a national cinema been so vital. The industry managed this conversion remarkably well, providing both propaganda and entertainment for receptive civilian and military audiences, and in the process the industry enjoyed record profits in a five-year "war boom."

This effective integration of Hollywood's ideological and commercial imperatives during World War II underscores both the proficiency of the studio system during the classical era and also the savvy political instincts of President Franklin Delano Roosevelt. FDR decided against the complete conversion of the motion picture industry to war production, as occurred with other major U.S. industries such as steel, construction, and automobile manufacturing. He also stopped short of converting the film industry into a state propaganda agency, as had been done in Germany and Italy. Instead, Roosevelt allowed the movie industry to maintain commercial operations so long as it effectively supported the war effort. The industry readily complied, and within six months of Pearl Harbor fully one-third of Hollywood's output was directly related to the war.

Although eminently successful, Hollywood's conversion to war production and rapid formulation of war films was scarcely a uniform, coherent, or harmonious process. On the contrary, the conflicts and struggles involved were often as intense as the drama depicted on-screen. In producing war films, Hollywood had to accommodate various constituencies, from the Hays Office and the Production Code Administration (PCA) to the military, the War Department, and a bevy of newly created wartime agencies, notably the Office of War Information (OWI). The studios also squabbled continually with the nation's exhibitors over the popular appeal of war-related films, with theater owners lobbying for more upbeat and "escapist" war films—USO-style musicals, for instance, or war-torn love stories. Ultimately, Hollywood managed to satisfy all of these constituents, including the moviegoing public, with films designed to entertain as well as to mobilize and inform, to "emotionalize" the conflict at hand and to provide occasional diversion from that conflict.

This essay focuses on Hollywood's war-related genre films and filmmaking, from the industry's tentative move into war-related production before Pearl Harbor through its wholesale commitment to the war effort after the U.S. entered the war in December 1941. Early on, this involved the integration of "war themes" (in current industry parlance) into established genres, but the key to Hollywood's war-related output and the dominant formulation of the war film by 1942–1943 was the combat film—dramatizations of U.S. soldiers in actual battles like *Wake Island* (1942) and *Bataan* (1943), *30 Seconds Over Tokyo* (1944) and *The Story of G.I. Joe* (1945). These films were altogether unique on several counts—and not only as genre films but also as Hollywood features. First, they evinced an extraordinary sense of historical immediacy, far beyond that of any other cinematic genre or cycle in movie history. Second, the fictional combat film developed a genre in direct symbiosis with the war-related documentaries and newsreels, which also saw heavy production during the war. Indeed, Hollywood's fiction and nonfiction treatments of the war represented, in Lewis Jacobs's evocative terms, a "vast serialization" of the American and Allied war effort.

A third and related point involves the issue of Hollywood film style. In terms of cinematic technique, the combat film brought a new level of realism to the Hollywood feature film. With Hollywood's wartime features more focused than ever before on real-world events, the lines between factual and fictional films steadily blurred. This was most pronounced in combat films, which often included documentary footage and depicted events that were widely covered in various news media. The wartime developments in film style involved Hollywood's "classical narrative" formulation as well, in that the very structure and substance of motion picture stories changed during the war. This was most evident in the changing nature and depiction of the conventional protagonist and a significant (albeit temporary) shift away from the Hollywood cinema's usual emphasis on romantic coupling.

A final point worth making here regarding Hollywood's output of combat films—and war-related films generally—is how closely this period of filmmaking coincided with the actual war era itself. Prior to U.S. involvement in the war, Hollywood produced very few war-related features as a result of both market concerns and political pressures. That changed dramatically after Pearl Harbor, of course, as Hollywood remained utterly committed to war-film production "for the duration." But once the war ended in late 1945, Hollywood's war-related production ended even more abruptly than it had begun four years earlier. There were a few notable exceptions like *The Best Years of Our Lives*, a 1946 release that became the biggest commercial and critical hit of the entire decade. But the film only seemed to underscore the desire of the studios and exhibitors—and audiences as well, apparently—to put the war behind them and to get on with their lives in the prosperous postwar era.

The World War II combat film would stage a sudden and dramatic return at the decade's end with several huge hits: *Battleground, Twelve O'Clock High*, and *Sands of Iwo Jima* (all released in late 1949). These films reestablished the currency of the combat film, which would become one of Hollywood's more durable genres in subsequent decades. Indeed, the World War II combat film would see far heavier production than the Korean War films or Vietnam War films produced during (or after) those subsequent U.S. military conflicts. But no wartime period in twentieth-century American history saw anywhere the intensity of war-film production as World War II, and the postwar cinematic reconstructions of that war represent a far different enterprise than those produced during the war itself.

Prewar Hollywood and the
Changing Movie Marketplace

Though the Hollywood war film emerged virtually by government mandate after U.S. entry into the war, it's important to note that political and economic forces actually militated against war-film production in the late 1930s and early 1940s. As late as 1938–1939, with many overseas markets still open and isolationist sentiments at home still relatively strong, films criticizing fascism or advocating U.S. intervention in "foreign wars" were simply not good business. Holly-wood did make occasional forays into war-related production in the late 1930s as conditions in Europe steadily worsened. The most notable of these, perhaps, was Warner Bros.' early-1939 release, *Confessions of a Nazi Spy*, a quasi-documentary thriller involving German espionage in the U.S. that well indicates the hazards of political filmmaking at the time. *Confessions of a Nazi Spy* won critical raves, with the National Board of Review naming it "the best film of the year from any country."[1] But the public was less enthusiastic, and the film did only moderate business in the U.S. Moreover, it was either banned or heavily censored in its over-seas release, where it was a major commercial disappointment.[2]

This latter point was of considerable importance in the late 1930s, when the domestic market was still mired in a late-Depression recovery mode. At the time, foreign trade generally accounted for any net profits on major studio releases, and thus despite the myriad crises overseas, Hollywood relied much more heavily on foreign markets than did other major U.S. industries. As the *Wall Street Journal* noted, "The moving picture industry was one of the very few American businesses that had a vital stake in foreign trade when the war broke out [in September 1939]."[3] In fact, the Hollywood studio-distributors actually had bene-fited from the political and military crises in the late 1930s, which se-verely curtailed the production of feature films in England, France, Ger-many, and Italy, which were Hollywood's chief competitors overseas. These crises eventually undercut Hollywood's overseas trade, particu-larly in the Axis nations, which by 1937 were severely limiting both the number of U.S. film imports and the portion of box-office revenues "re-mitted" to the studios.[4]

By the time the war broke out in late 1939, Hollywood had all but lost the Axis markets on the Continent and in the Far East. But the studios still realized roughly one-third of their revenues from overseas, thanks largely to England and the United Kingdom. According to a *Variety* survey of the global marketplace in September 1939, Hollywood's chief overseas clients at the time were Britain (45 percent of foreign trade) and Australia (11 percent), with all of Continental Europe contributing roughly 20 percent.[5] With the escalation of the war and the fall of France in June 1940, Hollywood's European market would fall to virtually nil—leaving England standing alone by late 1940, not only in the face of Nazi aggression, but also as Hollywood's last significant foreign market.[6]

The studios had little trouble adjusting to these changing market conditions abroad, since Britain traditionally had been Hollywood's chief foreign client and generated the lion's share of Hollywood's overseas income.[7] Hollywood films historically had accounted for over 80 percent of the screen time in England, and by the late 1930s Britain was becoming something of a direct extension of the American market.[8] As the war intensified in 1940–1941, Hollywood was continually on the verge of writing off its British income. But once England survived the Battle of Britain and the German Luftwaffe's "London blitz" in 1940, it was clear that the nation was in for a long haul against the Nazis. It was clear, too, that England was undergoing a wartime boom in moviegoing, and that Hollywood would be the chief beneficiary of that boom.[9]

The steady increase of Hollywood's filmmaking and marketing focus on England in 1940–1941 coincided with Roosevelt's political and economic agenda. During this period, FDR developed his "lend lease" policy to support the British war effort against Nazi Germany (which gained congressional approval in March 1941), and the prospect of U.S. intervention on the side of Britain became increasingly likely—despite protests from isolationists and proneutrality advocates.

Roosevelt also initiated a massive defense buildup in the U.S. in 1940–1941, which revitalized the American economy and brought a definitive end to the Great Depression of the 1930s. The defense buildup marked the first stage of an extended war boom for the U.S. economy in general, with the motion picture industry among the prime beneficiaries. The boom was most acute in the urban-industrial centers where war-related production was gearing up at a furious pace and where Hollywood did most of its business.[10] The full force of the defense buildup hit the movie industry in midsummer of 1941, and by the autumn the sustained box-office surge had become an accepted way of life for the studios and the nation's exhibitors.[11] Indeed, the prospects were virtually unlimited as new factories, urban labor migration, the draft, new army camps, and rearrangement of work schedules (night shifts, swing shifts, and the like) pushed movie attendance and ticket sales ever upward.[12]

This defense boom clearly indicated America's intensifying prewar mentality, which was further manifested by the public's growing appetite for news about the war overseas as well as U.S. "preparedness." By late 1940, Hollywood newsreels, documentary shorts, and features were increasingly devoted to war-related subjects. The public was buying, and in fact news-hungry audiences were changing the very nature of moviegoing. By spring 1941, theaters routinely interrupted their programs to provide news bulletins, and some houses began scheduling radio broadcasts of FDR's Tuesday evening "Fireside Chats," which were drawing total radio audiences of up to seventy million, fully one-half the U.S. population.[13] Another barometer of war-related public interest was the newsreel theater, which enjoyed its heyday before and during World War II. By late 1941, twenty-five of these theaters were in operation in the largest U.S. cities, with most of the news directly related to the war.[14]

The Emerging War Film

Though Hollywood produced hundreds of what might be termed "war films" during the prewar era, there was very little formal or thematic coherence to this effort, particularly in terms of feature films. On-screen treatment of the war developed in very different ways and at a different pace, with nonfiction films taking the lead in covering both the war overseas and the war-related events at home. The treatment of war-related themes and issues in feature films occurred in a remarkable array of genres and cycles, from slapstick farce and romantic comedy to female gothic and family melodrama, and most prominently in spy films and suspense thrillers. Noticeably lacking were the combat films and home-front melodramas that would dominate Hollywood's war-related production after Pearl Harbor.

Despite this rather uneven and haphazard treatment of the war in 1940–1941, most of the industry's war-related output shared one common thematic emphasis. After the outbreak of war in Europe, Hollywood's fiction and nonfiction films tended to be firmly prointerventionist, promilitary, and antitotalitarian. The newsreels, documentaries

Jerry Plunkett (James Cagney). *The Fighting 69th*, William Keighley. © Warner Bros., 1940.

(studio-produced shorts and imported features), and dramatic features released in the U.S. from 1939 through 1941 consistently portrayed the Axis powers, especially Nazi Germany, as a threat to the interests of America and its allies and to the American way of life. These films also depicted U.S. preparedness as absolutely necessary because of what came to be perceived as America's inevitable entry into the war.[15] There were a few pro-Nazi films in circulation, most of them German-produced documentaries released by independent distributors on a very limited basis. These virtually disappeared from the U.S. market by 1941, which by then was dominated by pro-Allied and interventionist pictures produced either in the U.S. or Britain.[16]

Hollywood's interventionist and promilitary—if not to say prowar—stance was rarely evident in its feature films before 1940, beyond those rare exceptions like *Confessions of a Nazi Spy*. The outbreak of war in Europe in late 1939 and the escalating U.S. defense buildup induced the studios to deal with the war in dramatic features, but it was well into 1940 before the results reached the screen. Among the earliest of these was Warners' *The Fighting 69th*, released in January 1940. The World

War I drama starring James Cagney was important because it depicted Americans in combat against a German enemy (albeit a quarter-century earlier); and also because it involved the successful adaptation of both a Warners star and an established formula into a war story. *The Fighting 69th* depicts the conversion of Cagney's swaggering, self-centered tough guy, so familiar from crime and action films, into a team player on behalf of the war effort. Significantly enough, the conversion is sparked by a priest played by Pat O'Brien—recalling O'Brien's similar efforts to reform Cagney's gangster in *Angels with Dirty Faces* (1938). Cagney's character "saw the light" before going to the electric chair in the earlier film, and in *The Fighting 69th* his character's conversion results in a more heroic demise: he gives up his life for his fellow soldiers by throwing himself on a German grenade.

The Fighting 69th was among Warners' biggest hits in 1940, and its popular and commercial success enhanced Hollywood's general shift to war-related features that year. By the spring and summer, as the Nazi blitzkrieg overran Europe and pushed to the English channel, Hollywood had begun a blitz of its own—although few movies dealt directly with World War II. Indeed, one of the more interesting aspects of Hollywood's own conversion to war film production in 1940–1941 was its continued avoidance of the current war and its tendency, à la Warners in *The Fighting 69th*, to treat the war by indirection. According to one industry survey, Hollywood from September 1939 through August 1940 released 129 features (including twenty-seven from Britain and France) and sixty shorts "dealing with the war and the troubles in Europe, national defense and preparedness, patriotism and Americanism, dictators and democracies." [17] But this included a remarkably wide range of genres, from Civil War epics and foreign legion films to westerns. In terms of features directly related to World War II, however, Hollywood's output was still quite limited. According to an in-depth study by Russell Earl Shain, Hollywood produced only six World War II–related films in 1939 (1.2 percent of its 483 releases), and twelve in 1940 (2.5 percent of 477 releases). [18]

Most of those appeared later in the year, as the industry shifted noticeably to more militaristic, nationalistic, and political themes and to a heavier emphasis on U.S. preparedness. "By 1940 Hollywood had crossed an important threshold," note Clayton Koppes and Gregory Black in *Hollywood Goes to War*. "Some studios had begun to make explicitly interventionist films." [19] In September Thomas Brady of the *New York Times* observed that "only in recent months" had the movies begun "proposing active American counteraction" to Nazi aggression.[20] Later that month Bosley Crowther, surveying the schedule of 1940–1941 films, noted the coming "wave of propaganda pictures" and that "films are fast assuming the role predestined for them in time of crisis."[21]

While Hollywood turned increasingly to war-related subjects in 1940, the studios tended to rely on established genres to dramatize those subjects. *Foreign Correspondent*, for instance, produced by Walter Wanger and directed by Alfred Hitchcock, rehashed Hitchcock's earlier quasi-political thrillers, *The 39 Steps* (1935) and *The Lady Vanishes* (1938), and gave the espionage thriller a twist by adding a familiar 1930s screen figure, the crusading, wise-cracking reporter (Joel McCrea). MGM's *The Mortal Storm* and Fox's *Four Sons* were domestic melodramas about families (in Germany and Czechoslovakia, respectively) torn asunder by the Nazi regime. Another interesting 1940 genre variation was Warners' *The Man I Married*, which cast Joan Bennett in a female gothic about a woman whose German-American husband gradually is won over by Nazi propaganda during a trip to Europe. The film is also notable for being one of the first mainstream features to actually use the word *Jew* in dealing with Nazi anti-Semitism.[22] A more sanguine variation was *Arise My Love*, an offbeat romantic comedy about two reporters (Claudette Colbert and Ray Milland) who fall in love while covering the war.

The most significant war-related genre variation in 1940 was Chaplin's *The Great Dictator*, with the familiar Little Tramp transposed into a meek Jewish barber who is mistaken for dictator Adenoid Hynkel. Released in October, *The Great Dictator* was a huge critical and commercial hit, and it went on to become the number two box-office hit of 1941—a year during which Hollywood moved more aggressively into war-related feature film production. The top box-office hit in 1941 was *Sergeant York*, Warners's biopic of reluctant World War I hero Alvin York. Among the other top-ten hits that year were *A Yank in the R.A.F.*, *Dive Bomber*, and *Caught in the Draft*, all of which dealt directly with World War II. According to Shain, thirty-two of the studios' 492 releases (6.5 percent) in 1941 dealt with the current war. Most of these were spy films, as the espionage thriller proved ever more amenable to war-related reformulation. In fact, eighteen of the fifty Hollywood features produced from 1939 to 1941 that dealt with World War II were spy films, and only three of those fifty films depicted soldiers in actual combat.[23]

The remainder of the war-related films dealt with the home front, and most of these (thirteen in all) focused on military training and preparedness. By 1941, training pictures were dominated by two popular cycles: aviation dramas and service comedies. The former cycle, which included *A Yank in the R.A.F.* and *Dive Bomber* as well as *I Wanted Wings, Flight Command*, and *International Squadron*, introduced two dominant motifs that were crucial to the World War II combat film. One was the overt celebration of military armament and technology and the Allies' superior know-how. The other was the further refinement of the war-related "conversion narrative," as the training pictures invariably traced the fate of the self-assured individualist—Tyrone Power in *A Yank in the R.A.F.*, Robert Taylor in *Flight Command*, Ronald Reagan in *International Squadron*, and so on—who in the course of military training learns to subordinate his own interests to those of the group.

The prewar service comedies provided a very different view of U.S. preparedness. In 1941, with enlistment on the rise and the draft reinstated, Hollywood turned out a number of comedy hits focusing on military training. The most successful of these service comedies were *Caught in the Draft*, starring Bob Hope, and three Abbott and Costello vehicles: *Buck Privates, In the Navy*, and *Keep 'Em Flying*. The Abbott and Costello comedies obviously were geared to each of the military branches, and although they caused some concern within the military, the films were regarded as effective recruiting tools. It's worth mentioning, however, that after the release of *Keep 'Em Flying* in November 1941, only weeks before Pearl Harbor, Universal (which produced the pictures) announced that, out of respect for the war effort, the duo would turn from service comedies to more "escapist" fare (as in the Hope-Crosby "road pictures" of the era). It's also worth mentioning that the Abbott and Costello service comedies were so successful that they vaulted the duo to third place among the top box-office stars in the U.S. in 1941.[24]

Whereas Hollywood was somewhat tentative in its direct treatment of the war in feature films, there was extensive prewar coverage of war-related subjects in documentaries and newsreels. The most notable of these were the *March of Time* newsreels, produced by Louis de Rochemont. Issued monthly, usually at about fifteen minutes in length but occasionally longer, these newsreels provided an international news service and covered an array of issues and events—including the war. Virtually the only direct mention of Hitler and Nazi Germany on American movie screens before 1939 came via the *March of Time*, notably in a sixteen-minute May 1938 issue, "Inside Nazi Germany." From September 1939 to December 1941, over twenty newsreels covered the war and related events in Europe and the Far East.[25] In 1940, the *March of Time* produced its first feature-length documentary, *The Ramparts We Watch*, which combined a celebration of small-town American life with a biting critique of fascism. In 1941, the *March of Time* and other newsreels turned increasingly to U.S. preparedness, the defense buildup, and other domestic concerns (espionage, the disruption of shipping, and so on). De Rochemont resumed the anti-Nazi, anti-isolationist push in September 1941, two years after the outbreak of war, with "Peace—By Adolph [*sic*] Hitler," which traced the German leader's record of broken promises and devastation of Europe.

A very different form of war-related nonfiction filmmaking in Hollywood involved military training and informational films. The studios began to regularly produce these one- and two-reel films in late 1940, primarily through a Hollywood-based reserve unit of the Army Signal Corps comprised of some two dozen officers and three hundred GIs trained in film production. The unit was headed by Lt. Col. Nathan Levinson, who also acted as vice-chair (under chairman Darryl Zanuck) of the Motion Picture Academy Research Council, an organization that coordinated industry support for the Signal Corps's production efforts.[26] By 1941 these efforts were well under way, and Zanuck was increasingly involved. In fact Zanuck himself made a trip to Washington in August to meet with army brass about Hollywood's military-related filmmaking operations. Zanuck brought with him six of the one hundred or so training films already completed, including John Ford's one-reeler, "Sex Hygiene." (Another forty were currently in production, including Frank Capra's "Combat Counter-Intelligence.") The military leaders were favorably impressed, and Zanuck was forthright about the industry's promilitary, anti-isolationist stance—a position he and other studio heads would publicly defend before the Senate only a few weeks later.[27]

The occasion of Zanuck's Senate testimony was the so-called propaganda hearings, held in Washington in September 1941. The hearings were convened by a cadre of isolationists who decided to take on the movie industry in a grandiose (if somewhat desperate) stand against the tide of interventionism. Gauging Hollywood as an ideal target, Senators Burton K. Wheeler and Gerald P. Nye demanded that the Interstate Commerce Committee investigate what Nye termed the "propaganda machine" in Hollywood, which was run by the studios "almost as if they were being operated by a central agency." The committee hearings focused on seventeen "war-mongering" feature films, twelve of which were produced in Hollywood—including *Foreign Correspondent* and *The Great Dictator*—along with four British imports and one other studio-released foreign picture.[28]

Actually, Hollywood had been struggling both internally and publicly with the issues of politics and propaganda for several years. Among the more notable of these struggles involved *Foreign Correspondent* some two years earlier. In early 1939, Walter Wanger was battling Hollywood's self-censorship agency, the PCA, over various political aspects of the story. Wanger made little headway and was still livid over what he considered the PCA's mutilation of *Blockade*, a 1938 film set against the Spanish Civil War, so he decided to go public with his concerns, lambasting the Hays Office and the PCA in a series of speeches and editorials.[29] In a February 1939 letter to the *New York Times*, Wanger accused the PCA of being wedded to a "formulated theory of pure entertainment . . . making impossible the honest handling of important truths and ideas."[30] Days later, Will Hays issued his annual Motion Picture Producers and Directors of America (MPPDA) report, which reasserted that theory: "the screen has handled successfully themes of contemporary thought in dramatic and vivid form and presented the subject matter as splendid entertainment, rather than propaganda."[31]

By 1940–1941, however, as the war in Europe intensified and as the prospects for U.S. intervention increased, neither Hays nor the PCA could discourage filmmakers from taking on geopolitical and war-related subjects. Indeed, Roosevelt himself had appealed to the movie industry in 1940 to support both the defense buildup at home and the Allied effort overseas. The industry had complied, eliciting both a public display of gratitude from FDR (via a letter of appreciation to be read at the Academy Awards banquet in early 1941) and the increased wrath of the nation's isolationist contingent. The term *propaganda* now was being invoked in the debate—a loaded term at the time, given the status of the German and Italian film industries as state propaganda agencies.[32]

Thus Wheeler and Nye and the remaining isolationists in Congress engineered the 1941 Senate propaganda hearings to provide a national forum to reassert their cause. As the hearings opened on September 9, Senator Nye set the tone of the investigation by describing the movies in question as "the most vicious propaganda ever unloosed on a civilized people," which he suggested were the result of a veritable conspiracy by a cabal of foreign-born Jews—the "movie moguls" who owned or operated the major studios. Several top executives were called to testify, as was Will Hays, but the key figure in hearings was Wendell Willkie, the renowned jurist and former Republican presidential nominee who served as Hollywood's counsel.

Willkie deftly reframed the terms of the isolationists' argument, putting the senators on the defensive from the outset. Public and press support quickly swung to Willkie and the movie industry, and soon there was open support from Washington as well. FDR praised Hollywood's war effort and Senator Ernest McFarland threatened to ask the Dies Committee on Un-Americanism to investigate the isolationists.[33] By October Nye and Wheeler had completely lost the initiative, and the hearings lapsed into a series of adjournments and postponements; in November they were postponed indefinitely with no plans for resumption.[34] The Japanese attack on Pearl Harbor and U.S. entry into the war rendered the entire question moot, as the federal government mandated that Hollywood immediately begin producing precisely the kind of propaganda films that the Senate hearings had challenged.

Hollywood's Conversion to War Production

In late December 1941, within days of the U.S. entry into World War II, Roosevelt appointed Lowell Mellett coordinator of government films. In that role, Mellett would act as liaison to the film industry and would advise the studios on war-film production. In the letter of appointment, FDR wrote: "The American motion picture is one of the most effective mediums in informing and entertaining our citizens. The motion picture must remain free in so far as national security will permit." This meant, in effect, that the industry could continue commercial operations without direct government control. But FDR clearly expected the industry's full support of the war effort, and he conveyed to Mellett six war-related subject areas that he wanted Hollywood to focus on in its films: the issues ("why we fight"), the enemy, the allies, the home front, the production front, and the U.S. armed forces.[35]

Washington eventually would formalize this "advisory" and monitoring process, creating the OWI in June 1942, with Mellett as head of the Bureau of Motion Pictures (BMP).[36] But by then the movie industry's voluntary support of the war effort was altogether evident. Indeed, it was nothing short of phenomenal, with every sector of the industry undergoing a rapid transformation. In the exhibition sector, movie theaters became wartime community centers, sponsoring events for the Red Cross, the March of Dimes, United Nations Relief, Army-Navy Emergency Relief, and many others.[37] Thousands of movie theaters became official bond "issuing agents" for the U.S. Treasury, and roughly one-fifth of the War Bonds sold during the war were purchased in theaters. Theaters also became collection centers for various "critical materials" such as blood plasma, rags and paper, copper, scrap metal, and rubber.[38]

In terms of distribution, the studios—mainly through the Hollywood-based War Activities Committee (WAC)—worked with the government to set up a worldwide distribution system, shipping 16 mm prints of nearly two thousand Hollywood features and another one thousand shorts in the course of the war to military bases, makeshift theaters, and "beachhead bijous" all over the globe.[39] By 1945, ten million military personnel per week saw Hollywood features under these conditions. WAC also helped secure distribution for government-produced documentaries and informational shorts—including, for example, Capra's "Why We Fight" films.[40]

Hollywood's conversion to war production in terms of actual filmmaking was equally impressive. Within weeks of Pearl Harbor, and with the Senate propaganda hearings only a few months past, Hollywood shifted from outspoken denial of any active promotion of U.S. involvement in the war to aggressive on-screen support of that effort. Within six months roughly one-third of the features in production dealt directly with the war, with a much higher proportion treating the war indirectly, as a given set of social, political, and economic conditions. In terms of the output of war-related films throughout the World War II era, consider these figures compiled by Russell Earl Shain.[41] Shain notes that during the sustained peak in Hollywood's war-related output from 1942 to 1944, one-fourth of all features (312 of 1,286 releases; 24 percent) dealt with the war. According to Shain, Hollywood released 340 war-related features during the four war years, or 20 percent of the industry total. Shain's figures relate only to films dealing directly with World War II and do not include films related to, say, World War I or the Spanish Civil War. Thus studies dealing with all war-related films indicate an even heavier overall output. Dorothy B. Jones of the OWI's Film Reviewing and Analysis Section found that over 28 percent of Hollywood's total output from 1942–1944 (376 of 1,313 releases in her sample) were war-related.[42]

Figure 6. WWII-related Hollywood Features, 1940–1947

	Total War Films	Total Films	% War Films
1940	12	477	2.5
1941	32	492	6.5
1942	121	488	24.8
1943	115	397	29.0
1944	76	401	19.0
1945	28	350	8.0
1946	13	378	`3.4
1947	2	369	0.5

Both Shain's and Jones's figures clearly indicate how rapid and aggressive Hollywood's conversion to war production after Pearl Harbor actually was. What they do not indicate, however, was the overall success of this effort in terms of both box-office revenues and popular response. In 1942, nineteen of the 101 films that returned at least one million dollars in rentals were war-related. The number and proportion of war-related hits more than doubled in 1943, when they comprised forty-one of the ninety-five releases returning one million dollars or more.[43] War-related films also included the top two hits in both 1942 and 1943: *Mrs. Miniver* and *Yankee Doodle Dandy* in 1942, and *This Is the Army* and *For Whom the Bell Tolls* in 1943. The war-related film's box-office currency peaked in 1944, when they comprised eleven of the nineteen releases returning three million dollars or more. For the entire wartime period, a remarkable thirty-two of the seventy-one three-million-dollar-returning releases were war-related—including ten musicals, nine combat films, and six home-front comedies or dramas.[44]

Considering the number of musicals and comedies in this total, it is clear that war-related films did not always depict combat or deal directly with war conditions. What Hollywood termed *war themes* were likely to show up in any number of genres, while the term *war film* took on steadily narrower connotations as Hollywood refined specific war-related formulas. The dominant formula was the combat film, although espionage films and home-front dramas involving military training or the day-to-day experiences of wartime Americans were significant cycles as well. Among the more interesting developments of Hollywood's war film production was the prominence of spy, espionage, and war-related crime thrillers in the early years of the war, especially 1942, and the subsequent surge in home-front dramas and combat films in the later war

Figure 7. WWII-related film by type, 1942–1945

	1942	1943	1944	1945
espionage	59.5%	22.0%	15.6%	17.7%
combat	24.8	41.5	51.4	60.7
home front	16.0	36.7	32.7	18.0

years. As the numbers from Shain's study clearly indicate, by 1944–1945 the combat film was by far the dominant war-related type (see figure 7).[45]

As we look at the reasons behind these figures, and especially the discrepancies between 1942 and the subsequent war years, it becomes evident that the first years of the war, and particularly the first six to eight months after Pearl Harbor, was a singularly odd, exceptional period in terms of Hollywood's war-film production. Predictably enough, perhaps, Hollywood's initial response to the war and to FDR's call to arms was to convert established stars and genres to war production. As noted earlier, Abbott and Costello stopped doing service comedies in late 1941 in deference to the war effort. That turned out to be a singular exception; the vast majority of stars and genres underwent just the opposite progression, converting to cinematic war production as soon as the U.S. entered the war. The result was a melange of genre hybrids and star-genre reformulations in 1942, with the term *war film* applying as little more than a useful generalization.

Significantly enough, most of the films directly related to the U.S. war effort were B pictures. Because Hollywood had been fairly tentative in its treatment of the war until Pearl Harbor, and because top features took nine to twelve months to produce and release, very few A-class pictures depicting U.S. involvement were released in 1942. *Casablanca*, for instance, was optioned within weeks of Pearl Harbor and went into immediate preproduction but did not go into general release until January 1943. Most of the war-related A-class films released in 1942 were initiated in 1941, and they tended to take one of three tacks: they focused on the British war effort (*Mrs. Miniver, This Above All*); they depicted Americans or "good" Europeans dealing with Nazis (*To Be or Not To Be, Desperate Journey*) or Japanese (*Somewhere I'll Find You, Across the Pacific*); or they featured American fliers fighting for other nations (England in *Eagle Squadron*; Canada in *Captains of the Clouds*).

There were B-grade versions of these trends in 1942 as well, such as

MGM's *Journey for Margaret*, a low-cost knockoff of *Mrs. Miniver*, and Republic's *Flying Tigers*, with John Wayne leading a group of fighter pilots assisting the Chinese against Japan. The majority of B-grade war films in 1942, however, had little in common with Hollywood's A-class films, nor were they prone to historical accuracy or the depiction of actual combat. The B film's rapid production and penchant for exploitation enabled low-budget filmmakers to scoop their A-class counterparts in terms of war-related topicality; in fact, on-screen references to Pearl Harbor began turning up in B films within only weeks of Pearl Harbor.[46] But this invariably occurred in jingoistic celebrations of American heroism and superior know-how, depicted in terms of B-movie formula rather than the conditions at hand.

Hollywood's rapid conversion of various B-grade series to war production in 1942 was in its own way quite remarkable. Espionage and sabotage films dominated, as a result not only of genuine public concern but also of the easy reformulation of low-grade crime formulas. G-men and undercover cops simply turned their sights from gangsters to foreign agents, with the trappings of the story—from props, sets, and costumes to cast and plot structure—remaining much the same. A few A-class 1942 features dealing with spies and sabotage, notably Hitchcock's *Saboteur*, gave the formula a certain legitimacy. But shrill, jingoistic B-grade thrillers were far more prevalent. Gangster and spy formulas were refitted in pictures like *Sabotage Squad, Unseen Enemy*, and *Counter-Espionage*, while Sherlock Holmes and Dr. Watson were updated into wartime sleuths in *Sherlock Holmes and the Voice of Terror* and *Sherlock Holmes and the Secret Weapon*. B western series were recruited in films like *Valley of Hunted Men*, with Republic's Three Mesquiteers battling Nazi spies, and *Cowboy Commandos*, with Monogram's Range Busters pursuing Nazi saboteurs.[47] Even the Universal horror film was converted to war production in *Invisible Agent*, as Jon Hall's "invisible man" took on both Nazi and Japanese spies.

Many 1942 B-grade spy and crime thrillers exploited the American public's anger about Pearl Harbor and its anxieties about the Japanese threat—as evidenced by such titles as *A Prisoner of Japan, Menace of the Rising Sun, Danger in the Pacific*, and *Remember Pearl Harbor*. These and other 1942 Bs demonized the Japanese and embellished the "stab-in-the-back" thesis that was haphazardly applied to all Japanese—including Japanese-Americans.

The OWI was alarmed by these trends and issued a much-publicized report in September 1942 that openly criticized Hollywood's B-grade war films. "The emphasis of the entire industry is still too much on the exciting blood-and-thunder aspects of the war," asserted the OWI, and the report went on to note that thirty-one war-related espionage and sabotage pictures had been released in the previous six months, which "tended to give the public an exaggerated idea of the menace."[48] In October the OWI's BMP reported that seventy of 220 pictures in the past six months were war-related, but that few of these substantially advanced the war effort. A *Variety* headline in November blared, "OWI Frowns on 'B' Types," and the subhead noted the agency's "Drive to get the studios to lay off cops-and-robbers formula." That story noted that whereas six "saboteur-spy type" war films were released in October 1942, there were none in the OWI's "all-important 'The Issues—What Are We Fighting For' category."[49]

This latter refrain would persist throughout the war years, as Hollywood continually avoided dealing with the conflict in sophisticated social or political terms. As the OWI's Dorothy Jones pointed out in a 1945 assessment of Hollywood's war-related films, no more than fifty or so had "aided significantly, both at home and abroad, in increasing understanding of the conflict." Jones accused the Hollywood community of thinking only in terms of escapist entertainment, and that "when faced with the task of making films which would educate the public about the war, most Hollywood movie makers did not know where to begin."[50] The industry's defense, of course, was that the primary obligation of commercial filmmakers is to make pictures that sell. Walter Wanger, then the Academy president, outlined that rationale in the spring 1943 issue of *Public Opinion Quarterly*: "Film with a purpose must pass the same test that the escapist film more easily passes," said Wanger. "Theatergoers must want to see the picture." Convinced that the kind of pictures the OWI espoused "can effect no purpose except to empty theaters," Wanger argued that any "truths" about war-related issues "had better be skillfully integrated" into the drama.[51]

We should note here that Mellett and the OWI's BMP had become increasingly combative in their relations with the Hollywood studios and with the industry's self-censorship outfit, the PCA. Though Mellett generally abided by FDR's assurances that there would be no government censorship of movies, the BMP became actively involved in analyzing and evaluating movie projects, in actively promoting particular subjects and plot lines, and in applying various pressures on the studios to cooperate. By late 1942 the BMP had developed something of a "second production code" and a PCA-style review process in an effort to rectify the situation.[52]

The BMP and the PCA (and their respective codes) were politically and ideologically at odds, not only on the treatment of the war but on other issues as well, from their respective notions of a "good society" to their views of what constituted a "good movie." As Koppes and Black point out in *Hollywood Goes to War*, the PCA's extreme conservatism and obsessive concern over moral and sexual issues did not jibe with the OWI's ethos of "mild social democracy and liberal internationalist foreign policy."[53] Moreover, the PCA had considerably more experience than the BMP in dealing with studio executives and filmmakers, and it also had a much clearer understanding of how to work social and political themes into films. Thus the OWI and the PCA often gave the studios conflicting and even contradictory input on the making of war-related films.

The OWI's ideological bent also conflicted with the views of Congress—particularly after the November 1942 election, which brought a more conservative-leaning group to Capitol Hill. The newly elected Congress viewed the OWI in general and the BMP in particular as blatantly pro-Roosevelt and dangerously liberal. And so in 1943 Congress cut off almost all funding for the OWI's domestic operations, which resulted in the resignation of Mellett and his key associates and left the BMP with little to do on the home front beyond the routine distribution of government shorts. But that did not mark the end of the BMP in Hollywood. On the contrary, the agency gained a stronger hand by shifting its liaison activities to its still-active overseas branch, which had developed a strong accord with the Office of Censorship. With its regulatory control over film exports, the Office of Censorship effectively put teeth in the BMP's advisory role, providing a post hoc threat to deny export to those films that blatantly disregarded the bureau's input on important political matters.[54]

The Hollywood War Film Comes of Age

By late 1942 a growing number of politically correct and commercially viable A-class war films rolled out of the studios. Though Hollywood would never quite satisfy the OWI, there was a clear improvement in the overall quality of war films when the ambitious first-run features made after Pearl Harbor finally reached the theaters in late 1942. Perhaps the most significant of this first wave of quality war films was *Casablanca*, a Warner Bros. release that premiered in November

1942 and provides an illuminating example of Hollywood's high-end conversion on several levels.

The initial impetus for the picture came via a story analyst report filed on December 8, 1941, the day after Pearl Harbor, which included coverage of an unproduced play, "Everybody Comes to Rick's." The story centered on American expatriate Rick Blaine, whose cafe in French Morocco is a haven for European war refugees, and whose life is disrupted by the unexpected arrival of Lois Meredith, the wanton American beauty who, years before, had broken up Rick's marriage and family and had cost Rick his law practice in prewar Paris. The story analyst considered the property a "box-office natural" and a suitable vehicle "for Bogart, or Cagney, or Raft in out-of-the-usual roles and perhaps Mary Astor." [55] A few days later the report reached Warners production chief Hal Wallis, who saw the property as an ideal prospect for a high-class war film. He tapped Michael Curtiz to direct and assigned several top writers to overhaul the story, strengthening both the political and romantic angles. He also entered negotiations with David Selznick for the services of his fast-rising contract star, Ingrid Bergman, to costar with Warners's own emerging star, Humphrey Bogart.

Thus began production on *Casablanca*, Hollywood's seminal wartime "conversion narrative." The conversion of studio operations and the retooling of established story formulas into war films were crucial here, but the key aspects of this conversion involved the narrative itself. The love story was recast in terms of wartime separation and duty by reworking the female lead: the American seductress Lois was transformed into an innocent European refugee, Ilsa, whose commitment to French Resistance leader Victor Laszlo motivated her earlier betrayal of Rick. And the most crucial conversion, finally, is Rick's. Early on, Bogart's Rick Blaine is very much the hard-boiled Warners hero: cynical and self-reliant, repeatedly muttering, "I stick my neck out for nobody." But in the course of the story he rediscovers his own self-worth, along with his love of woman and country. Rick's final heroics—sending Ilsa away with Laszlo, killing the Nazi officer, and leaving to join the Free French—crystallized the American conversion from neutrality to selfless sacrifice.

On a more abstract level, *Casablanca* also signaled the wartime conversion of Hollywood's classical narrative paradigm. As Dana Polan suggests in his study of 1940s film narrative, Hollywood's classical paradigm with its individual protagonist and clearly resolved conflicts underwent a temporary but profound shift to accommodate the war effort. [56] The

Victor Laszlo (Paul Henreid), Ilse Lund (Ingrid Bergman), and Rick Blaine (Humphrey Bogart). *Casablanca*, Michael Curtiz. © Warner Bros., 1942.

two most fundamental qualities of Hollywood narrative, one might argue, were (and remain) the individual goal-oriented protagonist and the formation of the couple. During the war, however, these two qualities had to be radically adjusted: the individual yielded to the will and the activity of the collective (the combat unit, the community, the nation, the family); and sexual coupling was suspended "for the duration," subordinated to gender-specific war efforts that involved very different spheres of activity (and conceptions of heroic behavior) for men and women.

Of course, Hollywood always had found conflict in its contradictory conception of the idealized male and female—the untrammeled man of action and of few words (and well-concealed sentiments) who's gotta do what he's gotta do; and the supportive, sensitive but stoic Madonna, whose natural (even biological) destiny is to tame that free-spirited male for the higher cause of civilization. The resolution of the classical film narrative invariably involved the overcoming of that contradiction in the lovers' final embrace. But the war effort created radically different requirements, indefinitely postponing the climactic coupling while celebrating the lovers' dutiful separation and commitment to a larger cause—the lesson learned from Rick in the final moments of *Casablanca*.

That lesson clearly played with movie audiences. *Casablanca* was shot during the summer of 1942 and previewed in November. The studio considered adding a "tag scene" to clarify the fate of Bogart's hero at film's end, but those plans were abandoned when the Allies began Operation Torch, a massive offensive in North Africa in the very region where the film was set. So Warners rushed the film out for a Thanksgiving premiere, clarifying the ending simply by redubbing Bogart's final line ("Louis, this could be the beginning of a beautiful friendship").[57] *Casablanca* officially opened in January 1943, just as Roosevelt and Churchill began a series of summit talks in Casablanca, further exploiting the picture's topical appeal. The film was one of Warners' all-time biggest hits, returning over four million dollars and winning an Oscar for best picture of 1943.

Casablanca was the first of many A-class war films that hit the nation's theaters with enormous impact in 1943. These included big-budget musicals such as *This Is the Army, Star-Spangled Rhythm*, and *Stage Door Canteen;* "resistance" dramas such as *Watch on the Rhine* and *The Moon Is Down;* wartime romantic comedies such as *The More the Merrier;* romantic dramas such as *For Whom the Bell Tolls;* and wartime family melodramas such as *The Human Comedy*. There was a marked increase in both the quantity and quality of Hollywood's A-class combat films, and a number of British war films also were successfully released in the U.S.—notably *In Which We Serve, The Way Ahead, The Invaders* (British title, *The 49th Parallel*), and *One of Our Aircraft Is Missing*. Critics responded favorably to this 1943 surge in A-class war films. The National Board of Review's top ten films included seven war-related pictures, and every film on the top-ten list via the *Film Daily's* poll of over four hundred critics was war-related (including *Random Harvest* with a World War I story and *For Whom the Bell Tolls* with its

Spanish Civil War context).[58] The Academy's ten nominees for best picture likewise included seven war-related films.

Though a number of Hollywood's high-end genres had been successfully reformulated for war production by 1943, it grew increasingly clear that the musical and the woman's picture were especially amenable. The musical was perhaps the most effectively enlisted to the war effort, primarily via a cycle of musical revues such as *Star Spangled Rhythm* (1942), *Thank Your Lucky Stars* (1943), *Stage Door Canteen* (1943), *Thousands Cheer* (1944), and *Hollywood Canteen* (1944). These were essentially filmed versions of military stage shows, laden with top talent—following the popular and well-publicized USO tours both at home and overseas—but thin on plot. Widely disparaged or dismissed by critics, the wartime revue musicals were among the most popular and commercially successful films of the era. As filmed stage shows, they were relatively inexpensive films by musical standards and thus highly profitable.

The most successful wartime revue musical—and in fact the single biggest box-office hit of the war era—was *This Is the Army* (1943), which had a rather curious pedigree. Created for the stage by the War Department as an all-soldier musical revue (with music by Irving Berlin), *This Is the Army* premiered on Broadway on July 4, 1942, and was a huge hit. Warner Bros. purchased the screen rights and began production in early 1943, while the stage version continued to play to record audiences. Producer Hal Wallis and director Michael Curtiz (between stints on *Yankee Doodle Dandy* and *Casablanca*) fleshed out the play's paper-thin plot about army recruits staging a big show for the troops, incorporating about a dozen second-rank studio stars (such as George Murphy, Joan Leslie, Alan Hale, Ronald Reagan) along with a few cultural icons such as boxer-soldier Joe Louis. On both stage and screen, *This Is the Army* ran uninterrupted throughout the war, and Warners' film version returned eight and a half million dollars in rentals.[59]

Meanwhile, the woman's film was effectively reformulated as well, with the war and related social conditions providing ready-made themes and conflicts, particularly in maternal and romantic melodramas. *Mrs. Miniver* established the currency of the family drama centering on a powerful wartime matriarch, and in fact David Selznick produced a hugely successful "American Miniver" in 1944, *Since You Went Away*. Hollywood produced a number of multigenerational or highly elliptical maternal melodramas that managed to incorporate war themes, notably *Random Harvest, Mr. Skeffington* (1944), and *The White Cliffs of Dover* (1944). There were numerous melodramas about separated, soon-to-be separated, or otherwise troubled couples, as in such 1945 hits as *I'll Be Seeing You, The Clock*, and *The Enchanted Cottage*. The working-girl dramas often involved both war-strained romances and war-related female labor. *Tender Comrade* (1943), for instance, focused on women war-plant workers sharing a home and the pain of loss and separation, and *So Proudly We Hail* (1943) honored army nurses serving and dying in the Pacific alongside male soldiers. Of the various women's subgenres, only the gothic thrillers such as *Suspicion* (1942) and *Gaslight* (1944) consistently avoided the war, although these carried wartime implications regarding hasty marriages and psychologically scarred male protagonists.

The Combat Film

The most direct and pervasive treatment of the war emerged in the combat film. The seminal picture in this cycle was *Wake Island*, a Paramount "near-A" released in August 1942 starring Brian Donlevy, William Bendix, Macdonald Carey, and Robert Preston, which dramatized the devastating December 1941 defeat of a marine contingent on a remote island outpost near Hawaii. As Jeanine Basinger suggests, *Wake Island* was a watershed release and in many ways the first true World War II combat film. Incorporating many traits of earlier war films, *Wake Island* "begins to relate the meaning of these 'old' devices directly to World War II." [60] Key factors, according to Basinger, were its focus on an actual U.S. military battle and its treatment of the combat unit, "that unique group of mixed individuals, so carefully organized to represent typical Americans." [61] The film also established the conventions of the World War II "last stand" drama. In *Wake Island* and subsequent films such as *Manila Calling* (1942) and *Bataan* (1943), a small, isolated unit of American soldiers fight to the death against impossible odds, with the narrative invariably concluding just before the last American is killed.

Wake Island was a solid critical and commercial hit, finishing among the top ten box-office hits of 1942 and scoring four Oscar nominations, including best picture. Bosley Crowther in the *New York Times* called it "a realistic picture about heroes who do not pose as such," and *Newsweek* called it "Hollywood's first intelligent, honest, and completely successful attempt to dramatize the deeds of an American force on a fight-

Wake Island, John Farrow. © Paramount, 1942.

ing front." [62] Made in cooperation with the Marine Corps and endorsed by the OWI, the film clearly established the viability of the violent, downbeat, hyperactive combat film, while toning down the jingoistic flag-waving, blatant racism, and gross historical distortions of the B-grade war films. However, these qualities were not eliminated altogether. Most of Hollywood's wartime combat dramas were set in the Pacific and depicted the Japanese enemy as not only uncivilized but essentially inhuman—a view that pervaded the American media and mindset in general. As war correspondent Ernie Pyle wrote: "In Europe we felt that our enemies, horrible and deadly as they were, were still people. But out here [in the Pacific] I soon gathered that the Japanese were looked upon as something subhuman or repulsive." [63]

With *Wake Island* serving as both a narrative template and an economic incentive, Hollywood's output of A-class combat films picked up considerably in 1943 with pictures such as *Air Force, Action in the North Atlantic, Bataan, Guadalcanal Diary, The Immortal Sergeant*, and *Sahara*. Two key films in this effort were *Air Force* and *Bataan*, which solidified the essential conventions of the World War II combat film while establishing its two dominant variations. *Air Force*, an early 1943 release shot on location (at a Florida air base) and made in cooperation with the army air corps, won critical praise for its semidocumentary style. The story focused on a group of men isolated within a powerful warship—in this case an authentic B-17 Flying Fortress—which was involved in various air-sea battles in the Pacific during the early months of the war. In the course of the film, the men learn both the value of group cooperation and the finer workings of their bomber, which gradually emerges as the crew's mother, lover, and sacred vessel. The finale of *Air Force* is relatively upbeat, with the warship taking part in the Allied victory in the Battle of the Coral Sea.

Bataan also involved an early battle campaign in the Pacific theater, but it was a more stylized, studio-bound production, and was considerably more brutal and downbeat as well. The story centers on a combat unit of thirteen men in an isolated jungle outpost on Bataan, which is being overrun by invading Japanese troops. The unit is assigned to destroy a bridge and prevent the Japanese from rebuilding it; in carrying out that assignment the men are killed, one by one, by the relentless, faceless enemy. The consummate last-stand picture, *Bataan* ends with the unit leader and lone survivor (Robert Taylor) throwing curses at the swarming Japanese and swinging his machine-gun fire directly into the camera for the film's powerful closing image.

These two narratives, one centering on the warship and the other on the infantry unit, coalesced into Hollywood's two standard, war-issue combat formulas. The group dynamic and celebration of technology of *Air Force* recurred in all manner of warships, from submarines and ships to tanks and aircraft, whereas the infantry films after *Bataan* traced the horrors of combat and the psychopathology of soldiering in increasingly grim terms. For Basinger, *Air Force* and *Bataan* defined the "new genre" of the World War II combat film. "They contain the new genre," she states. "In fact, they *are* the new genre. They are the two most important films . . . because they are the first that are totally in and about World War II combat."[64] Basinger contends, however, that the infantry variation represents "the truest and purest combat format," because it is so relentlessly "about" actual fighting. Whereas the bomber can take its crew back to the relative security and domesticity of the barracks, and even the submarine has its social and hospitable attributes, the infantry film offers "no relief from the war."[65]

Basinger singles out *Bataan* as "clearly the seminal film" of the World War II combat genre, citing three main reasons for her view.

Bataan, Tay Garnett. © MGM, 1943.

First, unlike all of the previous combat films made during the war, *Bataan* provided no "denial" of the war via furloughs, returns home, or other noncombat situations; it focused only on soldiering and combat. Second, the nature and composition of the combat unit in *Bataan* became a veritable paradigm for subsequent films. This applied along various social and cultural lines—the ethnic, racial, and religious background of unit members; their ideological, economic and class-related status; and their geographical and regional origins. It also applied in terms of military rank, experience, and professionalism. As Basinger notes, *Bataan* set the standard not only for the composition of the group in infantry combat films, but also the structure of authority, the likelihood of death, and even the order in which the unit members are killed.[66]

Third and perhaps most important, *Bataan* integrated these conventions into a dramatically compelling narrative—and thus into effective propaganda. The group constituted what Lewis Jacobs has termed "a national collective hero," although Basinger aptly notes that the unit's "democratic ethnic mix" necessarily included a leader "who is part of the group, but is forced to separate himself from it because of the demands of leadership." [67] Those demands generally include a military objective (in this case, the bridge) related to a specific military campaign, while also dealing with inevitable internal conflicts of the group. Meanwhile the individual group members partake in the myriad rituals of infantry life, the articulation of what they are fighting for, and the necessary horror of fighting and dying. With *Bataan*, asserts Basinger, "the foundation of the World War II combat film is in place," with the various "generic requirements" of the form "firmly established and repeated" in the films that followed, as was readily apparent by late 1943 with films such as *Sahara, Guadalcanal Diary, Cry Havoc,* and *Destination Tokyo.* [68]

Though Basinger provides an insightful analysis of one crucial strain of the combat film, her relatively inflexible schema tends to downplay or dismiss the rich variations in the war film's development. Consider briefly the similarities evident in two seemingly disparate war films, *Air Force* and *Since You Went Away.* The most basic similarity between this combat film and this home-front melodrama is their mutual celebration of distinctive American "fortresses"—one a Boeing B-17 bomber and the other a two-story brick colonial home—while valorizing the occupants and the special wartime rites of each domain. Whereas *Air Force* presents the saga of a B-17 Flying Fortress and its crew during the first disastrous months of the Pacific war, *Since You Went Away* involves an epic of a very different sort. Dedicated in its opening credits to "the Unconquered Fortress: the American Home," *Since You Went Away* charts a year in the lives of a woman and her two daughters, beginning in early 1943 with the departure of the husband and father for active duty. The lives of the three are transformed by the war effort and war-related experiences at home, as well as the fate of the absent patriarch—who is reported missing-in-action midway through the film, and whose reported return to safety provides the story's climactic moment.

In *Air Force*, the conversion theme operates on several levels. In a general sense, the warship itself (the *Mary Ann*) is converted from a training ship into a fighting machine, and the crew members into functional components of that machine. In the course of the story, the *Mary Ann* emerges as a distinct character and veritable member of the combat unit—and one that actually is "wounded in action" and must be nursed back to health in order to continue fighting. In terms of human drama, the story focuses on two converts: Winocki (John Garfield) is a surly loner and flight school washout who eventually accepts his role as a team player and gunner; in fact he is credited with inventing the tail gun for the B-17. Tex Rader (James Brown) is a professional loner, a pursuit pilot forced to ride in the *Mary Ann* when his fighter is shot down. Tex initially denigrates bombers (the crew, in turn, dismiss his "pea shooter"), but he eventually takes command of the plane after the pilot is killed and the copilot wounded.

In precise counterpoint to *Air Force, Since You Went Away* presents an idealized portrait of the fight waged by women, individually and collectively, on the home front. Unlike many woman's pictures and home-front dramas that invoked the war more indirectly, *Since You Went Away* was quite clearly a war film, tracing the conversion of home and family— the American community in microcosm—to the war effort. Thus *Since You Went Away* is very much a wartime conversion narrative, as the Hilton females as well as the family home and the community at large are utterly transformed by the war. As Koppes and Black suggest, the film presents "a virtual compendium of OWI-approved vignettes of American life as changed by the war." [69] And it was also the wartime woman's picture par excellence, focusing directly on the American female's experience of World War II. Though the absent patriarch's departure and reported rescue define the film's narrative trajectory, the principal dramatic concerns involve the travails of the Hilton women. In this sense it is quite a bit different from the "American *Mrs. Miniver*" that Selznick set out to produce. Whereas *Miniver* focuses on the initial impact of the war (and a direct Nazi attack) on a fully intact British family, *Since You Went Away* depicts the wartime experiences of a distaff "combat unit" on the home front facing battles that their male counterparts would never know or understand.

The similarities between *Air Force* and *Since You Went Away* are illuminating. Both are conversion narratives that trace the adjustments and sacrifices that American women and men had to make for the war effort to succeed. Both redefined family and community, positing a new (albeit temporary) kinship system based on mutual need and commitment to the task at hand. Both depicted epic journeys, although of a very different sort: the men in a Flying Fortress, traveling through space and externalizing their war-induced anxieties by fighting and killing; the women in an American domestic fortress, traveling through time and internalizing their anxieties by loving and nurturing—and waiting. Both films end in moments of triumph, although these are only momentary triumphs that scarcely resolve the larger social and military conflicts faced by the characters (and the audience).

Though this cursory comparison of *Air Force* and *Since You Went Away* suggests the kinds of cross-genre variations that developed in war-film production, we might also consider the variations that emerged within individual combat films. Among the more notable of these was *Sahara*, an underrated combat film of the war era. *Sahara* is significant on several counts, particularly the nature of the "warship" and the military unit involved, the deft blending of the warship and infantry variations, and the heightened realism of the production.

Sahara was a late-1943 Columbia release starring Warners loanout Humphrey Bogart as the leader of a disparate band of Allied soldiers (Dan Duryea, J. Carroll Naish, Rex Ingram, Lloyd Bridges, and others) who cross the Libyan desert aboard a U.S. tank and eventually make a stand at a desert well against an entire Nazi division. The film opens with Bogart's tank commander, Sgt. Joe Gunn, and his two-man crew crossing the North African desert alone in their tank during the chaotic retreat after the fall of Tobruk. At a bombed-out military hospital, they come across a British medical officer and five infantrymen: two British, two Australian, one South African, and one French. Gunn offers them assistance, but the British dismiss the tank as an "old scow" and a "tin hearse." Gunn takes offense, not only extolling his tank but romanticizing and feminizing it in the process. "She's an M3 air-cooled job that can cross two hundred miles of desert as easily as you'd walk around in that Piccalilli Circus of yours," he says. "When I go into Berlin I'll be riding that tank, the same one that's standin' there with the name Lulubelle on her." With no real choice, the soldiers climb aboard, riding atop the tank while Gunn and his crew (a radioman and a gunner) ride inside.

Sahara is clearly a star vehicle for Bogart, whose hero is a familiar wartime synthesis of rugged individualist and team player. Yet here the conversion to the collective war effort has long since been made, and he is presented as the ideal leader; in fact, the ranking British officer readily cedes authority to Gunn's tank commander early in the film. The soldiers eventually are won over by Gunn and the *Lulubelle*, as are a black British-Sudanese soldier and his Italian prisoner (a sympathetic figure with relatives in America) who join the rag-tag unit in its desert journey. *Lulubelle*'s efficiency is further evinced when the crew shoots down a German fighter plane and captures the pilot, adding a dedicated Nazi to the group. Thus the group is complete, a diverse amalgam of eleven

Sahara, Zoltan Korda. © Columbia, 1943.

Allied soldiers and their two Axis prisoners, comprising one of the more remarkable units in any wartime combat film and clearly representing the war's principal Western combatants in microcosm.

The first half of *Sahara* involves the delineation of these various characters—and the varied stakes and views of the nations they represent—along with an increasingly desperate search for water and fuel. The group eventually finds water at a modestly fortified well, where they decide to dig in and try to hold off a division of some five hundred parched Nazis en route to El Alemein. Thus *Sahara* shifts to a last-stand drama; the Allies are killed one after the other by the Germans, who themselves die in massive numbers in their repeated assaults on the well. The two prisoners also are killed under telling symbolic circumstances. The German pilot murders the Italian for defaming Hitler and Nazism, and then while trying to escape, he is killed in a desperate hand-to-hand struggle with the black Sudanese—an obvious comment on Aryan superiority. Eventually the Allied force is down to only two men (including Gunn) and low on ammunition. But the Germans, succumbing to thirst and unaware of the Allied numbers because of Gunn's successful ploys, suddenly surrender. So *Sahara* veers from last-stand drama to an updated version of *Sergeant York*, and its upbeat outcome is underscored as the two survivors and their Nazi prisoners are met by Allied troops who inform them of the victory at El Alemein.

Despite its star-vehicle status, careening patchwork plot, and upbeat resolution, *Sahara* is an altogether effective war film. Much of this is a function of the style and visual treatment of the narrative by a production unit that was nearly as diverse as the military unit in the film. Of particular note are director Zoltan Korda and cinematographer Rudolph Mate, two Hungarian-born émigrés to Hollywood from war-torn Europe (Mate via Germany and France; Korda from England where he had worked with his brother, producer Alexander Korda). The two achieved a quasi-documentary style in their treatment of soldiering and combat, while bringing a more stylized "poetic realism" to the depiction of the otherworldly desert milieu. Mate's camera work was nominated for an Oscar, and critic James Agee wrote of *Sahara*'s distinctive style: "It borrows, chiefly from the English, a sort of light-alloy modification of realism which makes the traditional Hollywood idiom seem as obsolete as a minuet." [70]

Wartime Documentary and the Issue of Realism

As Agee suggests, the realism in *Sahara* can be attributed in part to European influence, which was a function not only of the filmmakers directly involved but the growing number of émigrés working in Hollywood, as well as the number of British films currently in U.S. release. Equally important, however, was the documentary influence that became increasingly pronounced in Hollywood's combat films of the later war years. Crucial to the combat film's 1943 surge were the massive advances in news coverage of the fighting overseas, not only in the print media and on radio, but also in motion picture newsreels and documentaries.

In 1942 roughly 80 percent of all newsreels were devoted to the war; in 1943 that total rose to nearly 90 percent.[71] The six newsreel companies vastly improved their coverage in 1942–1943, moving beyond a "headline service" role to provide timely and graphic images of actual combat. This was facilitated by the easing in late 1942 (at FDR's behest) of military restrictions over the filming of combat and by rapid improvements in the technology and logistics of combat reporting.[72] Documentary film coverage improved as well, as in-depth nonfiction war films—both shorts and features, many of them created by top Hollywood filmmakers then in the military—became standard screen fare in 1943. In addition, several British war documentaries enjoyed widespread U.S. release and favorable critical response. In fact, the Academy Award for best documentary feature in 1943 went to *Desert Victory*, a British-American co-production on the Allied campaign in North Africa, and the award for best documentary short went to John Ford's *The Battle of Midway.*

Advances in nonfiction war coverage encouraged Hollywood filmmakers not only to dramatize combat but to do so with a greater degree of verisimilitude and historical accuracy. In the process, the narrative and dramatic emphases of combat dramas as well as the number of Hollywood filmmakers doing documentary work clearly influenced nonfiction war films. Thus by 1943 fiction and nonfiction war films were entering a stage of remarkable symbiosis, with combat dramas providing a (belated) fictional counterpart to the newsreel and documentaries, all of which not only depicted major military engagements but also defined and dramatized the war experience for millions of Americans at home.

This symbiotic interplay of fiction and nonfiction war films is noteworthy on several counts. The breakthrough combat film *Wake Island* was released in 1942 within weeks of Ford's *Battle of Midway*, which itself was precedent setting as the first document of an actual U.S. military engagement and the first to use 16 mm Technicolor photography. Moreover, it was the first "battle record" by an established Hollywood director, with Ford's handheld camera work setting the early standard for first-person combat coverage.

In 1943, as more Hollywood filmmakers did documentary work, they introduced dramatic qualities and narrative strategies that brought the nonfiction war film into a curious kinship with its fictional counterparts. Consider William Wyler's film treatment of bombing runs over Germany from a Flying Fortress in *Memphis Belle* (1944) and John Huston's treatment of fierce infantry fighting in the Liri valley in Italy in *The Battle of San Pietro* (1945). Among the more important and critically acclaimed wartime documentaries, both films effectively integrate fiction and nonfiction techniques. They extend and intensify the first-person technique of *The Battle of Midway*, and as hour-long documentaries they develop strong narrative and dramatic lines to delve into the human as well as the military stakes involved. Moreover, the two are documentary versions of Hollywood's dominant combat trends—the specialized unit operating (and confined within) a high-tech warship, and the isolated, interdependent, war-weary infantry unit trudging from one deadly engagement to another.

As documentarians like Ford, Wyler, and Huston dramatized and humanized their wartime subjects, fictionalized accounts of combat developed a more pronounced "documentary realism." In 1944–1945, interestingly enough, the number of fictional and documentary combat films released was almost identical (numbering sixteen and fourteen, respectively), and some have argued that these two forms of combat film can (and should) be considered as manifestations of the same genre.[73] Critic James Agee, for instance, named *San Pietro* and a dramatic feature, *The Story of G.I. Joe*, as the two best films of 1945, and for essentially the same reasons: their direct, unsympathetic, antiromantic portrayal of professional soldiers in combat, and the gauging of military conflict and outcome in human terms.[74]

Released in October 1945, *The Story of G.I. Joe* was in fact the dramatic counterpart of Huston's *San Pietro*, a grim depiction of an American unit in the Italian campaign directed by William Wellman and starring Robert Mitchum as the reluctant unit leader and Burgess Meredith as war correspondent Ernie Pyle (who had been killed in combat a year earlier). For Agee, *The Story of G.I. Joe* was "the first great triumph in the effort to combine 'fiction' and 'documentary' film"—an effort he had been tracing since the release of *Air Force* in 1943. Besides Wellman's direction, the "great triumphs" of the film also included its "antihistrionic casting and acting," which Agee considered crucial to this kind of war film. Indeed, Agee's one misgiving about the otherwise effective *Objective Burma* (1945) was that, for him, it could never quite overcome the onus of being an Errol Flynn picture—a criticism that might be leveled at *Sahara* (and Bogart) as well.[75]

Remarkably, both *The Story of G.I. Joe* and *San Pietro* were regarded as antiwar films by some critics, because they were so downbeat in their portrayal of men at war and so sensitive to the psychological and physical trauma involved. *The Battle of San Pietro*, in fact, so concerned military officials in Washington that it was withheld from distribution until the end of the war in Europe, and then was released only in an abridged version under the (also abridged) title, *San Pietro*.[76] Agee noted the debate that had arisen over the antiwar issue in his October 1945 review of *The Story of G.I. Joe*, and his own take was appropriately ambivalent: "Nobody [in the film] is accused, not even the enemy; no remedy is indicated; and though every foot of the film is as full an indictment of war as I ever expect to see, it is clearly also demonstrating the fact that in war many men go well beyond anything which any sort of peace we have known, or are likely to know, makes possible for them. It seems to me a tragic and eternal work of art." [77]

Two other fictional war films released just after the war, *They Were Expendable* (December 1945) and *A Walk in the Sun* (January 1946) also displayed the documentary-style realism of *The Story of G.I. Joe*, as well as its tone of grim resignation and weary professionalism. Few critics gauged these as antiwar efforts, however. As Roger Manvell points out, the Ford-directed *They Were Expendable* clearly accepts "the fatalism bred of combat conditions," while it also "brings out the ancient ethos of war, the aspiration to heroism, a profound acceptance of self-sacrifice for the 'cause' of the nation, the near-worship of the charisma of military authority implicit in such terminology as *high command* and *supreme command*." [78] At the same time, however, these films are willing to consider both the possible breakdown of the group cohesion as well as the price—in both individual and collective terms—of military victory.

Ultimately, the more "realistic" and somewhat disillusioned combat films of the later war era marked a significant departure from infantry dramas such as *Wake Island, Bataan, Sahara*, and *Guadalcanal Diary*. Though sharing many qualities with their flag-waving, heroic, and aggressively prowar antecedents, the later combat films clearly differ in style and tone. Again James Agee offers a useful distinction. In his review of *Bataan* (in July 1943 in *The Nation*), Agee termed the film a "war melodrama" much like *Wake Island*, and went on to describe it as "a small triumph of pure artifice," constrained as it was by its star, its obvious studio setting, and its utterly predictable heroic posturing.

Agee found this anything but realistic, but still he recognized the power and appeal of films like *Wake Island* and *Bataan*: "We may not yet recognize the tradition, but it is essentially, I think, not a drama but a kind of native ritual dance. As such its image of war is not only naive, coarse-grained, primitive; it is also honest, accomplished in terms of its aesthetic, and true." [79] Hollywood sustained this type of ritualized war melodrama with films such as *Destination Tokyo* (1943), *Winged Victory* (1944), *Thirty Seconds Over Tokyo* (1944), *God Is My Co-Pilot* (1945), and *Back to Bataan* (1945)—all of which were sizable hits. And whereas critics praised the documentary-style combat films, audiences clearly preferred the energetic hokum of war melodramas such as *A Guy Named Joe* over the grim realism of *The Story of G.I. Joe*.

As noted earlier, Hollywood's production of combat films ended abruptly after the war because the industry perceived the audience as disinterested.[80] By late 1945, exhibitors and studio executives alike had developed a firm conviction that the genre's currency for a war-weary populace—not to mention the millions of returning veterans—ended with the war itself. So as the government and the military rapidly dismantled the nation's vast war machine, the movie industry began reconversion as well, mustering out the war-related themes and formulas that had prevailed for the past four years. This was most evident in terms of the combat film, but the home-front drama also underwent a postwar decline as Hollywood shied away from stories of returning vets, postwar rehabilitation, and the domestic "return to normalcy."

The World War II combat film hardly disappeared altogether, of course. After laying dormant for fully three years, the genre would undergo a remarkable and quite unexpected resurgence in 1949, keyed by three major hits released late in the year: *Battleground, Twelve O'Clock High*, and *Sands of Iwo Jima*. As mentioned at the outset, the World War II combat film would remain a significant Hollywood genre for decades to come, utterly dominating war-film production through the Korean and Vietnam wars. Moreover, the war films that focused on those subsequent military conflicts looked to the World War II combat films for their structural and thematic features—although none portrayed the same kind of "heroic" action or the same kind of "good war." Indeed, even the World War II combat films produced after the war itself carried a different narrative and thematic charge—affected by the Cold War, as well as the active military conflicts and the changing social and political currents of the postwar era.

Thus the World War II combat film remains a special species of war film. From 1942 to 1945, Hollywood created a parallel universe for a nation at war, an odd amalgam of information and entertainment, of fact and propaganda, of realism and collective national fantasy. In that sense, Hollywood's war-related output, and particularly the wartime cycle of combat films, represents a body of films and a collective cultural experience that is altogether unique in American movie history.

Notes

This essay is excerpted and adapted from my book *History of the American Cinema*, Vol. 6: "Boom and Bust: The American Cinema in the 1940s,"

1. *1940 Film Daily Year Book* (New York: The Film Daily, 1941), 81.

2. Clayton R. Koppes and Gregory C. Black, *Hollywood Goes to War* (Berkeley: University of California Press, 1987), 30. Warners released a similar film in September 1939, *Espionage Agent,* starring Joel McCrea; it too fared better critically than commercially, despite the outbreak of war in Europe that same month.

3. *Wall Street Journal,* 2 January 1941, p. 48.

4. *Motion Picture Herald,* 4 February 1939, p. 38; 11 March 1939, p. 6; 13 January 1940, p. 8; *Variety,* 19 July 1939, p. 11.

5. According to *Variety* (6 September 1939, p. 6), the market shares of Hollywood's overseas clients in September 1939 were:

Great Britain—45 percent
France and Belgium—13 percent
Australia—11.2 percent
Central and South America—9 percent
Scandinavia—4.2 percent
Holland—1.5 percent
Bulgaria, Greece, and Turkey—1.2 percent
Neutral Central Europe—1 percent

Variety routinely reported that Hollywood realized up to half of its income from overseas. More conservative estimates placed the figure at about one third. The *Wall Street Journal* (3 October 1939, p. 1) reported: "The situation may be summed up as follows: American film producers obtain about 30 percent to 35 percent of their total film rentals from abroad. This varies somewhat from year to year. Around half of the foreign income . . . comes from Great Britain. South America supplies 10 percent to 15 percent and the rest is scattered. The Continent of Europe, due to government regulation and exchange difficulties, has provided little profit in recent years."

6. *1941 Film Daily Year Book,* 57. *Wall Street Journal,* 2 January 1941, p. 48.

7. *Wall Street Journal,* 2 January 1941, p. 48.

8. *Variety,* 4 January 1939, p. 5.

9. The major Hollywood studios took in nearly fifty million dollars in rentals in both 1940 and 1941—record figures that increased in the ensuing war years. *Motion Picture Herald,* 7 June 1941, p. 18; *Wall Street Journal,* 7 July 1941, p. 1.

10. On the impact of the defense buildup on the movie industry, see *Motion Picture Herald,* 22 June 1940, p. 8, and *Wall Street Journal,* 2 January 1941, p. 48.

11. See *Variety,* 9 July 41, p. 5; *Wall Street Journal,* 10 September 1941, p. 1.

12. *Motion Picture Herald,* 1 November 1941, p. 13; *Variety,* 26 November 1941, p. 7.

13. *Motion Picture Herald,* 3 May 1941, p. 9.

14. Douglas Gomery, *Shared Pleasures: A History of Movie Presentation in the United States* (Madison: University of Wisconsin Press, 1992), 152.

15. See chapter 2, "Hollywood Turns Interventionist," in Koppes and Black, *Hollywood Goes to War,* 17–47.

16. *Motion Picture Herald*, 15 April 1941, p. 9.

17. *Motion Picture Herald*, 7 September 1940, p. 47.

18. Russell Earl Shain, *An Analysis of Motion Pictures about the War Released by the American Film Industry, 1939–1970* (New York: Arno, 1976), 31, 61.

19. Koppes and Black, *Hollywood Goes to War*, 32.

20. *New York Times*, 8 September 1940, p. X3.

21. *New York Times*, 22 September 40, p. X3.

22. Bosley Crowther in his *New York Times* review of 3 August 1940 suggests that *The Man I Married* was in fact the first Hollywood film to use the term *Jew*. *New York Times Film Reviews*, vol. 3 (New York: The New York Times and Arno Press, 1970), 1724.

23. Shain, *An Analysis*, 31, 61.

24. *Motion Picture Herald*, 27 December 1941, p. 13.

25. Roger Manvell, *Films and the Second World War* (New York: Delta, 1974), 15–17, 86–92.

26. *Motion Picture Herald*, 2 November 1940, p. 9.

27. *Motion Picture Herald*, 30 August 1941, p. 15.

28. *Motion Picture Herald*, 9 August 1941, p. 26; 16 August 1941, p. 8; 30 August 1941, p. 8.

29. Note that *Foreign Correspondent* was based on a then-recent nonfiction best-seller, *Personal History*. The "Hays Office" refers to the Motion Picture Producers and Directors of America (MPPDA), the industry trade organization headed by Will Hays. The PCA was actually a subagency of the MPPDA.

30. *New York Times*, 26 February 1939, p. X4.

31. *Motion Picture Herald*, 1 April 1939, p. 22.

32. Koppes and Black, *Hollywood Goes to War*, 33–34. See also *Motion Picture Herald*, 18 January 1941, p. 9; 15 February 1941, p. 9; and *New York Times*, 19 January 1941, p. X5.

33. See *Variety*, 10 September 1941, p. 1; *Motion Picture Herald*, 13 September 1941, n.p; *Motion Picture Herald*, 4 October 1941, pp. 12–18.

34. *Motion Picture Herald*, 15 November 1941, p. 8; 29 November 1941, p. 9.

35. FDR's letter of appointment quoted in *Motion Picture Herald*, 27 December 1941, p. 17. See also Garth Jowett, *Film: The Democratic Art* (New York: Little, Brown, 1976), 311. According to several sources, Roosevelt himself specified the six subject areas.

36. Koppes and Black, *Hollywood Goes to War*, 58–60; *Motion Picture Herald*, 20 June 1942, p. 9.

37. *Look* magazine, *From Movie Lot to Beachhead* (Garden City: Doubleday, 1945), 204.

38. Ibid., 205; *1946 Film Daily Year Book*, 145–46.

39. *Motion Picture Herald*, 29 July 1944, p. 9; *Motion Picture Herald*, 13 January 1945, p. 9; *Motion Picture Herald* 6, October 1945, p. 8; *1946 Film Daily Year Book*, 147–48.

40. Garth Jowett, *Film*, 357; *Motion Picture Herald*, 3 January 1942, p. 16; *1946 Film Daily Year Book*, 145.

41. Shain, *An Analysis*, 31.

42. Dorothy B. Jones, "The Hollywood War Film: 1942–1944," *Hollywood Quarterly* 1, no. 5 (October 1945): 2–3. Note that Shain's and Jones's total release

figures for the period vary somewhat, which is not surprising given inconsistencies between the official and actual release dates.

43. *Variety*, 6 January 1943, p. 58; *Variety*, 4 January 1944, p. 54.

44. Figures are taken from an accounting of Hollywood's leading all-time box-office hits organized by decade in *Variety*, 24 February 1996, pp. 168–69.

45. Shain, *An Analysis*, 61. Note that the figures from 1945 do not total 100 percent; Shain does not explain this discrepancy.

46. The first reference, according to various sources, was in a Rapf-Schary B picture, *A Yank on the Burma Road*, which was reviewed in the *New York Times* on 29 January 1942. See Richard R. Lingeman, *Don't You Know There's a War On?* (New York: Putnam's, 1970), 176; and Jeanine Basinger, *The World War II Combat Film: Anatomy of a Genre* (New York: Columbia University Press, 1986), 26, 281.

47. Edward Buscombe, ed., *The BFI Companion to the Western* (London: BFI Publishing, 1988), 243–44; Koppes and Black, *Hollywood Goes to War*, 61.

48. *Motion Picture Herald*, 19 September 1942, p. 9.

49. *Variety*, 25 November 1942, p. 7.

50. Jones, "The Hollywood War Film," 12–13.

51. Walter Wanger, "The O.W.I. and Motion Pictures," *Public Opinion Quarterly* (spring 1943): 103–4.

52. *Motion Picture Herald*, 19 September 1942, p. 9.

53. Koppes and Black, *Hollywood Goes to War*, 69.

54. Ibid., 323.

55. Report of 8 December 1941, *Casablanca* production files, Warner Bros. collection, University of Southern California. For an excellent analysis of the story and script development of the film, see chapter 9 in Rudy Behlmer, *America's Favorite Movies* (New York: Ungar, 1982), which is devoted to the film. Wallis recalls first reading the play on December 12. For Wallis's account, see his autobiography (with Charles Higham), *Starmaker* (New York: Macmillan, 1980), 83–93.

56. Dana Polan, *Power and Paranoia: History, Narrative, and the American Cinema, 1940–1950* (New York: Columbia University Press, 1986).

57. According to Hal Wallis, he came up with Bogart's closing line. See Wallis, *Starmaker*, 91.

58. *1944 Film Daily Year Book*, 105. The films were *Random Harvest, For Whom the Bell Tolls, Yankee Doodle Dandy, This Is The Army, Casablanca, The Human Comedy, Watch on the Rhine, In Which We Serve, So Proudly We Hail*, and *Stage Door Canteen*.

59. The stage show enjoyed a thirty-nine-month run from July 1942 to October 1945, generating nineteen million dollars for army-navy relief and playing to an estimated two and a half million servicepeople. *Motion Picture Herald*, 27 October 1945, p. 8.

60. Basinger, *The World War II Combat Film*, 30.

61. Ibid., 37.

62. *New York Times*, 2 September 1942, in *New York Times Film Reviews*, 3:1887; *Newsweek*, 13 August 1942, p. 260.

63. Quoted in Koppes and Black, *Hollywood Goes to War*, 248.

64. Basinger, *The World War II Combat Film*, 42.

65. Ibid., 21–22.

66. Ibid., 37–55.

67. Ibid., 37; Lewis Jacobs, "World War II and the American Film," *Cinema Journal* 7 (winter 1967–1968), 19.

68. Basinger, *The World War II Combat Film*, 62–63.

69. Koppes and Black, *Hollywood Goes to War*, 156. See also Andrea S. Walsh, *Women's Film and Female Experience, 1940–1950* (New York: Praeger, 1984), 99.

70. James Agee, review of *Sahara*, *The Nation*, 8 October 1943, in Agee, *Agee on Film*, vol. 1 (New York: Grossett and Dunlap, 1958), 53.

71. *1943 Film Daily Year Book*, 152; *1944 Film Daily Year Book*, 144. The figure for 1943 in the latter is 87.7 percent.

72. *Motion Picture Herald*, 11 September 1943, p. 8.

73. The figures on fiction and nonfiction war-film output are from Basinger, *The World War II Combat Film*, 281–83. She is among the critics and historians who treat these two forms as variations of the same narrative paradigm.

74. James Agee, "The Best of 1945," *The Nation*, 19 January 1946, in Agee, *Agee on Film*, 1:186. Note that Agee wrote for both *The Nation* and *Time* magazine during World War II.

75. James Agee, review of *The Story of G.I. Joe*, *The Nation*, 15 September 1945, in Agee, *Agee on Film*, 1:173.

76. Richard Meran Barsam, *Nonfiction Film* (New York: Dutton, 1973), 196; Agee, *Agee on Film*, 1:186.

77. Agee, *Agee on Film*, 1:174.

78. Manvell, *Films*, 190.

79. James Agee, review of *Bataan*, *The Nation*, 3 July 1943, in Agee, *Agee on Film*, 1:45.

80. See, for example, *Variety*, 8 August 1945, p. 1; *Motion Picture Herald*, 18 August 1945, p. 19; *Motion Picture Herald*, 8 September 1945, p. 18; *Variety*, 31 October 1945, p. 1; *Motion Picture Herald*, 29 December 1945, p. 9.

Lounge Time

Postwar Crises and the Chronotope of Film Noir

VIVIAN SOBCHACK

*[A] definite and absolutely concrete locality serves as the starting
point for the creative imagination. But this is not an abstract
landscape. . . . No, this is a piece of human history, historical time
condensed in space.*

M. M. Bakhtin

*"Have you ever noticed if for some reason you want to feel
completely out of step with the rest of the world, the only thing to
do is sit around a cocktail lounge in the afternoon?"*

Lizabeth Scott to Dick Powell in *Pitfall*

My aim in this essay is to locate and ground that heterogeneous and ambiguous cinematic grouping called film noir in its contemporaneous social context.[1] This may, at first, seem a redundant
project, given the extremely large body of scholarly work that has been
published on noir, nearly all of it, in one way or another, attempting to
relate the films to changes in American culture during the second World
War and its aftermath.[2] As Joan Copjec points out in the introduction
to her recent revisionist anthology, *Shades of Noir:*

Film noir criticism correlates filmic elements with historical "sources":
World War Two, an increase in crime, mounting paranoia regarding the
working woman's place in society, and so on—thinking that it has thereby
located the "generative principle" of the films. But this reference to external sources in no way resolves the question of the internal logic of the
films.[3]

I would argue, then, that my project here is less redundant than it is radical. That is, I want literally—not metaphorically or allegorically—to locate film noir in its historical and cultural context. I want to look at the films' concrete and visible premises—premises that, in existing concretely and visibly in both the films and the culture, materially ground both the internal logic of the films and the external logic of the culture and allow each to be intelligible in terms of the other.

Thus, in speaking of grounds and premises, I am speaking radically, concretely, materially of the prereflective phenomenological conditions for the intuitive reading of film noir as "about" its historical and cultural moment—a reading we've done all along and yet whose logic still eludes us. These radical grounds and material premises figured concretely before us and to which we should pay heed are the cocktail lounge, the nightclub, the bar, the hotel room, the boardinghouse, the diner, the dance hall, the roadside cafe, the bus and train station, and the wayside motel. These are the recurrent and determinate premises of film noir and they emerge from common places in wartime and postwar American culture that, transported to the screen, gain hyperbolized presence and overdetermined meaning. In sum, to locate the historical and cultural intelligibility of film noir, I want not to allegorize or resort to metaphor, but "to return to the things themselves."[4]

To begin, it seems important to rehearse a certain amount of "canonical" knowledge about both noir and its context—if only to highlight how right our intuitions feel about the relationship between the two and yet how difficult it is to explicate the grounds of this perceived connection, this phenomeno-logic.

I

Let us start with the context. It is now a commonplace to regard film noir during the peak years of its production as a pessimistic cinematic response to volatile social and economic conditions of the decade immediately following World War II. Whether considered a genre or a style, the films circumscribed as noir are seen as playing out negative dramas of postwar masculine trauma and gender anxiety brought on by wartime destabilization of the culture's domestic economy and a consequent "deregulation" of the institutionalized and patriarchally informed relationship between men and women. The social context in which noir emerged is marked as "transitional," and its overarching themes are the recovery of a lost patriarchal order and the need for the country to literally and metaphorically "settle down." The national scenario and its cast of characters are by now familiar: returning veterans trying to reinsert themselves both into the workplace and family life after a long absence; working women who had realized themselves as economically independent during the war being remanded, not always willingly, to the hearth and motherhood; official rhetoric establishing the family unit and the suburban home as the domestic matrix of democracy even as divorce rates and personal debt escalated; economic and social ambivalence about the future deepening as the home front was reconfigured from a wartime economy that promoted the social unity of production and self-sacrifice to a peacetime economy emphasizing the privatized pleasures of consumption. All of these elements were entailed in a newly-troubled domestic economy that had previously determined American domestic life by separating the public and private sectors across gender lines into the workplace and the home. Furthermore, grounding this postwar domestic melodrama were first implicit and then explicit anxieties and imperatives brought on by that novel form of international political enmity called the Cold War—an enmity that motivated the further coalescence of the military-industrial complex and gave rise, as a substitute for a phenomenological sense of personal and national security, to the paranoid structures and nationalist sensibilities of the security state.

Thus, between 1945 and 1955, the years generally (if problematically) acknowledged to bracket film noir's most significant period of production and reception, themes such as the impossible return to a highly mythologized "home front," attempts to "settle down," and the desire for "stability," "security" and "loyalty" (rather than mere loyalty oaths) resonate and mark to an extraordinary degree the lived sense of insecurity, instability, and social incoherence Americans experienced during the transitional period that began after the war and Roosevelt's death in 1945, lasted through the Truman years (1945–1952), and declined as the Eisenhower years (1952–1960) drew to a prosperous close. By Eisenhower's second term, the country had learned to love the security state and the Bomb and had, indeed, settled down—into what David Reid and Jayne L. Walker describe as "a cold torpor" that now, for some, "passes in national mythology as the United State's golden age."[5]

However, the early postwar period, identified with film noir's "classic phase," was marked not by torpor but by domestic anxiety and political purpose. Domestic anxiety was informed not only by the constantly rising prices of food, clothing, and other necessities (blamed by manufacturers on labor's successful bid for wage increases), but also by increasing rents and a nationwide housing shortage. Indeed, in 1947, President Truman publicly focused on the housing crisis as "the foremost of the many problems facing the nation."[6] As Dana Polan has noted in *Power and Paranoia: History, Narrative, and the American Cinema, 1940–1950*:

During the war 50 percent of the American population is renting and frequently doing so in habitations far below needs and expectations. There is a dramatic housing crisis (lack of available sites, the absence during most of the war of any sort of rent control) that is frequently represented in narratives of the time (*Since You Went Away* [1944], *Twin Beds* [1942], *The More the Merrier* [1943]). The housing problem continues on into the postwar period when a new suburbia will suddenly be offered as the necessary solution.[7]

The political aim of the administration in the early postwar period was to consolidate America's hold on the European and world imagination and to secure a preponderance of power, but—against the ground of domestic problems—official rhetoric did not necessarily translate into a sense of social security. As Reid and Walker point out:

Despite bravado in the Truman White House, the public mood by any measure (Gallup or even novelistic) was fearful and apprehensive: fearful of a renewed Great Depression (at least up to 1947); fearful afterwards of international communism (the Attorney General's list of "subversive organizations" was drawn up in 1947). . . . The temper of the times was jittery and skittish. Respectable opinion was pursued by a host of phantasms.[8]

It is within this context of postwar fear and present apprehension of the future that the wartime past becomes secured in national memory as itself safe and secure. Reid and Walker note how quickly the war and the home front became the objects of national nostalgia—the former "sentimentalized into 'the good war'" and the latter characterized as having achieved a "chain-mail solidarity" in the social sphere:

How swiftly forgotten were the thousands of work stoppages, including hate strikes, racial strife . . . John L. Lewis's duel with Roosevelt, the congressional attack on the New Deal, and the bitter and morose 1944 presidential election (now remembered only for FDR's "Fala" speech).

Paradoxically, it was precisely the success of "wartime nationalism" and its subsequent deflection into the . . . crusade against communism and the national security state that dissolved these memories.[9]

Thus it is that, in the decade that follows World War II and gives us the Korean War and an ongoing Cold War, both wartime and the home front together come to form a re-membered idyllic national time-space of phenomenological integrity and plenitude. A mythological construction, this chronotope (a concept developed by Soviet literary theorist Mikhail Bakhtin to which I return later) emerges in postwar culture itself and becomes the lost time and place of national purpose, cohesion, and fulfillment.[10] Indeed, the chronotope of the idyllic wartime home front stands as this country's lost object of desire until Camelot—that other mythological spatiotemporal construction about loss (though not of a past but a future)—replaces it in the national mythology after John F. Kennedy's assassination in the early 1960s.

Within the context of the postwar period's national (and personal) insecurity about the future and its longing for the purposefulness, unity, and plenitude of a mythologized national past, film noir provided— or so film historians, critics, and anecdotal experience have told us— the cinematic time-space in which contemporaneous cultural anxieties found vernacular expression. Dark in tone (if not always chiaroscuro in lighting), twisted in vision (if not always in framing), urban in sensibility (if not always in location), impotently angry and disillusioned in spirit (if not always in execution), noir circumscribed a world of existential, epistemological, and axiological uncertainty—and inscribed a cinema that film critics and scholars saw as an allegorical dramatization of the economic and social crises of a postwar period they located roughly between 1945 and 1958.

In *Film Noir: The Dark Side of the Screen*, Foster Hirsch gives us a litany of selected titles that locate us in terms of place and mood and, as he puts it, "conjure up a dark, urban world of neurotic entrapment leading to delirium": *Murder My Sweet* (1944), *Scarlet Street* (1945), *Detour* (1945), *The Woman in the Window* (1945), *The Dark Mirror* (1946), *The Dark Corner* (1946), *The Black Angel* (1946), *The Big Sleep* (1946), *Kiss of Death* (1947), *Possessed* (1947), *Ruthless* (1948), *They Live by Night* (1948), *The Naked City* (1948), *Cry of the City* (1948), *Street with No Name* (1948), *The Window* (1949), *Caught* (1949), *The Dark Past* (1949), *D.O.A.* (1950), *Panic in the Streets* (1950), *Night and the City* (1950), *Edge of Doom* (1950), *No Way Out* (1950), *The Narrow Margin* (1952), *Jeopardy* (1953), *Killer's Kiss* (1955), *The Killing* (1956).[11] In the same vein we could add *Double Indemnity* (1944), *Cornered* (1945), *Out of the Past* (1947), *Pitfall* (1948), *The Night Has a Thousand Eyes* (1948), *The Set-Up* (1949), *On Dangerous Ground* (1951), *The Big Heat* (1953), *Nightmare* (1955), *Touch of Evil* (1958) and, of course, those titles that evoke noir's femmes fatales: *Phantom Lady* (1944), *The Blue Dahlia* (1946), *Fallen Angel* (1946), *Gilda* (1946), *The Lady from Shanghai* (1948), *The File on Thelma Jordan* (1950), *Angel Face* (1952). There are, of course, many more—along with corollary discussions about the criteria for their inclusion and exclusion as noir.

Making the extremely apt point that it is "tricky" to "read *noir* . . . as a series of social notations either in sympathetic response to or in reaction against a national frame of mind . . . because it is not primarily a social form, in the way that the stories of gangsters in the thirties were," Hirsch nonetheless—like the rest of us—cannot refrain from doing so.[12] Rehearsing the national scenario during the noir years and pointing to the "disoriented," "disconnected," "amnesiac and somnambulist" veteran as the only noir character "connected directly to the period, without any symbolic exaggeration," he tells us nevertheless:

Specific social traumas and upheavals remain outside the frame. *Noir* never insisted on its "extracurricular" meanings or its social relevance. But beneath its repeated stories of double and triple crosses, its private passions erupting into heinous crimes, the sleazy, compromised morality of many of its characters, can be glimpsed the political paranoia and brutality of the period. In its pervasive aura of defeat and despair, its images of entrapment, the escalating derangement of its leading characters, *noir* registers, in a general way, the country's sour postwar mood. This darkest, most downbeat of American film genres traces a series of *metaphors* for a decade of anxiety, a contemporary apocalypse bounded on the one hand by Nazi brutality and on the other by the awful knowledge of nuclear power.[13]

2

Recent revisionist scholarship has called into question both the historical periodization of noir as well as the historical and stylistic specificity of those textual features that circumscribe the films as an object of study and, as Fred Pfeil notes, are "conceded to be . . . constitutive . . . even by critics who otherwise disagree over where it belongs and what it means."[14] In the first instance, in an extraordinary essay in the previously mentioned *Shades of Noir*, Marc Vernet persuasively "undoes" film noir as a historical and stylistic coherence and interrogates the logic that underlies its "postwar" periodization and the critical linkage of noir texts to their historical context. He notes how the various bracketings of noir are variously "stretched back a bit (to 1941 for the father, *The Maltese Falcon*, or even 1940 if *Stranger on the Third Floor* is recalled) and forward a bit (to 1958 if *Touch of Evil* is to be included)."[15] And here, in support of Vernet's critique of the historical elasticity that marks noir criticism and has interpretive consequences, we might consider that Raymond Borde and Etienne Chaumeton's seminal *Panorama du film noir américain* locates noir between 1941 and 1953, Amir Karimi's *Toward a Definition of the American Film Noir* more narrowly between 1941 and 1949, and Robert Ottoson's *A Reference Guide to the American Film Noir* most expansively between 1940 and 1958. One way around the dilemma such elasticity poses in terms of linking noir specifically to postwar culture has been to further segment it and speak of its "classic period"—most often the decade between 1945 and 1955. However, as Vernet suggests:

this way of breaking up time has no real validity whatsoever. 1945 marks the end of World War Two, which is not a cinematographic event, and 1955 marks either the appearance of the book by Borde and Chaumeton or the year that RKO studio sold its stock of films to television, events that are totally incommensurable with the historical weight of the first date.[16]

In the second instance, Vernet also challenges the specificity of those stylistic and narrative features that are critically agreed upon as constitutive of noir and catalogued by Pfeil in his contribution to Copjec's revisionist volume:

[I]conographically they stretch from the dark city streets and lurid jazzy bars to the privatized, alienated space of the car and the modern urban apartment, and down to the close-up level of the cigarette, drink, swanky dress, trenchcoat and slouch hat; stylistically, from the use of voice-over and flashback to expressionistic lighting and decentred and unstable compositions, often in deep space; narratively, they include a new emphasis on deviant psychological motivation, the deviousness and frustrating confusion of the male protagonist's project or quest, and the outright hostility, suspicion and sexual attraction between the often confused and weary male protagonist and the duplicitous, powerful femme fatale (with a good asexual wife-mother figure optionally dead or waiting in the wings); and thematically, they consist above all in the "absurd" existential choice of moral behaviour according to one's own individual ethical code, in a hopelessly dark universe in which more consensual authorities are ineffectual, irrelevant, or corrupt.[17]

Vernet calls the basic historical and generic specificity of this circumscription into question. His strategy is to track those stylistic and narrative noir elements taken as constitutive and canonical (expressionist lighting and framing supposedly derived from German cinema; convoluted emplotment, characterization, and moral universe supposedly derived from hard-boiled American detective fiction) back to silent cinema and across generic lines. Breaking down the historical coherence of style and narrative topoi, he further interrogates the logic that has linked noir's supposed textual coherence to its historical context. Though he concedes that American films made after the war are different from those made before, these differences are so broadly located that they cannot be seen as constitutive features of a generic coherence. Postwar films are marked by "a more serious tone, a shrinking of the frame, a change of style in the physical appearance of the actors and décor, and finally the weakening of censorship."[18] Thus, Vernet—who has earlier reminded us that *film noir* is a French term coined by French *cinéastes* within the historical specificity of a particular moment of French social and political relations with America and American culture—diffuses noir's always already tenuous coherence.

Indeed, his overarching argument is that "*film noir* has no clothes": invented by French critics and elaborated by American scholars, it is a "cinephilic ready-made."[19] His iconoclastic conclusion is that as "an object or corpus of films, *film noir* does not belong to the history of cinema; it belongs as a notion to the history of film criticism," and his evaluation of that criticism is harsh:

Film noir presents a fine example of cinema history and aesthetic reflection that is founded on distribution (in France at a certain point in time) and critical discourse, and not on production (in the United States during several decades), in a complete ignorance of the larger cultural context. This is not only because the history of the cinema that already exists works with very short periods . . . , but also because no one has sufficiently reflected on the ideological conditions that could have presided over the advent of a kind of fiction. The result is a sort of imaginary enclosure in which what appeared to be evident to spectators becomes a venerable concept for feminists and historians, and in which the resulting critical work ends up occulting the films themselves and their production.[20]

And yet if film noir is shown to have no clothes, its body remains—even for Vernet. There are, after all, "the films themselves"—and, even for Vernet, the perception of at least a minimally sufficient historical coalescence (if not coherence) to suggest that there is, indeed, a "there" there. Criticizing the "complacent repetition" of the inherited topoi of noir, even Vernet admits: "Doubtless there is something true there, but what that truth relates to remains a question."[21]

3
_____

What is the "there" there of film noir? And what is its "truth"—or, more precisely, the force and charge of its phenomeno-logical presence to us as meaningful and relevant to human lives lived off the screen and outside the theater? Noir's substantial "there" and its cultural truth are grounded and come together, I would argue, in its material premises. As Dean MacCannell points out, "*Film noir* established democracy's dark side, not as an articulated message but as a critically constructed *mise en scène*."[22] Thus, the phenomeno-logic of noir and its experienced truth are to be found concretely in the visible "heres" that are brought together there on the screen and "co-here" in what is perceived as a comprehensible and particular world. This coherence cannot be completely subsumed under the more overarching and therefore somewhat more abstract thematic of "the city" so significant to noir criticism. What "co-heres" are more particular places, and they exist both in the city and the small town where they concretize an existential world in which (if I may offer a serious double entendre) "there is no place like home."

Robert Siodmak's *The Killers* (1946) is exemplary in this regard. It is telling that not a single scene in the film occurs in what could be considered a normal (that is, culturally normative) domestic space. The film begins in an inhospitable small-town diner (where much of what is on the menu is unavailable). It moves to an anonymous room in a boardinghouse where the "Swede" waits to be murdered. Then, in flashbacks, its characters occupy a variety of self-similar, nearly denuded hotel rooms, cocktail lounges and cafes, and yet more hotel rooms relieved only by a pool hall, a prison cell, a hospital room, and office space. If one stretches it a bit, we do enter the empty vestibule of the Colfax mansion to watch its owner die on the stairs at the film's end. And there is a scene earlier when Reardon, the insurance investigator cum noir detective, talks to Lt. Lubinsky, a former friend of the Swede, that takes place outdoors on Lubinsky's Philadelphia apartment rooftop where, in a supposedly domestic off-hour, he is painting kitchen chairs.

In a moment so startling as to be uncanny, emerging from a space that has no place in this film, Lubinsky's wife steps out of a door holding a pitcher of lemonade that seems to have come from another dimension. Indeed, that pitcher of lemonade functions much like Barthes's photographic "punctum," compelling and disturbing us with its evocation of an idyllic time and domestic space that doesn't belong and can gain no admittance to such a world as the one in which *The Killers* takes place. The lemonade comes from a coherent space and time that must stay forever off-screen here, behind a door, always out of visibility and beyond reach of characters such as the double-crossed Swede, femme fatale Kitty Collins, and even Reardon, the insurance investigator who travels from place to place seeking answers and cannot be imagined sitting at rest on a porch somewhere else than here. Evoking the pastoral, the familial, the generational, the secure and stable world of an idyllic time-space that we will—in the historical context of noir—(re)call the "home front," that pitcher of lemonade slakes no ironic thirst for something slightly sour but rather serves an unquenchable nostalgia for the sweetness of an America forever lost from view. This is lemonade from *Mrs. Miniver* (1942), *Meet Me in St. Louis* (1944), or *Centennial Summer* (1946). Indeed, the uncanny wrongness of the offer of lemonade from another time and place in *The Killers* is matched only by the unutterably sad rightness of the fact that the beneficiary of the Swede's tiny life insurance policy is someone who turns out to be a hotel chambermaid.

In *Power and Paranoia*, Dana Polan underscores a "negative existentialism" in American films of the 1940s that is constituted, in part, as a relation to environment: "one in which environments . . . don't reflect back to a character his/her personality or values—that is, his/her freedom to shape externality according to individual desire—but, quite the contrary, rather demonstrate the radical externality and even resistance of environment to the imprinting of a self upon environment." [23] That "radical externality" and "resistance" are nowhere made so concrete and visible as in the Swede's denuded boardinghouse bedroom—the only markers of human presence are the Swede himself, awaiting his death on the bed, and Kitty Collins's silk scarf. Such radical externality and resistance can also be found in the cocktail lounges, hotel bars, diners, roadhouses, and motels that spatialize film noir—those rented rooms or tables or counter stools that resist individual particularity and are made for transients and transience, those quasi places that substitute perversely for the hospitable and felicitous places and domesticity of a "proper" home in which such necessary quotidian functions as sleeping and eating and drinking are secured and transfigured into intimate social communion.

In terms of Polan's description, it is clear that although there are occasional houses in film noir, there are hardly any homes. As he points

out, "the imperatives of war invest themselves in a particular representation of home."

At the extreme, the forties home is not simply a haven against the outside
world but a separate world of its own, a vast act of the imagination. . . .
Home becomes a self-enclosed environment . . . with its own rules, its own
language games, its own memory . . . and its own rituals. . . . Home here
works rigorously to close out the world of ambiguous interaction, of ambivalent meanings. It is the mark of a certain surety and security.[24]

Thus, in noir, homes are given to us only in glimpses—as something
lost or something fragile and threatened. (Here, 1949's *Reckless Moment*
comes to mind). Indeed, the few homes that do appear seem anachro-
nistic, evoking the retrospectively idyllic and mythic time-space of the
war years and the home front. Unlike the noir house, the rare noir home
is furnished and lit in the overstuffed and chintzy manner of *Mrs. Miniver* and *The Best Years of Our Lives* (1946). In this regard, it is telling to
remember a pre- and protonoir moment in *Since You Went Away* (1944)
in which such a wartime home visibly diminishes, its private domesticity
fragmented and depersonalized into a mere house. Claudette Colbert's
housewife not only leaves home to take a job as a welder but also breaks
up and transforms the spatial and emotional integrity of the family's
home by taking in a paying boarder. This economic purchase, disintegration, and depersonalization of the domestic space and function of
the home is heightened in wartime and postwar culture as much as it is
in the period's films, and it exists as the concrete ground for the retroactive fantasy of the home front. The housing shortage is phenomenologically informed by a sense of the larger, irrevocable loss of home that
runs throughout the war and postwar years, however different its specific material causes in each period. Thus we can understand the hysterical edge to various wartime and postwar comedies of mishap surrounding housing—the most exemplary, perhaps, *Mr. Blandings Builds
His Dream House* (1948).

Both the culture and noir's retroactive fantasy of home in this historical period constitutes, as Gaston Bachelard might put it, a "felicitous
space," a "eulogized space," a space "that may be grasped, that may be
defended against adverse forces, the space we love."[25] Evoking the poetic and felicitous image of the house (what we identify here as the
home), Bachelard phenomenologically describes a particular form of to-
pophilia. The image of the house puts us "in possession of a veritable
principle of psychological integration" and provides us a "topography

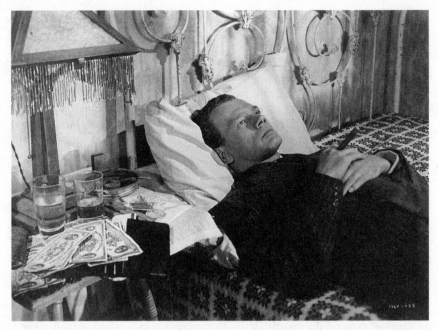

Uncle Charlie (Joseph Cotten). *Shadow of a Doubt*, Alfred Hitchcock. © Universal, 1943.

of Intimate being."[26] As he elaborates in an extraordinary passage that resonates in the context of the culture's lost home front and the absence of hospitable spaces of "intimate being" in film noir:

[T]here is a ground for taking the house as a *tool for analysis* of the human soul. With the help of this tool, can we not find within ourselves, while dreaming in our own modest homes, the consolations of the cave? Are the towers of our souls razed for all time? Are we to remain, to quote Gérard de Nerval's famous line, beings whose "towers have been destroyed"? Not only our memories, but the things we have forgotten are "housed." Our soul is an abode. And by remembering "houses" and "rooms," we learn to "abide" within ourselves. Now everything becomes clear, the house images move in both directions: they are in us as much as we are in them.[27]

In this context, wartime and postwar American culture's loss of home and the spatial and psychological integration it imaginatively and mythically provided is historically—and cinematically—poignant. Thus, as Dean MacCannell points out: "To better understand the opposition *noir*/homeless, it is necessary to sustain examination of the unusual moment in *film noir*, its glimpses into the interior of allegedly normal

Uncle Charlie (Joseph Cotten). *Shadow of a Doubt*, Alfred Hitchcock © Universal, 1943.

homes and communities."[28] In this regard, he suggests Hitchcock's *Shadow of a Doubt* (1943) as exemplary. Linked regularly by scholars to noir (however problematic such linkage is in terms of periodization, thematics, and iconography), *Shadow of a Doubt* visibly contrasts the impersonal, radical externality of Uncle Charlie's urban hotel room with the emotional intimacy of his namesake niece's small-town home and bedroom. Compared to young Charlie, Uncle Charlie's soul has no abode, is not "housed"; it lives in existential—and life-denying—negativity. Following MacCannell, we might look also to the "unusual moment" in films of the wartime and postwar period not usually linked to noir in which the loss of home and the ability to "abide" in one's soul is literalized and suddenly transforms the mise-en-scène into the concretely particular premises that ground the noir world. Here, *It's a Wonderful Life* (1946) is exemplary. In the sequence in which George Bailey, presumably ruined and contemplating suicide, is taken by his guardian angel, Clarence, to look upon a Bedford Falls from which George's existence and his existential acts have been erased, we see not only the concretization of Polan's "existential negativity," but also the literal

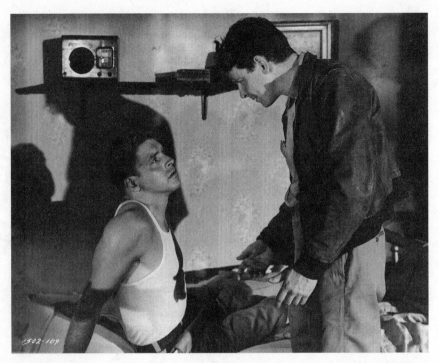

Swede (Burt Lancaster). *The Killers*, Robert Siodmak. © Universal, 1946.

transformation of Bedford Falls from the quintessential fantasy site of home and home front to a nightmarish and radically external site of domestic and social fragmentation. In the film's most "unusual" and powerful moment, Bedford Falls is grounded in the mise-en-scène of noir: there are sleazy bars, shoddy boardinghouses, cheap music, and disconnected and homeless people. For a brief but punctal moment, the "towers" of Bedford Falls' souls have been "razed for all time." *It's a Wonderful Life* is hardly a noir film in its final recuperation of home, intimacy, and abiding souls. Nonetheless, in making visible for a brief, conditional moment a world in which there is no place like home, it condenses and concretizes the impersonal and incoherent premises of noir with such unveiled hysteria that it is unsurprising (if still quite startling) that Bedford Falls and the Baileys provide the dark center for David Thomson's extraordinary noir novel, *Suspects* (described by the *Los Angeles Times* as both "a movie fan's delight" and "a mordant commentary on the loss of national innocence"[29]).

Polan's discussion of the "negative existentialism" of forties cinema

Swede (Burt Lancaster) and Kitty Collins (Ava Gardner). *The Killers*, Robert
Siodmak. © Universal, 1946.

considers the other—the less felicitous—side of Bachelard's phenomenological poetics of space. He tells us:

[I]f the *project* (to use the existentialists' term) is a narrative activity through
which human beings work to come to terms with an environment and make
it their own, forties narrative can serve as the site of a kind of reversibility of
meaning—what we might call a *symbolics* of narrative space—in which environment ceases to be a reflection or object of human projects and turns instead into a potential disruption, subversion, dispersion of projects. . . . Such
a symbolics is . . . the measure of a gap between intention and realization.[30]

Thus, the Swede's boardinghouse room with its sparse furnishings and
the myriad hotel rooms, cocktail lounges, bars, roadside diners, and
even the cold interiors of the houses of the rich and corrupt that constitute the environment of *The Killers* particularly and film noir's environment generally all refuse individual subjectivity and intimacy (as they
encourage individual isolation and secrecy). As Polan points out, this is
not an expressionist mise-en-scène:

Where a number of critics have argued the influence on forties film (and especially on *noir*) of an expressionist aesthetic, it is important to emphasize that the expressionism here is most often not the triumph of a subjectivity in which environment somehow reflects back to a character his/her own internal nature but, quite the contrary, an expressionism that demonstrates the radical externality and alterity of environment to personality.[31]

In noir, then, a house is almost never a home. Indeed, the loss of home becomes a structuring absence in film noir. It is particularly telling to think here of the ironic "domesticity" that runs through *Double Indemnity* (1944) or *Mildred Pierce* (1945)—films that are linked irrevocably to noir but pose problems to its particular urban iconography. The suburban house into which Phyllis Dietrichson invites insurance agent Walter Neff is merely a house: its furniture plain, its decorations sparse and impersonal, motel-like. It doesn't look lived in. Indeed, its interior decoration is best described in a line of dialogue offered by a character about a house in a later film noir, *The Big Heat* (1953): "Hey, I like this. Early nothing." And, even in her domestic beginnings, Mildred's home is also figured as merely a house: drab, plain, unmarked by the people who live there and supposedly constitute a family. The kitchen in which Mildred bakes her pies has none of the warmth and coziness of Norman Rockwell's kitchens and is hardly a felicitous space. And this lack of felicity is echoed in the bitterness of her voice-over narration that accompanies a flashback: "I was always in the kitchen. I felt as though I'd been born in a kitchen and lived there all my life except for the few hours it took to get married."

The irrevocable loss of the home in noir is also figured in the "radical externality" and cold glitter of the houses of the rich, where money buys interior decoration and fine art but no warmth, no nurturance. As Bachelard puts it, quoting Baudelaire, "in a palace, 'there is no place for intimacy.'"[32] Thus, there is a wonderful irony in the absolute precision of Waldo Lydecker's comment about his house to detective Mark McPherson in the protonoir *Laura* (1944): "It's lavish, but I call it home." Although we can trace the negative imagery of the empty and emotionally hollow houses of the rich and successful back to certain women's melodramas of the 1930s such as *Craig's Wife* (1936) where the wife's obsessive and hostile perfectionism constructs her husband as an unwelcome intruder in the house, the impersonal homes of the rich figure frequently in noir as signs of empty acquisition. (It is more than coincidental, then, that *Craig's Wife* is remade in 1948 as *Harriet Craig*, starring the post-*Mildred Pierce* Joan Crawford.) After her marriage to

Monte, Mildred Pierce's house is bigger and more furnished than the cold little parody of a home in which she lived her first marriage to Bert, but its size existentially echoes the hollowness of a space that is not inhabited emotionally, that is lived in display or deceit rather than in intimacy or authenticity. It is apposite that, in *The Killers*, all we see of the Colfax mansion is a huge empty vestibule marked by a cold and geometrically tiled floor. "Inhabited space transcends geometrical space," Bachelard tells us. "A house that has been experienced is not an inert box." [33] In his phenomenological topo-analysis, he concedes the house as "first and foremost a geometrical object" that, if analyzed rationally, "ought to resist metaphors that welcome the human body and the human soul." Nonetheless, he continues, "transposition to the human plane takes place immediately whenever a house is considered as space for cheer and intimacy, space that is supposed to condense and defend intimacy." [34]

Cheer and intimacy, however, are hardly the stuff of noir houses, of noir hotel and motel rooms. This is made as explicit in the dialogue as it is in the mise-en-scène. The sentiments expressed by Dana Andrews in *Fallen Angel* (1946)—"What a dump!"—echo throughout the films. *The Little Black and White Book of Film Noir* provides us the oddity (unique in American film) of a genre in which both male and female characters explicitly and regularly comment (usually with sarcasm) on the decor.

—You call this dump a hotel?
—That's what the sign says. Fresh sheets every day, they tell me.
—How often do they change the fleas?

Alan Ladd and desk clerk, The Blue Dahlia

—Well, the place looks lived in.
—Yeah, but by what?

Richard Erdman and Dick Powell, Cry Danger

—What a place. I can feel the rats in the wall.

Franchot Tone to Elisha Cook Jr., Phantom Lady

—Quite the hacienda.

John Maxwell to Van Heflin, The Prowler

—I hear you're living in the same old dump.
—*House* is what it's called.

Robert Ryan and Robert Mitchum, The Racket

—A neglected house gets an unhappy look. This one had it in spades.

William Holden, *Sunset Boulevard*

—Tell me, you think I'm going to like this rat trap we're going to?
—The Antlers? You betcha. It's a swell place. It's got a dining room, plenty of class, everything, and besides that it's the only hotel in town.

Ida Lupino and bit player, *Road House*

—But I like goldfish. I'm gonna get a couple for the room—you know, dress it up a little bit. It adds class to the joint, makes it a little homey.

Tom D'Andrea to Humphrey Bogart, *Dark Passage*[35]

In sum, the intimacy and security of home and the integrity and solidity of the home front are lost to wartime and postwar America and to those films we associate at both the core and periphery of that cinematic grouping we circumscribe as noir. Both during and after the war, the phenomenological coherence of the domestic life of family and home was shattered, dispersed, and concretely re-membered elsewhere: in hotels and boardinghouse rooms and motels, in diners, in bars, in swanky and seedy cocktail lounges and nightclubs, all places for transients, all fragmented, rented social spaces rather than coherently generated places of social communion, all substitutes for the intimate and integral domestic space of home. Polan quotes a telling line of dialogue from a non-noir, wartime film, *All Through the Night* (1942), in which a nightclub owner cynically remarks: "If my customers start thinking about home and mother, I'm a dead duck." Polan goes on to point out: "much of forties cinema stages the impossibility of . . . spiritual redemption through the forces of domesticity—through the imposition of a domestic space" that has become "unavailable in an America for whom innocence is becoming a mark of a vanished past."[36] Thus home in the postwar period exists only through reminiscence and in the nostalgic imaginary of *A Tree Grows in Brooklyn* (1945) or *I Remember Mama* (1948).

This perception of the loss of home—this new American homelessness of a kind historically different from its counterpart in the present day—does not find its expression as mere metaphor. It is not simply the hyperbolic trope of filmmakers and film critics (and, here, definitely not of French critics for whom the American notion of home is unimportant and, perhaps, unintelligible). The wartime and postwar period's myth of home and its loss are, in fact, grounded historically in the concrete social reality and material conditions that constitute a life-world. Focusing on contemporary film noir and relating its renaissance to the consequences of capitalist domestic politics during the Reagan and Bush presidencies and to a new era of American homelessness, Mac-Cannell emphasizes the disparity between the actual mise-en-scène of the contemporary urban landscape (with its gentrification, "renewals," and erasure of proletarian areas and housing for the poor) and the nostalgic (and guilt-ridden) mise-en-scène of contemporary noir films, which replicates the urban spaces of the forties (and forties' noir cinema). He tells us:

Following a logic that is something more than historical coincidence, the current Technicolor *film noir* renaissance (*Public Eye, The Two Jakes,* even *Barton Fink,* etcetera) occurs exactly as the interior space of classic (1945–55) *film noirs* is being excised from the American city. All but gone is the kind of hotel room in which Philip Marlowe once regained consciousness—the torn window shade, the single bare lightbulb hanging from a twisted wire, the iron bedstead, the water pitcher and basin used for shaving. There are no longer blocks of poor-but-respectable families living in faded tenements for the hero to wander through, looking for some undefined thing that he will recognize on first sight. There are no more characteristically appropriate offices for the hard-boiled detective; and no more by-the-week rooms for the femme fatale to rent, no questions asked.

Whilst the disappearance of the actual spaces of *film noir* has been highly consequential for those forced into homelessness, it has not presented a problem to the makers of revivalist *film noirs,* who can reconstruct virtual gritty reality in the form of film sets. Now we have a fictional recuperation of the proletarian city just as the actual proletarian space is historically lost.[37]

During the wartime and postwar forties and fifties, however, these actual spaces were not historically lost and their virtual presence on the screen did not stand in direct contradiction to the space outside the theater. These spaces were not the objects of nostalgia as were the home and the home front—nor were they merely metaphors. Rather, these were actual spaces charged with particular temporal meaning for the culture's life-world, and their representations on screen foregrounded a phenomenological expression of that life-world's insecurity and unsettledness, its transitional and hence transient status.

I should like to suggest that film noir's relation to its historical and social context can be best described not as metaphoric but as synecdochic and hyperbolic.[38] That is, actual spaces and places in American culture are not sublimated on the screen through the substitutions of metaphor (although they may lead to metaphorical thinking), but neither are they quite articulated according to the prevailing conventions of realism, exemplified by a film such as *The Best Years of Our Lives.*

Rather, noir represents concrete parts of the whole landscape of American wartime and postwar culture—but its synecdochic selectivity and partiality result in a hyperbolic textual exaggeration of aspects of that context's actual life-world. This is to argue that the baroque qualities of noir's visual style, the particularities of its narrative thematics and structure, emerge as an intensified form of selection, foregrounding, and consequent exaggeration of actual cultural spaces charged with contingent temporal experience.

Film noir's concrete spatiotemporal articulations are concretely found (if in less exaggerated form) in the extratextual life-world. Transported to the screen, attended to with an intensity that borders on hysterical fixation, they tell us not only about the limits placed on noir's narrative possibilities, but also about their significance in the cultural world from which they were selected and against which they are turned from ground to figure in a peculiar and revealing reversal. The hotel or boardinghouse room, the cocktail lounge, the nightclub, the diner or roadside cafe, the bar and roadhouse, the cheap motel—these are the recurrent and ubiquitous spaces of film noir that, unlike the mythic sites of home and home front, are actual common-places in wartime and postwar American culture. Cinematically concretized and foregrounded, they both constitute and circumscribe the temporal possibilities and life-world of the characters who are constrained by them—and they provide the grounding premises for that cinematic grouping we have come to recognize as noir.

4

At this point, as a way to comprehend how the concrete premises of noir ground its narrative possibilities, I turn to Mikhail Bakhtin's elaboration of a concept he called the *chronotope*. Simply put (by Michael Montgomery, one of very few scholars to have used the concept for film analysis), the chronotope "may be defined generally as any topological pattern in the artistic work that possesses the characteristics of a semantic field or grid."[39] At the least, chronotopes "constitute a set of template schemata that invest a causal chain with 'real' social contexts."[40] At the most, however, the chronotope—a term derived from physics—is meant to emphasize not only the absolute interdependence of time and space in the constitution of narrative and its significance but also the human "relativity" of their "ratio"—or, if you will, their historical rationality. As Bakhtin puts it, the chronotope is the "organizing center" of "fundamental narrative events," the "place where the knots of narrative are tied and untied." For him, "without qualification," to the chronotope "belongs the meaning that shapes narrative."[41]

First outlined during 1937–1938 and subsequently developed in two major essays—"Forms of Time and Chronotope in the Novel" and "The *Bildungsroman* and Its Significance in the History of Realism (Toward a Historical Typology of the Novel)"—the chronotope, as Michael Holmquist glosses it, is

literally, "time-space." A unit of analysis for studying texts according to the ratio and nature of the temporal and spatial categories represented. The distinctiveness of this concept as opposed to most other uses of time and space in literary analysis lies in the fact that neither category is privileged; they are utterly interdependent. The chronotope is an optic for reading texts as x-rays of the forces at work in the culture system from which they spring.[42]

Charged by Bakhtin with a variety of connotations and functions, the chronotope is a tool for synthetic analysis, not only for identifying and reasserting the force and information of concrete space on the temporal structure of the novel but also for comprehending historically the phenomenological relation between text and context in a way richer than that afforded by traditional generic analyses. As Montgomery notes, "One of Bakhtin's express purposes in developing the chronotope in the first place is to work past conceptions of genres he perceives as being too limiting to explore the more fundamental discursive patterns from which artistic works take their shape and which permit them to be understood and analyzed as cultural artifacts."[43] Although Bakhtin clearly distinguishes "a sharp and categorical boundary line between the actual world as a source of representation and the world represented in the work," he sees the chronotope as a spatiotemporal structure of meaning that links both worlds, and he tells us: "Out of the actual chronotopes of our world (which serve as the source of representation) emerge the reflected and created chronotopes of the world represented in the work."[44] The power of the chronotope is that it "references real-life situations with everyday associations for audiences, helping to create a sense of shared place. Through longstanding artistic usage, chronotopes also become associated with 'fixed expressions' and metaphorical patterns of thinking. . . . addressing the relationship of the represented locale to the community site." [45] Thus, the categorical boundary line between text and context is "not something absolute and impermeable." Text and context, the represented and the real world, "are indissolubly tied up with each other and find themselves in continual mutual interaction" in a continual process of "uninterrupted exchange." [46] Chronotopes serve as the spatiotemporal currency between two different orders of existence and discourse, between the historicity of the lived world and the literary world (here, the world of cinema).

In regard to the chronotope's structure and function as inherently specific and historical, it is worthwhile quoting some fairly lengthy passages from Bakhtin's *Bildungsroman* essay on Goethe:

[E]verything is intensive in Goethe's world; it contains no inanimate, immobile, petrified places, no immutable background that does not participate in action and emergence (in events), no decorations or sets. . . . [T]ime, in all its essential aspects, is localized in concrete space, imprinted on it. In Goethe's world there are no events, plots, or temporal motifs that are not related in an essential way to the particular spatial place of their occurrence, that could occur anywhere or nowhere ("eternal" plots and motifs). Everything in this world is a *time-space*, a true *chronotope*. . . .

Time and space merge here into an inseparable unity, both in the plot itself and in its individual images. In the majority of cases, a definite and absolutely concrete locality serves as the starting point for the creative imagination. But this is not an abstract landscape, imbued with mood of the contemplator—no, this is a piece of human history, historical time condensed in space. Therefore, the plot (the sum of depicted events) and the characters do not enter it from the outside, are not invented to fit the landscape, but are unfolded in it as though they were present from the very beginning. They are like those creative forces that formulated and humanized this landscape, made it a speaking vestige of the movement of history (historical time), and, to a certain degree, predetermined its subsequent course as well, or like those creative forces a given locality needs in order to organize and continue the historical processes embodied in it.

Such an approach to locality and to history, their inseparable unity and interpenetrability, became possible only because the locality ceased to be a part of abstract nature, a part of an indefinite, interrupted, and only symbolically rounded out (supplemented) world, and the event ceased to be a segment of the same indefinite time that was always equal to itself, reversible, and symbolically embodied. The locality became an irreplaceable part of the geographically and historically determined world, of *that* completely real and essentially visible world of human history, and the event became an essential and non-transferable moment in the time of this particular human history that occurred in this, and only in this, geographically determined human world. The world and history did not become poorer or smaller as a result of this process of mutual concretization and interpenetration. On the contrary, they were condensed, compacted, and filled with the creative possibilities of subsequent *real* emergence and development.

And it is this new sense of space and time that has led to an essential change in the orientation of the artistic image: that image felt an irresistible attraction to a particular place and to a particular time in this world that had become definite and real.[47]

What Bakhtin emphasizes here about the concretion of time and space in the charged chronotopicity of the artistic image resonates in relation to my earlier evocation of Bachelard's phenomenological "poetics of space." And Bakhtin's insistence that time is realized—and read—in space, that the two interpenetrate and allow for the "emergence" of meaning, recalls Erwin Panofsky's delineation of the uniqueness of cinema as its correlative and correspondent "dynamization of space" and "spatialization of time."[48] We may think, too, of Polan's discussion of narrative and the meaningful (negative) correlation of existence and environment. However, what is unique about Bakhtin's chronotopic phenomenology is—as indicated in the passage above—its structural provision of historical specificity, relativity, and dynamism. As Holmquist points out, Bakhtin "thought of himself less as a literary critic than as a 'philosophical anthropologist,' for the questions he seeks to answer . . . are less those that occupy historians of literature than questions about the nature of human consciousness under particular cultural and historical conditions."[49]

For Bakhtin, then, chronotopes are much more than topological patterns. Never merely the spatiotemporal backdrop for narrative events, they provide the literal and concrete ground from which narrative and character emerge as the temporalization of human action, significant in its diacritical marking of both cultural and narrative space. It is in this diacritical valuation of concrete space and its circumscription of temporal activity that chronotopes are not merely descriptive but rather constitutive of what we apprehend as genre. As Gary Morson and Caryl Emerson suggest: "It is as if each genre possesses a specific field that determines the parameters of events even though the field does not uniquely specify particular events."[50] Thus, certain chronotopes come to be associated with specific genres, although it is also possible for several chronotopes in complementary and contrary relation to combine in a single generic structure.

For Bakhtin, an exemplary—albeit minor—chronotope is the road, a spatiotemporal structure that has much resonance in film studies but that, like film noir, poses certain problems to the circumscriptions of traditional generic analysis. (The road picture is often—and uncomfortably—considered a subgenre of the adventure film, itself broad and ill-defined, or it is dealt with as a discrete category, discussion of which tends to elide issues of its generic status.) The chronotope of the road concretely structures and limits the nature and process of narrative events that temporally figure against the ground of its spatialization.[51] It radically inscribes time as passage and journey and thus tends to exclude (or especially privilege by virtue of their exceptionality and contrast) those temporal structures that emerge from a cultural space oppositionally articulated as self-contained and self-sustaining—like, for example, the "home." Only certain kinds of characters find their way onto the road or can be met along its way stations and resting places— and the road's particular spatialization will circumscribe temporal interactions among those characters, the nature and depth of their encounters and social relations. The road is, of course, a single and deceptively simple example of the many novelistic chronotopes Bakhtin identifies and explores. Furthermore, in part because of his extended focus on more general chronotopic structures such as folkloric time and adventure time, the chronotope of the road remains underelaborated and underhistoricized. There are consequential differences between the road of the picaresque and the road of the Winnebago, between a meandering country road and a tollroad or urban freeway. And, as Michael Montgomery asks, "What study of the 1960s road film, for instance, could afford to neglect Western landscapes, California, Zen, biker films, rock and roll tours, or psychedelic trips?"[52] Nonetheless, because it speaks to us so immediately of comprehended possibilities and limitations, of a phenomeno-logic of both personal and cinematic narrative, Bakhtin's chronotope of the road is extremely suggestive of how concrete spatiotemporal articulations generate narrative structures, figures, characters, and tropes.

Carnivals and Commonplaces, Montgomery's singularly sustained effort to relate Bakhtin's concept of the chronotope to film genre, explicates a number of Bakhtinian chronotopes and does an illuminating chronotopic analysis of a variety of films. However, Montgomery also criticizes the generality of many of Bakhtin's "master chronotopes" and suggests that any application of chronotopic analysis "must strive to give Bakhtin's chronotopes the cultural specificity they lack." In sum, "classical forms" of such chronotopes as adventure time or folkloric or idyllic time need "a great deal of fleshing out if we are to speak confidently of the semantic associations they continue to engender for audiences." [53] Furthermore, he suggests the investigation of "new chronotopes as they emerge throughout distinct periods of filmmaking to determine whether they possess their own peculiar 'narratibility.'" [54]

What, then, can be said of the select and hyperbolically articulated chronotopes of film noir and their less isolate and therefore less exaggerated sources in wartime and postwar American culture? What novel form of temporal existence do the cocktail lounge and nightclub (both tony and seedy), the anonymous hotel or motel room, or the cheap roadside cafe, spatially generate and concretize for character and culture alike in the 1940s?

If we look at films of the 1930s (whether comedies or gangster films), cocktail lounges and nightclubs and hotels are generally figured as celebrated and glamorous spaces—the places where sophisticated and affluent people display their wit, strut their stuff upon a polished dance floor that reflects the grace of Fred and Ginger, amuse themselves with all the fluff and romance of a feather boa, and gamble with money and hearts they can afford to lose. As Lewis Erenberg points out in an essay on the "legitimization of nightlife" after the repeal of Prohibition, "actual nightclubs continued to exist, and in some cases expanded during the Depression." [55] *Life Magazine* ran features on various nightclubs like the Stork Club throughout the 1930s. During the Depression,

syndicated stories, gossip columns and [motion] pictures showed couples at play in a world of ease and fun, spending money and enjoying life at a more intense level. The vision of consumption, personal freedom and fulfillment, though hedged in by many consoling messages that money was not everything, kept alive the dreams of nightclubs as the epitome of smart city living. [56]

Featured in film comedies such as *My Man Godfrey* (1936), *The Awful Truth* (1937), or *Bringing Up Baby* (1938), the "moderne" art deco nightclub exists as an idyllic capitalist chronotope. Most middle- and upper-class people don't work at night, and so labor is elided and time becomes spatialized as a place of "leisure"—dynamized, narrativized in a concrete and "clubby" space of socially lavish and lavishly social display. This chronotope is not belied by the nightclub in the gangster film but rather, focusing on the "night work" of those staging the scene, figured from its other side.

Erenberg notes that the mediated but very real legitimization of the nightclub, which started in the 1930s after Repeal, culminated during the war years: "The prosperity brought by defense spending and the rootlessness of a nation at war, made World War II the biggest era for the nightclubs." [57] Through reference to the Cocoanut Grove Fire in 1942, he also notes the expanded range of classes, professions, and ages that then constituted the nightclub clientele. He summarizes:

Clearly, by 1942, the nightclub had become part of the promise of American life. Perhaps this is what the large number of service men in attendance represented. These young men were celebrating inductions or furloughs, and they were part of a national trend during the War. Uprooted from their homes with money to spend, ordinary soldiers from around the country for the first time had the chance to patronize nightclubs. Fueled by wartime expenditures, the nightclub achieved the height of its prosperity. [58]

In some ways, the nightclubs and cocktail lounges as they are figured in various representations of the period as lavish places of social leisure, romantic encounter, and public display bear a strong resemblance to Bakhtin's "salon," a chronotope he discusses briefly as a fundamentally new time-space that finds its full significance in the novels of Stendhal and Balzac but is drawn from the real historical "parlors and salons of the Restoration and July Monarchy." [59] Pointing to the mix of social types—from politicians and businessmen to "courtesan-singers"—who mingle in the salon, Bakhtin notes that it is here that "webs of intrigue are spun, denouements occur" and "dialogues happen" that reveal the "ideas" and "passions" of the characters. [60] And he continues:

here in their full array [that is, brought together in one place at one time] are all the gradations of the new social hierarchy; and here, finally, there unfold forms that are concrete and visible, the supreme power of life's new king—money.

Most important in all this is the weaving of historical and socio-public events together with the secrets of the boudoir; the interweaving of petty, private intrigues with political and financial intrigues, the interpenetration of state with boudoir secrets, of historical sequences with the everyday and biographical sequences. Here the graphically visible markers of historical time as well as of biographical and everyday time are concentrated and condensed; at the same time they are intertwined with each other in the tightest possible fashion, fused into unitary markers of the epoch. [61]

Thus, the salon bears resemblance to the nightclub and cocktail lounge as they are figured in film genres of the 1930s and 1940s, from gangster films and comedies in the earlier decade to the darker intrigues and boudoir secrets of noir in the later. Indeed, as Montgomery notes, the "unstable blends of public and private spheres of influence" that characterize the salon also evoke the tight intertwining of "petty, private intrigues with political and financial intrigues" in Rick's Café Americain of the prewar *Casablanca* (1943) and the restaurant and cocktail lounges of the postwar *Mildred Pierce* (1946).[62] It is historically apposite that, in *This Gun for Hire* (1942), a nightclub singer (noir actress Veronica Lake) wants to settle down and get married but continues her "club spectacle in order to seduce a possible traitor and discover his secrets"[63] —or that, in *Casablanca*, the denouement of the political question concerning America's isolationism or involvement in World War II is not only tightly intertwined with a private romantic triangle, but that its temporalization is generated and resolved through the chronotope of the nightclub where the "ideas" and "passions" of the characters are revealed in the "dialogue" the salon allows. Indeed, as Erenberg points out, "That such a question could be posed in terms of a nightclub and its quixotic 'New Yorker' owner is a measure of how much a part of American culture the nightclub had become."[64]

In the salon spaces—nightclubs, cocktail lounges, and bars—of the postwar period, private, domestic intrigue and the "secrets of the boudoir" are more often intertwined with financial intrigue than with patriotism or political intrigue (except when the latter is characterized through the former in the fairly frequent person of a corrupt and greedy politician). Indeed, from the postwar period onward into the 1950s, in the salon spaces of films like *Mildred Pierce* or *Gilda* or *The Blue Dahlia* (all 1946) or *The Big Heat* (1953), the corruption of political life is not so much temporalized as is the financially based corruption of domestic life. It is pertinent here that in the non-noir *The Best Years of Our Lives* (also 1946), the one irresolvable postwar relationship in the film is that between the veteran pilot and his restless wife—figured as a nightclub singer.

Corollary to the nightclub and the cocktail lounge and their confusions of public and private spheres of influence, of business and personal intimacy, of financial and boudoir secrets, are those other re-membered places that fragment and substitute for domestic space much as Mildred's restaurant replaces her kitchen—namely: hotels, motels, and even cheaper boardinghouse rooms. Though not precisely salon space like the nightclubs and lounges and bars that share some of their qualities, in noir and in the culture of the period with its rented housing and housing shortages, the rooms of hotels and motels and boardinghouses figure as spaces of social dislocation, isolation, and existential alienation.

They also function in noir and in the culture as spaces where financial intrigue and boudoir secrets come to rest—albeit, if we think of the Swede, lying on his bed holding Kitty Collins's scarf and awaiting his murder, never in peace. Noting the character of the essentially urban space of the hotel and its extension into the countryside in the form of the motel (and, we might add, into the provincial town in the form of the boardinghouse), Polan writes:

If Gyorg Lukàcs (in the . . . preface to *History and Class Consciousness*) saw the hotel as a perfect image of an old Europe's fall into chaos and despair, the motel seems an appropriate image for a later moment where the elegant decadence of an aristocracy has given way to a mass-life run through with petty crimes, petty intrigues. The motel is the figure of furtiveness and a life dominated by the endless but transitory interaction of people all with something to hide. Significantly, the years from the thirties on witness a discourse on the motel not as adventure or romance spot, but as the place of festering, wasteland rot.[65]

(And here it is impossible not to think of the resolution of this social degradation of space and personal relations in the Bates motel in 1960's *Psycho*.)

Thus the petty crimes and the petty intrigues of the salon, where public and private business intertwine and constitute deals and dangerous liaisons as the ground of narrative action, move from city to country, from glamorous thirties' hotels and nightclubs and restaurants to "Mildred's" and then to shabbier hotels, seedy motels, and boardinghouses, to roadside diners (see *The Postman Always Rings Twice*, 1946), bars, and cafes (see *Roadhouse*, 1948). Salon space is reconstituted and fragmented in the historical period that begins during the war and lasts into the 1950s. Rather than bend out of shape the time-space of a chronotope whose own novelty is historically linked to "the Restoration and July Monarchy" and to the novels of Stendahl and Balzac to fit the cultural and imaginary spaces of America in the 1940s, a new and historically intelligible chronotope is called for.

What I suggest is a larger chronotopic structure, akin to Bakhtin's major and more general ones, that includes the privileged spaces of wartime and postwar American culture transported and hyperbolized on the screen in film noir. Specifically, I designate the life-world (both cultural and narrative) spatialized from nightclubs, cocktail lounges, bars, anonymous hotel or motel rooms, boardinghouses, cheap roadhouses, and diners as constituting the temporalization of what I call *lounge time*. The spatiotemporal structures and smaller chronotopic units (or

Frank Chambers (John Garfield) and Cora Smith (Lana Turner). *The Postman Always Rings Twice*, Tay Garnett. © MGM, 1946.

motifs) like the cocktail lounge or the hotel room that constitute lounge time emerge in their historical coherence as threats to the traditional function, continuity, contiguity, and security of domestic space and time. They substitute for and fragment into "broken" status the nurturant functions of another and more felicitous chronotope discussed earlier: the home. They transport spatially contiguous and intimate familial activity (eating, drinking, sleeping, and recreating) from private and personalized to public and anonymous domain. They substitute impersonal, incoherent, discontinuous, and rented space for personal, intelligible, unified, and generated space. They spatially rend and break up the home—and, correlatively, family contiguity and generational continuity.

Children do not normally—or normatively—find their way into these spaces. (It is telling that the psychotic babysitter in the hotel in *Don't Bother to Knock* [1952] attempts to kill her charge in order to keep a date in the hotel bar.) Women at home in these spaces are rarely mothers (although they may yearn to be like Veronica Lake's character in *This Gun for Hire*), nor are men fathers. (Only after the homicide detective sells his house and sends his daughter away after his wife has been killed by a bomb meant for him is the world of *The Big Heat* transformed to noir.) The cycles and rituals of family continuity and generation have no place, and therefore no temporal articulation, in cocktail lounges and hotel rooms.[66] No weddings, no births, no natural deaths (although plenty of unnatural ones), no familial intimacy and connection can be eventful in lounge time. Here, women have no anchor in domesticity and men no clearly defined work. Women do not make babies and bread (although, like Mildred, they may perversely create a business empire making pies), and their sexuality remains undisciplined. Men have no fertile fields to sow and reap, no occupation to sustain both family and patriarchal kingdom and mark their masculinity in signs of labor and amassed capital, no private retreat from the public sphere in which to relax and recreate and enjoy the fruits of socially sanctioned labor. The "traditional" divisions of the prewar domestic economy—re-membered and mythified as the idyllic patriarchal kingdom—are impossible in such places.

Correlative to the fragmentation of the coherence of domestic space and its temporalization in idyllic narratives, the cultural space-time isolated and intensified in the lounge time of film noir also radically transforms recreational time, making leisure more a condition to be suffered than pleasurably embraced. Indeed, leisure, as lounge time in the mise-en-scène of noir, is temporalized not as idyllic and regenerational activity (nor even the frivolous expenditure of energy figured in the nightclubs of the 1930s). Rather, it is temporalized negatively as idle restlessness, as a lack of occupation, as a disturbing, ambiguous, and public display of unemployment. Very few men (or women) can be said to labor in film noir. Most of them wait, hang on and hang around, making plans that go up in the smoke of a torch song or too many stubbed-out cigarettes. The men and women who inhabit the urban lounges, hotels, and isolated roadside cafes and diners of noir are restless, are transients. (Hence, in terms of chronotopic motifs, lounge time could well include bus and train stations and their waiting rooms.) Without real roots and occupation, they meet by chance, act impulsively, have no strong social curbs on their passions and fears. In sum, they embody and narrativize the very quality of the spaces in which they spend aimless time: they are centers for emotional activity without social commitment, are fractured by random appeals to their basic drives and desires. Both their life-world and their characters do not cohere. Indeed, like the bars, hotel rooms, and roadside cafes they frequent, they are literally and semiotically incoherent—a threat to the very language of patriarchal and capitalist culture (even as they are its perverse production). In sum, dispossessed, displaced from the culture's "traditional" signifiers of social place and function, their actions are temporalized as socially problematic, ambiguous, and dangerous (and, of course, often for those very qualities, extremely attractive).

The threat that lounge time poses to the traditional domestic economy dictates that its spatiotemporal boundaries limit and contain its "loose" women and "idle" men in what can only be described as a hermetically sealed—quarantined—social space. The dramas temporalized within it and determined by it are not allowed integration with the culture's traditional—by this time, retrospectively mythified—spaces of domesticity and labor. At most, events generated by and in lounge time briefly contaminate the spatiotemporal coherence of what is perceived to be and figured as the traditional and idyllic life-world of the (prewar) culture. Hardly seen at all, that idyllic life-world of domestic peace and harmony, of proper occupation for both sexes, is a structuring absence that contributes to the closed off yet unstable spatiotemporal nature of lounge time. That world previously described in the chronotopes of the supposedly stable prewar home and the retroactive and nostalgic postwar fantasy of the unified wartime home front are constructed on convention and its maintenance, on clearly defined and hierarchically valued sexual identities correlated with a specific division, valuation, and reward of domestic labor along gender lines, and on the contiguous relation of family and community that promises—through spatial and temporal integration—cultural regeneration and continuity.

In "Forms of Time and Chronotope in the Novel," Bakhtin devotes substantial discussion to a master chronotope that he identifies with folkloric time: the idyllic chronotope. His gloss on the positive and "special relation time has to space in the idyll" is particularly relevant both to the felicitous chronotopes of home and the wartime home front that provide the structuring absences of film noir and to the negative and infelicitous master chronotope of noir that I describe as *lounge time*. The idyllic chronotope includes a variety of pure and mixed types that focus on "love, labor, or family." No matter what the types and their variants, however, Bakhtin sees them as having "several features in common, all determined by their general relationship to the immanent unity of folkloric time" (which undoes historical time by focusing on basic life processes and temporal cycles rather than on the transience and variety of cultural forms).[67]

Idyllic chronotopes, then, are characterized by "an organic fastening-down, a grafting of life and its events to a place, to a familiar territory, . . . and one's own home." The events generated within the life-world of the idyll emerge from the secured familiarity of its spaces and the hermetic and integral wholeness of its temporality. As Bakhtin describes it:

This little spatial world is limited and sufficient unto itself, not linked in any intrinsic way with other places, with the rest of the world. But in this little spatially limited world a sequence of generations is localized that is potentially without limit. . . . [The] blurring of all the temporal boundaries made possible by a unity of place also contributes in an essential way to the creation of the cyclic rhythmicalness of time so characteristic of the idyll. (225)

Whereas the idyllic chronotope has relevance to the familiarity, stability, and rootedness of home and the familial and generational and even national solidarity of the wartime home front, the noir chronotope of lounge time evokes the life-world and space-time of a parallel, yet anti-nomic, universe. Though it constitutes a hermetic whole, its internal constituents and potential contiguities are fragmented and unfastened down. Furthermore, its spaces are visibly unfamilial, unfamiliar, and anonymous. Yet, isomorphic with the structures of the idyllic world, lounge time is also limited spatially, also self-sufficient, also sealed off from contact with the rest of the world. (Here it is worth recalling the line of dialogue from *Pitfall* [1948] used as an epigram at the beginning of this essay: "Have you ever noticed if for some reason you want to feel completely out of step with the rest of the world, the only thing to do is sit around a cocktail lounge in the afternoon?") The sequence of events as they occur and take on significance in lounge time also becomes cyclical—but instead of generating and continuing kinship relations, lounge time generates their denial and betrayal. (Here, one might remember Mildred Pierce and her treacherous daughter Veda as exemplary.) Undoing generational time in repetitive patterns in which the past and future collapse, lounge time de-generates.

In terms of narrative events and their repetitious temporal nature, Bakhtin further elaborates the idyllic chronotope as "severely limited to only a few of life's basic realities. Love, birth, death, marriage, labor, food and drink, stages of growth." And he goes on to say:

Strictly speaking, the idyll does not know the trivial details of everyday life. Anything that has the appearance of common everyday life, when compared with the central unrepeatable events of biography and history, here begins to look precisely like the most important things in life. But all these basic life-realities are present in the idyll not in their naked realistic aspect . . . but in a softened and to a certain extent sublimated form. (226)

Such a description evokes the idyllic, homey, cyclical and softened space-time of family meals and holidays and stages of growth characteristic of, for example, *Meet Me in St. Louis*. It does not evoke Phyllis Dietrichson in *Double Indemnity*, pushing a shopping cart up and down the aisles of a supermarket, wearing dark glasses and planning the murder of her husband with Walter Neff over canned goods. And yet this extraordinarily ironized scene of domesticity sits in a highly structured—if perverse—relation to the idyllic chronotope described by Bakhtin.

Lounge time creates a parallel emphasis on basic life-realities, but these are antinomous to those of the idyllic chronotope. Bakhtin identifies the love idyll and sees its richest "conjunction with the family idyll . . . and with the agricultural idyll." Here—and this is particularly poignant set against the unemployment, the lack of occupation, of so many of the characters in noir—Bakhtin notes:

The labor aspect . . . is of special importance . . . ; it is the agricultural-labor element that creates a *real* link and common bond between the phenomena of nature and the events of human life. . . . Moreover—and this is especially important—agricultural labor transforms all the events of everyday life, stripping them of that private petty character obtaining when man is nothing but consumer; what happens is that they are turned into essential life *events*. (226–27)

Hence we see the association of the idyllic with the pastoral—an association that reverberates both in the offer of lemonade in *The Killers* and in noir's primarily urban mise-en-scène. Furthermore, alienated from a connection to the kind of work that elevates the quotidian into eventfulness, figured only as petty consumer, characters in lounge time avoid labor—seeking the fast buck and easy money, talking about the deal and the plan and the big fix or score.

Bakhtin also points to the idyll's elevation of basic realities such as eating and drinking because of their connection to nature and labor and family:

Wine is likewise immersed in . . . its cultivation and production, and drinking it is inseparable from the holidays that are in turn linked to agricultural cycles. Food and drink in the idyll partake of a nature that is social or, more often, family, all *generations* and *age-groups* come together around the table. For the idyll the association of *food* and *children* is characteristic. (227)

Not only are children underage and not generally allowed in the spaces of lounge time, but the characters who sit around the tables in night-clubs, cocktail lounges, and roadside cafes hardly know each other. And although the spaces of lounge time are spaces in which food and drink are foregrounded, hardly anyone actually eats (although almost everyone drinks), no one is nourished, no "natural" thirst is slaked. Indeed, in *Clash by Night* (1952), one character ironically asks another: "Do you think beer has food value, Miss Doyle?"

Furthermore, "in the idyll, children often function as a sublimation of the sexual act and of conception; they frequently figure in connection with growth, the renewal of life, death" (227). Focus in lounge time and noir is on passion, libido, hate, vengeance, and boredom rather than on love and the sublimation of sexuality in family. Childlessness, whether from selfish choice, barrenness or sterility, abortion, or a child's death, reverses the idyll's happy concern with birth and regeneration. In *Mildred Pierce*, one of Mildred's two children dies from illness, and she is despised and betrayed by the other. Her best (and unmarried) friend tells her: "Personally, I'm convinced that alligators have the right idea. They eat their young." Death, of course, is never natural in lounge time, but murder is. Hence, we have noir's ironic emphasis on life "insurance." Marriages are institutions not to be nurtured and revered, but to be gotten out of—through infidelity, separation, divorce, or murder. There are also no stages of growth in lounge time—not only because there are no children in its spaces, but also because behavior is compulsive and repetitive and thus becomes cyclical even as it seems initiated by chance and in impulse.

Bakhtin notes that in the idyll all these basic life-realities are "softened," take a certain "sublimated form," and are represented in "non-literal" fashion. Like their appealing counterparts in the idyll, the perverse basic life-realities that provide the focal events of lounge time and noir are also represented in nonliteral fashion. However, rather than being "softened" and "sublimated," they are intensified and hyperbolized through baroque visual style and convoluted narrative structure. Thus, a certain mode of hysteria and overwroughtness becomes the norm of lounge time and noir's everyday life.

Though all these elements of lounge time seem structured in direct opposition to the pastoral idyllic chronotope, there are ways in which lounge time parallels the idyll. Given our particular interest here in the historical relation of lounge time and noir to its specific context in wartime and postwar America, most significant, perhaps, is the idyll's relation to history. Bakhtin describes the idyll as structured in folkloric time. That is, the specificity of history is subordinated to and disavowed by regeneration and repetition, cyclical activity. Lounge time also focuses on repetition (however obsessive or compulsive), on cyclical activity (however unagricultural) like sitting around hotel rooms planning heists or in cocktail lounges listening to torch songs. And one of the primary narrative enterprises of noir is to subordinate and disavow the "central, unrepeatable events of biography and history" that rarely find their articulation or make their mark in the anonymity of a hotel room or a nightclub or a diner. However, unlike in the idyll, the hermetic spaces and cyclical temporality of lounge time and noir are threatened by a return of the repressed that—because of the hermetic spaces and repetitive temporality—has no other place to go. Characters keep attempting to escape their specific biography or the particulars of history, and they live in fear of the revelation of shady individual pasts to those in their amorphous present. Earlier crimes, betrayals, failures, and infidelities are desperately hidden and generate new crimes, betrayals, failures, and infidelities, but return nonetheless from *Out of the Past*. Indeed, the space-time configuration of lounge time generates the flashbacks characteristic of noir as a perverse formal manifestation of the repetition and cyclicity of a folkloric time that ultimately overcomes and undoes history—and the possibility of change. Thus, its characters are forever fixed, paradoxically, in a transitional moment. If lounge time and noir undo historical time, they are, nevertheless, informed by it, and it is most particular.

Bakhtin tells us that the idyll "assumed great significance in the eighteenth century when the problem of time in literature was posed with particular intensity, a period when precisely a new feeling for time was beginning to awake." He points to the development of special forms of the idyll in which the "real organic time of idyllic life is opposed to the frivolous, fragmented time of city life or even to historical time." And he mentions the appearance of the idyllic "elegy." For Bakhtin, the significance of the idyll to the development of the novel is enormous, and he decries the fact that "its importance as an underlying image has not been understood and appreciated . . . , and in consequence all perspectives on the history of the novel have been distorted" (228). Its influences can be seen across a range of novelistic types from the provincial novel to the idyll-destroying *Bildungsroman*, from the sentimental novel to the family novel and the novel of generations. In the latter, he notes, the "idyllic element undergoes a radical reworking":

Of folkloric time and the ancient matrices only those elements remain that can be reinterpreted and survive on the soil of the bourgeois family and family-as-genealogy. Nevertheless the connection between the family novel and the idyll is manifested in a whole series of significant aspects, and that connection is precisely what determines the basic—family—nucleus of this type of novel. (231)

Bakhtin goes on to discuss the "destruction of the idyll," which "becomes one of the fundamental themes of literature toward the end of the eighteenth century and in the first half of the nineteenth" (233). The hermetic nature and organicity of the idyllic world is still valued, but its "narrowness" and "isolation" are emphasized:

Opposed to this little world, a world fated to perish, there is a great but abstract world, where people are out of contact with each other, egoistically sealed-off from each other, greedily practical, where labor is differentiated and mechanized, where objects are alienated from the labor that produced them. It is necessary to constitute this great world on a new basis, to render it familiar, to humanize it. (234)

Furthermore, the *Bildungsroman* shows up the idyllic world and its psychology as "inadequate to the new capitalist world." In this new novelistic form, we see:

the disintegration of all previous human relationships (under the influence of money), love, the family, friendship, the deforming of the scholar's and the artist's creative work and so forth—all of these are emphasized. The positive hero of the idyllic world becomes ridiculous, pitiful and unnecessary; he either perishes or is re-educated and becomes an egoistic predator. (234–35)

If different in its phenomenological inflection and, thus, its inscription, time was also felt in some new way and represented with great intensity in the 1940s as the United States first debated its entry into the

war and then went off to fight the good fight and to come home after it
to a troubled capitalist domestic economy. It is during this period that
the idyllic chronotopes of home and the wartime home front take on
particular significance, that special forms of the idyll emerge in which
the "real organic time of idyllic life is opposed to the frivolous, fragmented time of city life or even to historical time." As Montgomery
points out, "In the two years following the War, as Americans readjusted
to peace, they reverted to the small town ideal. In mainstream Hollywood, a similar reactionary movement took place, with war themes suddenly out and several new film versions of 'timeless' literary classics in
the works." [68] There also appears during this period specific forms of the
idyllic "elegy"—here, again, we can look to the likes of *Centennial
Summer* or *Meet Me in St. Louis* or *I Remember Mama*.

As Dana Polan suggests, "the imperatives of war invest themselves in
a particular representation of home." This investment is in the chronotopic structure that informs the idyll, in precisely the ahistorical quality
of folkloric time. Using as example *The Big Clock* (1948), a film whose
very title represents an intensified awareness of time, he discusses home
as "a self-enclosed environment . . . with its own rules, its own language
games, its own memory . . . and its own rituals." It closes out ambiguity and ambivalence and closes in security. Polan goes on, however, to
expand this notion of home as an existential phenomenon: "as a sign,
'home' is something not necessarily limited to a specific locale, a specific building. It is an attitude—a way of perceiving environment. . . .
Home's values can extend outward—through the stability of a job,
the camraderie of friends, through places invested with the succoring
warmth of the home." [69]

Given the labor disputes, given the economic instability experienced
both in terms of the basic life-realities like food, clothing, and housing
and the destabilization of the gender lines that had staked out the domestic economy in its proper place, given actual unemployment and the
fragmentation of families and the dispersal of friends, if home was as
much a way of "perceiving the environment" as it was a concrete place,
then—in the world of the 1940s both during the war and after—many
Americans were homeless.

And yet they couldn't move on. Where, in the Cold War and paranoid
security-state culture, could they go? What were the motivations that
spoke to the temporalizing of a concrete future and its anticipation?
Like the characters of noir, much of America was fixed, paradoxically, in
a transitional moment—looking back toward a retrospectively idyllic
world that could not be historically recuperated (even if it could be rep-

resented), looking forward, like the Swede, with a certain inertial apprehension of a probable dead end. Indeed, as Bakhtin describes the economic and existential question posed by a capitalist economy to the "positive hero of the idyllic world," the Swede stands as the putative hero of a *Bildungsroman* frustrated—he must exist as "ridiculous, pitiful and unnecessary" or he "either perishes or is re-educated and becomes an egoistic predator." The Swede is indeed reeducated both by Kitty and by Colfax, but his new knowledge—capitalist to the core and all about love for money—is unbearable. He finally opts for death.

The boundaries of lounge time stand, then, as more than the four walls of the Swede's hotel room—or of the nightclubs and cocktail lounges and bars that he and Kitty and Colfax and all the characters of film noir so often frequent. They are the concretion of a historical, existential situation. As Montgomery points out: "The chronotopic analysis of film locales may illustrate the 'boundaries' of an audience's world as they were perceived to exist, the society's attitudes toward 'change,' or the exclusionary practices that denied certain members full participation in their community's plans for the future."[70] Thus, although its motifs can be traced backward into the 1930s and forward to the present renaissance and radical reworking of noir, lounge time is one of the dominant—or master—chronotopes of the historical period that begins in the early 1940s with the rumblings of war and declines in the 1950s as the "security state" becomes a generally accepted way of life. As such, it provides us the concrete ground, the premises, that frame and create a "global viewpoint" from which the period's films may be "judged" and "set against the world outside the text."[71]

Emerging out of actually lived cultural spaces, the represented space of lounge time is a perverse and dark response, on the one hand, to the loss of home and a felicitous, carefree, ahistoricity and, on the other, to an inability to imagine being at home in history, in capitalist democracy, *at this time.* It is no wonder that in noir so many people need a drink or try to get lost in a bottle. A master chronotope that grounds both the period's texts and contexts and makes them intelligible each to the other, lounge time represents the nether side of Bakhtin's idyll. It represents both the historical necessity and the historical failure to constitute the "world on a new basis, to render it familiar, to humanize it." Thus, noir's characters are forever fixed in a transitional moment—stabilized negatively in space and time, double-crossed by history.

The noir world of bars, diners, and seedy hotels, of clandestine yet public meetings in which domesticity and kinship relations are subverted, denied, and undone, a world of little labor and less love, of threatened men and sexually and economically predatory women—this world (concretely part of wartime and postwar American culture) realizes a frightening reversal and perversion of home and the coherent, stable, idealized, and idyllic past of prewar American patriarchy and patriotism. In short, lounge time is the perverse "idyll of the idle"—the spatial and temporal phenomeno-logic that, in the 1940s, grounds the meaning of the world for the uprooted, the unemployed, the loose, the existentially paralyzed. Lounge time concretely spatializes and temporalizes into narrative an idle moment in our cultural history—a moment that is not working but, precisely because of this fact, is highly charged. Evoking George Bailey at the moment he looks not only at the conditional loss of all the safety and security that was Bedford Falls but also at the loss of his own identity, noir historicizes in the most concrete manner the moment when the idyllic and "timeless" identity and security of the patriarchal American "home" was held hostage to a domestic future beyond its imagination.

Notes

1. For the source notes citations, see M. M. Bakhtin, "The *Bildungsroman* and Its Significance in the History of Realism (Toward a Historical Typology of the Novel)," in *Speech Genres and Other Late Essays*, trans. Vern W. McGee (Austin: University of Texas Press, 1986), 49; and *Pitfall*, dir. André de Toth, screenplay Karl Kamb (United Artists, 1948).

This essay is a major revision and elaboration of a much shorter essay delivered at the annual meeting of the Society for Cinema Studies in 1984 and circulated among colleagues in the following years. Portions of it have been cited prior to publication in Robert Stam, *Subversive Pleasures: Bakhtin, Cultural Criticism, and Film* (Baltimore: Johns Hopkins University Press, 1989), 12; Robert Stam, Robert Burgoyne and Sandy Flitterman-Lewis, *New Vocabularies in Film Semiotics: Structuralism, Post-Structuralism, and Beyond* (London: Routledge, 1992), 217–18; and Fred Pfeil, "Home Fires Burning: Family Noir in *Blue Velvet* and *Terminator 2*," in *Shades of Noir: A Reader*, ed. Joan Copjec (London: Verso, 1994), 229–31.

2. By now, not only is the literature on noir too extensive to be exhaustively listed here, but it also overlaps with a good deal of writing on the crime and detective film as well as with feminist work on melodrama. The seminal French texts that elaborated noir after the term was first coined by Nino Frank in *Ecran français* 61 (28 August 1946) are Jean-Pierre Chartier, "Les Américains aussi font des films noirs," *La Revue de cinéma* 2 (November 1946): 66–70, and Raymond Borde and Etienne Chaumeton, *Panorama du film noir américain (1941–1953)* (Paris: Editions de Minuit, 1955). Key early works in English on noir published in the 1970s include Colin McArthur, *Underworld U.S.A.* (New York: Viking

Press, 1972); Paul Schrader, "Notes on *Film Noir*," *Film Comment* 8, no. 1 (spring 1972): 8–13; Raymond Durgnat, "The Family Tree of Film Noir," *Film Comment* 10, no. 6 (1974): 6–7—as well as several other pieces in that issue; J. A. Place and L. S. Peterson, "Some Visual Motifs of Film Noir," *Film Comment* 10, no. 1 (January-February 1974): 30–35; Robert Porfirio, "No Way Out: Existential Motifs in the Film Noir," *Sight and Sound* 45, no. 4 (1976): 212–17; J. S. Whitney, "A Filmography of *Film Noir*," *Journal of Popular Film* 5, no. 3–4 (1976): 321–71; Amir M. Karimi, *Toward a Definition of the American Film Noir, 1941–1949* (New York: Arno Press, 1976); James Damico, "Film Noir: A Modest Proposal," *Film Reader* 3 (February 1978): 48–57; E. Ann Kaplan, ed., *Women in Film Noir* (London: BFI, 1978); Alain Silver and Elizabeth Ward, *Film Noir, An Encyclopedic Reference to the American Style* (Woodstock: Overlook Press, 1979); Jack Shadoian, *Dreams and Dead-Ends: The American Gangster/Crime Film* (Cambridge: MIT Press, 1979); and Paul Kerr, "Out of What Past? Notes on the B Film Noir," *Screen Education* 32–33 (1979/80): 45–65. These have been followed by several book-length works: Foster Hirsch, *The Dark Side of the Screen: Film Noir* (San Diego: A. S. Barnes, 1981); Robert Ottoson, *A Reference Guide to the American Film Noir* (Metuchen: Scarecrow Press, 1981); Jon Tuska, *Dark Cinema: American Film Noir in Cultural Perspective* (Westport: Greenwood Press, 1984); Dana Polan, *Power and Paranoia: History, Narrative, and the American Cinema, 1940–1950* (New York: Columbia University Press, 1986); J. P. Telotte, *Voices in the Dark: The Narrative Patterns of Film Noir* (Chicago: University of Illinois Press, 1989); Frank Krutnik, *In a Lonely Street: Film Noir, Genre, Masculinity* (London: Routledge, 1991); and most recently Ian Cameron, *The Book of Film Noir* (New York: Continuum, 1993), and Copjec, *Shades of Noir*.

3. Copjec, introduction to *Shades of Noir*, xi–xii.

4. Edmund Husserl, *Cartesian Meditations*, trans. Dorion Cairns (The Hague: Martinus Nijhoff, 1960), 12–13. (The phrase in German is *zu den Sachen selbst*.)

5. David Reid and Jayne L. Walker, "Strange Pursuit: Cornell Woolrich and the Abandoned City of the Forties," in Copjec, *Shades of Noir*, 88.

6. Truman quoted in Gorton Carruth, *The Encyclopedia of American Facts and Data*, 8th ed. (New York: Harper and Row, 1987), 550. For more on housing in the period covered in this essay, the reader is directed to *Call It Home: The House That Private Enterprise Built* (New York: Voyager, 1992); this videodisc covers the history of privately built housing in America from the 1920s to the 1960s through archival materials that address both real and imaginary relations to house and home.

7. Polan, *Power and Paranoia*, 254.

8. Reid and Walker, "Strange Pursuit," 88, 90.

9. Ibid., 60.

10. M. M. Bakhtin, "Forms of Time and Chronotope in the Novel: Notes toward a Historical Poetics," in *The Dialogic Imagination: Four Essays by M. M. Bakhtin*, ed. Michael Holquist, trans. Caryl Emerson and Michael Holquist (Austin: University of Texas Press, 1981), 84–258.

11. Hirsch, *Film Noir*, 10.

12. Ibid., 17.

13. Ibid., 21. (Emphasis mine.)

14. Pfeil, "Home Fires Burning," 229.

15. Vernet, "*Film Noir* on the Edge of Doom," in Copjec, *Shades of Noir*, 4.

16. Ibid., 4.

17. Pfeil, "Home Fires Burning," 229.

18. Vernet, "*Film Noir* on the Edge of Doom," 20.

19. Ibid., 2.

20. Ibid., 25–26.

21. Ibid., 2.

22. Dean MacCannell, "Democracy's Turn: On Homeless *Noir*," in Copjec, *Shades of Noir*, 288.

23. Polan, *Power and Paranoia*, 208.

24. Ibid., 253.

25. Gaston Bachelard, *The Poetics of Space*, trans. Maria Jolas (Boston: Beacon Press, 1964), xxxi. In regard to the "eulogized space" of the home in this period, see also Stephanie Coontz, *The Way We Never Were: The American Family and the Nostalgia Trap* (New York: Basic Books, 1992).

26. Ibid., xxxii.

27. Ibid., xxxiii.

28. MacCannell, "Democracy's Turn," 297 n. 12.

29. David Thomson, *Suspects* (New York: Vintage Books, 1985). *Los Angeles Times* commentary is taken from the back cover of the first Vintage Books Edition, 1986. (It is also worth noting in the context of the present discussion that the novel has a sole illustration used as a frontispiece: a photograph by Wright Morris titled "Reflection in Oval Mirror, Home Place, Nebraska, 1947." In the mirror we see the interior of a room, a closed door, and a small table covered with photographs; given its presentation, the space of the intimate is transformed by the photographer into "radical exteriority.")

30. Polan, *Power and Paranoia*, 209.

31. Ibid., 210.

32. Bachelard, *The Poetics of Space*, 29.

33. Ibid., 47.

34. Ibid., 48.

35. Peg Thompson and Saeko Usukawa, ed., *The Little Black and White Book of Film Noir: Quotations from Films of the 40s & 50s* (Vancouver, BC: Arsenal Pulp Press, 1992), 10–12, 35.

36. Polan, *Power and Paranoia*, 249. On this topic, see also Elaine Tyler May, *Homeward Bound: American Families in the Cold War Era* (New York: Basic Books, 1988).

37. MacCannell, "Democracy's Turn," 281–82.

38. Here, I would direct the reader to Harold Bloom, *A Map of Misreading* (New York: Oxford University Press, 1975), 83–105, in which the author links various figural devices such as synecdoche and metaphor to specific psychic structures.

39. Michael V. Montgomery, *Carnivals and Commonplaces: Bakhtin's Chronotope, Cultural Studies, and Film* (New York: Peter Lang, 1993), 5–6.

40. Ibid., 84.

41. Bakhtin, *The Dialogic Imagination*, 250.

42. Michael Holmquist, glossary to Bakhtin, *The Dialogic Imagination*, 425–26.

43. Montgomery, *Carnivals and Commonplaces*, 125 n.2.

44. Bakhtin, *The Dialogic Imagination*, 253.

45. Montgomery, *Carnivals and Commonplaces*, 6.

46. Bakhtin, *The Dialogic Imagination*, 254.

47. Bakhtin, "The *Bildungsroman*," 42, 49–50.

48. Erwin Panofsky, "Style and Medium in the Motion Pictures," in *Film Theory and Criticism: Introductory Readings, Second Edition*, ed. Gerald Mast and Marshall Cohen (New York: Oxford University Press, 1979), 246.

49. Michael Holmquist, introduction to Bakhtin, *Speech Genres and Other Late Essays*, xiv.

50. Gary Saul Morson and Caryl Emerson, *Mikhail Bakhtin: Creation of a Prosaics* (Stanford: Stanford University Press, 1990), 370.

51. Bakhtin, *The Dialogic Imagination*, 243–45.

52. Montgomery, *Carnivals and Commonplaces*, 84.

53. Ibid.

54. Ibid., 85. (Here it should be mentioned that Montgomery's last chapter is in response to this issue of "new" chronotopes; it focuses on the chronotope of the shopping mall in films of the 1980s.)

55. Lewis A. Erenberg, "From New York to Middletown: Repeal and the Legitimization of Nightlife in the Great Depression," *American Quarterly* 38, no. 5 (winter 1986): 761.

56. Ibid., 773.

57. Ibid., 774.

58. Ibid., 774.

59. Bakhtin, *The Dialogic Imagination*, 246–47.

60. Ibid., 246.

61. Ibid., 247.

62. Montgomery, *Carnivals and Commonplaces*, 20. (Montgomery discusses the nightclub, bar, and hotel as salon space in relation to *Written on the Wind* [1956]. See pp. 67–72.)

63. Polan, *Power and Paranoia*, 80.

64. Erenberg, "From New York to Middletown," 775.

65. Polan, *Power and Paranoia*, 232–33. For historical discussion of the extension of the hotel—via the motel—into nonurban America, see also John A. Jable, "Motels by the Roadside: America's Room for the Night," *Journal of Cultural Geography* 1, no. 1 (fall-winter 1980): 34–49.

66. For a discussion of the "structuring absence" of the family in film noir, see Sylvia Harvey, "Woman's Place: The Absent Family of Film Noir," in Kaplan, *Women in Film Noir*, 22–34. In relation to more contemporary articulations of the family and its relation to noir, see also Pfeil, "Home Fires Burning," an essay that draws upon an earlier version of this present one.

67. Bakhtin, *The Dialogic Imagination*, 224–25; page numbers hereafter cited parenthetically.

68. Montgomery, *Carnivals and Commonplaces*, 23.

69. Polan, *Power and Paranoia*, 253.

70. Montgomery, *Carnivals and Commonplaces*, 121–22.

71. Ibid., 81.

"Democracy and Burnt Cork"

The End of Blackface, the Beginning of Civil Rights

MICHAEL ROGIN

The New Deal, what historian would disagree, brought the immigrant to the center of American politics; shifting the orientation of the majority party from the hinterland to the metropolis, Roosevelt's victories were foreshadowed by the Catholic Al Smith's 1928 run for the presidency. With the coming of talking pictures, the 1930s and 1940s were also the golden age of the Hollywood studio system. In the standard film history accounts, urban, Americanizing immigrants watched mass-produced, studio, genre films purveying the quintessential national narratives—gangster pictures, musicals, screwball comedies, domestic melodramas, and westerns. The 1930s left its mark on the genre mix, from this point of view, in the urban milieu of gangster films, the class reconciliation of screwball comedy, the populist politics of Frank Capra's movies, and the depression-fleeing escapism of cinema entertainment.

Some of the most important and popular films of the period are missing from this picture, films grounded on race. As the jazz age came to an end, Al Jolson's blackface *The Jazz Singer* (1927) and *The Singing Fool* (1928) broke all existing box-office records. At the same time that Jolson was the top Hollywood box-office star, *Amos 'n' Andy* was the most popular radio show. The Motion Picture Exhibitors' coveted top-ten list of stars was headed in 1934 by Will Rogers, who put on Stepin Fetchit's blackvoice in the southern *Judge Priest* (1934); from 1935 through 1938 by Shirley Temple, who starred in a series of Civil War southerns with Bojangles Robinson (and put on blackface in one of them); and in 1939 by Mickey Rooney, who led a blackface minstrel show that year in *Babes in Arms.* Far from being a blockbuster exception to New Deal cinema, David O. Selznick's *Gone with the Wind* (1939), the most popular film in Hollywood's history, proves the rule.[1]

Far from excluding ethnicity in its concern with race, New Deal cinema makes visible the relationship between the two. The New Deal coalition, an alliance of northern ethnics and southern whites, appears on screen with the former Jakie Rabinowitz singing "My Mammy" in blackface in New York and the Irish O'Haras making, losing, and struggling to revive a southern plantation. Race also Americanizes white immigrants in both films. African Americans ground the O'Haras in the great American historical epic of slavery, Civil War, and Reconstruction. Blackface moved Jakie Rabinowitz in *The Jazz Singer* and Jolson in life from immigrant Jew to American, as it had earlier functioned for Irish immigrants on the cultural border between black and white. Their status as migrants from the countryside (South) to the city (North) also provided a point of identification for immigrant fans of *Amos 'n' Andy*.[2]

Al Jolson, the most popular entertainer of the first half of the twentieth century, was the first Jew to become an American mass idol. He belonged to the white immigrant group that, in the first half of the twentieth century, was most involved both in the struggle for civil rights and in the dominant American mass-entertainment forms, blackface and motion pictures. American politics was organized around antiblack racism rather than anti-Semitism. That was hardly without consequence, however, either for European immigrants in general facing nativist pressure as they made themselves into white Americans, or for Jewish moguls, blackface entertainers, and songwriters, in particular, putting their American dream on the screen during Hollywood's golden age. Jewish Americans neither invented blackface nor, anti-Semitic fantasies notwithstanding, made the motion picture industry into a tool of Jewish power. On the contrary, Jewish immigrants inherited and often struggled against the racial representations that signified American belonging. But they also made those representations their own. Jews were the most black-identified immigrant group, and one form of that identification, blackface, defamiliarizes the other—the Jewish-black civil rights alliance—as it is made visible on the Hollywood screen. The shared and divergent situation of immigrant Jews and native African Americans brings together the two New Deal genres that are the subject of this essay, the blackface musical and the racial social problem, or civil rights, film.[3]

Gone with the Wind and *The Jazz Singer* synthesize genres that separate before and after them. Moving back and forth between silence and sound, blackface and whiteface, Jew and gentile, street and stage, *The Jazz Singer*'s genre liminality is part of its generic liminality. The first talking picture unites the subgenre of the social problem film that it climaxed, the generational conflict-intermarriage-passing motion picture, with the genre it originated, the musical, more particularly, the self-reflexive movie musical about making musicals or making music, which encompasses at its foundation the blackface musical.[4]

As Jim Kitses insists about the western, even within established genres, with their own formal rules, building blocks, and symbolic structures, film presents itself as history.[5] The social problem and musical genres may seem to offer opposed historical visions, as tragedy and comedy, realism and escape, narrative and spectacle, or heavy and light. But where escapist entertainment puts on the mask of the oppressed, it exposes, in itself, the social problem. Moreover, the mixture of the two genres in the first talking picture—the use of musical blackface to encapsulate and solve the social, generational problem by Americanizing the immigrant son—supports the suggestions by Robin Wood and Vivian Sobchack that placing apparently opposed genres together illuminates ideological work hidden by exclusive attention to a single genre.[6] From one perspective the racially inflected social problem film supplies the reality escaped from in blackface musical utopia. However, not only do blackface stereotypes carry over into race relations movies, but the blackface celebration of performance infects the social problem film as well, since role-playing and identity transformation organize both genres. Both offer the Hollywood method to cross the racial-ethnic divide.

The two genres separated again after *The Jazz Singer*, as the generational-conflict social problem film went into decline and was supplanted by the blackface musical. The Jewish novelist and screenwriter Fanny Hurst supplied the major examples of the generational conflict film, *The Younger Generation* (1928) and *Symphony of Six Million* (1932) on the Jewish side, and *Imitation of Life* (1934) for black passing. Blackface, keeping black actors off the screen, had done duty in social problem silent films and other genres of narrative cinema. Talking pictures, a large step toward narrative realism, ended the practice of whites playing black in dramatic roles, but sound's ability to capture the singing voice revived blackface minstrelsy. Serving music in the Vitaphone shorts and *The Jazz Singer*, synchronized sound originally called attention to performance rather than supporting illusionistic cinema. Musicals continued the spectacle side of sound. If *The Jazz Singer* ended the use of black-face as unself-conscious method of impersonating African Americans (as in *Birth of a Nation*), it introduced to feature films blackface as conscious film subject. White performers put on burnt cork in self-reflexive celebrations of American entertainment itself. Beginning with *The Jazz Singer*, blackface musicals established Hollywood's roots in the first and most popular (before Hollywood) American mass-entertainment form, blackface minstrelsy.[7]

Although there were some roles for black people as entertainers in the 1930s (usually combined with the narrativized minstrel roles of mammy, tom, and coon, particularly in the genre that *Gone with the Wind* climaxes, the southern, for example in the Shirley Temple and Bojangles Robinson series, John Ford's *Judge Priest*, and *Jezebel* [1938]), blackface musicals sustained the tradition of whites playing blacks as spectacle. In the classic period of Hollywood narrative realism, with its claims to verisimilitude and focus on individual, interiorized character development, the musical in general and the blackface musical in particular retained the gestural, playing-to-audience, theatrical, self-reflexive, nonrealistic, utopian side of silent film.[8]

A family melodrama, *The Jazz Singer* used music to evoke conflict and loss, and in the first years of talking pictures other musicals followed its example. By the mid-1930s the genre had transformed itself, according to Rick Altman, associating music with pleasure rather than pain; the blackface musical is an instance.[9] Most musicals using blackface in the 1930s and 1940s fall into two subcategories, both derived from *The Jazz Singer:* either backstage musicals about putting on a show, or biographies of the central figures in the history of American popular music. The first group includes such unsuccessful Jolson vehicles as *Mammy* (1930) and *The Singing Kid* (1936), Fred Astaire's *Swing Time* (1936), Mickey Rooney and Judy Garland's *Babes in Arms* (1939) and *Babes on Broadway* (1942), Fred Astaire's and Bing Crosby's *Holiday Inn* (1942)—the film that introduced what was for half a century the best-selling song in history, Irving Berlin's "White Christmas"[10]—and Ronald Reagan's *This is the Army* (1943). The second group, the retrospective, nostalgic films that, from 1939 to 1949, took blackface from its antebellum origins to post–World War II America, recounted the lives of Stephen Foster (*Swanee River*, 1939; the movie also features the blackface minstrel E. P. Christy, played by Jolson); Dan Emmett, who along with Christy was the most popular minstrel in the early years of the form (*Dixie*, 1943); George Gershwin (*Rhapsody in Blue*, 1945; Jolson, whose blackface rendition of "Swanee" made Gershwin famous and helped launch the jazz age, repeats that performance); and Jolson (*The Jolson Story*, 1946, and *Jolson Sings Again*, 1949). *The Eddie Cantor Story* and the Danny Thomas *Jazz Singer* remake (both 1953), critical and box-office failures, bring the subgenre to an end, though it came back from the dead in Neil Diamond's *Jazz Singer* (1981).[11]

As framed by *The Jazz Singer* and *Gone with the Wind*, and culminating in the immense postwar popularity of *The Jolson Story* and *Jolson Sings Again*, the blackface musical was among the most important genres of New Deal cinema. *The Jolson Story* was one of two films to monopolize the 1946 Academy Awards nominations and, coming at the apex of Hollywood's wartime boom, one of three to follow *Birth* and *Gone with the Wind* as, until the 1960s blockbusters, Hollywood's all-time money-makers. *Jolson Sings Again* led all films of 1949 in box-office receipts. But the other 1946 movie that combined academy awards with box-office success, apparently at the opposite pole from *The Jolson Story*, was *The Best Years of Our Lives*, the social problem film about returning World War II veterans. The film second to *Jolson Sings Again* in 1949 box-office receipts was the racial social problem film *Pinky*. *Home of the Brave*, which combined *Best Years'* war subject with *Pinky's* racial theme, was also among the top thirty grossers of the year, remarkable for a low-budget, independent production. That the race-ethnic social problem film, both in its original generational conflict and later racial prejudice forms, is the underside of the blackface musical, that the social problem and musical genres are split halves of a common ur-film, is suggested not only by their common *Jazz Singer* roots, but also by the conjunction of *Jolson Story* and *Best Years*, *Jolson Sings Again* and *Pinky*.[12]

For a brief period after World War II, when the popular front overlapped with early civil rights Cold War liberalism, Hollywood produced six films exposing racial prejudice, the industry's first two movies on anti-Semitism, *Crossfire* (1947) and *Gentleman's Agreement* (1947), and then in 1949, in a literal transfer, four movies about antiblack racism, *Pinky, Lost Boundaries, Home of the Brave*, and *Intruder in the Dust*.[13]

These civil rights movies are the stepchildren of the generational conflict films. Unwilling to show nativist hostility to immigrants, the earlier motion pictures displaced anti-Semitism in the wider society onto generational conflict within the Jewish family: resistance to Jews becoming American in *The Jazz Singer* comes from the Jewish father, not the gentiles. The end of mass immigration to the United States and the destruction of European Jewry produced nostalgia for a lost Jewish world instead of the menace, however tragic, of old world figures blocking the path to Americanization. This shift takes place visibly in the black-face musical, where *The Jazz Singer* patriarch metamorphosizes into the adorable, supportive, old people dolls—Stepin Fetchits a later critic would call them—of the Jolson biopics.

However sentimentalized the postwar depiction of Jews, the Holo-caust nonetheless turned Hollywood attention to anti-Semitism. The extermination of European Jews also called attention to the racial op-pression of African Americans. Racism and anti-Semitism, the unac-knowledged condition for blackface musicals and generational conflict films from *The Jazz Singer* to *Jolson Sings Again*, are made visible on the screen in the civil rights movies. But these films also expose the under-side, in blackface stereotypes and relative Jewish privilege, of Jewish black identification.[14]

The doubled postwar genre films—Jolson biopics and racial social problem pictures—straddle the fissures that would ultimately shatter the New Deal coalition around race and war, and one could foresee that political coming apart by identifying the southern nostalgia in the Jol-son films as Dixiecrat and identifying *Crossfire* (whose director, pro-ducer, and writers would soon fall victim to the House UnAmerican Activities Committee) as (Henry) Wallaceite. Not only do the Jolson biopics hold together the southern-Jewish alliance, however, but the so-cial problems films are also inside it. The continuation of the New Deal coalition for two decades after the war, in spite of pressures from white supremacists on the right and from civil rights and anti–Cold War movements on the left, shows up in the way the two genres in the late 1940s are not polarized but interpenetrated. The racial social problem film, although it poses itself against the blackface musical, is actually an inheritance from it.

What, then, is the genre, "blackface musical"? There is an ideology of its content, i.e., organic nationalism, and an ideology of its form, that is, self-making, performance, artifice. In content the blackface musical offers regression as national integration. Mammy is at the childhood and southern root, supporting the ease of transfer from white to black and back again, whether as Judge Priest doing Stepin Fetchit's black voice, or Dan Emmett performing a blackface "Dixie," or Bing Crosby and Marjorie Reynolds celebrating Lincoln's birthday in blackface in *Holiday Inn*. The wide-open, maternal or infantile, blackface mouth—Jolson's singing "My Mammy," Larry Parks's in closeups in the Jolson biopics—is, as in *Dixie*, the stage door from which blacks make every-

The open blackface mouth in *Dixie*, A. Edward Sutherland. © Paramount, 1943.

thing available to whites. In the vision of interracial harmony to which these nostalgic films return, the Civil War rather than race relations is the source of division in American life. Blackface heals that division in the white ability to playfully expropriate black under conditions of hierarchical, interracial harmony. Southern domestic repose supports northern acquisitive self-making, the southern parvenu and redneck replace the black beast, and Warm Springs, Georgia (FDR's southern home), joins with Tammany Hall to perpetuate the Democratic Party politics out of which blackface had originally sprung: Martin Van Buren's alliance between the planters of the South and the plain republicans of the North.[15]

The entertainment business, from blackface to Hollywood, was itself the vehicle for national integration in the blackface musical. When the *New Yorker* reviewed *Dixie* alongside the war movie *Pilot Number 5*, its "Democracy and Burnt Cork" title implied blackface's contribution to the war effort.[16] In defining Americanness as entertainment, however, blackface musicals slid from content to form, to presenting American identity as performance and self-making. Calling attention to their nostalgia, blackface musicals are self-reflexive at their core. They self-consciously make not the world they represent but themselves as performances the basis for American patriotism. Synecdochical for Hollywood, blackface gives America its meaning, self-making through role-playing, in *Holiday Inn, Swanee River,* and *Dixie.*

"Fifteen nights a year Cinderella steps into a coach and becomes queen of Holiday Inn," says Marjorie Reynolds as she applies burnt cork to her face. The cinders transform her into royalty. Although blackface was often justified as disguise, as in the *Holiday Inn* scene, that was itself a ruse, for the audience was always in on the secret. Dirt was the magical, transforming substance in blackface carnivalesque (particularly transgressive for the blackface Jew, since the term *ham actor* originated from the use of ham fat to wipe off burnt cork.) On the one hand the filthy mask ("Dirty hands, dirty face," sings young Jakie Rabinowitz) brought the performer down to the earthy substrate, the ape he aped. But on the other, the masquerade identified him not with the mammy but with the trickster. Orality in its performed form was less the sucking mouth of nurture and more the signifying mouth of changing identity. Black mimicry, black performance, the black mask, the technique by which the subjugated group kept its distance from and mocked its oppressor, was itself expropriated and made into a blackface performance for whites.[17]

There is a primal scene in every blackface musical; it shows the performer blacking up. The scene lets viewers in on the secret of the fetish: I know I'm not, but all the same. The fetish condenses the unanalyzed magical significance assigned to black people, as to the substitute phallus in Freud's analysis and the commodity in Marx's. Although blackface is detachable and reattachable, like Freud's fetish, the fact that the films make visible the pleasure of putting on and taking off burnt cork may seem to violate the Marxian-Freudian rule that demystifying the fetish stops it from doing its work. What remains hidden, however, are the historical crimes embedded in the fetish's invidious distinction: here white over black parallels man over woman (if we revise Freud to make the phallus itself a fetish) and capitalist over worker. In a culture that mythicizes self-making, moreover, the blackface fetish acquires power by being shown to be put on; blackface joins white power over black to personal mobility and self-expression. But what looks like uncovering origins, exposing how the magic works, is the deepest mystification of all, for it attributes the ability to change identity to individual construction of the self.[18]

Blackface self-awareness, the instrument of identity transfer, always defined minstrelsy, but over time an increasing self-consciousness indicated that the form was in trouble. Putting blackface into history reveals the pressure being placed on both the ideology of the content and the ideology of the form.

Insisting on the blackface roots of American entertainment, the blackface musical wanted to create a seamless tie to the past. But attempts to incorporate the past opened up a fissure between the gone with the wind plantation and the present of racial conflict, between domestic service and military service, and between the plantation darkey and the urban, self-assertive New Negro of the war. *Life*'s photographs authenticating *Dixie*'s historical accuracy may have used surface imitation to hide historical lies, but history took its revenge in the pictures of the Detroit race riot of 1943 that appeared in the same issue, for there would have been a smaller gap between an accurate account of antebellum America and the race conflicts during World War II.[19] *Swanee River* and *Dixie* conclude with the Civil War, but their exercises in national reconciliation through blackface undermined blackface as racially reconciliatory during World War II.

The modern civil rights movement, of black militance and mass protests, was born during World War II. Since it was African American self-representation from which blackface nostalgia sought escape, blackface came under growing criticism during and after the war. The context remained one of compliance among blacks and almost universal endorsement among whites: Eleanor Roosevelt and the cosmopolitan journalist and socialist Heywood Broun loved *Amos 'n' Andy*; Larry Parks, soon to be blacklisted leader of the left wing of the Screen Actor's Guild (which opposed "discrimination against Negroes in the motion picture industry" and the stereotyping of African Americans), played Jolson in blackface. But by 1949 the form was in trouble.[20]

There was a growing sense after the war, captured in Martha Wolfenstein's term *fun morality*, that spontaneity took work, that the natural had to be made.[21] Blackface captured that paradox perfectly but could no longer, in the face of civil rights disapproval, carry it. *Holiday Inn* incorporated artifice into its love story, at once celebrating Crosby's Holiday Inn as a retreat from show business fakery and making his trickysterdom—genetically blackface—the method for winning back his girl. Crosby theatricalizes domesticity; the spokeswoman for simple love and devotion is the real African American, Mamie (Louise Beavers), and fortunately Crosby does not follow her advice. But the infinite regress of self-referentiality seven years later, in *Jolson Sings Again*, has a mannerist feel; blackface, made too self-conscious by civil rights scrutiny, is reaching the end of its line.

Jolson Sings Again made blackface method the subject as had no film before it, generalized it to Hollywood special effects, and left it behind. No longer the carrier for a Jewish self, divided between parental past and American future, and increasingly suspect from a civil rights perspective as the insulting doubling of blacks, blackface in its film apotheosis moves entirely off the street and onto the stage, out of society and into entertainment. Self-consciousness, going too far, turns back on itself instead of going out into the world. *Jolson Sings Again* introduced the postwar Hollywood paradise of consumption and special effects, the increasingly self-enclosed musicals of the 1950s that separate art from life. But the film's self-reflexivity cuts the present off from the past as most 1950s musicals avoided doing. Although the theft of black music and performance styles energized 1950s popular culture, it could no longer root itself in open blackface display.[22]

Jolson Sings Again climaxes with the making of *The Jolson Story*, and the introduction of Larry Parks as the actor who will play Jolson has two unsettling features. The first is that the Parks who appears as himself has already been playing Jolson for most of two movies, so that the Jolson who watches Parks play Jolson is Parks playing Jolson. The second is that Jolson's agreement to put his songs through his impersonator's mouth, by displaying Hollywood's lip-synch technique, separates the singing voice from the image that produces it as if it were its own. When Larry Parks as Larry Parks mouths the words of "Toot, Toot, Tootsie," he is presenting the song that, first to join voice to lips in a feature film, introduced talking pictures. But whereas *The Jazz Singer*'s "Toot, Toot, Tootsie" expressed spontaneity and integration, echoed in *Jolson Sings Again* it introduces splitting and self-consciousness. Hollywood normally employed lip-synch to create the illusion of unity between image and sound. By showing off lip-synch, the motion picture industry was exposing not only the Larry Parks who had already been playing Jolson, but also itself.[23]

There was a further irony hidden in this scene, of which Jolson followers would be aware, for his career foundered on lip-synching. Primitive sound techniques restricted the use of voice in Jolson's first two, immensely successful, part-talkies, and required him to be filmed while he actually sang. He did not lip-synch "Toot, Toot, Tootsie." When prerecording of songs developed, and sound took over the entire set, Jolson mouthed his own previously-recorded voice. Since he never sang a song the same way twice, however, lip-synching inhibited his spontaneity. Talking pictures technique, Jolson's apotheosis, thus brought about his decline. The blackface mass idol would return only as the voice behind someone else's face.[24]

Al Jolson (Larry Parks). *Jolson Sings Again*, Henry Levin. © Columbia, 1949.

That was poetic justice, as the movie was perfectly aware, because he had reached stardom as the voice behind another's (black)face. We get our first view of blackface immediately after the lip-synch scene, through the eyes of Parks as Jolson watching a screen test of Parks under burnt cork.[25] (For Parks as Jolson in *Jolson Sings Again* watching Parks play Jolson in blackface in the *Jolson Story*, see illustration above.) Looking at Parks, we hear Jolson sing "Toot Toot Tootsie." Jolson had not sung "Toot Toot Tootsie" in blackface in *The Jazz Singer*; *Jolson Sings Again* wanted to underline the connection between blackface and speaking one's own words. But in making that link, the film undercut it. Blackface, which creates visual doubleness, is introduced in the context of calling attention to the separation of voice from body. But burnt cork, self-consciously using doubling to create spontaneity, had freed the jazz singer to be himself and not only the child of his Jewish father. Lip-synching redivided that self in two identical doubles of the singer that created consciousness of self rather than providing access to difference. Instead of being heard through blackface, and so acquiring an interior, the lip-syncher was silenced as he was seen. Burnt cork gave Jolson the

Parks as Jolson meets Parks as Parks. *Jolson Sings Again*, Henry Levin.
© Columbia, 1949.

voice he lost with lip-synching. Now lip-synching gives him back his
motion picture voice at the price of his visual absence from the screen.
It enlists this more universalized and technologized "I am what I am
not" in the service of what is exposed as the authenticity effect.

Far from hiding the triple doubling—cork and skin, voice and body,
Jolson and Parks—the film makes the most of it; after displaying lip-
synch and blackface for Parks's-as-Jolson's eyes, it has Jolson meet the
actor who will play him. Two identical images of Larry Parks shake
hands; there is no effort to make one look older or otherwise different
from the other. Parks as Jolson begins the story of his life as he wants
it to appear on film. The camera cuts to Parks as Jolson before a mirror, showing Parks as Parks (the actor who will play Jolson) practice
the classic Jolson moves. The mirror effect puts four images of Larry
Parks on the screen; cut to Parks as Parks moving his lips in blackface,
then back to Parks as Jolson watching his blackface double sing. The
whiteface Parks as Jolson throws himself silently into the song, rooting

on and applauding the blackface Parks as Parks. (To those who knew that the real Jolson had never accepted not playing himself, and had finally been thrown off the set of *Jolson Sings Again*, the Parks foursome, excluding the real Jolson as it multiplied images of him, would have been particularly ironic.[26])

Jolson Sings Again has two more doublings to come: Jolson's with the spectator and its own with *The Jolson Story*. Parks as Jolson watches the premiere of *The Jolson Story* as a member of the motion picture audience. Parks sings "My Mammy," the song that ended *The Jazz Singer*, and when the actor playing Jolson in blackface interrupts his number with the apparently spontaneous but completely familiar line, "It's my mammy I'm talking about," it takes no postmodern critic to grasp that it's doubly not his mammy. The mammy isn't Jolson's, and Parks is no Jolson. The power of the scene comes from the magic by which the performer has made his not-mammy, for the space of the performance, his own.

After a long medley of Jolson classics, some in blackface, some not, *Jolson Sings Again* ends. Twice. When "The End" fills the screen the first time, it turns out to announce the end of *The Jolson Story*. The film comes to its second and final end with Parks playing Parks as Jolson, reenacting the benefit that we earlier saw (with Parks playing Jolson) as the inspiration for *The Jolson Story*. This time Parks as Jolson goes out with "Dixie Melody," the tune that incorporates musical homages to "Old Black Joe," "Swanee River," and other signifiers of the American southern plantation that is the ancestral home not of the North, not of most of the South, not of post–World War II America, not of the immigrant Jew, transformed from the nightmare home of black Americans to the cornucopia of whites in blackface—and thus retrospectively, through history as fantasy, transubstantiated by cinders into the home of all those who had not come from there—the home that may be gone with the wind, but that Jolson, or rather Parks as Jolson, can bring back to life.

But the return of the South after the mirror stage produces an alienation effect that confirms Lacan's analysis. The child, here son, who sees himself in the mirror experiences separation of his bodily self not only from his ideal self but from his mother.[27] The mirror in *Jolson Sings Again* marks the absence not just of Jolson but of his mammy. When the movie brings them back, after the film within the film has called attention to the medium, the ideology of the form has undermined the ideology of the content, because mammy organic nationalism is now solely in the past and on the stage. In the present is the social problem film.

Yet the social problem film is hardly the binary opposite of the blackface musical. The two most popular racial problem films, *Gentleman's Agreement* and *Pinky*, and *Lost Boundaries* as well, concern putting on an identity not one's own. All three are passing films. Phil (Gregory Peck) in *Gentlemen's Agreement* is an old-family Protestant passing down. Pinky (Jeanne Crain) is a light-skinned Negro who has gone North and passed up. But since the actress playing Pinky is herself white, her skin privilege is what allows white viewers to share the suffering she endures as black.[28] Moreover, Pinky is not passing as white in the North but suffering as black in the South for the entire duration of the film. Both passing movies, like the blackface musical, are vehicles for passing down. Blackface supposedly opens the door to essential racial difference, passing to the experience of suffering for a stigmatized difference that is not real, but that distinction eventually breaks down too.

No one passes in *Home of the Brave*, where a Jewish doctor treats a black soldier for partial amnesia and hysterical paralysis. But at crucial moments the doctor plays the roles of significant figures in the soldier's mission. As with blackface and passing, Hollywood celebrates itself in *Home* by making acting redemptive. With Jewish assimilation and upward mobility, ethnic performance—putting oneself in another's place, the empathic trying on of multiple identities—was moving from blackface and vaudeville to journalism (in *Gentleman's Agreement*) and the helping professions (a nursing school in *Pinky*, the psychiatrist in *Home*). Instead of teaching immigrants to be Americans through blackface, *Home*'s role-playing is the method by which the immigrant son, the doctor, heals his patient's divided self. Middle-class professionals—journalist, doctor, and nurse—substitute for theatrical performers in the racial problem film. Hollywood, inheriting and universalizing blackface in the blackface musical, celebrated itself as the institutional locus of American identity. It allied itself with the therapeutic society in the social problem film. Generic overlap suggests institutional overlap, as Hollywood was not just Hortense Powdermaker's dream factory but also the American interpreter of dreams, employing role-playing as national mass therapy.[29]

Because both the blackface musical and the social problem film change identities through masquerade, the binary opposition resides not between the genres but between the two most popular racial problem films, whose contrast goes back to the split upon which the original mixed genre film, *The Jazz Singer*, depends, between the Jew who can change his identity and the African American who cannot change hers.

Darryl Zanuck and Elia Kazan, NAACP allies from the single major studio, Twentieth Century Fox, without a dominant Jewish presence at the top, established Hollywood's terms for Jewish and black mobility. Filming *Pinky* after their success with *Gentleman's Agreement*, they turned from a Protestant journalist masquerading as Jewish to a light-skinned southern Negro who has passed as white. That identical structure creates a stunning difference. At the moment when his fiancée can no longer endure the trouble Phil's passing has brought into her life, Cathy (Dorothy McGuire) blurts out, "It's no use Phil. . . . You're doing an impossible thing. You are what you *are* for the one life you have. You can't help it if you were born Christian instead of Jewish." The movie, and the favorable review in *Commentary*, the organ of the American Jewish Committee, reject that insistence on unalterable identity, because it would not only prevent gentiles from understanding how Jews feel, but also deprive Jews of the right to assimilate. *Pinky*'s Miss Em, the southern aristocrat who shares her old family, upper-class background with Phil's Darien, Connecticut, fiancée, makes a similar speech to Pinky, and this time the movie is on the aristocratic, fixed-identity side. Submitting to her grandmother's emotional blackmail, Pinky has agreed to nurse the dying matriarch, whose laundry her grandmother (Ethel Waters), now herself too old to serve, had done for years. Pinky still plans to return North and marry the white doctor to whom she is engaged. But by the end of the film she has followed Miss Em's admonition, "Be yourself," and, with a black doctor, opened a training school for black nurses in the mansion Miss Em has bequeathed her. "I'm a Negro and I don't want to be anything else," she tells her fiancé as she sends him away. As a white actress playing a light-skinned Negro, Jeanne Crain can, like Gregory Peck, pass down; as a Jew, Phil can pass up; as a black woman, Pinky cannot.[30]

Ralph Ellison pointed out in the review of the four 1949 race movies that gave its title to his classic essay collection, *Shadow and Act*, that what Pinky is not is a segregation-accepting, southern Negro; to return to southern segregation she has to change what she has become, and in the name of the givenness of identity, the film endorses that choice. Going beyond the Barthian "principle of myth" that "transforms history into nature," *Pinky* attacks history as unnatural, reversing Pinky's historical change in the name of racial nature.[31]

There may be a different political valence to that choice now than in 1949; the light-skinned African American nationalist student with whom I saw the film was far more sympathetic to it than her integrationist Jewish professor. Like Pinky, she did not want to stand with the fiancé, the white professional man who insisted that the southern blacks were "not your people," and "told me there'd be no Pinky Johnson after I was married." But in counterposing loyalty to one's people to integration, *Pinky* was accepting the dichotomy of the passing and generational conflict films, now overcome, as the Jolson films and *Gentlemen's Agreement* would have it, for Jews. The postwar Jewish films, whether with Parks as Jolson or Peck as a Jew, flee any possible conflict between group distinctiveness and loyalty on the one hand and integration on the other. *Pinky* insists on that conflict to justify segregation.

Movie endings cannot erase what has come before; they do not obscure what *Pinky* and *Gentleman's Agreement* share with each other and with blackface: the fascination with racial masquerade. Nonetheless, the contrasting endings are also decisive. As in blackface, Jews rise and blacks serve. Because the condition of white ethnic mobility was that black people be kept in place, mobility cannot extend from blackface to black passing.

Pinky opts for southern segregation, the fixed black identity on which white play with identity depends, whereas *Gentleman's Agreement,* in the name of mobility, attacks the idea that Jews are any different from other people. That contrast, realized in the endings, also works throughout the films. There is a black milieu in *Pinky,* but only a few isolated Jews in *Gentleman's Agreement.* That departure from the original generational conflict films, which embedded ethnics in old-world communities, redistributes black fixity and Jewish transfer into two separate movies. And that is a sign that blackface is in trouble, for neither film can hold together, play with, simultaneously reinforce, and dissolve racial difference.

Both films ground themselves on racial masquerade's play with identity, the ability to move back and forth, but both reject mutability in their climaxes. When Phil's son is subjected to anti-Semitic insults, Cathy reassures the boy, "It's not true. You're no more Jewish than I am." Phil is furious at this distinction, central to blackface, between those who can and those who cannot stop being members of the stigmatized group. Cathy wants Phil's Jewface to be a magazine assignment, a game. For Phil the conditions that gave rise to that game must end. Pinky's choice of segregation leaves the same message behind, not to dissolve the difference between Jew and gentile but to insist on the difference between white and black. Unlike musical blackface, these movies, to use the title of Chester Himes's fictional exposé of racial passing, are proposing "To End All Stories," to abolish the conditions that enable their own storytelling.[32]

Gentleman's Agreement stands for the northern, Jewish solution to the race problem, *Pinky* for the southern one imposed on blacks, but the contrast between the movies is also underlined by a third term, gender. As in both versions of *Imitation of Life* (1934, 1959), the African American daughter who wants to pass is drawn back into the body of her mammy.[33] Women are what they are; men are what they do. Women, especially black women, are embodied; men transcend. Just as white ethnic mobility requires black fixity, so men need women. Mammy allows the blackface Jew, the jazz singer, to move forward; she pulls the whiteface African American back to her maternal roots.

As men, both Phil and his Jewish friend move forward in *Gentleman's Agreement*, to marriage, integrated housing, and middle-class careers. The woman moves backward in *Pinky*, to gender and racial solidarity. Allying community with segregation, *Pinky* reflects social reality through a distorting mirror. Blocked in their efforts to win white social and political acceptance in the decades after the Civil War, members of the lighter-skinned elite allied themselves with the people they might otherwise have left behind. But that alliance produced, in the years surrounding *Pinky*, not the acceptance of segregation but the fight for integration.[34]

Under the sign of Mammy, *Pinky* stood for female community as well as segregation, like *Imitation of Life*. *Pinky* was the first Hollywood film to portray an interracial romance, but instead of the traditional, two-parent family that propels exogamy, Miss Em and Granny together pull Pinky away from heterosexual and interracial relations into a community of women.[35] They do what Miss Bea and Delilah had done to Peola in *Imitation of Life*. But the more rebellious Peola requires a dead mother to pull her back. In the claustrophobic final shot of Douglas Sirk's remake, white mother and daughter embrace the returning prodigal in the car at her own mother's funeral. This love that feels like death and confinement deprives the reformed racial passer of the social space of Miss Em's nursing home; psychological melodrama, here as elsewhere, may convey a deeper truth than social realism.

The light-filled hospital room tells its own truth, to be sure, about the institutions that black professionals, significantly women, built under the sign of segregation. Nonetheless, to make Mammy signal female community as submission was no favor to black women. Making history, the combination of Pinky and Ethel Waters produced a figure opposite to the black nurses changing white bed linen at *Pinky*'s segregated finale. Six years after *Pinky*, Rosa Parks's refusal to move to the back of the bus initiated the most significant American mass protest movement of the second half of the twentieth century.

Do gender and regional differences explain the divergence of *Pinky* from *Gentleman's Agreement*, or is the black-Jewish contrast more fundamental? A thought experiment would imagine changing the black protagonist from woman to man, moving him North instead of returning her South, and transforming the gentile as Jew into a Jew as black. Stanley Kramer and Carl Foreman carried out that experiment as *Pinky* was being filmed; turning black the Jewish protagonist of Arthur Laurents's Broadway play, they made *Home of the Brave* into a film.[36]

Why did Kramer and Foreman black up Laurents's Peter Coen? It looked like better box office, after two films on anti-Semitism, to shift from Jews to blacks. In addition, to "daringly substitute a Negro" for a Jew, in the prose of *Time* magazine, was, so the *Saturday Review* thought, to make a more radical choice.[37] However vicious, American anti-Semitism was not the racism that organized the society. As the United States defeated Nazism with a Jim Crow army, there was growing recognition that American Negrophobia was the counterpart of European anti-Semitism. The NAACP journal, *Crisis*, warning against the "kernel of fascism" in the South, exposed "Southern Schrecklichkeit." "These are not wrecked Jewish establishments in Nazi Germany, but Negro businesses in democratic America," ran the caption under pictures of a "Kristallnacht" in Columbia, Tennessee. Both *Crisis* and *Commentary* campaigned against discriminatory college admissions policies and restrictive covenants that excluded Jews and African Americans from white Christian neighborhoods, the plot device on which *Gentlemen's Agreement* turns.[38]

These parallels served the black-Jewish civil rights alliance. The most virulent racists were also anti-Semites, *Crisis* reminded its readers. Racists blamed Jewish judges for tolerating black criminals. Reporting a Klan revival in the South and an increase in southern anti-Semitism, *Crisis* quoted Tennessee Kleagle Jesse M. Stoner's "Anti-Semitism and white supremacy go hand in hand."[39]

But although shared opposition to racism generated the civil rights alliance of the two diaspora peoples driven from their homelands, that alliance also exposed the more privileged position of Jews, both in society and in the civil rights organizations themselves, where most of the money, legal resources, and social scientific expertise—though, crucially, not all—were in the hands of Jews, and where integrationist goals and legal means would work better for Jews than for blacks.[40] Kramer's film marked that difference when, in painting its Jewish soldier black, it turned its doctor into a Jew, not explicitly but by replacing his gentile name with no name at all, giving him a Jewish nose and appearance, photographing him from angles and in closeups that emphasized his facial look, and, unlike the play, hinting at his own experience of racial prejudice. One massive social fact, however, ought to have made impossible the transfer of victim from Jew to black, even in Hollywood. And yet not a single reviewer named it, not even those most critical of the film for avoiding the real character of racial oppression in the United States. In the Jim Crow American army of World War II, no black soldier could have been in the company of whites. Not only were the American armed forces entirely segregated during the war, but the postwar debate over integration could not have been missed by anyone concerned about civil rights. A 1946 army report proposing that an occasional black technician enter white units "where Negro personnel with special skills can be utilized to advantage as individuals" might, though retrospectively, have explained the black soldier's presence among white soldiers, since he's brought in as the only available surveyor. However, that report not only postdated the war, but its suggestion was never implemented. Civil rights forces pressed for military integration in the year before *Home* was filmed, and A. Philip Randolph and the NAACP threatened black draft resistance if the army remained Jim Crow. When, under pressure, Truman finally issued his executive order in 1949 looking forward to military integration, the army dragged its feet. It did not place black and white troops together until the Korean War.[41]

By blocking out Jim Crow instead of endorsing it like *Pinky, Home* took its lone black man out of a black milieu. Textually the African American alone is vulnerable to racial hate; subtextually, as with blackface, he is vulnerable to racial love. In the film's plot, Peter Moss (né Peter Coen) has suffered partial amnesia and a hysterical paralysis after his best friend, who is white, is killed on a mission to map a Japanese-held island. Through drug-induced narcosynthesis, depicted in flashback, the doctor elicits the story of the five soldiers on the island. *Home* thereby does what the Office of War Information wanted and most war films failed to do: unite combat to the larger issue of why we fight.[42]

Stanley Kramer named his black soldier for Carleton Moss, the Hollywood journalist who had attacked *Gone with the Wind* in the *Daily Worker*, and then written and starred in the World War II propaganda film *The Negro Soldier*. The army dropped Moss in 1946 for "my un-American past," as the black writer put it; three years later he promoted the film on race prejudice in the military made by his leftist friends.[43]

To serve Carleton Moss's goal of promoting democracy, however, the film cripples Peter Moss; it humiliates him in extended and visually intrusive ways. Although the announcement that Moss cannot walk is made at the beginning of the film, the camera initially shows him, in flashback, as arguably the first dignified, erect, nonstereotyped, intelligent black leading man to appear on the Hollywood screen (excepting certain Jim Crow films, and depending on one's view of James Lowe in *Uncle Tom's Cabin* and Paul Robeson in *Emperor Jones*). Unlike the white soldiers, Moss has already volunteered for the mission in the scene where he meets them. As the white men hunch over, fearful and vacillating, not wanting to join the mission but afraid to refuse, he towers above them.

That opening scene sets off the painfulness of Moss's fall. Most of the movie analyzes him as brought down by racism. But the film does not show what it tells, for Moss can close himself off to racial insults. Made abject by the Jewish doctor's interventions, he becomes abject again, in flashback, through his love for and loss of his white friend. The doctor injects him, forces tears from his eyes and words from his mouth, hovers over him while he's lying in bed, lectures him, berates him, sneaks behind his back to scare him with the voice of T. J., his persecutor, and the voice of Finch, his dead friend, holds him, cures him, and is the recipient of his devotion. The film puts unsympathetic racist stereotypes, including a reference to Finch and Moss as Amos and Andy, into T. J.'s mouth. That method of distancing itself from blackface allows *Home* to do its own blackface on a far more powerful, because loving, level.

A fundamental contradiction runs through this film. Its ideology is "Jewish" on the *Gentleman's Agreement* model: northern, male, and integrationist, the film insists there is no difference between black and white. But its spectacle, its affect, enforces black difference as bodily excess. Assimilated to Jew at the high level of mind, Moss is made emotion-ridden and female at the low depth of body. As hysterical body, Moss (né Coen) blackened an anti-Semitic stereotype that troubled the assimilating Jew. Was it integrationist identification with the victim of racial oppression that made the film so powerful a viewing experience for two white male adolescents, one Jewish, one not, watching the film a continent and a decade apart? Was it aspiration to the position of power in which Jew-white helps black? Or was it male adolescent anxiety about tears, the open body, and gender confusion, brought again into play when these now grown men watched the film together with the leading (and female) film authority on cross-gender identification?[44]

In forcing words and tears out of the black face, the Jewish doctor, imitating the jazz singer before him, is putting on blackface. He is making the black face and body perform emotions that once took over the Jewish man. Turning Moss into an infant and mammy, he also joins the doctors who invade women in innumerable postwar psychological films, doctors who heal women's divided identities as this doctor heals Moss. (James Agee reviewed one such film, *The Dark Mirror*, alongside of *The Jolson Story*, perhaps sensing the invasive doubling that doctor-and-female-patient movies share with blackface.) As a doctor film, *Home* participates in the postwar turn to psychology and the faith in the professional expert to solve the country's postwar maladjustment.[45]

"How must a fellow like Dave [John Garfield, his Jewish friend] feel?" Phil wonders when he is looking for an angle for his series on anti-Semitism. Maybe he should ask Dave what happens to him inside "when you hear about Jewish kids getting their teeth kicked in by Jew-haters in New York City." But, Phil decides, "There isn't any way you can tear open the secret heart of another human being," so he takes on a Jewish identity himself. *Home*'s Jewish doctor, opening up the black soldier's heart, makes the other choice. The privileged subject position within the film, nonetheless, will turn out, as in the woman's films, to reside not with the doctor but with the patient.

The move from the stage to the hospital, from the blackface musical and *Jolson Sings Again* to the postwar psychological film, may seem extreme; in fact, by way of Phil's Jewface and Jolson's army entertainment, it is doubly mediated. *Gentleman's Agreement* aligns passing with illness. His mother's heart attack generates Phil's decision to put on the mask of the Jew. Phil "was scared. I was a kid again. My mom was sick," and that propels him to realize he'll "know the answer [to anti-Semitism] only when I feel it myself." Phil has to be scared before he can understand. Then, like Jolson in *The Jazz Singer* and *Jolson Sings Again*, he stares at himself in the mirror. The blackface Jolson saw the mirror reflection of his father; Parks as Jolson saw himself. The gentile Peck sees in himself a face that could be Jewish. He describes to his mother his resemblance to Dave—dark hair, dark eyes, no accent, no mannerisms—as she lies in her bed. Camera cuts and Phil's agitated movements break down the distance between mother and son, as Phil wins his mother's approval for Jewface. She calls his masquerade "the best medicine I could have had." The boundary breakdown of blackface and passing is derived from the mother-son symbiosis, from the time before a stable, self-enclosed, male identity is in place. Mammy supports mutable identity in the blackface musical; the ill mother blesses Jewface in one social problem film; *Home* takes the next step and makes the victim of racial prejudice sick.

Home belongs with the postwar focus on psychology in advertising, industrial relations, and child rearing, as the production of private desire served regulatory and consumption functions for corporate, state, and professional institutions. The turn to psychology, reestablishing the home front division of labor interrupted by depression and war, targeted women in particular. But damage repair began with the soldiers themselves. Jolson ends up in a hospital bed in *Jolson Sings Again*, victim of a lung collapse while entertaining World War II troops. The entertainer as war casualty reminds us that *Home* is a combat film. The war film's effort to intensify immediate experience, through combat semantics and the documentary effect, moves into the social problem film by way of passing and psychological invasion. The combat wounds of returning veterans, in such films as *The Best Years of Our Lives* and *The Guilt of Janet Ames*, signified internal disturbance. They were read through the psychological tests administered to soldiers during the war and through the pervasive wartime discourse about the psychological disabilities that made so many soldiers unable to fight. The poetic line that is *Home*'s leitmotif, "Coward take my coward's hand," asks what it means when, in the home of the brave, soldiers are rendered unfit for combat. But if psychological disablement is a universal problem of the World War II fighting man, what does race—the land of the free—have to do with it?[46]

It's in the space between the specificity of racial disablement and the universality of male lack (exhibited, for example, by the armless veteran in *Best Years*) that *Home* locates itself. The doctor's psychological detective-work makes Moss and the audience experience how race prejudice has turned the black soldier into "half a man" (the title of NAACP leader Mary Ovington's book on the Negro problem). Racial slurs, by T. J. in the Pacific and from Moss's memories of his prewar past, are brought home when Finch starts to call Moss a "yellow-bellied nigger" for not wanting the white soldier to return for the maps he left behind. The film looks like it is saying that, unable to respond aggressively to racial intimidation, Moss unconsciously wanted his best friend to be hit. When Finch died, the analysis would go, Moss turned his racial anger inward. This psychology of the oppressed, anticipating Frantz Fanon's *Wretched of the Earth* by a decade, seems confirmed when the doctor finally gets Moss to walk by calling him a yellow-bellied nigger. Moss, exemplifying the Fanonian solution, moves forward in anger.[47]

Fanon's goal is rebellion, however, race-conscious and violent, a direction in which *Home* can hardly go, both for political reasons and because it would acknowledge the legitimate anger blacks feel toward sympathetic whites.[48] Finch wants Moss's reassurance that he is not like all the others; it turns out that he is. Having exposed black rage, *Home* must dissolve it. On the one hand, not Moss but the invisible Japanese enact the violence of people of color. On the other hand, between the diagnosis and the walking cure intervenes the rejection of the analysis on which the film depends. The doctor has told Moss he was glad when Finch was shot not because of the racial slur, but because all soldiers are relieved when the man next to them takes the bullet. As with *Pinky*, the ending cannot undo the film, but as in *Pinky* the ending that seems to undercut the film is also its telos.

Washing Moss white is insufficient to wipe away white guilt for his suffering, however, and so the film also elicits African American forgiveness. The first part of *Home* deprives Moss of his black milieu as racial specificity, on the *Gentleman's Agreement* model (there are no other blacks either in the neighborhood where Moss grows up or in his army), but insists on the racial specificity of the wound to his psyche. By the film's end, this distribution has been reversed. As the message deprives Moss of his difference as racial prejudice, by a compensatory logic the story restores his racial difference as less than whole. The racist source of his disability is denied only after the movie turns Moss into the racially abject.

Home subjects Moss to three primal scenes of abjection. The first, climaxing his love of Finch, shows the black soldier and his mutilated white friend in extended closeup, as Dimitri Tiomkin's mysterious, menacing, wartime music mixes with the strains of "Sometimes I Feel Like a Motherless Child." The first shot in this scene shows Moss alone before Finch crawls to him, falling on the ground and crying, "Nigger, nigger, nigger, nigger." Supposedly a sign that he's been broken by racist slurs, the incantation announces the racist stereotype that, however

Pinky (Jeanne Crain) and Granny (Ethel Waters). *Pinky*, Elia Kazan.
© Twentieth Century Fox, 1949.

sympathetic, is about to take Moss over. His head on Finch's chest, Finch's head on his chest, hysterically rocking and cradling his friend's dead body, Moss is enacting a black and white pietà. He is thereby, as is evident from comparing Moss with Finch to Pinky with her granny, playing mammy. The abject is gendered feminine; Moss has united on his own body the mammy and Mary (name of his gentile girl friend) to whom Jolson sang in *The Jazz Singer*'s climax.[49] Having become a mammy, he will lose the use of his legs.

James Edwards plays a mammy in *Home of the Brave*, Mark Robson. © United Artists, 1949.

The second scene, consummating the cure through tough love, shows the doctor supporting Moss and calling him "Peter" after his racial insult has finally provoked the paralyzed soldier to walk. No one in the army has ever called him Peter, Moss gratefully tells the doctor, but the first name the doctor now incessantly repeats is no advance over "Mossie," the name given the African American in dialogue and on the cast list, because no white soldier is ever called by his given name.

Moss's final abjection ends the movie, as he goes off to open a bar and restaurant with Mingo, the white soldier who, doubly castrated, has lost his arm and his wife. Moss knows in his head that the doctor is right, that his survivor guilt makes him like other soldiers, but he only believes it in his heart when Mingo describes a similar feeling of relief. Paternal authority alone can't heal Moss; he needs interracial comradery as well.

Home of the Brave, Mark Robson. © United Artists, 1949.

In bleeding black man into white, against the traditional model of closed off and invulnerable manhood, *Home* provoked nervousness about homoeroticism among white male reviewers. The movie and Leslie Fiedler's "Come Back to the Raft Ag'n, Huck Honey!" appeared at the same time. As Ellison responded to Fiedler, however, the scandal lay not in interracial male love but in its route through black humiliation. The problem lay not in cross-gender liminality but in the need to color black the bearer of the identificatory wound. The maternal black man would offer a less contaminated healing were he not invented to care for whites. Tying Moss to the disabled veteran, the movie intends to dissolve the stigmas attaching to racial difference and amputation, but in proclaiming that two damaged men could make a postwar life together, the movie was allying the black man with the cripple.[50]

In making Moss abject, *Home* was blacking up social problems' Hollywood. It was completing the movement of exposed emotionality from the Jews—publicly displaying their hysterical excess in generational conflict films like *The Jazz Singer*—to African Americans. *Home*'s doctor orchestrates abjection rather than being subject to it, but Jews in motion pictures had not escaped the danger of self-exposure once and for all. In the House UnAmerican Activities Committee (HUAC) investigation of communist influence in Hollywood, which began two years before *Home*'s filming, they were a major target. The Hollywood Ten (more than half of them Jewish) refused to participate in HUAC's degradation ceremony. Their anger protected them from psychological invasion; they went to jail instead. Larry Parks, the gentile who'd risen to stardom playing a blackface Jew, was also scheduled to testify; his reprieve enabled him to make *Jolson Sings Again*. When the committee reopened its investigation in 1951, its first "cooperative witness" was the now-repentant Parks. In a way far worse than he had anticipated, HUAC fulfilled Parks's fear that he had "entered so completely into the part [of Jolson that he would] never have a recognizable personality of his own again." Parks's testimony—Eric Bentley calls it "perhaps the most pathetic in all the annals of the Committee"—is the fourth scene of abjection surrounding *Home*, because, like *Home*, HUAC was turning social problems' Hollywood into blackface.[51]

Parks "opened himself as wide as possible to" the committee, a phrase he repeated seven times, in the hope that HUAC would not make him inform. The actor defended his Communist Party membership during the war as the product of youthful idealism and sympathy for the underdog. "If a man doesn't feel that way about certain things, he is not a man," Parks explained as his manhood was being taken away. The Jolson movies, by raising Parks to stardom, had made him a committee target. "My career has been ruined because of this," Parks said, begging the committee—and here Gregory Peck's words from *Gentleman's Agreement* echo in the mind—not to "tear open the secret heart of another human being." "I'm asking you as a man, having opened myself as wide as I know how," Parks pleaded; "forcing me to name names is like taking a pot shot at a wounded animal." "Don't present me with the choice of . . . going to jail or forcing me to really crawl through the mud [like the dying Finch crawled to Moss]." "He feels so bad about what he has to do," Parks's lawyer, Louis Mandel, explained. If the committee forced him to name names, Mandel implied, Parks would go along, although "what he is going to give you will only eat up his insides." "He may have to sacrifice the arm with gangrene in order to save the body. Even though he doesn't like it, he will walk around the rest of his life without an arm." *Home*, whose protagonist was also crippled because he betrayed his friend, wanted to redeem the condition of the one-armed man; Parks spoke the cost of amputation.[52]

And then, from out of the wide-open mouth of "the most completely ruined man you have ever seen," the names poured out. "Morris Carnovsky. Joe—" "Will you spell that name," interrupted Committee Counsel Frank Tavenner, who knew perfectly well how to spell *Carnovsky* but wanted to call attention to the alien ethnicity. Parks pushed on. "I couldn't possibly spell it. Carnovsky, Joe Bromberg, Sam Rossen, Anne Revere, Lee Cobb"—four Jewish men and a gentile woman—and more and more. "Gregory Peck?" asked Tavenner. "I have no remembrance of ever attending a meeting with Gregory Peck."[53] Peck, never a convincing Jew, was no subversive either. Even as the star of *Gentleman's Agreement* escaped exposure, however, the open blackface mouth of the Jolson biopics took over Parks's whole body. Forced to repeat his Jewish blackface routine, Parks was singing once again before HUAC.

The committee bludgeoned Parks into opening himself up; love produces that effect and affect in *Home*. *Home*, on the blackface model, placed a role-playing Jew in charge of a hysterical black; HUAC, mocking *Home*'s aspiration to universality, abased the American from Kansas as a blackface Jew. *Home*'s ending announced a victory, as if sending Moss and his one-armed white friend out into an unchanged society was not setting them up to be knocked down again. Parks knew he had suffered defeat. James Edwards, the actor who played Moss, joined the successful NAACP campaign to remove *Amos 'n' Andy* from television. But in rejecting the path of abjection Parks shared with Moss, Edwards entered not Moss's rosy future but Parks's unhappy Hollywood ending. Victim of the Cold War witch hunt that would set back racial progress and drive Hollywood even from the ground staked out in *Home*, Edwards refused to name names before HUAC and was blacklisted.[54]

Home's final scene was meant to be redemptive, making a new community out of the breakdown of racial barriers in the wake of the loss of the old. Melodrama more convincingly restores lost innocence than makes something new, however, a difficulty underlined by the historical obstacles in 1949 to Moss and Mingo's interracial community.[55] A solution plausible in the play, given Jewish assimilation, discredited the movie that replaced the Jew with the African American.

Retaining black difference, *Home* creates an African American man who nurtures and forgives whites. The repressed social position of black soldiers in the Jim Crow army, largely confined to supply, medical aid, and cleanup, returns in the black man as mammy.[56] But racial polarization encourages the male adolescent viewer to cross over from black difference to black identification, not because of universal survivor guilt but out of the longing to give up, by crossing the racial divide, the self-enclosed, closed-off, invulnerable male identity.

In turning the problem of racism into its psychological effect on the victim, *Home* was a creature of its period, because it was under the sign of psychological damage that support for civil rights reentered American politics after the three-quarter-century silence with the end of Reconstruction. The Supreme Court declared segregated schools unconstitutional five years after *Home* because of their harm to black children's self-esteem. The classic 1950s discoveries of the race problem in social psychology and history, Kardiner and Ovesey's *Mark of Oppression* before *Brown v. Board of Education* and Stanley Elkins's *Slavery* after it, presenting African Americans as victims without agency, indicted racial oppression as a psychological wound. (Elkins, as if paying homage to *Home*, not only made Jewish concentration camp inmates his model for slaves, but also came to the debilitating effects of total institutions by analogy with his own experience in the wartime army.) The damage hypothesis, as Elkins called it, would shortly produce the Moynihan *Report on the Negro Family* and subsequent treatments of ghetto pathology that consign racism to history. Looking for past trauma rather than present injustice, the psychological turn may seem to have taken race relations in the wrong direction.[57]

From another perspective, however, it was not so much psychological interpretation that made the black man vulnerable to whites as his isolation from other African Americans on the one hand, and, on the other, the refusal to face the actual source of his material and psychological vulnerability, the structure of authority itself. In part a flight from army racism, that evasion was also in keeping with the condition under which World War II movies of the 1940s could convey immediate experience, that they not call into question the army chain of command.[58] Could psychological insight be brought into play when collective black soldiering in the Jim Crow army broke down? Just as *Home* inserts itself between *Gentleman's Agreement* and *Pinky*, so it bears comparison with a movie that was not made, a soldier's story of the Mare Island mutiny and court-martial of African American navy stevedores.

In turning a Jewish soldier black, *Home* entered a discourse that had cast its shadow over African Americans in the military since the Civil War, the debate over whether black soldiers had the ability and courage to endure combat. "Our fellow pale-face Americans would have us and the world believe that we make poor soldiers," wrote a *Crisis* book reviewer at the end of World War II. The NAACP condemned army claims during the war, endorsed by Secretary of War Henry Stimson, that black soldiers lacked the capacity to master modern military weapons. *Crisis* also rejected accusations that black men lacked the will to fight. Competence was one thing, however, and psychology another; instead of simply rejecting the psychological discourse, *Crisis*, like *Home*, turned it against discrimination. To deny that African Americans faced a motivational problem in the Jim Crow army played into the stereotype of the happy, submissive darkey. If there was psychological recalcitrance, in the NAACP view, racism not racial cowardice was to blame. *Home* created a psychologically incapacitated black soldier but, except at the end, attributed his weakness to racism. Militant African Americans had their own version of that analysis, whose similarity to the movie exposes the chasm between them.[59]

Racism was not a diffuse set of attitudes, as *Crisis* presented it, concentrated in one discontented soldier, but rather a property of the army structure of command. *Home*'s racist is a single private, and its colonel is more enlightened than its major. Army hierarchy was the problem for *Crisis*. With its high concentration of southern officers, the army was "running a plantation as far as Negroes are concerned," as black former army chaplain Grant Reynolds quoted one soldier. Reynolds "discovered the South more vigorously engaged in fighting the Civil War than in training soldiers to resist Hitler." Black soldiers were subject to daily racial insults and humiliations. That did not make them less willing to fight, but it would be understandable if they turned their resentments against the army rather than the army's enemy. Black militants wanted to hold out that threat for the future, if army racism did not change, without having it used against black soldiers in the present.[60]

This was no mere abstract discussion. Black soldiers at Mare Island, San Francisco, in 1944 were court-martialed for refusing to load munitions. The reason, as in *Home*, was the racially inflected response to military death. Already resentful of their place in the military and their treatment by the southern-dominated chain of command, many of the mutineers, wrote Reynolds, were survivors of the Port Chicago tragedy, where more than "200 Negroes were blown to bits" loading high explosives. In Reynolds's words, "They had gathered up the mutilated bodies of their former buddies. The psychological strain produced thereby, aggravated by the general resentment they have built up against the navy for the way they have been treated, must be considered in passing judgment against such men."[61]

The Mare Island soldiers, like Moss, had broken down. Mare Island, like *Home*, raised the question of cowardice, of whether black soldiers could serve. But for Reynolds, service was already their condition, under the auspices that "the traditional beast of burden has no right to complain." The Mare Island mutineers, moreover, recovered the remains of black comrades; Moss cradled the mutilated body of a single, white friend. The mutineers chose to resist; they did not develop hysterical symptoms. If they were "rendered psychologically unfit to give their best service to the country," in Reynolds's words, it was by army racism not survivor guilt. Their mass court-martial contrasted with Moss's individual narcosynthesis, and Reynolds proposed substituting for the law not therapy but "justice," turning the tables, and court-martialling "those responsible for the miserable plight of the Mare Island mutineers." Within a few years, as *Home* was going into production, Reynolds and A. Philip Randolph were planning their own mutiny, mobilizing the threat of draft resistance to force army integration. In a period of growing black collective militancy, *Home* generated sympathy for its African American soldier by making him an isolated victim. Unseen, menacing, interchangeable Japanese fill the anxious space of *Home*'s community of color. The price for white sympathy for the lone, unthreatening African American was the elision of the actual conditions of black military service, the bonds among black soldiers, the collective life, resistance, and punishment of African Americans in uniform.[62]

The army punished African American solidarity on Mare Island; *Home* advocates solidarity across racial lines. For the phallic display of traditional minstrel transvestitism, where white men in blackface, some in drag, made much of black male sexual power, *Home* substitutes tenderness. But since the condition of that tenderness was black emasculation, the repressed was going to return. *Home* wants to take the integrationist *Gentleman's Agreement* path against *Pinky*. But with its nurturing black soldier and disabled male solidarity, *Home* is closer to the *Pinky* matrix than the integration versus segregation, North versus South, male versus female oppositions suggest. And that spoke to the intractability of racial division in the United States.

The Jewish blackface promise of changing identities flowered from black difference in the white imaginary and from the privileged position of Jewish compared to African Americans. Those were the very conditions to which the civil rights promise of changing identities, not to deny its achievements, fell victim. *Gentleman's Agreement* would prove more prophetic than *Home of the Brave* about the solution to each film's racial problem. But the very commonality between *Home* and *Pinky*, by the law of the return of the repressed, turned the opposition between them—integration versus segregation—in a direction neither film desired, foreshadowing the split between Jews and militant blacks that would bring the civil rights period to an end, now under the sign of neither the Jewish professional man nor the black working woman but of the figure repressed not only in these films but in all of Hollywood since his demonic appearance in *Birth*. Did that figure finally overthrow blackface, or was he performing it one more time—the aggressive black man, the Black Panther, Malcolm X?

Notes

Originally conceived as a contribution to the research group on film genre at the Humanities Research Institute, University of California, Irvine, this essay was first published in *representations* 46 (spring 1994). A much expanded version is now part of *Blackface, White Noise: Jewish Immigrants in the Hollywood Melting Pot* (Berkeley: University of California Press, 1996).

1. Michael Rogin, *Blackface, White Noise: Jewish Immigrants in the Hollywood Melting Pot* (Berkeley: University of California Press, 1996), 13–16; Melvin Patrick Ely, *The Adventures of Amos 'n' Andy: The Social History of an American Phenomenon* (New York: Free Press, 1991); Thomas Schatz, *The Genius of the System: Hollywood Filmmaking in the Studio Era* (New York: Pantheon, 1988), 243, 261.

2. See David R. Roediger, *The Wages of Whiteness: Race and the Making of the American Working Class* (London: Verso, 1991); Rogin, *Blackface, White Noise*, 56–58; Ely, *Amos 'n' Andy*, 64–96.

3. Neal Gabler, *An Empire of Their Own: How the Jews Invented Hollywood* (New York: Crown, 1988); Rogin, *Blackface, White Noise*, 430–48.

4. Rogin, *Blackface, White Noise*, 117; Jane Feuer, "The Self-Reflective Musical and the Myth of Entertainment," in *Genre: The Musical*, ed. Rick Altman (London: Routledge, 1981), 160.

5. Jim Kitses, *Horizons West: Anthony Mann, Budd Boetticher, Sam Peckinpah: Studies of Authorship within the Western* (London: Thames and Hudson, 1969), 8; Thomas Schatz, *Hollywood Genres: Formulas, Filmmaking, and the Studio System* (Philadelphia: Temple University Press, 1981); John G. Cawelti, "*Chinatown* and Generic Transformation in Recent American Films," in *Film Theory and Criticism: Introductory Readings*, 3d ed., ed. Gerald Mast and Marshall Cohen (New York: Oxford, 1985), 515.

6. Vivian Sobchack, "Child/Alien/Father: Patriarchal Crisis and Generic

Exchange," *camera obscura* 15 (1986): 6–34; Robin Wood, "Ideology, Genre, Author," in Mast and Cohen, *Film Theory*, 475–85.

7. Patricia Erens, *The Jew in American Cinema* (Bloomington: Indiana University Press, 1984), 43–97, 140–45; Thomas Cripps, *Slow Fade to Black: The Negro in American Film, 1900–1942* (New York: Oxford, 1977), 269; Daniel J. Leab, *From Sambo to Superspade* (Boston: Houghton Mifflin, 1975), 116; Charles Wolfe, "Vitaphone Shorts and *The Jazz Singer*," *Wide Angle* 12 (July 1990): 58–78; Robert Toll, *Blacking Up: The Minstrel Show in Nineteenth Century America* (New York: Oxford, 1974), 1–5.

8. Edward D. C. Campbell, *The Celluloid South: Hollywood and the Southern Myth* (Knoxville: University of Tennessee Press, 1981); Warren French, ed., *The South and Film* (Jackson: University Press of Mississippi, 1981); Donald Bogle, *Toms, Coons, Mulattoes, Mammies, and Bucks: An Interpretive History of Blacks in American Films*, 2d ed. (New York: Continuum, 1989), 26–90; Cripps, *Slow Fade to Black*, 254–96, 357–59; Altman, *Genre: The Musical*.

9. Rick Altman, "A Semantic/Syntactic Approach to Film Genre," in *Film Genre Reader*, ed. Barry Keith Grant (Austin: University of Texas Press, 1986), 34–35.

10. Geoffrey Perrett, *Days of Sadness, Years of Triumph: The American People 1939–1945* (Madison: University of Wisconsin Press, 1985), 243.

11. 1930s comedian comedies, descended from vaudeville and driven by virtuoso performances rather than plot, also often featured blackface, usually in musical numbers. Eddie Cantor was the major film blackface comedian, and examples of the genre that employ blackface include his *Whoopee!* (1931), *Palmy Days* (1931), *Roman Scandals* (1933), and *Ali Baba Goes to Town* (1937), as well as Bert Wheeler's and Robert Woolsey's *Diplomaniacs* (1933), and The Marx Brothers' *Day at the Races* (1937). See Henry Jenkins, *What Made Pistachio Nuts? Early Sound Comedy and the Vaudeville Aesthetic* (New York: Columbia University Press, 1992), and Rogin, "Making America Home," 1072–77.

12. Doug McLelland, *From Blackface to Blacklist: Al Jolson, Larry Parks, and "The Jolson Story"* (Metuchen, N.J.: Scarecrow Press, 1987), 79; Robert Edelman, *"Home of the Brave,"* in *McGill's Survey of Cinema*, 2d series, 6 vols., ed. Frank V. McGill (Englewood Cliffs, N.J.: Prentice-Hall, 1981), 3:1047; Douglas Gomery, "Al Jolson," in *Actors and Actresses*, ed. James Vinson (New York: St. Martin's, 1986), 335–36; Don Miller, "Films on TV," *Films in Review*, July 1962, in *The Jolson Story* file, Margaret Herrick Library, Motion Picture Academy of Arts and Sciences, Beverly Hills, California (hereafter abbreviated as MPAAS); undated, unidentified clipping, *Jolson Sings Again* file, Pacific Film Archives, University Art Museum, University of California, Berkeley. The third top grossing film of 1946 and the following decade was another film with a racial theme, *Duel in the Sun*. That *The Jolson Story* and *Best Years* could hold their own against Selznick's heavily-hyped blockbuster underlines their audience appeal.

13. Abraham Polonsky's *Body and Soul* (Enterprise, 1948), a social problems boxing film focusing on the Jewish-African American bond rather than race prejudice directly, comes at the beginning of the cycle, which continued with *No Way Out* (1950), Sidney Poitier's first film. There are few other examples until the end of the decade, with Douglas Sirk's remake of *Imitation of Life* and Stanley Kramer's successor to *Home of the Brave*, *The Defiant Ones* (both 1959).

14. I do not mean to identify the civil rights film with the perspective of all Jews fighting for civil rights. When I refer to the "Jewish solution" to the problem of discrimination, I mean that imagined for Jews by Hollywood civil rights films. Many Jews in the 1940s endorsed neither the separation of Jewish achievement from radical, collective struggle nor Hollywood's form of the Jewish-black homology. Nonetheless, these movies expose trouble in the civil rights perspective and the Jewish-black alliance that goes beyond motion pictures.

15. Bernard Wolfe, "Uncle Remus and the Malevolent Rabbit," *Commentary* 8 (July 1949): 31–32; Alexander Saxton, *The Rise and Fall of the White Republic* (London: Verso, 1990), 165–82.

16. David Lardner, "Democracy and Burnt Cork," *New Yorker* 19 (July 3, 1943): 38.

17. Columbia Pictures *News*, "Film Actors Learn the Origins of 'Ham,'" undated [1946] clipping, *Jolson Sings Again* file, MPAAS; Henry Louis Gates Jr., *Figures in Black: Words, Signs, and the "Racial" Self* (New York: Oxford, 1987), 235–46; Ralph Ellison, "Change the Joke and Slip the Yoke," *Shadow and Act* (New York: Random House, 1964), 45–59.

18. See Karl Marx, *Capital*, 3 vols. (New York: Charles Kerr, 1906), 1:82–83; Sigmund Freud, "Fetishism," *Collected Papers*, 5 vols., ed. and trans. James Strachey, Joan Riviere, Alix Strachey (London: Hogarth Press, 1959), 5:199; Marjorie Garber, *Vested Interests: Crossdressing and Cultural Anxiety* (New York: Oxford, 1992), 121, 249–50. .

19. *Life* 15 (July 5, 1943): 8–10, 80–90; Joseph Boskin, *Sambo: The Rise and Demise of an American Jester* (New York: Oxford, 1986), 89–90.

20. Perrett, *Days of Sadness*, 11; Ely, *Adventures of Amos 'n' Andy*, 202–44; Marjorie P. Lasky, "Off-Camera: A History of the Screen Actor's Guild during the Era of the Studio System" (Ph.D. diss., University of California, Davis, 1992), 278–79, 301–309, 315; Boskin, *Sambo*, 198–200; *Motion Picture Herald*, March 15, 1947, in Jolson file, MPAAS.

21. Martha Wolfenstein, "The Emergence of Fun Morality," *Journal of Social Issues* 7 (November 1951): 15–25.

22. See Jane Feuer, *The Hollywood Musical* (Bloomington: Indiana University Press, 1982), 102–8; George Lipsitz, *Time Passages: Collective Memory and American Popular Culture* (Minneapolis: University of Minnesota Press, 1990); W. T. Lhamon, *Deliberate Speed: The Origins of a Cultural Style in the American 1950s* (Washington, D.C.: Smithsonian Institution Press, 1990).

23. Compare Leo Braudy, *The World in a Frame* (Garden City: Doubleday, 1976), 238–39.

24. Herbert G. Goldman, *Jolson: The Legend Comes to Life* (New York: Oxford, 1988), 230–31; McLelland, *From Blackface to Blacklist*, 87; Alan Williams, "The Musical Film and Recorded Popular Music," in Altman, *Genre: The Musical*, 147–50.

25. The real Jolson was in this scene, too, as an anonymous member of the audience of actors watching (along with the man playing him) the man playing him. See Braudy, *World in a Frame*, 238–39.

26. Goldman, *Jolson*, 285.

27. Jacques Lacan, "The Mirror Stage as Formative of the Function of the I

as Revealed in Psychoanalytic Experience," in *Ecrits* (New York: Norton, 1977), 1–7.

28. James Baldwin, "The Image of the Negro," *Commentary* 5 (April 1948): 379–80; Bogle, *Toms, Coons*, 213–15.

29. Compare Charles Musser, "Ethnicity, Role-Playing, and American Film Comedy: From *Chinese Laundry Scene* to *Whoopee!* 1894–1930," in *Unspeakable Images: Ethnicity and the American Cinema*, ed. Lester D. Friedman (Champaign-Urbana: University of Illinois Press, 1991), 39–81; Hortense Powdermaker, *Hollywood, The Dream Factory* (Boston: Little, Brown, 1950); Philip Rieff, *The Triumph of the Therapeutic* (New York: Harper and Row, 1966).

30. Thomas R. Cripps, *Making Movies Black: The Hollywood Message Movie from World War II to the Civil Rights Era* (New York: Oxford, 1993), 55; Elliot Cohen, "Mr. Zanuck's *Gentleman's Agreement*," *Commentary* 5 (January 1948): 51–56; "Ladies, What Would You Do?" *Life* 27 (October 17, 1949): 112–15. Thanks to Herbert Hill for the reminder about Twentieth Century Fox.

31. Ralph Ellison, "The Shadow and the Act," in *Shadow and Act*, 279–80; Roland Barthes, *Mythologies* (New York: Hill and Wang, 1957), 129. Ellison was the first to bring together the four 1949 films for analysis, and I am indebted throughout to "The Shadow and the Act."

32. Chester Himes, "To End All Stories," *Crisis* 55 (July 1948): 205–7, 220.

33. Loren Berlant, "National Brands/National Body: *Imitation of Life*," in *Comparative American Identities*, ed. Hortense J. Spillers (New York: Routledge, 1991).

34. Joel Williamson, *New People* (New York: Free Press, 1980), 142–70.

35. Bogle, *Toms, Coons*, 150.

36. Arthur Laurents, *Home of the Brave* (New York: Random House, 1946).

37. *Variety*, May 4, 1949, in *Variety Film Reviews*, 16 vols. (New York, 1983); *Time* 53 (May 9, 1949), 100; John Mason Brown, *Saturday Review of Literature* 33 (June 11, 1949), 26–27. For the contrary view, see Manny Farber, *Nation* 168 (May 21, 1949), 590.

38. Daniel James, "A New Coalition in U.S. Politics," *Jewish Frontier* 19 (November 1952): 5–9. From *Crisis*, see Jacob Panken, "A Northern Judge Looks at the South," *Crisis* 54 (February 1947): 42; *Crisis* 53 (September 1946): 276; "What Happened at Columbia," *Crisis* 53 (April 1946): 110–11; Joseph H. Genrie, "Roosevelt College and Democracy," *Crisis* 55 (February 1948): 45–46; *Crisis* 54 (October 1947): 297. From *Commentary*, see Felix S. Cohen, "The People vs. Discrimination," *Commentary* 1 (March 1946): 17–22; Malcolm Ross, "The Outlook for a New FEPC," *Commentary* 3 (April 1947): 301–8; Charles Abrams, "Homes for Aryans Only," *Commentary* 3 (May 1947): 421–27; Maurice J. Goldbloom, "The President's Civil Rights Report," *Commentary* 4 (December 1947): 559–67; Felix S. Cohen, "Alaska's Nurenberg Laws," *Commentary* 6 (August 1948): 136–38; James A. and Nancy F. Wechsler, "The Road Ahead for Civil Rights," *Commentary* 6 (October 1948): 297–304; Charles Abrams, "The Segregation Threat in Housing," *Commentary* 7 (February 1949): 123–26.

39. Panken, "Northern Judge," 60; Harold P. Reese, "The Klan's 'Revolution of the Right,'" *Crisis* 54 (July 1946): 202–3.

40. See David Levering Lewis, "Parallels and Divergencies: Assimilationist

Strategies of African American and Jewish Elites from 1910 to the Early 1930s," *Journal of American History* 71 (1974): 543–64.

41. Roy Wilkins, "Still a Jim Crow Army," *Crisis* 53 (April 1946): 106–8; Richard Polenberg, *One Nation Divisible: Class, Race, and Ethnicity in the United States Since 1938* (New York: Viking, 1980), 76, 112–14. However, *Bataan*'s black soldier among whites from the army corps of engineers was precedent for *Home*. See Cripps, *Making Movies Black*, 72.

42. I rely here on Tom Schatz, presentation on the war film to the Film Group, Humanities Research Institute, University of California, Irvine, November 11, 1992, and Clayton R. Koppes and Gregory D. Black, *Hollywood Goes to War* (New York: Free Press, 1987).

43. Cripps, *Making Movies Black*, 22, 106–8, 125, 222–23.

44. Watching *Home of the Brave* with Tom Schatz and Carol Clover decisively influenced my understanding of the film. See Carol Clover, *Men, Women, and Chain Saws: Gender in the Modern Horror Film* (Princeton, N.J.: Princeton University Press, 1992).

45. Mary Ann Doane, *The Desire to Desire: The Woman's Film of the 1940s* (Bloomington: Indiana University Press, 1987); James Agee, *Nation* 163 (November 19, 1946): 536–37; Siegfried Kracauer, "Psychiatry for Everything and Everybody," *Commentary* 5 (March 1948): 222–28.

46. Tom Schatz, seminar on the war film, Humanities Research Institute, University of California, Irvine, November 1992; Rebecca Plant, "The Menace of Momism: Psychiatry and the Anti-Woman Backlash in the Post World War II Era" (seminar paper, Johns Hopkins University, 1992), 16–21; Dana Polan, *Power and Paranoia: History, Narrative, and the American Cinema, 1940–1950* (New York: Columbia University Press, 1986); Kaja Silverman, *Male Subjectivity at the Margins* (New York: Routledge, 1992), 52–90.

47. Silverman, *Male Subjectivity at the Margins*, 52–54, 63–90; Mary Ovington, *Half a Man* (New York: Longmans, Green, and Co., 1911); Frantz Fanon, *The Wretched of the Earth*, trans. Constance Farrington (New York: Grove Press, 1965).

48. Although Fanon interprets racial oppression psychoanalytically, he cites *Home of the Brave* to illustrate his distrust of most "talk of psychoanalysis in connection with the Negro." See Frantz Fanon, *Black Skin, White Masks*, trans. Charles L. Markmann (1952; New York, Grove Press, 1967), 150–51. Fanon had yet to develop his *Wretched of the Earth* alternative.

49. On the abject being rendered feminine, see Clover, *Men, Women, and Chain Saws*, 18.

50. Richard M. Clurman, "Training Film for Democrats," *Commentary* 8 (August 1949): 182; Robert Hatch, "Good Intention," *New Republic* 120 (May 16, 1949): 22; Leslie A. Fiedler, "Come Back to the Raft Ag'n, Huck Honey!" in *An End to Innocence* (Boston: Beacon Press, 1952; the original date of the article's publication [in *Partisan Review*] is June 1948); Ellison, *Shadow and Act*, 51. Two recent critical and popular successes that offer variations on the caretaking, feminizing theme are *Driving Miss Daisy* (1990) and *The Crying Game* (1992).

51. "'Jolson Sings Again,'" *Life* 27 (September 12, 1949): 96; Gabler, *An Empire of Their Own*, 351–386; Victor Navasky, *Naming Names* (New York: Viking,

1980); Eric Bentley, ed., *Thirty Years of Treason: Excerpts from Hearings before the House Committee on Un-American Activities, 1938–1968* (New York: Viking, 1971), 299; Garber, *Vested Interests*, 224. Thanks to Leo Braudy for suggesting that I look at Parks's HUAC testimony.

52. Bentley, *Thirty Years of Treason*, 309–40.

53. Ibid., 340–45.

54. Clurman, "Training Film," 183; Lipsitz, *Time Passages*, 64–65; Edelman, "*Home of the Brave*," 1047.

55. On melodrama and innocence, see Peter Brooks, *The Melodramatic Imagination: Balzac, Henry James, Melodrama, and the Mode of Excess* (New Haven: Yale University Press, 1976), applied to American racial melodrama in Linda Williams's presentation to the Film Group, Humanities Research Institute, University of California, Irvine, November 18, 1992.

56. Perrett, *Days of Sadness*, 37.

57. Abram Kardiner and Lionel Ovesey, *The Mark of Oppression* (New York: Norton, 1951); Stanley Elkins, *Slavery, A Problem in American Institutional and Intellectual Life* (Chicago: University of Chicago Press, 1959); Lee Rainwater, *The Moynihan Report and the Politics of Controversy* (Cambridge, Mass.: M.I.T. Press, 1967). Elkins labels his contribution the damage hypothesis in his third edition (Chicago: University of Chicago Press, 1976), pp. 267–70. He described the army genesis of *Slavery* to me in personal conversation. For Ralph Ellison, the flight from acts of racial injustice to psychological shadows produces a phantom Negro in the white mind, the shadow who substitutes for actual black Americans. See *Shadow and Act*, 277–78. For Ellison's critique of Elkins see "'A Very Stern Discipline': An Interview with Ralph Ellison," *Harper's* 234 (March 1967): 76–95. See also *Shadow and Act*, 303–17.

58. Schatz, seminar on the war film, Humanities Research Institute, differentiates World War II films from Vietnam War movies on this score.

59. Amy Kaplan, "Black and Blue on San Juan Hill," in *Cultures of United States Imperialism*, ed. Amy Kaplan and Donald Pease (Chapel Hill: Duke University Press, 1993); Saxton, *Rise and Fall of the White Republic*, 370–76; J. Wilvey, *Crisis* 53 (September 1946): 281; Roy Wilkins, "Still a Jim Crow Army," *Crisis* 53 (April 1946): 106; Grant Reynolds, "What the Negro Soldier Thinks about This War," "What the Negro Soldier Thinks about the War Department," "What the Negro Soldier Thinks," *Crisis* 51 (September, October, December 1944): 289–91, 299, 316–18, 328, 342–43, 353.

60. Reynolds, "What the Negro Soldier Thinks about the War Department," 317; Reynolds, "What the Negro Soldier Thinks about This War," 289.

61. Reynolds, "What the Negro Soldier Thinks," 353.

62. Ibid.; Max Lerner, *Crisis* 55 (May 1948): 155.

Genre Anxiety and Racial
Representation in 1970s Cinema

GEORGE LIPSITZ

*Genres hold the world in place, establishing and enforcing a sense
of propriety, of proper boundaries which demarcate appropriate
thought, feeling, and behavior and which provide frames, codes,
and signs for constructing a shared social reality.*

Michael Ryan and Douglas Kellner

*Genres are at once fluid and static. Their boundaries continually
shift and adapt, but once they announce themselves, genres depend
on distinct icons and codes. In addition, because generic icons
encode ideology, a genre's form and content express ideological
traces (what Fredric Jameson has called "sedimented ideolo-
gemes") through structure, plot, and characterization.*

Paula Rabinowitz

Generic pleasures are familiar pleasures.[1] Genre conventions encourage the repetition, reconfiguration, and renewal of familiar
forms in order to cultivate audience investment and engagement. Created mostly for the convenience of marketers anxious to predict exact
sales figures by selling familiar products to clearly identifiable audiences,
genres also have ideological effects. Their conventions contribute to an
ahistorical view of the world as always the same; the pleasures of pre-
dictability encourage an investment in the status quo.

But sometimes small changes in generic forms serve as a register of
broader alterations in society at large. In moments of crisis, old stories
may seem inadequate or at least incomplete. Pressing problems of the
present may intrude into seemingly fixed genres. Even in less hectic

times, the marketing imperatives of mass culture that generate genres in the first place can also encourage change because the need for novel ways to attract new audiences works against the promise of predictable pleasure implicit in any generic form.

Because genres involve classification and categorization, they have important ideological effects. Jacques Derrida connects generic thinking to the kinds of binary oppositions that divide people by gender, race, and class. "As soon as genre announces itself," he argues, "one must respect a norm, one must not cross a line of demarcation, one must not risk impurity, anomaly, or monstrosity."[2] Generic codes often connect activity to identity, reserving clearly defined roles for distinctly gendered, classed, and raced characters. Their conventions often encode social hierarchies as necessary and inevitable; they emerge within what Nick Browne calls "a gender-racial-economic system built as much on what it prohibits as on what it permits."[3]

Race plays a crucial role in generic representations. Hollywood westerns, war movies, detective stories, melodramas, and action-adventure films often rely on racial imagery, underscoring the heroism of white males by depicting them as defenders of women and children against predatory "Indians," Asians, Mexicans, and black people. They use racial differences to signal zones of danger and refuge; they move toward narrative and ideological closure by restoring the white hero to his "rightful" place in the cinematic system. As Browne contends, race is the political unconscious of American cinema, and it is important to see that in any given time period consistent changes in cultural texts are not purely aesthetic gestures, but also reflections of broader structural and social changes. Browne points out how increased representations of Asians and Asian Americans in Hollywood films after World War II emerged in tandem with U.S. economic and political interests in Asia. It will be my contention in this essay that the racial crises of the 1960s in the U.S. gave rise to "genre anxiety," to changes in generic forms effected by adding unconventional racial elements to conventional genre films.[4] The emergence of those films, their eclipse later in the 1970s by changes in Hollywood's marketing and production strategies, and their subsequent return in many films about "minority" issues during the 1980s and 1990s, can best be understood not as aesthetic changes alone but as a register of dynamic changes in social relations.

Filmmakers from aggrieved racial communities have a particularly complicated relationship with genres. To attract audience investment and engagement, they need to cater to the conventions of genre expectations. But often they find it necessary to displace the conservative effects of previous representations, not just by adding on new racial characters or settings but by using race as a way of disrupting and re-structuring genre conventions themselves. The tasks confronting oppo-sitional filmmakers from aggrieved racial communities come into sharp relief when we study the images and genre conventions they have to displace in order to tell their stories their way.

John Avildsen provides a particularly vivid example of what they are up against, of the conservative consequences of generic traditions, in the opening credits of his 1989 film *Lean on Me*. Through a series of vignettes depicting a world out of control, the director introduces view-ers to life in Paterson, New Jersey's Eastside High School. With the heavy metal song "Welcome to the Jungle" playing in the background, titles announcing the names of the actors and production personnel ap-pear superimposed over scenes of violence in the graffiti-covered hall-ways and classrooms of the high school. Black thugs surround a white male and rough him up. A well dressed black teacher opens his executive briefcase and takes out drugs to sell to a student. A group of black girls humiliate a white classmate in the bathroom, ripping her blouse off her body. When she runs screaming into the crowded hallway, a black fe-male teacher tries to cover and console her, fending off the advances of leering and grinning black males who surround the two women. A white teacher tries to break up a fight in the cafeteria, but winds up getting his head cracked open as one of the students brutally pounds it against the concrete floor. Finally, older black boys push a rotund black youth into a locker, close the door on him, and walk away. As he pounds on the door and yells, "Somebody help, please, somebody help," a black janitor reading a newspaper aimlessly ambles down the empty hall, un-concerned about the student in the locker or his cries for assistance.

In this montage, Avildsen offers us images that prefigure his film as a story about pollution and violation. Litter and graffiti in the school building provide a background of dirtiness and decay for the violations of persons, property, and propriety that follow. The student's plea for help that closes the credits prepares us for a drama about a black princi-pal who brings law and order to this inner-city high school. Although the story is a contemporary one, the images that activate it rely on genre conventions that reach back to the early days of film.

The scenes behind the opening credits for *Lean on Me* portray black people as boisterous, brutal, licentious, and lazy. In order to underscore the danger and disorder in Eastside High School, Avildsen employs im-

Lean on Me, John G. Avildsen. © Warner Bros., 1989.

agery originally used by D. W. Griffith in his 1915 film *The Birth of a Nation*, as a means of discrediting Reconstruction Era reforms that allowed black people to vote, serve on juries, and hold elective office in the postbellum South. Drawing on minstrel show stereotypes, Griffith showed black legislators devouring pieces of fried chicken, sneaking nips of alcohol from flasks, propping their bare feet on their desks, and casting lascivious glances at white women when discussing legislation allowing interracial marriage. Griffith even depicts freedmen whipping a black "faithful soul" for remaining loyal to his old master, so that he can introduce the Ku Klux Klan as an organization formed to restore respectability to the legislature and to save "good" black people from the physical brutality of the "bad" ones.

In *The Devil Finds Work*, James Baldwin argues that *The Birth of a Nation* "cannot be called dishonest; it has the Niagara force of an obsession."[5] The obsessive force of *The Birth of a Nation* comes as a logical consequence of its function as film legitimating the "common sense" of white supremacy.[6] It has to go to great extremes in storytelling, turning racist vigilantes into innocent victims, presenting slave owners and the Ku Klux Klan as the "protectors" of African Americans and saving them from the evils of Reconstruction. But *The Birth of a Nation* also articulates the common sense of patriarchal power in American life and film form alike. The solitary white male figure whose heroism maintains social order and social boundaries needs both adversaries and dependents of other races and genders to secure his own status.

As Michael Rogin explains, *The Birth of a Nation* not only mobilizes patriarchal heroism in defense of white supremacy, but also recruits the narrative of white supremacy on behalf of patriarchy, underscoring the threat to the family and the need for patriarchal authority by making the threat racial.[7] The conventions of Hollywood film function here as Browne describes them—as nodes in a network of a gender-racial-economic system built on what it prohibits as much as on what it permits.

Avildsen updates Griffith's imagery without really revising it. He attributes the demise of discipline in Eastside High School to the power over school policy won by black female parents and teachers as a result of the civil rights movement, and he substitutes a black principal for the role played by the Klan. ("This is known as progress," explains James Baldwin sarcastically in describing a similar switch in the racial economy of *In the Heat of the Night* in 1967).[8] Both *The Birth of a Nation* and *Lean on Me* summon up patriarchal power as the necessary cure for a wide range of black misbehavior—ranging from lascivious attacks on white women to the laziness of public employees, from boisterous sounds, body movements, and speech to uncontrollable brutality against white authorities and "innocent" black people in need of white protection. Avildsen's use of the song "Welcome to the Jungle" as his theme invokes white racist associations between black people and "uncivilized" jungle life, although the song itself is actually a white heavy metal band's protest against exploitative and shallow commercial popular culture products like Avildsen's film.[9]

Like most Hollywood productions, *Lean on Me* borrows its conventions from more than one place. Elements of melodrama, comedy, and action-adventure characterize its key dramatic moments; story and spectacle combine to provide the pleasures of fused forms and genres. The plot and characters display clear debts to the "high school disruption" film genre that includes *The Blackboard Jungle* (1955), *High School Confidential!* (1958), *To Sir with Love* (1967), *Rock'n'Roll High School* (1979), and *Fast Times at Ridgemont High* (1982). But unlike the high school disruption films, *Lean on Me* has no sympathy for the subjectivity or subcultures of students and offers no critique of the broader social conditions that create disorder.

Lean on Me concerns itself solely with burdens of beset patriarchy,

Beverly Todd (Morgan Freeman) and Alan North (Robert Guillaume). *Lean on Me*, John G. Avildsen. © Warner Bros., 1989.

with the need to use physical force and intimidation to make teachers, parents, and students knuckle under to law and order as defined by Joe Clark. Although the film mixes elements of several genres, its role in the gender-racial-economic system is to insist on patriarchal power as the only answer to the disorder emblematized by the rampant subjectivity of black women and black teenagers.

The continuities that unite *The Birth of a Nation* and *Lean on Me* demonstrate the enduring power of genre conventions. Culture is cumulative; it builds like a barrier reef. Nothing from the past ever disappears completely; new stories often depend on our knowledge of old ones. Moreover, the pull of the past is powerful. Representations from the present often appear credible in proportion to their resemblance to those from the past. Just as John Ford's western films struck many viewers as the "real West" because he derived his images from western paintings, lithographs, and Wild West shows, Avildsen's depictions of race attain credibility by redeploying images about race from the minstrel show and from previous films including *The Birth of a Nation* and *Gone with the Wind*.[10]

The rigidity of genre conventions in *Lean on Me* perfectly complements its ideological conservatism. The film purports to tell the "true" story of an actual high school principal, Joe Clark. Yet, it displays more allegiance to genre conventions than to historical accuracy. Clark rose to prominence in the 1980s as part of a coordinated campaign by neoconservatives to hide the consequences of cuts in government spending on education encouraged by the Reagan administration. Hailed as a national hero by Reagan's secretary of education, William Bennett, Clark blamed liberals and the civil rights movement for the sorry state of inner-city schools and offered his own record as an administrator who ruled with an iron hand as a way of improving the schools without spending more money on education.

As principal at Eastside High School, Clark illegally expelled large numbers of "troublemakers," fomented factional fights among teachers, and roamed the halls carrying a baseball bat as a way of threatening students who misbehaved. Although all of these actions won praise from much of the press and from neoconservative pundits, Clark secured no increase in achievement on any level in his school. The costs of his incessant efforts at self-promotion became clear when employees under his supervision hired a stripper to perform at a school assembly and, even worse, Clark was out of town on a speaking tour the day of the performance. Clark then took a leave of absence from his educational post to pursue more lucrative employment as a full-time speaker before neoconservative audiences.

The choice of Clark as the "hero" of Avildsen's film helped determine its ideological and narrative trajectory. Unlike Jaime Escalante (the Los Angeles teacher celebrated in Ramon Menendez's 1987 *Stand and Deliver*), whose faith in his Mexican American students actually produced improvement in their knowledge of math and led to subsequent educational achievement, Clark's record consisted purely of punishing black students in a manner more appropriate to a prison situation than a high school. The message of this film is not so much "Lean on me" as it is "Step on them." Avildsen portrayed Clark as a hero by evading his real record at Eastside High School, by transforming the principal into a generic countersubversive patriarch saving white people from their own "fear of a black planet." By placing blame in the film for the crisis in inner-city education on the mostly black and mostly female parents and teachers at Eastside, Avildsen absolves his viewers of any responsibility for the consequences of deindustrialization and neoconservative economics on inner-city youth. Instead he demonizes these young people and their parents, imagining that they would welcome a figure like Clark, a man who makes them cower by threatening them with a baseball bat and who forces them to learn to sing the school song on his command. In this respect, *Lean on Me* grafts parts of *Dirty Harry* and *An Officer and a Gentleman* onto *The Birth of a Nation*, providing an ideologically conservative message within an aesthetically conservative use of dramatic genre conventions.

The iconography shared by *Lean on Me* and *The Birth of a Nation* demonstrates the durability of socially charged stereotypes and the clear connection between the ways in which we have learned to tell stories and their ideological content. *Lean on Me* is not alone; many films since the 1970s have embraced generic forms and displayed the blend of generic and ideological conservatism at the center of *Lean on Me*, especially the "blockbuster" films of the 1970s. Aimed at audiences in newly developed suburban multiscreen theaters and tailored for cross-marketing to upscale consumers in a variety of venues, these blockbuster films drew upon generic conventions to affirm continuity in an era of rupture and change.

For example, *Star Wars* (1977) affirmed patriarchal power through a recombinant mixture of generic icons from science fiction and western films, whereas the popularity of *The Godfather I* and *II* (1972, 1974), *The Deer Hunter* (1978), *Close Encounters of the Third Kind* (1977), *An Unmarried Woman* (1978), *Grease* (1978), *Jaws I* and *II* (1975, 1978) and *The Exorcist I* and *II* (1973, 1978) signaled similar resurgences in gangster and war films, romances, musicals, action-adventure, and horror stories that displayed the same tight fit between political ideology and fidelity to generic norms.

This emergence of blockbuster films firmly rooted in genre conventions during the 1970s and 1980s seems particularly surprising in retro-spect, because they followed a period of filmmaking in the late 1960s and early 1970s characterized by genre anxiety—by the intrusion of social tremors into cinematic representations in such a way as to ren-der traditional genre icons unsatisfying and incomplete. Anxiety here emerges as an epistemological principle, as a way of knowing. Like fear, the trope of anxiety signals that something is wrong even if we cannot fully formulate a description of the problem or of its solutions. Rather than presuming that culture merely reveals, conceals, reflects, or shapes social relations, an examination of anxiety as a focal point in films en-ables us to see how cultural creations indirectly engage social conditions by registering them in unexpected ways. The ambiguities illumined by anxiety and the inability of anxious representations to suppress them may allow us important new insights into the utility of film as indirect evidence about social life.

When placed in this context, we can see that *Lean on Me* emerges at the end of an era of reconsolidation of both genre and patriarchy in response to the oppositional forces of the 1960s and 1970s. Consider, for example, the contrast between *Lean on Me* and the 1972 American International Pictures release *Blacula*, by director William Crain. In *Blacula*, Crain puts a new spin on an old story. Like many other horror films, this one begins with an image of Count Dracula's castle in Tran-sylvania on a stormy night in 1780. But on this particular evening, the count's guests are a handsome black man and a beautiful black woman. "I've never before had the opportunity of entertaining guests . . . from the darker continent," the count tells the couple.

Dracula's statement locates the film within the history of previous Count Dracula movies, while simultaneously announcing its point of departure from them. Racial difference adds a new dimension to the Count Dracula story by bringing to the surface and to the present the legend's hidden metaphor about social relations. Vampires are, after all, aristocrats who terrorize and exploit ordinary people because of their blood. The history of racism in the U.S. adds an additional resonance to issues of "blood" and "blood sucking" in this film.

The black couple have journeyed to Transylvania as representatives of their nation, hoping to persuade the count to sign a petition calling for an end to the slave trade. The dignity and intelligence of the Africans (played by Shakespearean actor William Marshall and television favorite Denise Nicholas) contrast sharply with the boorish behavior of their host. When the black prince speaks about the "barbarity" of slavery, the

Michelle (Denise Nicholas) and Mamuwalde Blacula (William Marshall).
Blacula, William Crain. © American International, 1972.

count responds by enumerating its benefits and pleasures for slave owners—adding that he would not mind acquiring a possession like the African's wife.

Offended by Dracula's insult, the couple attempt to leave, but the
count's henchmen subdue the prince and hold him down while Dracula
sucks his blood. The count "curses" the prince, condemning him to
replicate Dracula's own suffering—to hunger for blood without satis-

faction. He then condemns the princess to an eternity of hearing her husband's anguished cries. To crown his victory, the count takes away the prince's African name and gives him a European one very much like his own, transforming Prince Mamuwalde into "Blacula."

As in its less accomplished sequel, *Scream, Blacula Scream!!* (1973), the racial specificity in *Blacula* transforms the film's generic conventions. Vampire films generally combine horror and sympathy; we fear the vampire even as we understand the sadness of his insatiable desires. But connecting the count's power to white supremacist beliefs makes the victimization of the prince and princess all the more terrifying, while at the same time augmenting our sympathy for their hunger. Accustomed to thinking of Dracula as European, watching this film makes us think of him as white. By addressing the context of inner-city life in the 1970s, *Blacula* also gestures to an even greater horror off-screen, to white racism with "the Niagara force of an obsession," even if the film addresses it only indirectly through generic expressions of horror and comedy.

A low budget "blaxploitation" film designed for inner-city theaters and the suburban drive-in circuit, *Blacula* presents a playful mix of the familiar and the unfamiliar; it attempts to create engagement and investment among audiences by inserting contemporary social concerns into a familiar genre. Although exceptionally attentive or imaginative viewers might have been able to develop more fully the film's intriguing premises about white responsibility for black criminality, Crain's film does not do so. Instead, it slips back into an uneasy amalgam of standard horror film conventions and 1970s urban black life. *Blacula* is not so much a social problem film as it is a spasm of genre anxiety—an uneasy hybrid created by the conflict between the conservative continuity reinforced by the persistence of generic forms and the ceaseless pattern of social change that makes almost all generic representations seem inadequate and obsolete.

The attempt in *Blacula* to inculcate new elements within an old genre raises important questions about the relationship between seemingly static generic conventions and the dynamic vicissitudes of social life. Of course, all genres change. Generic conventions offer guideposts for character zones and narrative resolutions; changes in genre form offer opportunities for product differentiation and for fusing new audiences together through recombinant forms that blend the western with science fiction, the musical with the social problem film, and action-adventure with comedy. Creative artists cultivate audience interest through small changes in generic expectations, even in times of social

Blacula, William Crain. © American International, 1972.

stability. But more dramatic ruptures in genre form often appear in moments of great historical change. In a sensitive study of 1940s film noir, Frank Krutnick argues that minor changes in the genre revealed significant stress in society at large over changing standards of masculine identity and behavior.[11] Similarly, Will Wright shows how tensions between individualism and community in western films between the 1930s and 1950s followed the contours of changes in corporate capitalism. Jonathan Munby's research reveals how Oedipal anxiety replaces ethnic anger as the motivating force in gangster films made between 1930 and 1949, and studies by Diane Waldman and Andrea Walsh demonstrate that gothic romances tended to arbitrate tensions between female aspirations and male expectations during and after World War II.[12]

These scholars provide examples of changes in single genres as clues about broader transformations and conflicts in society at large—about changes in gender roles brought on by wartime mobilization and postwar reconversion, or about changes in individual and group identity engendered by alterations in corporate capitalism and family form. All acknowledge the tendency for film genres to register and discursively transcode social tensions through slight variations in genre conventions.

But what happens when different genres show signs of the same anxiety? In the early 1970s, *Blacula* was not the only genre film displaying racial concerns. A number of westerns, comedies, and action-adventure dramas assumed unprecedented directions by combining racial issues with generic conventions. Unlike self-consciously avant-garde and anti-racist films like *Sweet Sweetback's Badasssss Song* (1971) and *The Spook Who Sat by the Door* (1973), these films added black characters and situations to traditional genres and then traced the attendant consequences. By moving black characters out of their generic homes in comedies and social problem and action-adventure films, they registered crises about racial relations in unexpected yet powerful ways. In many cases, foregrounding race did more than desegregate previously all-white genres. Rather, the prominence of race called the generic form itself into question, leaving filmmakers and audiences with no consistent guide to resolving familiar dilemmas.

Because the history of our own time has been so poorly told, the early 1970s may not seem like a particularly important period for examining the relationship between generic form and social change. But for black communities in the U.S., the early 1970s presented a crisis of catastrophic dimensions. The Nixon administration's cessation of the War on Poverty, its abandonment of public housing, and its retreat from efforts to desegregate education, housing, and employment exacted terrible costs on communities of color. The Federal Bureau of Investigation's COINTELPRO program, coupled with repression by local police departments all across the country, destroyed the infrastructure and leadership of self-help and activist organizations from coast to coast. The cumulative consequences of wasteful spending on the Vietnam War, capital flight overseas, and the "planned shrinkage" and austerity imposed on municipal governments by finance capital in the 1970s combined to create a severe crisis for the entire country, but one that had particularly harsh consequences in inner-city communities.

The social crisis in society at large during the 1970s shaped changes in generic representations on-screen. For example, in 1971 Sidney Poitier directed a revisionist western, *Buck and the Preacher*, for Columbia Pictures. Poitier's film contains many traditional western icons—a wagon train of settlers heading west, Native Americans on the warpath, and a troop of armed men wearing blue coats and hats with crossed cavalry swords on them. In a generic western, the settlers would turn to the blue-coated riders to protect them from the natives. But in *Buck and the Preacher*, the wagon train is made up of black people running away from the post–Civil War South. The men in blue coats and cavalry hats are white racist thugs, "labor recruiters" from Louisiana, seeking to intimidate the settlers and make them return to work as sharecroppers for their former slave masters. "There's a whole way of life back there [Louisiana] that's going down the drain," one of them vows, "we don't aim to see it frittered away." With enemies like these, the settlers see the Native Americans as potential allies.

An element of overdetermination infuses the force of the revisionism of *Buck and the Preacher* because of the presence of Poitier in the starring role. Having reaped critical and commercial reward for his dignified roles during the 1960s, Poitier found himself by the early 1970s under attack by many race-conscious African Americans for these same roles. Poitier's critics lambasted him as the black man whom white people loved to watch, as "St. Sidney," because his roles always had an antiseptic quality to them, rendering him soft-spoken, quiet, patient, asexual, and unthreatening. With *Buck and the Preacher*, Poitier, the director, not only attempted to transform the western genre, but he also tried to transform the image of Poitier, the star, by departing from audience expectations and giving himself a role that enabled him to display physical strength and courage and that presented him as a member of a devoted, loving, and sexual partnership with his black wife.

The opening credits of *Buck and the Preacher* announce its revisionist intentions. Even before an image appears on the screen, *Buck and the Preacher* begins with a musical pun, the sounds of a harmonica, slide guitar, and jaw harp played by Sonny Terry and Brownie McGhee in their traditional folk style, but sounding ambiguously like the contemporary synthesizer and electric guitar scores of other films about black people, such as *Shaft* and *Superfly*. The first visual images we see are sepiatone still photos of nineteenth-century western buildings and landscapes with the superimposed names of the film's stars (beginning with Sidney Poitier). Still black and white photos of black migrants to the Old West on wagon trains follow underneath the remaining credits. A printed introduction scrolls up the screen, telling the story of freed slaves subject to terror in the postwar South fleeing to the West to build a home for themselves and their families. The invocation of hard times, physical repression, and the disillusioned aftermath of a period of turmoil connects the 1970s to the 1870s and links the fate of the civil rights movement in 1971 to the betrayal of the freedom won during the Civil War in the 1870s. As the film itself begins, the stills turn to moving pictures, and as Poitier rides toward the camera, the black and white turns to color.

Buck and the Preacher does not merely reverse racial roles, making white men the villains and people of color the heroes. African Americans and Native Americans cannot so easily assume the heroic roles reserved for white people in western lore, largely because the virtues imputed to white people in these films depend upon the denigration or demonization of people of color. We learn how poorly the conventional western fares in representing these realities in a dramatic scene, when the wagon master (Sidney Poitier as Buck) speaks through an interpreter and asks for aid from the chief of a native tribe whose land the settlers must traverse in their flight to freedom. After paying a sum of money to guarantee safe passage and to compensate for the game they will kill on their journey, Buck tells the chief that his group needs guns to win their freedom. But the leader refuses. Buck attempts to assert a bond between African and Native Americans, pointing out that his wagon train cannot return to Louisiana and will have to fight its way to freedom. Buck claims that they have the same enemies, but the chief reminds him that black soldiers fought for the U.S. army against his people. "Tell him I ain't in the army no more," Buck asks the translator, but she just turns away and says, "He knows, Buck."

The scene has few parallels within the western genre, but an uncanny connection to events off-screen. In the midst of the Vietnam War, at a time when changes in civil rights laws and competition for scarce resources exacerbated tensions between African Americans and other communities of color, everyday life events seep into this scene in *Buck and the Preacher*. Although Buck eventually leads the wagon train to freedom, we know that neither the African Americans nor the Native Americans are really safe, that the broken promises of the Reconstruction Era that send the wagon train west in the film are much like the broken promises of the civil rights era in the lives of the audience. In addition, by challenging the integrity of the frontier myth and showing the internal and external contradictions of nineteenth-century U.S. society, *Buck and the Preacher* destabilizes the western itself, undercutting its status as a foundational story about origins in order to expose the contradictions it has always served to conceal. In *Buck and the Preacher* there can be no uninterrogated heroism, because the heroism of the frontier always depends upon genocide.

The African American settings and characters that subvert genre conventions in *Blacula* and *Buck and the Preacher* also manifest themselves in detective films, including *Cotton Comes to Harlem* (1970) and *Coffy* (1973); in action-adventure movies, including *Gordon's War* (1973) and *Black Caesar* (1973); and in comedy, including *Uptown Saturday Night* (1973), *Let's Do It Again* (1975), *A Piece of the Action* (1977), and—most notably— Michael Schultz's 1975 Universal Pictures release, *Car Wash*.

Slipping back and forth between a television-style ensemble comedy and self-contained short vaudeville performances by Richard Pryor, George Carlin, and Professor Irwin Corey, *Car Wash*'s unstable form mirrors the precarious social realities faced by its black working-class characters.[13] A terrific rhythm and blues sound track helps move the action from one scene to another, but the film remains a series of vignettes rather than a coherent linear narrative. Like Robert Altman's *Nashville* (1975), the film's vignettes simultaneously underscore the poignancy of individual stories while demonstrating the seeming impossibility of pulling them together into a coherent social vision.

But as in *Blacula* and *Buck and the Preacher*, making race a central element changes the contours of the genre. Hollywood has long built comedies around groups struggling for success—most immigrant ethnic comedy entails a certain element of self-making and upward mobility. But whereas film genres have not always shown these efforts to be successful, they have only rarely offered the level of fatalism and pessimism presented in *Car Wash*.

Like *Blacula* and *Buck and the Preacher*, *Car Wash* starts from a premise of promises unfulfilled—in this case the expectations for upward economic mobility sparked during the prosperity of the 1960s and stoked by the utopian goals of the civil rights movement and the War on Poverty. Stifled by the tedium, monotony, and the low pay they receive for their work, and divided from one another by jealousy, resentment, and petty rivalries, the characters in *Car Wash* plot an array of individual escapes. One assumes an Islamic name and presents himself as a black militant; another imagines himself as a comic book superhero. The white boss's son quotes Chairman Mao and convinces his father to let him work with the men, but they scorn his pathetic efforts to address them as fellow "revolutionaries." The script (by European American screenwriter Joel Schumacher) mocks all their efforts as foolish and self-deluding. Instead, it privileges the perspective of one character, a family man who pitches "constructive" ideas to the boss.[14] Denied the tragedy of *Blacula* as well as the heroism of *Buck and the Preacher*, the characters in *Car Wash* learn to accept their fate. Renouncing both individual and collective rebellion, the film implies that only obedience and resignation are appropriate responses to the social crisis that it addresses.

But if the generic disruption achieved in *Blacula* and *Buck and the Preacher* signals how racial identities can interrupt generic closure, *Car Wash* starts a new trend whereby the defeats suffered by aggrieved racial groups may have instructive power for the rest of society. Although the film's conclusions clearly seem headed in a conservative direction, *Car Wash*'s nonlinear uncentered story leads it to avoid the kind of narrative and ideological closure generally required of ensemble comedy films. Secure only in its cynicism, it ridicules the rebels and dreamers whose flamboyant actions engage our attentions most fully. Like the song by The Who that responds to the 1960s with a vow not to be fooled again, the conclusions of *Car Wash* seem motivated less by conservatism than by the protective cynicism of disillusioned idealists facing defeat. By 1975, the fiscal crisis of the state, deindustrialization, and economic restructuring had already started to reverse the modest gains made by African Americans and by low-income people until 1973. Factory shutdowns, cuts in social services, and a sharp decline in real wages undercut the infrastructure that sustained the civil rights movement, and increases in crime, delinquency, and drug addiction further fragmented the political and social fabric of African American communities. In its recognition of that reality and its resort to bemused detachment as a strategy for coping with rather than conquering community problems, *Car Wash* in both its content and form reflected the increasingly fragmented world inhabited by much of its audience.

The genre anxiety of the 1970s stemmed from a racial crisis so pervasive that it permeated films in genres usually isolated from political and social controversies. *Blacula, Buck and the Preacher*, and *Car Wash* challenged horror, western, and comedy genre conventions mostly because of the ways in which racial issues in the 1970s affected black people. But another set of films strengthened and reinforced genre conventions as a consequence of the racial crisis as seen by many whites in the early 1970s. In the wake of Richard Nixon's "southern strategy," which created an electoral majority by mobilizing white opposition to school busing, affirmative action, and other attempts at desegregation, urban crime films particularly took on a new tone and character.

Equally rooted in authoritarian and antiauthoritarian traditions, the urban crime drama has often been a contested zone of representation. It has been the domain of lone wolf private detectives as well as large efficient crime-fighting bureaucracies, a forum for physical combat as well as for individual intelligence. Crime films of the early 1970s, including Don Siegel's 1971 *Dirty Harry*, reflected "white anxiety" about the black self-activity and subjectivity of the 1960s as well as about economic stagnation by reconfiguring the genre to present authoritarian white male heroes as the only remedy for a disintegrating society.[15] Although the urban crime drama has a long history of both celebrating and implicating the rogue cop, in *Dirty Harry* the specter of social disorder inscribes within the text a celebration of the hero's sadism as a preferred alternative to that specter. Ambiguity disappears and sharp, simple binary oppositions distinguish the good guys from the bad guys. Crime comes from bad people, coddled by insufficiently authoritarian rules and regulations, whereas extralegal displays of force and violence by authority figures bring order and presumably justice. Gender serves as a major organizing principle in *Dirty Harry* as criminals and civil libertarians alike of both genders are coded as "female" forces undermining patriarchal power and its ability to protect the populace from harm.

With a voyeurism bordering on envy, *Dirty Harry* details the brutality and sadism of criminals in order to sanction violent revenge by the hero. But the scenario has racial implications as well. At a crucial moment in the film, Harry Callahan foils a bank robbery by a black gang. Firing his enormous .44 magnum, he disables the getaway car and wounds several of the robbers. Walking over to one lying on the pavement outside the bank, he stands over him as they both spot a gun lying near the robber's hand. The camera gives us Callahan's view of the black criminal cowering on the ground, looking up at him. A quick cut reverses the view and lets us look over the criminal's shoulder up the barrel of the officer's gun. Coolly taunting the robber, Harry softly raises the question whether he has expended all six bullets in his gun or whether he has one left. Confessing that he can't remember himself, Callahan reminds his victim that he is carrying the most powerful handgun in the world and encourages the thief to make a move for the gun on the ground, to ask himself, "Do I feel lucky?" Smiling, Harry asks softly, "Well, do you, punk?" When the criminal relents and lets Harry get to the gun, he tells the officer in exaggerated black dialect, "I gots to know." Harry raises his gun and points it at the wounded man on the ground. We see the criminal's mouth open wide and his eyes pop in terror as Callahan pulls the trigger, but there are no bullets left. Harry smiles triumphantly and walks away. We see the black man mutter "son

Dirty Harry (Clint Eastwood). *Dirty Harry*, Don Siegel. © Warner Bros., 1971.

of a bitch," and then the camera directs our gaze back to Callahan. Just in case we've missed the phallic power of this scene, Harry carries the two long guns by his sides, while a fire hydrant smashed by the foiled getaway car spews bursts of water up into the air.

To offset the racist pleasures provided by this scene, Siegel switches immediately to a hospital ward where a black doctor tends to Harry's wounds. We find that they are friends who grew up together, "absolving" Harry of any racist intentions in the previous scene. But Siegel takes an additional step. When Harry starts to tell the physician about his wound, the doctor asks affectionately, "Do I come down to the station and tell you how to beat a confession out of a prisoner?" We see that "good" blacks not only don't mind Callahan's actions, they approve of them.

The depiction of a black criminal cowering before white male authority in *Dirty Harry* brings to the screen an image prefigured by thousands of law and order speeches by politicians, but it also relies on our absolute faith in the rigidity of genre boundaries. Harry's ruthlessness and contempt for the law mirror that of the criminals; they are so evil, he must become just like them. Harry Callahan is a hero only because the strict binary oppositions of the urban crime drama establish him as one. But in order to win us to this position, Siegel cannot isolate the genre from events off-screen. He has to summon up the specter of social disintegration in order to have Harry protect us from it. At the conclusion of *Dirty Harry*, Callahan reenacts the "feel lucky, punk?" scene with an effeminate, long-haired serial killer. This time, the criminal resists and Harry kills him. But if our society needs Harry Callahan, it shows itself to have already failed as revealed in this film, just as much as in *Blacula, Buck and the Preacher*, and *Car Wash*.

Callahan needs the threat of social disintegration to justify his assertion of white male power. But more than race is at work here. The irreversible entry of women into the paid labor force, the reach and scope of popular culture, declining real wages that threaten the intergenerational transfer of wealth, and the emergence of a therapeutic and administrative bureaucracy of educators, psychologists, and social workers have all undermined the power of patriarchy in the U.S. since World War II. If the imagery summoned up by *Dirty Harry* evokes *The Birth of a Nation* in a manner similar to *Lean on Me*, it is not because patriarchy is triumphant and unquestioned, but rather that it must be affirmed all that much more emphatically in culture as it gradually loses its power in actual social life. Genre anxiety grows from social anxiety, but so might authoritarian genre renewal.

The directors of these 1970s films had different agendas, ideologies, and interests. None of them intended either a purely ideological statement or a self-conscious innovation in genre form. Each wanted to attract audiences, and they allowed social problems to seep into their cinematic representations because they thought that would help them do so. Whether acknowledged overtly or covertly, the social crises of the early 1970s suffused these films with an instability that posed serious challenges to traditional genre conventions.

By comparison, contemporary Hollywood offerings seem exceptionally conservative in both ideological content and aesthetic aspiration. But it would be a mistake to connect genre forms with social relations without examining how the commercial matrix in which Hollywood films are made helps determine their ideological and aesthetic dimensions. In his indispensable research on the motion picture industry, Thomas Schatz reveals that between 1969 and 1973 film studio profits fell drastically.[16] In addition, until 1974, Hollywood depended largely on receipts from ten thousand theaters in older downtown districts. Under those circumstances, experimental and innovative films might be worth backing, and motion pictures with appeal to African Americans in inner-city locations could play a significant role in studio earnings. But key changes in the film industry since the 1970s have worked against the production of films like *Blacula, Buck and the Preacher*, and *Car Wash*. Changes in tax laws in the mid-1970s discouraged investors from risking money on smaller films, driving them instead to seek secure returns from high budget "calculated blockbusters" featuring well-known stars and displaying potential for cross-marketing opportunities such as video games, toys, amusement park rides, and lunch boxes. Justin Wyatt identifies another important development at this time, the rise of the "high concept" film starting in the mid 1970s, by which he means films carefully crafted around style in production and designed to integrate the film with its marketing, what Wyatt calls "the look, the hook, and the book."[17] In addition, the construction of more than twelve thousand new theaters between 1975 and 1990, most of them in shopping malls located in white suburban neighborhoods, undercut the economic importance of black consumers to the industry.[18] The growing gap between income and wealth acquired by white people as opposed to people of color after 1973 disenfranchised large sections of the population as consumers while giving special place to others.

Many of the hits that emerged as blockbusters or high concept successes in the 1970s and 1980s stuck closely to genre conventions, in part to facilitate the strategy of marketing films to children as something new but selling those same films to parents as "nostalgia." *The Godfather* (1972), *Jaws* (1975), *The Exorcist* (1973), *Grease* (1978), *Saturday Night Fever* (1977), *Star Wars* (1977), and *Superman* (1978) among others suited the emerging financial structure of Hollywood better than small films with uncertain genre affiliations. As revenues from tape rentals emerged as an increasingly important source of profits, producers attempted to tailor their films to that market as well. Just as the content of D. W. Griffith's *Broken Blossoms* responded to the director's desire in 1919 to market films to an elite audience, today's films follow the forms that filmmakers believe will win favor among young white suburban viewers.[19] Richard Schickel complains that the need for blockbuster star vehicles with sideline product potential has led to a merger of genres, so that all Hollywood makes these days are comedies and action-adventure films.[20] If true, this would certainly prevent films displaying genre anxiety like those of the early 1970s from ever being made again.

Yet, it is clear that the new economic realities of filmmaking have not permanently stifled genre anxiety. Schatz notes that the emphasis on producing a few blockbusters reduces the supply and increases the demand for new films. Low-budget mainstream and independent filmmakers have taken advantage of that opportunity to produce films that challenge absolute generic boundaries. Independent filmmaking especially has opened up new vistas for directors and writers from aggrieved racial groups, and these artists often deploy recombinant and genre-bending forms. Social power relations bleed into their films in intentional and unintentional ways, evoking resemblances to the genre anxiety films of the early 1970s.

Hollywood's gender-racial-economic system has always been more than a matter of black and white; representations of Native Americans, Asian Americans, and Latinos have also been staples of generic oppositions. When filmmakers from those communities told their own stories in the 1970s and 1980s, they often engaged generic forms and characters as stereotypes that needed to be displaced in order to allow for the emergence of new images and identities on- and off-screen.

For example, Wayne Wang's low-budget 1982 film, *Chan Is Missing*, appears to be a mystery, but instead uses the conventions of the mystery genre to explore issues about identity among Chinese Americans in San Francisco. "I'm no Charlie Chan," the narrator admits at one point, making reference to the screen detective who defined so many stereotypes of Asian Americans for film audiences. Throughout the film, Wang highlights the disparity between Hollywood images of Chinese Americans and their lived experience. In searching for the disappeared Mr. Chan, the heroes make their way through a Chinatown that resists easy characterization. The Chinese Americans in this film are divided by politics, age, gender, consumer tastes, and values. Mr. Chan is missing, but so is Charlie Chan. Instead, the community is made up of complex and complicated characters—a Chinese man who dances to mariachi music at a Filipino senior citizens' center, a cook who drinks milk and wears a

"Samurai Night Fever" T-shirt, a taxi driver who imitates Richard Pryor and Mexican American gang members. The community is so composite that no picture can capture it accurately, certainly not the picture established in Hollywood's generic conventions. "I have Chan's picture," the narrator tells us at the film's conclusion, "but I still don't know what he looks like."

Similarly, Cheech Marin's 1987 *Born in East L.A.* engages with genre conventions only to call them into question. The film appears to be a comedy built around yet another version of the dope-smoking Chicano hustler that Marin has played throughout his comedy career. Yet in this film, the comedy takes a back seat to an inquiry into the meaning of the border for Mexicans and Chicanos, into Anglo insistence on seeing Chicanos as foreign, and on the plight of undocumented workers trying to enter the U.S. Like Wang, Marin makes an affectionate film about an ethnic group without essentializing them. The lead character speaks German better than Spanish, doesn't know why his community celebrates *Cinco de Mayo*, and only grudgingly acknowledges his ties to people from Mexico.

Marin also depicts genre conventions in order to subvert them. He presents stereotypical representations of Chicano identity that originated in many films about gangs and barrio life, but parodies them at the same time. As Rosa Linda Fregoso notes, he draws upon "insider" knowledge of the parodic tradition of Mexican comedians Tin Tan and Cantinflas to insert a sense of shared history and social criticism into what might otherwise seem a simple stereotype.[21] At the same time, his title and title song parody Bruce Springsteen's "Born in the USA," satirizing national identity on both sides of the border. In addition, through a scene where he teaches a group of Asian immigrants how to pass as Chicanos, he reveals the constructed nature of Chicano stereotypes.

Similarly, Jonathan Wacks's 1989 *Powwow Highway* combines the western, the social problem film, and the caper comedy into a new hybrid that also reveals ethnic identity to be unstable, constructed, contested, and composite. Although not made by Native Americans, its images and icons evoke the history of Hollywood's Indians only to demonstrate their inadequacy. Instead, we find that Native Americans are both united by a common history and divided by their responses to it, that social change requires diverse visions that address the entire community, and that just as some Native Americans can be villains, some white Americans can be allies to the Native American cause.

During the 1970s, films displaying genre anxiety gestured occasionally toward the growing perception that race in America did not just entail a binary opposition between black and white. Michael Schultz's *Which Way Is Up?* (1977), for example, depicted Richard Pryor as a black farmworker in the midst of militant Chicanos. In the 1980s and 1990s, filmmakers from aggrieved racial groups, including Wang, Marin, and Spike Lee, have emphasized the importance of intercultural communication and conflict, of recognizing the poly-lateral dimensions of racism and antiracism.

There can be no direct correspondence between political activity in any given era and aesthetic representations. No artistic form can remedy social problems all by itself, just as no movement for social change can guarantee a concomitant change in artistic representation. Challenges to generic conventions often serve emancipatory ends; renewals of generic conventions often signal social conservatism. But genre anxiety is more of a symptom than a critique; it can be a stimulus to social activism but not a substitute for it. Similarly, renewals of genre conventions signal a search for order in an unstable world. They may lead to reactionary politics, but at the same time they also display the anguish that people feel as they try to live what Robert Warshow described as the lives that happen to be open to them. They reflect the demands of marketers and the needs of investors but also the uncertainty and self-doubt of a society unable to face the political and social inequalities generated by the new economic realities of deindustrialization and economic restructuring.

Struggles over resources and power are always implicated in cultural stories. Instabilities in social life can never be divorced completely from aesthetic choices. Anxieties and tremors in generic forms do not necessarily signal social transformation, but they may provide the preconditions for it. Just as durable as the generic forms they challenge, efforts to alter genre conventions will continue as long as ordinary people discern the disparity between their aspirations for meaningful connection to other people and the poisonous legacies of hierarchy and exploitation that pervade our shared social life.

Notes

1. For the epigraphs, see Michael Ryan and Douglas Kellner, *Camera Politica: The Politics and Ideology of Contemporary Hollywood Film* (Bloomington:

Indiana University Press, 1988), 70; Paula Rabinowitz, *Labor and Desire: Women's Revolutionary Fiction in Depression America* (Chapel Hill: University of North Carolina Press, 1991), 66.

2. Jacques Derrida, "The Law of Genre," *Glyph* 7 (1980): 202–3.

3. Nick Browne, "Race: The Political Unconscious in American Film," *East-West Film Journal* 6, no. 1 (January 1992): 10.

4. See Nick Browne's important argument about how heterosexual coupling between white men and "nonwhite" women forms a semiotic subtext for this system. Ibid., 5–16.

5. James Baldwin, *The Devil Finds Work* (New York: Dell, 1990), 53.

6. Herman Gray, presentation at the "Emerging Majority or Warring Minorities" conference, Santa Cruz, California. March 5, 1994.

7. Michael Rogin, *Ronald Reagan, the Movie: And Other Episodes in Political Demonology* (Berkeley: University of California Press, 1987).

8. Baldwin, *The Devil Finds Work*, 61.

9. Rob Walser, *Running with the Devil* (Hanover: Wesleyan / University Press of New England), 1993.

10. William Howze, "John Ford's Celluloid Canvas," *Southwest Media Review* 3 (1985): 20–25.

11. Frank Krutnick, *In a Lonely Street* (London: Routledge, 1993), 88.

12. Will Wright, *Sixguns and Society* (Berkeley: University of California Press, 1976); Diane Waldman, " 'At Last I Can Tell It to Someone': Feminine Point of View and Subjectivity in the Gothic Romance Film of the 1940s," *Cinema Journal* 23, no. 2: 29–40; Andrea Walsh, *Women's Film and Female Experience* (New York: Praeger, 1984); Jonathan Munby, "Screening Crime in the U.S.A., 1929–1958: From Hays Code to HUAC; from *Little Caesar* to *Touch of Evil*," (Ph.D. diss., University of Minnesota, 1995).

13. Mark A. Reid, *Redefining Black Film* (Berkeley: University of California Press, 1993), 30, 31.

14. For conflicting interpretations of *Car Wash*, see Ryan and Kellner, *Camera Politica*, 124, and ibid., 30–31.

15. I first encountered this thesis in Ryan and Kellner, *Camera Politica*, 46.

16. Thomas Schatz, "The New Hollywood," 15.

17. Justin Wyatt, *High Concept: Movies and Marketing in Hollywood* (Austin: University of Texas Press, 1994), 21.

18. Schatz, "The New Hollywood," 20.

19. John Kuo Wei Tchen, "Modernizing White Patriarchy: Re-Viewing D. W. Griffith's Broken Blossoms," in *Moving the Image*, ed. Russell Leong (Los Angeles: University of California at Los Angeles Asian American Studies Center, 1991), 256.

20. Richard Schickel quoted in Schatz, "The New Hollywood," 33.

21. Rosa Linda Fregoso, "Born in East L.A. and the Politics of Representation," *Cultural Studies* 4, no. 3 (1990): 264–280.

Monster Roundup

Reintegrating the Horror Genre

DAVID J. RUSSELL

> *By the Ancients monsters are ascribed to depraved conceptions;*
> *and are defined to bee excursions of nature, which are vitious one*
> *of these foure wayes: In figure, situation, magnitude, or number.*
> John Sadler, 1636

Despite the easy recognition and popularity of modern horror movies with audiences and critics, the exact boundaries of their collective definition as a genre have become increasingly difficult to discern.[1] Horror's generic legibility nowadays endures an incessant three-front assault: first, as a result of its formal tendency to unceasingly mutate as an entertainment type defined by shock and novelty; second, as a consequence of the recognition of horror's potential social uses that has inspired an increase in and diversification of critical attention; and, third, a widespread critical indifference to and suspicion of a working definition of the genre as if a consistent critical vocabulary might be, somehow, a bad thing.

Jeffrey Sconce delineates his critical hesitation in this way:

What is at stake in valuing one film over another, or even in attempting to define systematically a group of films, is a struggle over cultural meaning and power. Just as representation, enunciation, and identification are political processes, so too are the cultural classifications and evaluation of texts. To say one film is "good" horror and the other is not, or even to say that one film *is* horror and the other is not, presents a situation where a critic occupying a certain social and cultural position passes judgement on the viewing experiences and values of other social groups.[2]

Whereas Sconce is quite right to point out that there is potential danger in "occupying" positions staked out by "other social groups," he seems to imply that any general (or generic) description or debate concerning horror as genre is impossible. The problem is that critics with this view, in avoiding the problem of deciding whether "one film *is* horror and the other is not," are effectively disabled as genre critics whose fundamental work is to make such distinctions.

For any film genre critic, horror movies (or "monster movies," as I prefer to label them) might alternatively stimulate or stymie classification efforts. On the one hand, the horror genre presents a weird zoo of tantalizing and bizarre imagery and themes that begs for a sane and sensible straightening out by a knowing critic (perhaps, with a lucid system of classifying cages that might corral such feral film fauna once and for all.) Over time, complex movie monster "eco-systems" (wildly spawned from the verdant jungles of film production studios) have continuously produced strange breeds of characters and stories (*Dracula, The Wolfman, Frankenstein*), which astute genre critics have often named, enumerated, and organized by character type (vampire, werewolf, monster), story and theme (magic, monster, manufactured), and so on.

More often, however, clear classification is confounded by the bewildering chaos and number of movie monsters appearing in all their confounding shapes and complicated evolutions. Because horror filmmakers innovate in extremis in order to profitably startle and amaze their intended audience, any rules regulating the "breeding" of movie monsters inevitably become counterproductive. This willy-nilly forging of individual movie monsters has resulted in a horror genre that resembles less a legible generic system than merely a "bunch of monsters" strewn across a disconnected series of film texts.[3]

Moreover, given the apparently uncontrollable flux and violence of the genre in its contemporary state, the appeal of a cool classical classification seems pitted against the aims of the inherently transgressive film group that it seeks to define. Acknowledging this dilemma, there has even developed a polarization among many horror critics that may be loosely identified as the *subjectivist* and *objectivist* camps. The objectivists generally aspire toward a totalizing description of the genre usually based in the formulation of clearly defined categories of iconography, content, or themes. In contrast, the subjectivists usually prefer a looser definition of formal elements and, instead, focus on the genre's less tangible emotional effects.

Subjectivists also generally downplay the function of visual conventions and iconographic elements (including types of monsters) and favor consideration of single or small groups of horror films in terms of the psychological effects that such films set in motion for the audience. The emotional effects of terror, horror, suspense, and, by extension, desire, perverse curiosity, and sexualized looking tend to emerge as the only clearly identified (and identifiable) consistent features of a genre otherwise defined as defiantly protean.

Aside from the tautological assertion that "horror movies horrify," the obvious drawback of the subjectivist approach is that by classifying horror films (singly or otherwise) merely in terms of fleeting emotional effects ends up reifying the audience as, to a large degree, fixed. One can presume that actual emotional responses must change significantly not only during the course of a film's life but with each audience. What might be genuinely frightening to one audience, or what might have seemed frightening at the time of a film's initial release, may appear for someone else, elsewhere or later on, as trite, stale, confusing, or even unintentionally funny.[4]

Alternatively, the more formal objectivist approach may show brave attempts to clearly map out the complex landscape of the horror genre in its entirety but has more often resulted in the devising of a limited and limiting range of nominative categories at once overly rigid and structurally disconnected. In 1954 William Everson stated with some assurance that "all horror films fall into one of seven categories. In the order of most frequent usage these are: scientific experiments; monsters; vampirism and lycanthropy; voodoo; 'old house'; necromancy and diabolism; ghosts and apparitions; and an unclassifiable group that includes 'stunt' thrillers and such infrequent near-spectacles as *The Phantom of the Opera*."[5] Aside from its uncanny resemblance to one of Jorge Luis Borges's imaginary encyclopedias, Everson's clearly outdated horror movie taxonomy illustrates many of the problems of later classifying systems that also take the form of thematic lists.[6] Though such generic filing systems often provide a method for pigeonholing horror films, they can be seriously limiting in several crucial ways.

Using Everson's list here as illustration, it is obvious that descriptive pigeonholing cannot account accurately for instances of potential thematic overlap among the given categories. For instance, hypothetically proposing the category of *undead* ends up (con)fusing at least four of Everson's given categories: *vampirism, voodoo, necromancy*, and *ghosts*. His system likewise blurs distinctions between horror and other related genres; how, for instance, can one distinguish Everson's *scientific experi-*

ments as belonging to the horror genre and not to science fiction (or even science-themed biopics or docudramas?) And how does one tell *old house* apart from mere suspense or melodrama?

Finally, the fixed nature of Everson's seven categories cannot anticipate possible and potential variations such as horror parody and horror comedies or, for that matter, any other potential (and in fact, now existing) intergeneric hybrids such as combat horror, horror musicals, romance horror, and horror westerns.[7] Likewise, the system is unable to anticipate the invention of character variations such as hybrid creatures like Freddy Krueger, who is a complex combination of demon, vampire, ghost, shapeshifter, and psychokiller.[8] Freddy, I suppose, would have to be placed in Everson's necessarily overly elastic category of *monsters*. However, practically every such organizational label system conceived by subsequent horror genre critics has remained a mere laundry list in some way. Random listmaking often betrays an inability to coordinate the various pieces of descriptive labeling into a coherent critical entity that may be convincingly called the "horror genre." This is the central weakness of horror film criticism to date.

Occasional efforts have also been made to combine critical attention both to issues of affect (defined in terms of viewer response or with reference to depth psychology) with content-oriented thematic or iconographic organizations of films and, by doing so, to cross-index the concerns of both the subjectivist and objectivist critical camps. Nöel Carroll's most recent attempt at a comprehensive analysis of the horror genre (*Philosophy of Horror*, 1990) proposes a basic formula that handily describes the latent processes presumed to govern movie monster creation. He proposes a basic formula of the "bio-physics" of artistic fusion and fission from which all monster characters, in some way, are generated. His "biological metaphorical" approach combines a description of the inherently disgusting materiality of the monster with the revulsion audiences feel when looking at it. For Carroll, who grounds his observations in Mary Douglas's classic anthropological study *Purity and Danger* (1966), audience (and, by extension, cultural) reactions to the sight of movie monsters relate, in a more socially pervasive sense, to deeply internalized fears concerning cultural disorder (or "dirt"), which the monster allegorically represents. Carroll's system, therefore, attempts to combine attention to the genre's formal elements ("monster physics") with an account of its cultural significance and affectivity.

Somewhat similarly, Robin Wood's seminal essay on the horror genre ("An Introduction to the American Horror Film," 1979) posits a correlation between a range of specific horror movie themes and monster types that he labels *Monster as psychopath, revenge of Nature, Satanism, Terrible Child,* and *cannibalism.*[9] The audience relates these horrific filmic entities to various anxiety-provoking ideological categories already culturally in place: social Others identified by Wood as *other people, Woman, the proletariat, Other cultures, ethnic groups, alternative politics and ideologies, deviations from sexual norms,* and *children.*[10]

Essentially, Wood defines the horror film genre in terms of its social function. The genre mediates between culture and ideology through an indirect mode of representation that formulates the tensions between the demands on the individual imposed by social order (as manifested through external social oppression) and by personal desire (internally held in check by emotional repression.) In Wood's estimation, horror films can function to reenact and reaffirm social repression and contain disorder and violence by eliminating the monster, which symbolically stands in for social disorder and rampant desire (as exemplified in so-called reactionary horror films).[11] Yet Otherness itself expressed through the horror film and its monsters may also serve to point to the breakdown and failure of repression as symptomatically expressed through a realization of unconscious desire for which the monster acts as a medium.

Though Wood and Carroll both propose complex analytical systems for the entire horror genre, offering clear definitions for both its formal and ideological functions, they nonetheless perpetuate several problems that occur in other classification systems. For Wood, the list is an obvious problem, which he resolves by conflating the related but certainly not identical themes of (cultural) monsters and (social) Others and boiling them down into a single condensed and overarching theme of politicized and homogenized sexual Otherness. His argument ends up proposing a libidinal "base metaphor" for horror that is overly reductive and, ultimately, too literal even by Freudian standards. Wood's Other-based model, as Ed Lowry has observed, also inadequately distinguishes the horror genre from other film genres where Otherness noticeably abounds (for example, established genres such as westerns, war films, comedies, melodramas, and the like.)[12] His overly rigid reliance on ideological causality (combined with libidinal determinism) fuses a complex constellation of generic elements into a single thematic trope (sexual Otherness), making it difficult to constructively apply his system beyond its overt ideological purposes.

Carroll equivocates even more than Wood in his claim to explain and define the horror genre in its entirety. Though much of Carroll's system remains compelling, it seriously falters in its blanket omission of an entire obvious subcategory of horror: the psychokiller horror film. His reliance on "fantastic biology" privileges mere visual extraordinariness as the sole defining trope for all monster characters, a descriptive rigidity that finally leads Carroll to observe, "Consider the case of Hitchcock's *Psycho*. One could imagine the claim that it ought to be regarded as an example of horror. But, of course, my theory does not count it as such, because Norman Bates is not a monster. He is a schizophrenic." [13] Though Carroll goes to great lengths to rationalize this astonishing elision of psycho horror, his system cannot be considered comprehensive if it fails to include what everyone else would indisputably define as a horror film (*Halloween, Friday the 13th,* and *The Texas Chainsaw Massacre* go entirely unmentioned in his book.)

Whereas Wood's model may be faulted for its conflation of formal variety into an external yet controlling formula of Otherness and unconscious activity, Carroll resolves the contradictions in his system by throwing out the contrary portions. Though Wood's and Carroll's studies still stand as the most thorough (and, arguably, the best) attempts so far to comprehensively delineate the horror genre, such a system, I propose, may be still further refined. [14]

As a beginning premise, there appears a general agreement among most horror critics that Robin Wood's basic formula for the horror genre, "normality is threatened by the monster," [15] is precisely appropriate (if variously put.) Michael Armstrong writes, "All horror films are based upon fear of the unknown." [16] Andrew Tudor states that "the 'threat' is the central feature of the horror movie narrative." [17] Even Noël Carroll avers that "humans regard the monster they meet as abnormal, as disturbances of the natural order." [18] Indeed, Wood's basic formula, as these and other critics seem to agree, has an advantage of focus and concision and, I would add, provides the basis for further construction of a new classification system.

Wood's formula breaks down easily into three basic constituents: *normality, threat,* and the *monster.* Wood defines *normality* as the ideological space where social order enacts itself and where the *threat* is identified as any person, thing, or action transgressing or refusing this social order—a position taken up in horror films by the *monster. Monster,* then, becomes contrasted to an insider-dominated normality facing an externalized threat (from an outsider-dominated abnormality), appearing in monster form as the material mediator of this internal-external

Freddy Krueger (Robert Englund). *Nightmare on Elm Street* series, 1984–1989.

antagonism. As formally represented, the monster may then be eradicated in order to abolish abnormality and restore order (normality).

However, this ideological formula can be expanded to include formal elements not stressed in Wood's essentially political account but that are no less important to genre description. First, the term *normality* may be used to refer not just to actual social and ideological effects (expressed through or as culture) but also to elements as formally represented in a work of fiction. *Normality* can be compared to *realism* (as in the film's "reality effect") with reference to the familiar traditional and pervasive aims of cinematic realism dominating most Hollywood filmmaking. Though horror films are themselves generally defined by their fantastical visual elements (especially the monsters), horror films are composed with stylistic elements that comprise fictional contemporary narrative cinema in general (spatial construction, invisible continuity editing, psychologically developed characters, and so forth.) What distinguishes the horror film is that the appearance of the overtly unreal monster directly challenges and perturbs the film's virtual construction and maintenance of a cinematic reality effect.

With reference to the literary genre of the fantastic, Rosemary Jackson writes, "Fantastic narratives confound elements of both the marvelous and the mimetic. They assert that what they are telling is real—relying upon all the conventions of realistic fiction to do so—and then they proceed to break that assumption of realism by introducing what—within those terms—is manifestly unreal." [19] In this sense, horror movie *normality* refers not only to social and cultural conventions recognized by the viewer as factually "real" but, more importantly here, to the artistic simulation of reality fashioned through conventions of realistic narration and cinematic trompe l'oeil, a "virtual reality" disrupted (or interrupted) by the intrusion of a patently unreal monster.

This "perturbed realism" is clearly manifested in the way space is handled in most horror movies. The story will promise a "real" (unthreatened) space, identified with and inhabited by the *normal* characters, which becomes violently disrupted whenever the monster figure enters the frame via a suspenseful alternation of the monster's on-screen presence and absence. Of this, Pascal Bonitzer writes,

filmic space is divided between two fields: on-screen space and off-screen space; we could say between specular and blind space. . . . Off-screen space, blind space, is everything that moves (or wriggles) outside or under the surface of things. . . . The point of horror resides in the blind space. In other words, if film produces, as it is said to do, a strong impression of reality, it is less because of photographic realism and movement than because it presents a dialectic between these two spaces (or fields.) [20]

Though Bonitzer's analysis does not necessitate the presence of an explicitly fantastical monster (for example, he illustrates his observations via reference to the "realistic" shark in *Jaws*), the filmic existence of the monster within the fiction nonetheless constitutes an attack on normality perceived as actuality (or truth) by the viewer. To sustain an enjoyable engagement with the film, the monster becomes accepted by the audience as real and presents to it a fictional-ontological or "pseudo-ontic" challenge to the more believable simulation of reality constructed through photographic realism and cinematic movement. The challenge to the film's pseudoreality presents an ontological paradox (perceived as threatening) resolved only by the monster's eventual elimination from (or, less often, incorporation into) normal space. It is the unacceptable presence of the unreal monster within an otherwise realistic frame that constitutes the basic instability within the horror genre (the "threat to normality") and provides the essential terms for the genre's comprehensive definition.

The present horror canon suggests only a few ways that monster characters can be categorically defined through their varying threats to film's distinctive mode of realism. Horror critics have already suggested typologies that reduce the genre to a handful of major film groups. Roy Huss and T. J. Ross have proposed the terms *Gothic Horror, Monster Terror*, and *Psychological Thriller* as the horror genre's three basic subcategories.[21] Likewise, Charles Derry and Bruce Kawin both break down the horror genre into three basic subgroups (Derry's *horror of personality, horror of Armageddon*, and *horror of the demonic*, and Kawin's *monster stories, supernatural stories*, and *psychosis stories*), whereas Will H. Rockett adds an additional group to these other tripartite patterns with his four groups: *slasher, bad science, supranatural*, and *supernatural.*[22]

These subcategorizing sets share a fairly consistent and manageable ensemble of subgroups that define the horror genre comprehensively and, helpful to our purposes, neatly correspond to the following three designations: the *real*, the *unreal*, and the *part-real* (or, alternatively stated, the *possible*, the *impossible*, and the *improbable*.) These three conditions likewise encompass all of the possible attitudes monsters may take in any horror film toward normal (pseudo-ontic) space.

The taxonomy for the horror genre I propose here shows a debt and resemblance to these other systems. But these other taxonomies are essentially formal and stylistic and lack reference to the forms of realism, what I call "pseudo-onticity," discussed here: *real, unreal*, and *part-real*. Some types of monsters may be explained as *"real"* as they originate wholly from within the realistic space of the film as this space conforms to the actual space inhabited by the audience watching the film. Such monsters are produced from and by normality in that they are not remarkable in any physical sense. Their threat to normality is manifested solely through abnormal behavior challenging the rules of social regulation through "monstrous" and transgressive behavior. Here, we locate human monsters who are constitutionally natural (ontologically speaking) but who exhibit dangerous and threatening behavior and, thus, appear to any on-screen normal character (and to most viewers) as real "monsters": psychokillers, maniacs, stalkers, slashers, and the like. Such monsters will be classified and labeled by the present system as *deviant*: monsters emerging from within normal space and threatening that space primarily through abnormal or "off course" behavior.

The second category of monsters is more explicitly *unreal* and originates from completely outside any recognizable frames of normal mundane reality. Their on-screen existence is attributable to magical origins completely at odds with known nature, and such abnormal origins are usually underscored by unnatural powers (such as sorcery, possession, resurrection, and so forth.) These unreal monsters contradict in every way the pseudo-ontic space of reality established on-screen and enter this space in order to occupy the same space as normal characters and settings only through direct invasion or the possession of normality's natural hosts. Thus they usher the metaphysical realm into the physical world. Such monsters will be classified here as *supernatural* and include creatures such as vampires, ghosts, witches and sorcerers, demons, and so forth.

Third and finally, types of monsters may be *part-real*, that is, partially related to normal space (as physical monsters) but having little or no relation to nature as "normally" experienced. Such nonquotidian monsters (monsters with unusual powers or origins) represent the transgressive and hypothetical permeability and weaknesses of those boundaries separating secure normal reality from unstable abnormal unreality. Their existence can be explained only by stretching the rules of everyday experience otherwise regulating the film's realistic (rule-bound) world. Such monsters—whose monstrous physical abnormality is posed in a tense and approximate juxtaposition to the familiar universe—will be classified here as *paranatural* and will include monsters from outer space, genetic mutations, bad science, technological monsters, creatures from other dimensions, and so forth.

To clarify this relationship of the three proposed monster groups to a given horror film's simulation of reality—its pseudo-ontic universe— these monster groups may be further defined according to their differing relationships to mortality (in other words, how they are finally eliminated from the narrative.) In the real world, all living creatures must reproduce or face extinction. In the traditional horror film, however, "reproduction" by the monster must be averted for the sake of normality and curtailed in order for the monstrous threat to be abolished in the service of narrative closure. In view of its mortality or immortality, each type of monster as defined previously relates to this formula (dangerous multiplication versus restorative containment) in three different ways. Each highlights the differing pseudo-ontic conventions governing these three monster groups.

The reproducibility of the first type of monster is the most familiar and, pursuant to its transgressive function, likewise the most obscene. *Deviant* monsters (being human) are always associated with natural, though dangerously twisted, modes of sexual behavior (for instance, witness the ubiquitous rape theme in the psychokiller subgenre), and their derangement is frequently and explicitly associated with degenerated or arrested sexual development (manifested in the voyeurism and stalking that usually precedes their individual murder sprees.) At the same time, deviant monsters can always be killed in familiar ways—such as by conventional weaponry—and are, therefore, explicitly shown to be mortal beings.

In contrast, *supernatural* monsters are always defined as "immortal." Even when their abnormal presence becomes manifested through a normal human host (as with demonic possession) or as former humans who have returned from the dead (as with vampires or ghosts), the ultimate destruction of the monster usually takes the form of the expulsion of an immortal presence from a mortal frame (such as when exorcism is used to evacuate demons or religious paraphernalia is used to end a vampiric curse.) For this reason, supernatural reproducibility is rarely related to sexual reproduction per se but is more often akin to a kind of infection (as in curses, possession, and the vampire's bite) that must be cured via magical means.

Finally, *paranatural* monsters may themselves originate from an "unknown" space and spread through "infection" (like supernatural types), but they nonetheless share many characteristics with their deviant cousins, insofar as they are always permanently killable with conventional weaponry. These monsters, however strange in appearance, are always explicitly mortal but enter normal space from an abnormal origin that bars concourse with humans except as alien invaders.[23]

The three basic categories of film monsters proposed here—*deviant, supernatural,* and *paranatural*—can be further illustrated through their three different but related spatial relationships to the pseudo-ontic space of the real as shown in figure 8. This simple yet coherent pattern organizing the three basic monster types previously defined suggests a coherency applicable to the entire horror genre.

Such a model does have evident limitations. First, the general nature of the scheme becomes useful only when it addresses specific film ex-

Figure 8

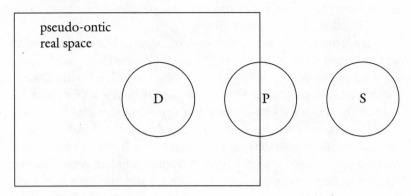

D = DEVIANT
P = PARANATURAL
S = SUPERNATURAL

amples. Second, some monsters obviously do not conform exactly to the space provided for them within one of the three designated categories.[24] Potential contradictions between the grouping system and the film examples require the possibility of adjustments at the level of the system to ensure that it remains flexible enough to anticipate challenges of unusual, but actual, examples. Third, the taxonomy should also be able to quantify film examples and account for the varying frequencies with which films populate one category or another (accounting for the distinction between common and rare movie monster types and their specific appearances.) Fourth and finally, the system should, in some way, be able to also address relevant social and cultural contexts so that the classifying system does not stall at the level of a purely formal description.

Let's consider these requirements in turn. First, the need to address existing individual film examples may be met by drawing on the previously mentioned "zoo model" or biological metaphor for classifying monster characters. This taxonomy may be permitted to mimic, to a certain degree, classifying systems employed to organize animals in the real world. In proposing this analogy, in spite of its general lack of popularity amongst some classification theorists, I am quick to add that this biological metaphor should remain simple and need not be scrutinized in terms of a capacity to account for every leg and bone of the

Figure 9

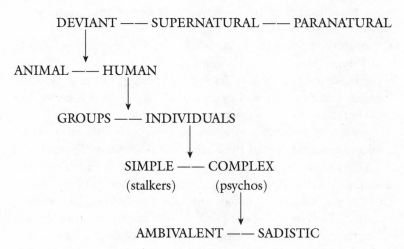

cinematic creatures it seeks to organize.[25] Conforming to a misplaced ideal of (pseudo)scientific exactness is certainly too confining for this (or any other) generic system addressing the looser processes of cultural creation.

Here, I use a more general classifying strategy to focus on the organization and interrelationships of characteristics and functions of monster types. Such general traits may be arranged along a descending sequence that proceeds with developing specificity until relevant film examples start to become recognizable under the given label. Taking as example the *deviant* main category (physically natural monsters), the lineage may proceed as shown in figure 9.

This "tree diagram" starts with a basic definition for the *deviant* group (as distinguished from the other main categories appearing at the top only) and proceeds through a descending order of alternating options in which "quantity" declines toward "quality" (or species.) This sequence then concludes with a category label corresponding with more or less precision to recognizable and specific film examples. The label *deviant human individual complex ambivalent* summarily describes psychologically troubled horror movie characters that have appeared in films like *Psycho* (1960), *Peeping Tom* (1960), *Repulsion* (1965), *Don't Go in the House* (1980), and a host of others. Alternatively, the sequence *deviant human individual complex sadistic* identifies somewhat similar yet psychopathically guiltless characters such as Jon Ryder in *The Hitcher* (1986), Hannibal Lecter in *The Silence of the Lambs* (1991), and Manny Coto's *Dr. Giggles* (1992).

Though this tree diagram method can usefully illustrate one strain of the *deviant* main category, as a comprehensive mapping strategy, tree diagramming has a major flaw. Tracing at once its many branches would ultimately result in a diagram so entangled that it would become difficult, if not impossible, to show in any manageable form.

However, under a given main category, subcategories can be composed and arranged around a repeating and descending tripartite routine. Drawing on the *deviant* category as illustration, this alternative pattern of subcategorical grouping is shown in figure 10 (with relevant film examples included). Though I use only the *deviant* category here to partially illustrate the horror genre in toto, the system works equally well for the remaining main categories (*supernatural* and *paranatural*), which a lengthier study demonstrates.[26] However, even outlined here in part and using only one of the three main categories, additional pitfalls of this classifying strategy may still be readily apparent to the discerning reader.

First, obviously important film elements are not really addressable within the terms of this character-based descriptive taxonomy. Falling out of the classifying equation are elements such as issues of authorship and style, plot structure, setting, the presence of nonmonster characters (such as heroes and victims), minor iconographic elements within the mise-en-scène (costume, weapons, vehicles, and so on), as well as lighting, framing, editing, sound, and so forth. Attempts to critically orchestrate at once this complex constellation of fundamental film elements have stymied even the most sophisticated of classifying systems, let alone one that addresses a class of films as protean as horror and monster movies.

Such complications, however, do not fundamentally contradict this taxonomy's concern with the establishment of pseudo-ontic space and its violation by the monster character as a mode of generic grouping. Further, the individual citation of such basic filmic elements, as they relate to the monster types organized here, reveals patterns entirely consistent with the positioning of specific films within the taxonomy's categorical system. For example, Vera Dika's study of the "stalker film" focuses particularly on this subgenre's narrative structure; but the monsters contained within these plot structures are entirely congruent with this system's *single deviant: robot* (I.A.2) subcategory as proposed

Figure 10

I. DEVIANT: natural monsters
  A. SINGLE DEVIANTS: human monsters acting as individuals
    1. LUSTMORD: ambivalent obsessionals; schizophrenics; serial murderers; Oedipal psychos
        FILMS: *Psycho, Repulsion, Manhunter, Henry: Portrait of a Serial Killer, White of the Eye*, etc.
    2. ROBOT: instinctual compulsives; mass murderers; rampaging killers; stalkers
        FILMS: *Halloween, Friday the 13th, Slumber Party Massacre, Silent Night, Deadly Night*, etc.
    3. SADIST: self-conscious psychopaths; killer geniuses
        FILMS: *Dressed to Kill, The Hitcher, The Silence of the Lambs, White of the Eye*, etc.
  B. GROUP DEVIANTS/FERAL FAMILIES: human monsters acting in groups
    1. CRIMINAL FAMILY: loose aggregate of criminal or countercultural types; rape/revenge dramas
        FILMS: *Last House on the Left, I Spit on Your Grave, Ms. 45*, etc.
    2. DEGENERATE FAMILY: isolated inbred family; cannibals
        FILMS: *2000 Maniacs, The Texas Chain Saw Massacre, Mother's Day, The People Under the Stairs*, etc.
    3. NEO-PRIMITIVE FAMILY: regressive isolated clans; religious or countercultural cults
        FILMS: *The Wicker Man, The Hills Have Eyes, Deadly Blessing*, etc.
  C. DEVIANT NATURE: naturally occurring errant animals
    1. SINGLE/LONE SHARK: single rogue animals
        FILMS: *Jaws, Cujo, Razorback*, etc.
    2. SWARM: leaderless nondistinct animal groups
        FILMS: *Wolfen, Frogs, In the Shadow of Kilimanjaro, Nightwing*, etc.
    3. TEAM: animal groups led by single rogue animals
        FILMS: *Willard, Arachnophobia*, etc.

---

in figure 10.[27] Dika's work is a close analysis of the plot structure of films featuring a monster type—as defined by this taxonomy. Likewise, Carol Clover's identification of the "final girl" character addresses almost exclusively *single deviant* (I.A) type monsters (especially *robots*), which are, again, clearly addressable through our taxonomy.[28]

Another, different problem occurs with the potential elision of important secondary characteristics pertaining to individual monsters. For example, though the deviant monster's natural status (human or animal), numerical appearance (individual or group), and presumed motivation for violence (compulsive or decisive) are all explicitly covered in figure 10, locating additional character traits appears uncertain: the deviant's national origin (for example, German psychokillers like Karl Gunther in *Crawlspace* [1986]); economic class (the blue collar types in *Henry: Portrait of a Serial Killer* [1989] as opposed to the white-collar professional psychiatrist Hannibal Lecter); ethnicity (the black supernatural psychokiller *Candyman* [1992]); gender (the female "stalkers" in *Ms. 45* [1980], *Lipstick* [1976], and *Basic Instinct* [1992]); sexual orientation (crossdressing in *Psycho, Dressed to Kill* [1980], and *The Silence of the Lambs*); and so forth.[29] Such characteristics are crucial to the analysis of any given monster but have frequently overpowered the interests of many horror film critics who prefer to examine such factors outside of the considerations of the wider horror film system. For an analysis of genre, such secondary specific characteristics remain addressable either through single film analysis or via a further subcategorization of the already given monster types (for example, further classifying *sadists* by gender or *lustmords* as straight or gay).

A more troubling problem lies in complex or overlapping variations of monster characters that straddle more than one main category. For instance, the deviant film *Willard* (1971) contains both a lustmord (I.A.1) and an intelligent rat-led team (I.C.3). *The Silence of the Lambs* features both a lustmord in the troubled "tailor" Jame Gumb, and a sadist (I.A.3) in Hannibal "the cannibal" Lecter. *Henry: Portrait of a Serial Killer* presents team serial killers in the characters Henry and Otis, who would be more accurately defined as two lustmords rather than as a true criminal family (I.B.1). Though multiple character types may occur within the same film, they do not constitute a contradiction of the taxonomy but a combination of its elements.

Aside from examples already noted in the *deviant* category, "cross categorical" movie monsters can combine within a single character elements derived from more than one of the three main categories (*deviant, supernatural,* and *paranatural*). This complication presents a potential subversion of and challenge to the entire premise of this system by complicating the exclusivity of the ontological designations (and, to be sure, horror filmmakers are constantly reinventing their monster types through the cross-fertilization of existing characters.) Rather than follow Noël Carroll's lead and ignore the contrary film examples, I argue instead that a comprehensive typology should account for, even anticipate, such often unpredictable reinvention.

In fact, this "hybridity problem" is easily resolved by a simple topological strategy. The circles in figure 8, which illustrate the three differ-

Figure 11

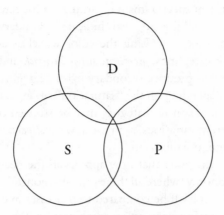

D = DEVIANT
S = SUPERNATURAL
P = PARANATURAL

ing relationships each main category has to pseudo-ontic reality, may be reintroduced, bent around, and overlapped to indicate the complex intersecting of the taxonomy, as shown in figure 11.

Through this simple overlapping, the existing triad of main categories produces three additional subcategories representing overlapping combinations. These *hybrid* categories can be further defined by assigning a priority of one set of characteristics over another. Using the intersection of the *deviant* and *supernatural* main categories as example, we may classify a monster character with delusions of vampirism (as in the films *Martin* [1976] and *Vampire's Kiss* [1988]) as *deviant supernatural*—such as psychokillers who delusionally imagine themselves to possess magical powers. Conversely, psychokiller monsters who actually have magical powers (such as Freddy Krueger in the *Nightmare on Elm Street* series and the killer doll "Chuckie" in the *Child's Play* series) may be classified as *supernatural deviant*. The simple combination of the three major categories produces, by extension and through relative weighting, six additional "hybrid" categories that expand the taxonomy to cover existing, recombinative variations.[30]

An additional benefit of this overlapping strategy is its ability to incorporate functions from other critical systems. For instance, the three intersecting circles call to mind the familiar "color wheel" that organizes the various tint spectra: main or primary color categories (blue—yellow—red) overlapping to also indicate secondary color values (green—orange—purple.) Using the color wheel as an analogy, the primary monster categories (*deviant, supernatural,* and *paranatural*) similarly combine to produce secondary hybrid categories as described previously and, depending on the "saturation" of one category over another, one primary monster category may be stressed over another to distinguish different variations, as in the *deviant supernatural* versus *supernatural deviant* organization.

Furthermore, the zone that now appears in the dead center of the overlapping taxonomy (where all three primary monster categories meet and intertwine) can itself be compared to processes in color photography where additive primary color combinations (all colors reflected back at once) will produce white, while subtractive combinations (no color reflected back) will produce black. Here, *additive-white* can refer to examples where elements from all main categories are combined together or appear in a potpourri (as in confusing or crowded "monster rally" films like *Monster Squad* [1987] or indecisive combinatory films such as *Prince of Darkness* [1987]). Alternatively, *subtractive-black* can refer to horror films where monsters are more indecipherable and tend to stymie clear generic categorization based on monster characters (as in *Eraserhead* [1978] or *Videodrome* [1983]).

Perhaps an even more evident organizational analogue to this system are "Venn diagrams" (developed by John Venn in 1894) familiar to set theory and symbolic logic. In the Venn system, three intersecting circles are also used to represent logical relationships between various sets of elements or operations in order to illustrate their shared (*intersecting*) or unshared (*disjoint*) features. For example, in application to the present taxonomy, the hybrid category *deviant supernatural* might intersect with *supernatural* on the basis of theme and iconography (as in delusions of vampirism) but remain disjoint with reference to the film's suggested pseudo-ontology (the characters are not actual vampires.)

However, there are good reasons not to pursue too inflexibly this genre system's surface resemblance to Venn diagramming. The aim of the Venn system is to represent a strict process of syllogistic reasoning rendered in pictorial form and is based around the declension of precisely determined premises advancing toward a logical conclusion. Though, for instance, the *paranatural* category may suggest a logical synthesis of the other two main categories in certain respects, the present taxonomy (though not arbitrary in its designations) is neither built from nor determined by pure logic. By no means do I wish to propose for the horror genre a set of rigid rules like that which Symbolic Logic demands for its purposes. The main use of this "Venn-like" system is to provide a descriptive tool to manage horror genre organization. Though I would defend this system as rational, it is not necessarily logical. It has the type of relations evident of cultural, as opposed to mathematical, ensembles.

This taxonomy has the ability to both quantify and locate the instances of the horror genre that appear from year to year and to chart in a clearly readable form the relative frequencies of particular monster appearances over time. Data produced by the taxonomy can be used to provide evidence to support claims concerning the relative popularity of particular monsters during any given year or era. Such statistical patterning opens a window that may relate the formal or ontological shape of the horror genre to social-historical contexts and provide the basis for a certain type of reader-response criticism.

The taxonomy can enable the mapping of the correlation of monster types to film production practices over time. For example, popular and profitable films (such as *Jaws, The Exorcist*, and *Alien*) resulted in a series of spin-offs as film studios strove to exploit successful film formulas. Using a monster typology, one can trace clearly the growth and decline of spin-off films and, correspondingly, infer the rise and decay of audience interest in the modalities of such creations as particular monsters appear then disappear.

Such correlations may also suggest more general concerns within society itself, supplying a kind of "anxiety index" that links the allegorical function of monsters by type to particular social and historical events. Correlations linking AIDS, for example, to monster types suggest a form of social or cultural "symptomology" that might test or prove current theories regarding the use of film culture as an accurate gauge of corresponding social crises. Conversely, particular social events themselves may clue us to examine more closely the range of horror films clustered around such events. Through noting and examining what horror films omit from their narratives, the presence of submerged anxieties may be constructively deduced (such as those related to economic pressures or to the almost totally repressed representation in horror films of white-black racial tension).

Through proposing this taxonomy, I attempt to offer a few general solutions to several of the issues that have heretofore beleaguered horror genre criticism. The basic definition of any horror film may be centered around its monster character, and the conflict arising in the fantastical and unreal monster's relationship with normality—as represented through a pseudo-ontic space constructed through filmic realism—provides the necessary basic terms for its (filmic) existence. This taxonomy (constructed elsewhere in its entirety) clearly and concisely maps all possible permutations of this relationship. The taxonomy of horror organizes a limited range of possible variations into three basic categories (*deviant, supernatural,* and *paranatural*) and is sufficient to provide a coherent critical mapping system from which further analysis of this most complex of genres may proceed.[31]

Notes

1. The epigraph comes from John Sadler's 1636 treatise on teratology, *The Sicke Womans Private Looking-Glasse,* cited in the translator's introduction to Ambrose Pare, *On Monsters and Marvels,* trans. Janis L. Pallister (1573; Chicago: University of Chicago Press, 1982), 133. Both Sadler's and Pare's works were part of a general teratological trend of the period and, as Pallister points out, "by the end of the sixteenth century treatises on monsters had become a veritable genre" (xxii).

2. Jeffrey Sconce, "Spectacle of Death: Identification, Reflexivity, and Contemporary Horror," in *Film Theory Goes to the Movies,* ed. Jim Collins, Hillary Radner, and Ava Preacher Collins (New York: Routledge, 1993), 119 (emphasis is author's).

3. Witness, for example, the more recent trends in horror film criticism where the usually essay-length focus is on only a single horror film, subgroup, or specific theme (such as gender issues). The value of individual insights aside, the now dominant short-essay format in horror criticism aptly expresses the disarray and disintegration of the genre.

4. The apparent inability to precisely define a real audience has frequently led to the formulation of ideal audiences used to maintain critical continuity. These fictional formulations, however, often conflate crucial distinctions that occur in real audiences, so that all horror film viewers are defined as "white adolescent male American heterosexual voyeurs" seeking to experience a rite of passage in the horror film's "roller coaster effect"—both assertions being two reductionist mainstays of horror genre audience studies.

5. William K. Everson, "Horror Films: Though Their Ingredients Vary They All Depend upon the Manipulation of Fear," *Films in Review* 5 (1954): 13.

6. Borges is also cited by Michel Foucault, *The Order of Things* (New York: Random House, 1970), xv, to illustrate the "monstrosity" of formal classification.

7. Everson tentatively allows for parody in this article by proposing an additional category: "Perhaps there is an eighth category of horror films—the horror

satire. Most of the categories already described have inspired at least one alleg-edly humorous takeoff" (Everson, "Horror Films," 20).

8. Freddy Krueger is, of course, the burned to death and later resurrected child murderer from the *Nightmare on Elm Street* film series. Since his initial appearance (Wes Craven, 1984), Freddy has gone on to become one of the most enduring (six sequels and counting) and recognizable monster characters in modern horror cinema.

9. Robin Wood, "An Introduction to the American Horror Film," in *American Nightmares: Essays on the Horror Film* (Toronto: Festival of Festivals, 1979), 16–17.

10. Ibid., 9–10.

11. Ibid., 23–28.

12. Edward Lowry, "Genre and Enunciation: The Case of Horror," *Journal of Film and Video* 36 (1984): 13.

13. Noël Carroll, *The Philosophy of Horror or Paradoxes of the Heart* (New York: Routledge, 1990), 38.

14. Approaches by other and more recent authors are either not significantly different or show no significant improvement over Wood's or Carroll's models.

15. Wood, "An Introduction," 14.

16. Michael Armstrong, "Some Like It Chilled," *Films and Filming* 17 (1971): 29.

17. Andrew Tudor, *Monsters and Mad Scientists: A Cultural History of the Horror Movie* (Oxford: Basil Blackwell, 1989), 8.

18. Carroll, *The Philosophy of Horror*, 16.

19. Rosemary Jackson, *Fantasy: The Literature of Subversion* (New York: Methuen, 1981), 34.

20. Pascal Bonitzer, "Partial Vision: Film and the Labyrinth," *Wide Angle* 4 (1981): 58.

21. Roy Huss, T. J. Ross, eds., *Focus on the Horror Film* (New Jersey: Pren-tice-Hall, 1972).

22. Charles Derry, *Dark Dreams: A Psychological History of the Modern Hor-ror Film* (London: A. S. Barnes, 1977); Bruce Kawin, "Children of the Light," in *Film Genre Reader*, ed. Barry Keith Grant (Austin: University of Texas Press, 1986); Will H. Rockett, *Devouring Whirlwind: Terror and Transcendence in the Cinema of Cruelty* (New York: Greenwood Press, 1988).

23. These three basic "monster mortality" variations are complicated in some films by monsters who depart from the usual formula (such as the *deviant* Jason's *supernatural* return from the dead in the later *Friday the 13th* installments or the permanently killed vampires appearing in *The Lost Boys* and in *Near Dark*.) Such instances indicate a mixture of these mortal relations, rather than a rejec-tion of them, and are, therefore, designated by the taxonomy as *hybrid* types.

24. This should not be surprising in that filmmakers rarely (if ever) conceive their monster creations with the aim of honoring this, or any other, critical system.

25. For classification theorists who object to this analogy, see, among others, George Lakoff, *Women, Fire, and Dangerous Things: What Categories Reveal about the Mind* (Chicago: University of Chicago Press, 1985); and Bernard E. Rollin, "Nature, Convention, and Genre Theory," *Poetics* 10 (1981): 127–143.

26. David J. Russell, "Parts of Darkness: A Rescue of the Modern Horror Film Genre through a Classification of its Monster Characters" (Ph.D. diss., University of California, Los Angeles, 1995).

27. Vera Dika, *Games of Pleasure*: Halloween, Friday the 13th, *and the Films of the Stalker Cycle* (New Jersey: Associated University Press, 1990).

28. Carol J. Clover, *Men, Women, and Chain Saws: Gender in the Modern Horror Film* (New Jersey: Princeton University Press, 1992).

29. *Candyman* would actually be reclassified as a *hybrid* monster but here serves as a way to illustrate a limitation of the *deviant* category as thus far defined.

30. One should also note that creative overlapping at the subcategorical level potentially produces even more elaborate (and, hence, potentially more specific) descriptive categories. However, space does not permit here further discussion of this point.

31. Russell, "Parts of Darkness."

"God Bless Juries!"

CAROL J. CLOVER

It was one of Tocqueville's great insights that because there were in America "no nobles or literary men, and the people are apt to mistrust the wealthy," it was men of law, lawyers and judges, who consequently formed "the highest political class and the most cultivated portion of society" and whose ways were emulated by the larger public much as the ways of the European aristocracy were emulated by common folk. And how did Americans come by their knowledge, such as it was, of lawyers and the legal system? In two ways, Tocqueville declared. One was through public life: because judges and lawyers frequently went into politics, they inevitably "introduce[d] the customs and technicalities of their profession into the management of public affairs." But a far more important mechanism for the generalization of legal thinking, Tocqueville claimed, was the jury system, and on this point his reasoning seems astonishingly modern. "The jury," he declared, "extends this habit to all classes. The language of the law thus becomes, in some measure, a vulgar tongue; the spirit of the law, which is produced in the schools and courts of justice, gradually penetrates beyond their walls into the bosom of society, where it descends to the lowest class, so that at last the whole people contract the habits and tastes of the judicial magistrate." By bringing common people to the law, the jury brings the law to common people, and hence the thought of the legal aristocracy "extends over the whole community and penetrates into all the classes which compose it; it acts upon the country imperceptibly, but finally fashions it to suit its own purposes."[1]

What interests me here are not so much the mechanism of discipline

255

and the process of political interpolation that Tocqueville so approvingly outlines as it is the shaping force he ascribes to the judicial system in the hands of a citizenry of once and future jurors.[2] That system constitutes a common language, a rhetorical and logical template that gives shape to all manner of social forms above and beyond the court of law. So it is that "scarcely any political question arises in the United States that is not resolved, sooner or later, into a judicial question," that "all parties are obliged to borrow, in their daily controversies, the ideas, and even the language, peculiar to judicial proceedings," and that "the jury is introduced into the games of schoolboys."[3]

Just what "games of schoolboys" Tocqueville had in mind we don't know, but the spirit of the remark is clear enough: so fundamental is the jury in the American imaginary that it turns up in and structures even the sheerest forms of play. No one even vaguely acquainted with American culture can help being struck by the truth of his observation. We watch television programs like *You Be the Judge* (which summarizes the arguments of real trials and has viewers call in their verdicts on a 1–900 number) and *Jones and the Jury* (in which audience members are "impaneled" to decide cases). We marvel at game-show gimmicks like the "OJ-ometer," an electronic register of the reactions—"good for OJ" as it rose and "bad for OJ" as it fell—of button-pushing audience members as they viewed the preliminary hearings of the Simpson trial. We read books like *You Be the Jury* or *You're the Jury: Solve Twelve Real Life Court Cases Along with the Juries Who Decided Them* and *Trial of the Century: You Be the Juror*, a guide to all the Simpson witnesses and the points of law that were engaged in their testimony ("See the OJ Trial through the Eyes of a Juror"). We play board and computer games based on trials, and we constitute ourselves as mock jurors on the internet (for example, www.cyberjury.com). Some of us attend real trials as so-called courtwatchers, producing and reading the *Courtwatchers Newsletter*. Others of us content ourselves with live-coverage television ("If I were on the jury" is the refrain of callers on Court TV's "Open Line"). And of course we watch and read what seems an endless stream of documentary and quasi-documentary forms (*The Trial of Lee Harvey Oswald, The Thin Blue Line*); courtroom dramas proper (*Witness for the Prosecution*), and finally, forms that duplicate the structure and operations of the trial though they may never actually set foot in the courtroom (lots of detective mysteries and thrillers). My interest in this essay is in the cinematic version of the next-to-last category, the courtroom drama or trial movie—a category widely acknowledged though never treated as a genre—and in the ways that it positions us not as passive spectators, but as active ones, viewers with a job to do.

It is perhaps no accident that the courtroom drama or trial movie that most clearly declares the relation between juries and audiences is probably the very first: the 1907 Biograph picture *Falsely Accused!* This short feature begins with the murder of an inventor in his studio. His daughter is found beside the body, clutching the murder weapon (an envelope opener), and she is arrested and charged with the crime. Her boyfriend believes her falsely accused and begins poking around the studio looking for clues. He notices a motion picture camera and realizes that it was running at the time of the murder.[4] He removes the film, takes it into a darkroom, and puts it in the chemical bath. We cut to a close-up of the chemical tray to see the film as it develops.[5] Armed with the film, the boyfriend rushes into court just as the daughter is about to be convicted and demands to project his footage. The judge agrees, and two men mount chairs behind the witness stand and stretch a sheet between them. On this screen, in the film's climactic scene, is projected the footage that reveals the murderer to have been someone else.[6]

The courtroom scene of *Falsely Accused!* has been noted as the first in which D. W. Griffith appeared in film (as one of the men holding the sheet),[7] but surely its greater significance lies in the way it prefigures, with startling clarity, the terms of a form that will be a staple of American cinema for a century to come. *Falsely Accused!* is not just a movie about a trial. It is a trial movie that spells out the natural fit between trials and movies. By having a motion picture give testimony (note the placement of the film screen at the witness stand), *Falsely Accused!* turns the courtroom into a movie theater and the jury into a film audience. And to the extent that we, the audience of *Falsely Accused!*, are aligned with the diegetic jury at that moment, both of us looking to the film for evidence, we too are in the geometry. At just the moment that the cinema of "attractions" began to give way to the cinema of "narrative integration," we get a courtroom drama—and not just any courtroom drama, but one that is as clear a program statement for the genre as we could ever hope to find.[8]

There is a difference between the diegetic and extradiegetic juries of *Falsely Accused!*: having witnessed the crime as it happened, we know more than they do. With the courtroom screening, they see for the first time what we see for the second. This split-knowledge arrangement, in which we know more than the jury does until the end, will persist and remains a standard format to this day, usually in films that turn on the question of why or how rather than who or whether (*Compulsion*, for example, or more recently *Mortal Thoughts*). But its alternative, in which the diegetic jury and the extradiegetic one are in the same position with respect to the evidence, also puts in an early appearance in cinema history. Consider the 1913 film *By Whose Hand?* (aka *Who Killed Simon Baird?*). As the AFI catalogue sums it up:

Edith and John Maitland will allow David Sterling to marry their daughter Helen as soon as he earns five thousand dollars, so David tries to sell one of his inventions to Simon Baird for that amount. Simon, unable to make up his mind, is found murdered the next day, and David is arrested with five thousand dollars of Simon's money in his possession. At the trial, Edith confesses to the murder, saying that Simon had wronged her years before, and that she took his money and gave it to David so that he could marry Helen. David refutes this testimony, though, and claims to be the murderer himself. In the end, the audience must decide for itself the identity of the killer.[9]

If *Falsely Accused!* announced the equations "film audience=jury" and "film diegesis=evidence," *By Whose Hand?* simply enacts them in such a way that the film diegesis is the sole iteration of the evidence, and the film audience and the jury are in the same shoes doing the same job— in this case, trying to figure out which of the four suspects is the culprit. The word *diegesis* is peculiarly appropriate in this connection, given its original Greek referent: the recital of facts in a court of law. The term was imported into film studies by Etienne Sauriau from Aristotle, who in the *Rhetoric* speaks of the "survey of actions," the account of "the actions themselves," in a lawsuit as a form of "narration."[10]

By Whose Hand? is an extreme case, but in degree, not kind. As contemporary reviews make clear, the you-are-the-jury, you-decide format was not unprecedented, though it was more familiar in serials than in feature films. (*The Trial of Vivienne Ware* [1932] appeared first as a six-part serial run simultaneously in a newspaper and on radio, accompanied by an offer of "money prizes for the best verdicts that listeners sent in.")[11] In our own day, the question mark ending is more characteristic of documentary or based-on-real-trial features—*The Trial of Lee Harvey Oswald* (1977), for example, which closes with a crawl that reads, "In creating the trial of Lee Harvey Oswald we have relied on documented fact. We have assumed the roles of prosecutor and defense attorney. We do not assume the role of the jury. The judgment is yours."[12]

Although overt "jury challenges" of this sort crop up periodically in the coming decades, most courtroom dramas after the early period eschew obvious forms of apostrophe in favor of devices more in keeping with the invisible apparatus of classical Hollywood narration. There is an interestingly intermediate form of jury address in MGM's first all-talking picture, *The Trial of Mary Dugan* (1931). A showgirl friend of Mary's who takes the stand keeps addressing her answers to the examining attorney, who is standing before her to her right—an arrangement that shows them both in semiprofile. He, in turn, keeps reminding her to "please address the jury" and with a bodily flourish directs her gaze away from himself to a focal point some 45 degrees to her left. Following his prompt, she turns directly to the camera and completes her testimony looking flatly into our eyes. This happens no fewer than four times in her short stint on the stand, each a more brazen breach of classical cinematic protocol than the one before. (Her extraordinary eyes make the moments all the more striking.) The point is driven home by the judge when, toward the end of the trial and film, he instructs the jury. "You," he says, pausing for emphasis, "are the sole judges of the facts in this case, of the guilt or innocence of this woman. You are not here to say who killed Edgar Rice. Your sole function is to determine the guilt or innocence of Mary Dugan. The jury will now retire and reach a verdict." Before this speech, he was looking in another direction, but with the word *You*, he turns emphatically to the camera and looks us straight in the eye, a position he holds until he is done. Direct address of this kind is hardly unprecedented in cinema, but what distinguishes this example and others like it is the naming of the addressee: "you," "the jury." [13]

The jury challenge has for the last couple of decades been largely relegated to promotional materials (videocassettes, posters, sometimes trailers), which by tradition speak the language of second-person address: "Was the 'Scarsdale Diet' doctor murdered, or was it a tragic accident?" or "Was Randall Adams murdered—or was he an innocent scapegoat?" or "What are the limits of justice? Of social responsibility?" or "Was she simply malicious, or was she sick?" and so on.[14] This is not to say that modern films jury-box their audiences any less. It is to suggest that with the fixing of the narrative and cinematic codes, we have come to need less overt discipline. We know our place and just what our job will be even before we take our seats.

Still, even the most discreet of trial movies may tip its hand now and then. At the end of *Compulsion*, the 1959 film based on the Leopold-Loeb case, defense attorney Wilk (based on Clarence Darrow and played by Orson Welles) delivers himself of what is said, at some fifteen minutes, to be the longest speech ever delivered on screen. In it, he begs in impassioned terms for a sentence of life imprisonment rather than the death penalty. "Life!" he exhorts. "Any more goes back to the hyena!"

Wilk came late to the case, only after the parents of the accused men had grasped the seriousness of the situation and also, as it turned out, after their sons' guilt had been irrevocably established, thus forcing Wilk to forgo a jury for a judge, to plead guilty by virtue of a species of insanity, and to beg for a merciful sentence. We saw the earlier jury: a bunch of flinty older men. But that jury is dismissed, and now, as Wilk takes over, the camera takes pains to show the jury box empty, almost lingering on the void. When Wilk-Darrow-Welles begins to speak, we see him in a frontal shot, as though he were addressing us or a space proximate to us. Because we know that the judge is the object of the performance, we feel ourselves positioned in his vicinity. But then, still facing us—virtually looking us in the eye—and without missing a beat in his peroration, Wilk changes his orientation somewhat, turning some 30 degrees to the right, and leans one forearm on the telltale rail. The space so insistently established as empty some minutes ago has now been filled, as it were, by us.

Again, the equations are clear. Although the diegesis, echoing the historical facts of the case, draws a strong distinction between judge and jury (dismissing the latter in favor of the former), the cinematography puts them together again. By positioning us first at the judge's bench and then, through a rotation, in the jury box, the camera links the two, reminding us that they are versions of one another and that a speech meant for the one will do for both. But even more striking is the equation the camera draws between the diegetic jury and the film's spectators. The fact that there is no diegetic jury in this sequence only makes more pointed the camera's invitation. It is as though the diegetic jury box, explicitly drained of diegetic jurors, has been extended out into the movie theater to embrace us. What we are asked to judge is not the facts of the matter, which are no longer in dispute, but the sentence. More generally, we are asked to pass judgment on the death penalty, that act that "takes us back to the hyena," in principle. Lest we doubt who the real addressee is of that fifteen-minute speech, we might recall that it was issued separately for sale as a phonograph record.

The homiletic tone of *Compulsion*, once a regular feature of trial movies, has fallen out of favor. But the trope of the empty jury box lives on. Consider *Presumed Innocent* (1990). The film opens with the shot of a vacant courtroom. Our vision pans ever so slowly to the right until it arrives at the jury box. We pause. Then, at an almost imperceptible rate, we start moving forward. The empty, ornate chairs of the jury loom larger and larger in our vision, and as the credits crawl over them, we hear a man's voice intone: "I am a prosecutor. I am a part of the business of accusing, judging, and punishing. I explore the evidence of a crime and determine who is charged, who is brought to this room and tried before his peers. I present my evidence to the jury, and they deliberate upon it. They must determine what really happened. If they cannot, we will not know whether the accused deserves to be freed or punished. If they cannot find the truth, what is our hope for justice?"

What is most striking about the voice-over here is not so much its words as its almost mantralike or incantatory tone. It is as though we are being ushered into that empty courtroom, directed to those empty chairs, and sworn in. Two hours later, we will revisit this scene—same shot of the empty courtroom and jury seats, voice-over in the same monotone. The time in between we spend not in the courtroom but following the fortunes of the speaker, District Attorney Rusty Sabich, as he investigates the murder of his colleague Carolyn Polhemus, with whom, it emerges, he had been having an affair. In fact, the finger of suspicion begins to point to him: the blood type matches his, and a glass found in her apartment has his fingerprints on it. The visualized story roams into Sabich's obsessive relationship with Carolyn, into his home life with his wife Barbara, a woman angry at the affair with Carolyn and dissatisfied with her role as bedmaker (she's at work on a dissertation, but it's slow going), into his relation with his lawyer Sandy Stern, and (typically enough) into District Attorney Horgan's political ambitions and shady connections. Even when we finally arrive in the courtroom, some eighty minutes into the film, our narrative and cinematic focus remains stubbornly on Sabich and Stern as we approach the bench with them, go to chambers with them, and so on.

Despite all this mobility in time and space, however, and despite our engagement with the figure of Sabich, we are functionally speaking never very far from the jury box of the opening scene. We study exhibits and demeanor, speculate on motive, consider other candidates, and wrestle with the presumption of innocence of the title.[15] In fact, when it comes right down to it, Sabich's own "work" is pretty much the work of the jury—at least until a point in the last third of the film, when something seems to dawn on him that does not dawn on us. At that moment, he splits off from us, leaving us behind with the diegetic jury, with whom we "vote," in the end, for a verdict of not guilty, not because we positively know otherwise, but simply because the prosecution did not meet the standard of reasonable doubt. The fact that we subsequently learn who really did it (Sabich's wife) does not mean that we have finally transcended our role as jurors in the rhetorical economy of the film; it only means that we are jurors who learned more after the fact, as jurors sometimes do. (*Presumed Innocent* lets us off easier than films like *Anatomy of a Murder*, in which we realize that we are jurors who may have screwed up, and *Witness for the Prosecution*, in which we learn that we are jurors who surely did screw up.) Our position and our predicament are slammed home in the film's closing scene, which returns us to the scene—same courtroom, same empty jury seats—and the sound—same flat voice-over—of the opening, the only difference being that this time the voice tells us, in effect, that the search for justice sometimes fails. At no time during the film's two hours do we catch so much as a glimpse of the jury actually trying the case—an omission all the more striking in light of the attention lavished on the empty seats in the beginning and again at the end. The point could hardly be clearer: we are it.

We are similarly ushered into and out of *Reversal of Fortune* (1990), but with a difference: the voice-over and images are those of the victim. Alan Dershowitz's account of Claus von Bulow's second trial for attempting the "insulin murder" of his heiress wife Sunny, *Reversal of Fortune* opens with a blue-tinted static image of Sunny, lying in a hospital bed in a coma. After a pause, a voice-over begins—hers, recounting the history of the first trial. This rather lengthy synopsis ends with the following words: "On March 16, 1982, he was found guilty on both counts. Even Alexandra Ives testified against him. You are about to see how Claus von Bulow sought to reverse, or escape from, that verdict." And then, in grave tones, " You tell me." Now, with history in place and the jury charged, the movie proper starts.

Reversal of Fortune plays a sly game. Its "you tell me" suggests a balanced two-story setup: the prosecution case, brought by the children, who believe that Claus murdered Sunny, versus the defense case, spearheaded by Dershowitz and his team of Harvard law students, who argue that Sunny overdosed. So the opening shots suggest, and so suggests the *Rashomon*-like visualization of different scenarios for how Sunny came to be lying in a faint on the bathroom floor with her gown hiked up to her waist. Both enact voice-overs. In the first, we see Sunny in the bedroom popping pills, then walking to the bathroom, turning on the sink faucet, lifting her skirt to use the toilet, and fainting. In the second, we see her overdose and Claus let it happen, after which he drags her to the bathroom (hence the hiked-up skirt) and deposits her on the floor. The sequences are of the same length and mode and both are plausible.

Nor does the film ever give us an answer. The crime is presented as a mystery and left as such. Claus is played (by Jeremy Irons) as inscrutable. "Is it the truth?" Dershowitz asks him. "Of course it's the truth," he answers. "But not the whole truth. I don't know the whole truth. I don't know what happened to her." The film's final dialogue line is spoken by Dershowitz to von Bulow as they part ways at an elevator: "One thing, Claus. Legally, this was an important victory. Morally, you're on your own." If that were not enough, we cut at the end to Sunny in her coma, her voice-over saying, "Claus von Bulow was given a second trial and acquitted on both counts. This is all you know, all you can be told. When you get where I am, you will know the rest." This is not quite the "you are the jury, you decide" ending of *By Whose Hand?* but it comes awfully close—the jury challenge in modern drag. It is in fact strikingly like *Presumed Innocent*, ending as it began with the same static image and the same flat voice-over. The similarity of that triadic structure, in which the ending is a version of the beginning and both of them are discursively different from the long middle, to the triadic structure of the Anglo-American jury trial is a subject I consider in detail elsewhere. Suffice it to note here that it is a standard structure of both trials and trial movies.

But *Reversal of Fortune* is not only about Claus von Bulow. It is also—even more so—about the business of defense lawyering. Long stretches of the film have a law-school how-to quality: how to value even the smallest detail, how to extract multiple meanings from a fact, how to question whether "facts" really are facts, and how to give oneself over to one's imagination in the creation of an alternative story. Piece by piece, we watch Dershowitz and his team of students construct another explanation for the set of givens: black bag, insulin levels, room temperature, and so on. We also get a dose of moralizing about the goodness of a system that guarantees everyone, even Claus von Bulow, the right to a defense. To judge from its proportions, *Reversal* is less interested in the case at hand—the guilt or innocence of von Bulow—than it is in criminal defense as a process and a moral project in American law. It is more than a best-possible-case-for-the-defense movie. It is also a best-possible-case-for-the-criminal-defense-lawyer movie. More particularly, it is a best-possible-case-for-Dershowitz movie, mounted by Dershowitz himself.[16] Thus the double-trial structure: the explicit diegetic trial of von Bulow and the implicit trial of defense lawyer Dershowitz. On the matter of von Bulow's guilt or innocence, the film claims, if not neutrality, then eternal mystery, which from the defense standpoint amounts to the same thing.[17] The Dershowitz trial, by contrast, urges us to a verdict of not guilty (of all the bad things people think about criminal defense attorneys).

The double-trial structure is fundamental to trial narratives. Films about rape or wife beating usually mount a second, unofficial trial on the legal system's ability to serve (female) victims of intimate crimes. *The Accused* (1988), for example, is about the New Bedford gang-rape trial, but its dramatic tension lies as much in whether one female lawyer can buck a male system set in its ways and a male law structurally biased against victims of rape. Consider films like *Burning Bed* (1984), in which the first trial turns on a wife's murder of her husband and the second on the failure of criminal law to appreciate what is now called battered wife syndrome; *The Murder of Mary Phagan* (1988), in which the first trial is based on the Leo Frank case and the second makes the case for a miscarriage of justice; *Sergeant Rutledge* (1960), in which the first trial has Rutledge charged with murder and the second asks whether a black man can get a fair trial. *Breaker Morant* (1979), like most court-martial and war-crimes movies, asks not only whether the accused committed the deed, but what is the nature of an order and what is the range of interpretation allowed the individual, and indeed, in this case, whether the convictions and executions were done in the name of law or of propaganda. *Class Action*'s (1991) official trial is a civil suit resembling the Ford Motor's Pinto case, but its unofficial trial turns on selling out to corporate big bucks. In the overwhelming majority of trial movies, from the beginning of cinema, the unofficial trial turns on an aspect of the legal system. Is the system fair across various social differences—class, race, and gender? Can it be corrupted? Does money buy people off? Are lawyers human? Should the death penalty exist ? Can the system really get at the truth? Can it distinguish between technical justice and real justice? Does it convict innocent people? Does it too often acquit the guilty?

What it almost never questions, however, is the institution of the jury. Even when the system has gone manifestly wrong, blame is laid at the door of a sleepy judge, an ambitious DA, a greedy lawyer, a dishonest witness, a misleadingly charming or offensive defendant, the general clubbiness of the legal profession, politics at large—but not the jury or the jury system. The institution of the jury has been much debated in the press in recent years, but it remains for the most part oddly secure in the movies.

It is also oddly invisible. We seldom see movie juries. When we do, it is usually momentarily and at a distance, often by way of a pan across the courtroom or in the occasional cutaway—a shot in either case too briefly held for us to register such vitals as gender, race, or ethnicity, much less individual characteristics. The faces that loom so large in courtroom sequences include those of just about everybody in the courtroom, even gallery spectators (wives, journalists, and so on), but not those of jurors. If we look carefully, we see a group of people (not focusing on any one) as nondescript as they are impassive: not too fat or thin, not too young or old, not too strangely dressed, and expressionless but for a certain look of attention. In either case, such shots usually add up to no more than a couple of minutes of the film's two hours. The avoidance of the jury box is all the more striking in light of the fact that courtroom camerawork is often rather inventive, as if to counter the claustrophobia that inheres in the situation.

The shunning of the jury as both visual object and political subject is too consistent and too patterned to be accidental. The reason that juries are largely unseen in trial movies and the jury system largely uncontested within the regime of cinema is surely that we understand the jury to constitute a kind of necessary blank space in the text, one reserved for us. To critique the system in a courtroom drama would involve us with jurors in a way that is incompatible with our own position in the text. To know about Juror Number Five in any detail would detract from the puzzle we came to solve, and add another dimension to what is to be interpreted. We can imagine an art film focused on the jury and individual jurors, but would we then perceive that film as courtroom drama? I suspect we would feel it as something else—that what we expect in a courtroom drama is a form that presents itself as a trial and us as its jury and that draws us into its text by addressing us visually (as in *Dugan* and *Compulsion*), by directing us to a vacant jury box (as in *Presumed Innocent* and *Incident at Oglala*), by gesturing to a jury so generic that we take it as not as a competing body but as a vague surrogate, or by simply skipping it altogether. The rule, in the televising of real trials, that the jury cannot be shown is a rule we have lived with in fiction for decades (and is arguably a rule we would not know how to live without).

Of course there are exceptions—movies in which a juror forms a relationship with someone he shouldn't (*Suspect*) as well as films like

Knock on Any Door, Rampage, and others, mostly generically offbeat. And then there is *Twelve Angry Men,* not only an exception, but a monumental one. Showing nothing but the jury and taking place entirely within the jury room, *Twelve Angry Men* not only breaks the rules, it reverses them utterly—and yet it is in the eyes of many the defining example of the courtroom drama as a category. How are we to explain the emergence and canonical status of such a deviant case?

Twelve Angry Men was written as a teleplay by Reginald Rose in 1953. It aired in 1954, and in 1956 Henry Fonda proposed to Rose that he expand it to feature length. He did so, and Sidney Lumet was assigned the project as his directorial debut. The film, which appeared in 1957, retains the teleplay's theatricality and sense of enchamberment. It opens with outdoor shots of the courthouse and courthouse steps, and the precredit sequence show us courtroom interiors, including a scene in which a bored judge instructs the jury and we get a haunting head-shot of the accused, a dark-skinned, large-eyed eighteen-year-old male. The credits roll over a shot of the jury room, empty in the beginning, into which the jurors file one by one. The credits end when the room is full, and the drama begins. It opens with a preliminary vote: eleven guilty and only one, Juror Number Eight (Henry Fonda) not guilty. Other jurors try to bring Juror Eight into line, but he will not be moved. Maybe the boy did do it, he says, but does the evidence really prove it beyond a reasonable doubt? So the debate goes for ninety minutes, with all the jurors' personalities and personal stakes slowly emerging. As Juror Eight questions the prosecution's evidence, piece by piece, others join him, one by one, in his doubt. Finally even the most recalcitrant of the group crumbles, and the jury delivers a verdict of not guilty. In yet another turn on the triadic structure, the film closes as it began, outdoors on the courthouse steps, as Juror Eight and the old-man juror exchange names on parting.

The first thing to be noted about *Twelve Angry Men* is that it appears to have been inspired by a French original: the 1950 film *Justice est faite,* written and directed by André Cayatte and distributed in the United States as *Justice Is Done* and *Let Justice Be Done.*[18] ("Strangely enough," writes Thomas J. Harris, "as of 1957 the subject of the jury had only received one serious treatment in all of world cinema—by French writer-director André Cayatte in his 1950 film *Justice est faite.*")[19] The film recounts a seven-member jury's deliberation in the trial of a woman doctor who euthanized her terminally ill lover at his request.[20] *Justice est faite* is perhaps as anomalous among French trial movies as *Twelve Angry Men* is among American ones in light of the fact that the jury is seldom used in France and has little place in the public imaginary, much less cinema. In any event, for whatever reason, Cayatte (himself a lawyer) made *Justice*, and perhaps just because the trial movie is not the chestnut of French cinema that it is of Anglo-American, he was not so bound by a tradition that he could not experiment with the dramatics of an underappreciated element of the system. And the result moved Rose to a similar experiment.

But if Cayatte's was an experiment in something like a vacuum, Rose's was one in what would seem a downright inimical context. To understand why *Twelve Angry Men*'s breach of the jury-avoidance rule did not disqualify the film with American audiences, we need to look more closely at its narrative operations. To begin with, there is the question it asks. The issue in *Justice est faite* is not who did it, which is clear, but why (out of mercy as his lover or out of greed as his heir), whether circumstances can ever be special enough to justify murder, and whether those entrusted with judging can ever come unbiased to their task. *Twelve Angry Men* asks the typical Anglo-American trial-movie question: did the accused man do it or not? More to the point, it goes about answering that question in the same way that trial movies have always gone about it: by casting it in strongly adversarial terms and by putting the audience through the steps and processes of the trial itself.

The discussion around and about the preliminary vote sets the terms. Eleven of the jurors agree more or less summarily that the evidence against the defendant, a young man accused of stabbing his father to death, is overwhelming: a woman saw him (from the other side of the elevated train tracks); an old man downstairs heard him; he had bought a switchblade that day; he was known to fight with his father and to shout that he wanted to kill him; and he had been in trouble with the law before. Juror Eight balks: he doesn't know whether to believe the defendant's story or not, but given his miserable life (dead mother, felonious father, orphanage) and the fact that a guilty vote would send him to death, they at least owe him a serious deliberation. He introduces in clear terms the cornerstone of every criminal defense when, in response to one juror's argument that the boy must be guilty because nobody proved otherwise, he declares, "Nobody has to prove otherwise. The burden of proof's on the prosecution. The defendant doesn't even have to open his mouth. That's in the Constitution." In other words, the first five minutes of the jury drama sound for all the world like opening statements in a trial: prosecution first (the evidence will show guilt beyond a reasonable doubt), and then the defense (the evidence does not meet the burden of proof beyond a reasonable doubt).

Lee J. Cobb, E. G. Marshall, Jack Warden, Ed Begley, Jack Klugman, Henry Fonda, Martin Balsam, Edward Binns [John Fiedler, George Voskovec, Robert Webber, Joseph Sweeney]. *Twelve Angry Men*, Sidney Lumet. © Orion-Nova, 1957.

With the two sides in place, the jury drama moves into a different phase. It is introduced by a second poll, in which each of the eleven pro-guilt jurors is to state his reasoning. Thus the text shifts from generalities to details, each of which is subject to dispute as the jurors interrupt one another with objections, questions, and, increasingly, insults. There is no order to the discussion of evidence: it comes in bits and pieces as they occur to jurors. But one by one, the items of evidence are submitted to the process of examination: first direct, then cross, and often redirect and recross as well. An exemplary exchange turns on the switch-blade knife with which the man was killed and that the defendant claimed to have bought and lost on the same day. One juror cites it, during the second poll, as the piece of evidence that seemed to him incontrovertible. They ask to see it, and it is brought in. The juror enumerates all the incriminating facts about the knife. He ends by stabbing it into the table so that it stands upright and declaring, "Take a look at this knife. It's a very unusual knife. I've never seen one like it, and nei-

Juror Number Eight (Henry Fonda). *Twelve Angry Men*, Sidney Lumet.
© Orion-Nova, 1957.

ther had the storekeeper who sold it to the boy. Aren't you [turning to Juror Eight] asking us to accept a pretty incredible coincidence?" "I'm just saying a coincidence is possible," Juror Eight replies, reaching into his pocket to produce an identical knife, which he stabs into the table next to the other one.

Point, counterpoint; direct examination, cross examination. So the film goes, with every piece of prosecution evidence effectively answered by one or another of the jurors: the eyewitness had indentations on the sides of the bridge of her nose, meaning she wore glasses and could not have seen what she claimed; the old man downstairs had a bum leg and couldn't have covered the space he said he did in the time available; the grip on a switchblade precludes a downward stabbing motion; and so on. At one point, the most vehemently pro-guilt juror becomes so angry at Juror Eight that he shouts, "I'm gonna kill him!"— thus undoing the force of the testimony about the defendant's having similarly shouted at his father. Piece by piece, what seemed a watertight assemblage of facts comes apart, and juror by juror, they change their votes, until at the end, we have moved from the prosecution view of the case to the defense side, which is to say the side of reasonable doubt.[21]

A full account of the ways that trial movies enact the structure and narrative procedure of real trials is beyond the scope of this essay. But even this short account should suffice to suggest that *Twelve Angry Men* is in all respects but one playing by the rules. It may transpire in a jury room (as other courtroom dramas may transpire in judge's chambers, police stations, lawyer's conference rooms, jail cells, or morgues) instead of a courtroom, and the players may be citizen jurors instead of lawyers, but in its triadic shape, adversarial mode, X-not-X opposition (and the insistence on the reasonable-doubt basis of not-X), the cross-examining quality of the discussions of evidence, the programmed shift from prosecution to defense, and the sense of truth-crisis that attends that shift, *Twelve Angry Men* is a consummate courtroom drama. Most crucially, despite its jury-room setting, it still plays to an off-screen jury. Perhaps it is because we sense our position as the film's object of address to be so secure that we can ignore or get beyond our diegetic competition. In any case, *Twelve Angry Men* is on closer inspection not quite the exception it at first seemed.

Perhaps *Justice est faite* is not quite the exception it seemed either. American commentators, in any case, found it too much interested in the characters of the jurors (whose lives are explored in detail) and too little in the trial and the crime. The *Variety* reviewer thought that the film put "too much emphasis on its jurists, detracting not only from the trial but from the killing itself."[22] Bosley Crowther was also bothered by the apparent absence of procedure (the "casualness" and the "conspicuous eccentricity of practices") in the trial scenes, but he concluded that "to enter an objection to these aspects might be ironic in its way, too, for the obvious theme of the picture is the doubtfulness of hard and fast rules. And the major fascination of the picture resides and is achieved, anyhow, in the brilliance and colorful variety with which it explores its jurors' lives."[23] These are telling remarks, for they suggest that by American lights what is wrong with *Justice Is Done* is that it is not a *trial* movie, as though any film that focused on a jury ought to be considerably, if not mainly, about the trial. Rather, it is a philosophizing set of character studies and, as such, not so different from other French and European films of its time. In naturalizing the jury story to Anglo-American expectations, *Twelve Angry Men* reversed the priorities, not only putting the trial front and center but also following the narrative procedures of the standard trial movie.

To say that we managed with *Twelve Angry Men* is not to say we loved it. The film was a great success among critics, but it was a box-office mediocrity, not even close to the ten top-grossing films of that year.[24] It apparently played best to the art-film crowd in that crowd's heyday. That those critics and that crowd won the day eventually is clear from the subsequent installation of *Twelve Angry Men* at the top of the court-room drama list. It may deserve that place. But it is important to re-member that the public at large demurred. Perhaps that was because of the film's staginess, its philosophizing, its refusal of romance and ac-tion—features that suited the tastes of the late fifties art-movie crowd but not of the public at large. But perhaps it was also because, for all its virtues, *Twelve Angry Men* got something wrong. In any event, it didn't start a trend.[25] The big dramas of the following few years—*I Want to Live!* (1958), *Anatomy of a Murder* (1959), *Compulsion* (1959), *Inherit the Wind* (1960), *To Kill a Mockingbird* (1962)—revert to the cipher jury formula. Again, there are exceptions, but they are occasional and brief. *Twelve Angry Men* remains a blip on the American scene—not such a blip as to be discursively unrecognizable (on the contrary, it is discur-sively old hat), but too much a blip to catch on.

Twelve Angry Men was widely reviewed as a "penetrating indict-ment" of the jury system.[26] Insofar as it reminds us how overdetermined jurors' reactions can be, it is indeed sobering. Were it not for one man in the right place at the right time, the defendant would have gone to the chair. Still, that one man was there, and all of the other men are rational enough to be brought around when the evidence is put before them. And we are also repeatedly reminded that twelve heads are bet-ter than one, an observation that has particular force in a film in which the one head, that of the judge, is so manifestly bored that it must be propped up with an arm—apparently because it regarded the conclu-sion as foregone. Not even this odd-duck film in the American cine-matic tradition—an art film with social-critical ambitions and a French prototype—seems to be able to take on the jury system in any real or sustained way. To take on the jury system seriously would be to repudi-ate the judgment of citizens in favor of the judgment of professionals, and that is not a step that *Twelve Angry Men* comes even close to taking. The judge's role is small, but it blows open the film's politics. Fright-ening though a jury may be, given the number of "angry men" in the world, it is better than the alternative.

The jury may be up for grabs in the world of law and politics, but in the world of popular culture, it remains serenely untouchable. In movies, citizen juries make mistakes only when the system misleads them (*Presumed Innocent*), not because they don't understand the issues or are irrational bigots. Surely this has to do with the fact, as Tocqueville might point out, that movie audiences are made up of citizen jurors—both actual ones (people who have served or almost served on juries) and generalized ones (movie viewers who identify with and do the work of juries). It is no surprise, given the effort of movies to suture audiences into the jury position and given the desire of audiences to be engaged as triers of fact, that films should be friendly to the idea of the citizen jury: to be otherwise would be to bite the hand that feeds them. What the editors of *Cahiers du Cinema* wrote of *Young Mr. Lincoln* (1939), that it is "America itself which constitutes the Jury, and who cannot be wrong, so that the truth cannot fail to manifest itself by the end of the proceedings,"[27] pretty much goes for trial movies in general, which indeed often show us, in a final shot, a monumental courthouse or an American flag or both. An American courtroom drama could no more critique the jury than a game of Cowboys and Indians could critique racism.

Such is our relation to the form and the tradition that when juries are discussed, we know to take it personally. When the lawyer Michael in *Class Action* (a film about a civil case that looks a lot like the Ford Motor's Pinto scandal) coaches a witness, "Keep your words short; don't talk above the jury—though that wouldn't be hard," we register the insult, sensing that at some level he means us, and mark Michael as the villain. By the same token, we know how to take it when, in *Anatomy of a Murder*, as the lawyers are waiting for the verdict to come in, one, a duffer named Parnell, philosophizes: "Twelve people, with twelve different minds, with twelve different sets of experiences . . . and in their judgment they must become of one mind—unanimous. That's one of the miracles of man's disorganized soul, that they can do it, and in most instances do it quite well. God bless juries!" The fact that this is one of those instances in which we're not at all sure the jury did do it quite well should not bother us unduly, because lead defense attorney Jimmy Stewart, in one of his most winning roles, is not quite sure either. We do the best we can with what we get, and much of the art of trial movies, like the much of the art of trials, lies in playing the ambiguity for all it's worth.

Tocqueville was right: we are a nation of jurors, and we have created an entertainment system that has us see just about everything that matters—from corporate greed to child custody—from precisely that vantage and in those structural terms. Just as the legal system has always drawn on the entertainment system, playing to the spectator in us all, so, from *Falsely Accused!* to *Philadelphia* and trial after trial on Court TV, the entertainment system draws on the legal system, playing to the juror in us all. If Tocqueville were to return tomorrow, he would no doubt relate the trial-mania of our current popular culture to the fact that, of the world's jury trials, 90 percent are now American. In any case, what he saw with such preternatural clarity is that the American legal imagination, as it plays itself out among the "common people," inhabits first and foremost not the judge's bench, not the attorney's chair, not the witness stand, not even the jail cell or the electric chair, but the jury box. The visible player, the protagonist, may be any of these other people (commonly one of the lawyers, in line with Tocqueville's observation that jurors are would-be jurists), and the fiction may take us into the judge's chambers, or back in history to the scene of the crime, or with the investigator on his quest for clues, but at bottom our stance with respect to the evidence is always that of the citizen asked to decide: the trier of fact. It is hard to imagine a more generative exercise in American popular culture than this one. Diegesis, in its first form, may be our most favorite kind of narrative.

Notes

This essay is adapted from a chapter of my *Trials, Movies, and the Adversarial Imagination* (Princeton, N.J.: Princeton Univ. Press, forthcoming, 1998).

1. Alexis de Tocqueville, *Democracy in America*, vol. 1 (New York: Random House/Vintage, 1990), 278–80.

2. Where modern readers will see the machinery of discipline and the means of political interpellation, Tocqueville saw a splendid form of education:

The jury contributes powerfully to form the judgment and to increase the natural intelligence of a people; and this, in my opinion, is its greatest advantage. It may be regarded as a gratuitous public school, ever open. . . . I think that the practical intelligence and political good sense of the Americans are mainly attributable to the long use that they have made of the jury in civil cases. . . . Thus the jury, which is the most energetic means of making the people rule, is also the most efficacious means of teaching it how to rule well.

Although Tocqueville is speaking here of the civil trial, his remarks apply in the main to the criminal one as well. Ibid., 285–87.

3. Ibid., 280, 318.

4. The topos of the accidentally photographed or filmed crime scene also has a long history. Dion Boucicault's *The Octoroon* is often cited as the literary an-

cestor. For early film examples, see especially Jim Lastra and Tom Gunning, "Tracing the Individual Body, aka Photography, Detectives, Early Cinema, and the Body of Modernity," in *Cinema and the Invention of Modern Life*, ed. Vanessa R. Schwartz and Leo Charney (Berkeley: University of California Press, 1995), and "What I Saw from the Rear Window of the Hotel des Folies-Dramatiques, or the Story Point of View Films Told," in *Ce que Je vois de mon ciné . . .*, ed. André Gaudreault (Paris: Klincksieck, 1988). That the idea is going strong after ninety years is clear from the 1996 ABC television serial *Murder One*. In the last two episodes (April 22 and April 23, 1996), the defense lawyer realizes that the murder in question must have been captured on videotape, finds and views the tape, and, in the series finale, plays it to the court, thus revealing the identity of the real murderer and establishing the innocence of his own client— the plot of *Falsely Accused!* updated for video.

5. This "skillful cut-in of film being developed in a darkroom tray" (John L. Fell, "Motive, Mischief, and Melodrama: The State of Film Narrative in 1907," in *Film Before Griffith*, ed. John L. Fell [Berkeley: University of California Press, 1983], 279) may be the first instance of what will become a standard gesture in evidence-based movies.

6. The surviving print is incomplete at this point (the screen in the courtroom has not yet been matted with the images of the murder sequence, which come next on the reel). Writes Fell: "The last sequence is visible in the Museum nitrate print, first with spectators staring at a blank sheet mounted behind the bench, then with the yet-to-be-matted-in murder footage positioned to accommodate the preceding image" (ibid., 279). See also Eileen Bowser, "Griffith's Film Career Before *The Adventures of Dollie*," in Fell, *Film Before Griffith*, 367–68.

7. Bowser, "Griffith's Film Career," 367.

8. "Attraction" and "narrative integration" are Tom Gunning's categories in his "The Cinema of Attraction: Early Film, Its Spectator, and the Avant-Garde," *Wide Angle* 8 (1986): 63–70.

9. *The American Film Institute Catalogue*, vol. F1 (Berkeley: University of California Press, 1988), q.v. *By Whose Hand?* It was a five-reel picture (Equitable).

10. Etienne Sauriau, "La Structure d'univers filmique et le vocabulaire de la filmologie," *Revue internationale de Filmologie* 7/8 (n.d.): 233. See also Edward Lowry, *The Filmology Movement and Film Study in France* (Ann Arbor, Mich.: UMI, 1985), 8–85. Aristotle writes:

There must, of course, be some survey of the actions that form the subject-matter of the speech. . . . One of the two parts of this speech is not provided by the orator's art, viz. the actions themselves. . . . Nowadays it is said, absurdly enough, that the narration [*diegesis*] should be rapid. Remember what the man said to the baker who asked whether he was to make the cake hard or soft: "What, can't you make it right?" Just so here. We are not to make long narrations, just as we are not to make long introductions or long arguments. Here, again, rightness does not consist either in rapidity or in conciseness, but in the happy mean; that is, in saying just so much as will make the facts plain, or will lead the hearer to believe that a thing has happened to some one, or that the man has caused injury or wrong to some one, or that the facts are really as important as you wish them to be thought: or the opposite facts to establish the opposite arguments.

The Rhetoric and Poetics of Aristotle (1954; reprint, New York: New York Modern Library, 1984), *Rhetoric* 1416b: 18, 1417a:3.

11. *American Film Institute Catalogue,* vol. F3, q.v. *The Trial of Vivienne Ware.* The serial ran first in New York and subsequently by the Hearst papers elsewhere in the U.S. The parts of judge and lawyers in the radio broadcast were played by well-known figures in the political and legal arena. The film, however, fixed the ending. The 1941 film based on Ayn Rand's play of the same name is a similar case: the stage play of 1935 used a jury recruited from the audience at each performance, and depending on their vote, one of Rand's multiple finales was played out; but the film chose one ending and played the case straight. Wrote the *Variety* reviewer, "The film version of 'Night of Jan. 16' will hardly emulate the success of the Ayn Rand play in '35–'36 because the show hinged on a trick of audience participation which the picture obviously cannot employ. Result is a moderate feature destined to play in support." *Variety Film Reviews* (New York: Garland, 1983), September 10, 1941.

12. For example, *Scene of the Crime* (1984–1985), "a trio of intricate and spine-tingling cases each presenting a rogues' gallery of celebrity suspects and asking you to discover whodunit," and *Free, White, and 21* (1963), described by Marlyn Robinson as follows: "The defense argues consent in the trial of a black hotel owner accused of raping a white civil rights worker. The trial culminates with both attorneys making their final arguments and the judge giving jury instructions directly to the camera. The screen fades to black, a clock appears, and the movie audience, having previously been handed a 'summons,' is asked to decide the verdict." "Law in Popular Culture: Feature Films; An Annotated List of Films in the Law and Popular Culture Collection, Tarlton Law Library, University of Texas School of Law," available from http://www.law.utexas.edu.

13. See, for example, Wheeler Winston Dixon, "It Looks at You: Notes on the 'Look Back' in Cinema," *Post Script* 13, no. 1 (1993): 77–87; and Marc Vernet, "The Look at the Camera," *Cinema Journal* 28, no. 2 (winter 1989): 48–63.

14. From the video boxcovers for *The Trial of Jean Harris, The Thin Blue Line, The Accused,* and from Court TV's *Prime Time Justice* tag for the Susan Smith Trial (July, 1995), respectively.

15. On the irony of the title, see Christine Alice Corcos, "Presuming Innocence: Alan J. Pakula and Scott Turow Take on the Great American Legal Fiction" (unpublished manuscript).

16. Dershowitz's novel, on which the film is based, is clear about the autobiographical stakes and is written in Dershowitz's first person; *Reversal of Fortune* (New York: Simon and Schuster/Pocket, 1986) esp. "Setting the Stage," xv–xxvi. The Magill's entry explains the film's defense bias as a function of libel law, a problem that often dogs films about still-living characters. Thus the stepchildren are sketchily drawn as "passive and almost nonexistent" because the filmmakers feared a lawsuit, whereas the Dershowitz father and son are depicted as fiery, passionate, emotional, and vibrant. "Because the film is based, for the most part, on Dershowitz's book of the same name and was co-produced by his son Elon, the filmmakers had little to worry about lawsuits from Dershowitz and his family and had more freedom to add substance to these characters and more fully dramatize their points of view"; *Magill's Survey of Cinema, English Lan-*

guage Films, 2d series (Englewood Cliffs, N.J.: Salem Press, 1981), q.v. *Reversal of Fortune*.

17. Said writer Nicholas Kazan of his open ending,

I certainly could never convince myself that this man was totally innocent in the more primitive sense of having nothing on his conscience. So I didn't want to make a film which wildly professed his innocence if, you know, when I met my maker I'd be tapped on my shoulder: "By the way, this is a dreadful thing, but Claus was guilty". . . . Hence the end of the film. . . . I did want to leave it open, because I feel the essence of the human condition is that we never know for sure.

From Suzanne Gibson [Shale], "The Conflicts of Law and the Character of Men: Writing *Reversal of Fortune* and *Judgment at Nuremberg*" (paper delivered at the conference Picturing Justice, University of San Francisco Law School, April 1996).

18. The evidence for influence is circumstantial but powerful and generally assumed. See Thomas J. Harris, *Courtroom's Finest Hour in American Cinema*, (Methuen, N.J.: Scarecrow Press, 1987), 2. Cayatte's film was released in France in 1950 and won the main Venice Film Festival award that year. It was also released and reviewed in the U.S. in 1950 and seems to have had a second run in 1952–1953. Rose's teleplay was first broadcast as a CBS Studio One production in 1954.

19. Ibid.

20. "Actually," R. Bosley Crowther wrote in his review of March 3, 1953,

this terse investigation of seven assorted jurors' private lives as they sit in solemn judgment on a woman accused of the mercy killing of her paramour is simply a study of the natures and the reactions of human characters when called upon to render a decision involving the straight interpretation of law and morals. It is a crisp and absorbing demonstration of how people generally respond to the moral aspects of a situation according to the sort of people they are. And, as such, it becomes an exposition of consummate social irony, for the question it leaves with the viewer is whether justice or unfairness has been done.

New York Times Film Reviews (New York: New York Times). The *Variety* review (November 1, 1950) also finds something amiss in the trial treatment: "The film puts too much emphasis on the jurists, detracting not only from the trial but the killing itself."

21. Writes United States Circuit Judge Alex Kozinski of his first viewing of *Twelve Angry Men*:

As I sat there watching, struggling a bit with the language, trying to figure out the jury's function in American law . . . my whole adolescent conception of certainty, of knowledge itself was shaken. The case against the defendant sounded so airtight; the reasons offered by the eleven sounded so irrefutable. I couldn't imagine how (or why) anyone could reach a different conclusion. Then, as one reason after another started to come apart, as inconsistencies crept into the picture, as Jurors began changing their votes, I came to understand that truth does not spring into the courtroom full-blown, like Athena from the head of Zeus.

In Paul Bergman and Michael Asimow, *Reel Justice: The Courtroom Goes to the Movies* (Kansas City: Andrews and McMeel, 1996), xiv. On the different status of truth in the adversarial and the inquisitorial systems as well as in the narrative entertainments derived from those systems, see chapter 4 of my *Trials, Movies, and the Adversarial Imagination*.

22. *Variety Film Reviews*, November 1, 1950.

23. *New York Times Film Reviews*, March 3, 1953.

24. "Released as a conventional booking in large theaters (rather than being distributed only to small art houses, where it might have gained a major following and run for months on the strength of the uniformly favorable reviews it received), the film failed to make a profit, and Fonda never received his deferred salary." Jay Robert Nash and Stanley Ralph Ross, eds., *The Motion Picture Guide* (Chicago: Cinebooks, 1987), q.v. *Twelve Angry Men*. After noting its commercial failure, Pauline Kael commented that "the social psychology of the film is attuned to the educated audience." Kael, *5001 Nights at the Movies* (New York: 1982), q.v. *Twelve Angry Men*. .

25. There have been occasional television programs (such as *Picket Fences* and *Happy Days*) that reenacted the "Twelve Angry Men" scenario. Similarly, in *Murder Most Foul* (1964), Miss Marple is the sole holdout juror. There is a Tony Hancock spoof and various international versions or remakes, including the Hindi *One Man Stopped the Action* (1986).

26. Harris, *Courtroom's Finest Hour*, 20.

27. "John Ford's *Young Mr. Lincoln*," in *Movies and Methods*, ed. Bill Nichols, vol. 1 (Berkeley: University of California Press, 1976), 519.

The Genre of Nature

Ceremonies of Innocence

LEO BRAUDY

The great poems of heaven and hell have been written and the great poem of earth remains to be written.
Wallace Stevens, "Imagination as Value",
The Necessary Angel

For more than a decade, both the popular and the political cultures of the United States have been preoccupied with the question of nature. Sometimes that nature is defined as the primitive essence of what it means to be human; sometimes it is the animal world over which we strive to dominate; sometimes it is the inanimate world of vegetation, rock, and earth. And sometimes it is all three. The continuing focus on environmental and ecological issues is only the most obvious example. Others include the controversies over genetic engineering, the biological basis of social forms, the moral and legal concerns over abortion, surrogate parenting, the molestation of children, and the sexual and psychological abuse of women.

Through all of these debates over the relation between public policy and private desire runs a deeply tinged imagery of nature. No matter what side partisans take, they are usually animated by a heightened sensitivity to the potential corruption of what is assumed to be a natural human innocence. Yet the same controversies also embody a profound uncertainty over whether such an innocence truly exists, how it can be represented, and how it should be protected.

Natural, innocent, primitive—such powerful words are complex, often contradictory terms, at once embodying both ideal and critique. In times of cultural nostalgia like the present, they are used almost interchangeably to designate all we have lost by becoming social beings, all we have failed to understand about the world and our true place in it. Even though they may have markedly different meanings for those who invoke them, they have nevertheless become the common vocabulary of a protest against the technology, reason, and order that since the industrial revolution of the eighteenth century have sustained a belief in civilization and progress.

In the polarized form that marks the public discussion of most of these issues, the underlying interconnectedness of their common beliefs and terminology is usually lost sight of. Yet in a surprisingly large group of films from the 1980s and after, the myths, metaphors, and motifs of nature stand out, sometimes in shadows and shadings, but often in bold relief. I want here to explore those films and their forebears not to determine a specific genre of nature with a codified group of characteristics, but to indicate first how powerful themes can inflect preexisting genres to create transgeneric hybrids and then to suggest how popular culture particularly acts as sounding board or lightning rod for deep-rooted audience concerns.[1]

My point is not to say that certain films are really "about" abortion or genetic engineering. Too much current interpretation, whether from the Left or the Right, assumes that popular films are only a crude but handy searchlight by which to read political and social conflicts: monsters in 1950s science fiction films, for example, are always really "about" the Red Menace. Such analysis continues to subordinate (and reduce) the products of popular culture to rationally determinable (and thereby superior) political or social meanings. But within our own minds and attitudes, there is a constant interplay between the stories told in film and fiction and the stories told in journalism, on television news, in casual conversation, and in classrooms. Many of these stories are not simply the by-products of more explicit and self-conscious political formulations, but voice deeper disquiets that cut across an entire cultural landscape.

In a society where mass culture touches everyone, it is archaic as well as uselessly paranoid to suppose that powerful people—who run studios or governments—are totally free of its ways of formulating issues, while everyone else is being manipulated. The debates over the coerciveness of patriarchal, colonialist European and Anglo-American cultures have, for example, paid more attention to the obvious ways their stories have been imposed than to the more subtle and complex mechanisms of their acceptance. In this way, the history of how the American film industry rose to domination in the world market in the 1920s, defeating the German, is told almost entirely in terms of an economic sway over the markets thereby crushed into obedience. Occasionally there is a nod toward the "system of Hollywood narrative." But even this perfunctory invocation of a bent for storytelling is treated as if it too were a premeditated imposition rather than evidence that Hollywood, aiming at its culturally mixed and lower-class audiences, might be telling stories in which individuals from very different cultures recognized enough of their desires and dreams that they went to see those films out of choice.[2]

One significant aspect of such stories is what might be called their "portability," the circumstances that allow the products of one culture to be absorbed and even co-opted by another. Edward Hall makes an intriguing distinction between a high-context culture, in which nearly everyone knows the rules and cultural messages are often inexplicit, and a low-context culture, in which little can be taken for granted and all codes need to be spelled out.[3] In these terms, the commercial need to attract a heterogeneous audience impelled the development of stories and genres that established or extracted a common narrative vocabulary underlying the attitudes of otherwise disparate (and high context) groups. The economic domination by Hollywood of the world film market therefore should not obscure the fact that for at least fifty years (1920–1970) American films were also giving audiences all over the world a good portion of what they at least thought they wanted.[4]

Historically in the United States, many of those myths and stories have focused on nature. This is hardly surprising, since native or newly arrived Americans were conditioned to look into nature for astonishment and rejuvenation, or to expect astonishment and rejuvenation as the sign that nature has been truly evoked. As Emerson never tired of asserting, Americans were and ought to be "nature's nation." The implicit but official American view of nature is thus a fundamental, even fundamentalist search for master myths through which nature can be both revealed and conquered by story. Audubon's paintings in *Birds of America*, Edward Curtis's photographs of Native Americans, the activities of Teddy Roosevelt, Gifford Pinchot, and John Muir to preserve natural parks and wildernesses, the travelogues of Burton Holmes—all partook of the necessarily mixed message of the effort of language, art, and politics to preserve an evasive and elusive nature.

Popular film especially furnishes an intriguing set of clues to such underlying cultural concerns because it is in film that the technological and the emotional have the uneasiest commerce—a replication of the tension underlying so many of the social issues that now upset people the most. Claude Lévi-Strauss has argued that all cultural action is the symbolic resolution of conflict, and Roland Barthes that the function of myth is to turn culture into nature. Unqualified, both principles postulate a static mythic world and assume an "opium of the people" approach to production that ignores the dynamic reciprocity between the sometimes pat resolutions of individual stories and the frequently gaping irresolution of their social implications. These views lead to the gloom that in the 1970s suffuses writing about genre, when critics despaired of being able to find a "coherent cultural myth" in the films they saw around them and hinted darkly of genre degeneration.

In place of this generally static view of the cultural function of film, I would rather consider film in general and genre film in particular as a field of contested themes, images, and other signifiers that cannot be neatly divided into text, subtext, and context because neither producers nor consumers have the final word on their meaning.[5] Similarly, the "genre" of nature that I propose to construct or discover is hardly transparent in the sense that French sociological and anthropological theory accords to the concept of naturalization. It has instead a double project: to foreground the process of epistemological confrontation between culture and nature, along with the subsequent evasions, cover-ups, and ellipses; and at the same time to pursue the elusive goal of finding a still point of innocence to be preserved. In their heyday from the early 1980s to the present, the films of nature appear to constitute something between a genre and a cultural node, neither an explicitly codified or codifiable form nor a bundle of thematic coincidences, but a product of the inadequacy of established narrative modes and systems of production to deal effectively with the new world the audience inhabits.

*   *   *

Looking to nature to revitalize civilization has been a constant urge in Western culture since Rome created the first self-conscious (and therefore defensive) urban culture in the last century B.C. A whole genre of Roman poetry, called pastoral and deriving from a handful of Greek precedents, featured jaded city-people in the guise of shepherds celebrating the virtues of the countryside. Pastoral also bequeathed to Christianity such long-lasting images as the lost lamb and the good shepherd who looks after the flock (in contrast with the ambitious and self-seeking

Roman politician). In these poems, the purer values of nature were opposed to the corruption of the political and social worlds. But in the right hands, nature could also authorize political power. In another favorite Roman story, Cincinnatus drops his plow and takes up the mantle of power when his country calls, and aristocracies through the ages have used the argument that their power is itself "natural."

For all its preoccupation with the land and the cycles of growth, the Roman pastoral world was less wild than restful. By the Renaissance, Montaigne, among others, had established an early vision of this primitive innocence in his essay "Of Cannibals," in whom he saw a human nature perhaps violent but also uncorrupted by European traditions and customs, and therefore more able to respond to the immediacy of life, because it was free of both civilization and history. Another crucial change, building on this celebration of a more savage world, occurred in the late eighteenth and early nineteenth centuries, when the rebellion against established social power in the name of nature became part of the polemic of the French and American revolutions.

In a noted article on the eighteenth-century uses of the word *nature*, Arthur O. Lovejoy reckoned up some thirty or forty major variations, most of which seemed logically contradictory. Nature could be what is outside you or inside you. It could be what is regular, efficient, and systematic, or what is irregular, abundant, and follows no theory. It could be the heart of things or it could be the surface of things. It could be what is inherently human or what is inherently animal. It could be opposed to society, politics, culture, and art, or it could be their essence. Politically, it could mean freedom (as a return to a lost or repressed human nature) or confinement (as the need to abide by an unchangeable human nature). Artistically, it could mean the need to follow eternal rules or the need to forget all rules. Theologically, it could mean what is permanent or what constantly changes, what is pure (and innocent of thought) or what is impure (and beyond any thought).[6]

Lovejoy's catalogue illustrates how the argument based on nature is inherently neither conservative nor liberal but radical and oppositional. Nature can thus be invoked by individuals with a whole range of political views, especially when they feel dispossessed and alienated from any status quo. This invocation of nature as a primitive power opposed to everything that civilization has created comes to us from the revolutionary and romantic period. Developed through such ideas as the "noble savage," who was unwarped by social forms and conventions, this praise of primitive life put down firm roots in a vision of America as the uncon-

ditioned landscape, the refuge from an unnatural Europe of rigid archi-
tectures and classes. To a large extent it was also a reaction to the revolution in empirical science, when the more spiritual view of the natural
world as an expression of God had been transformed into a countable,
analyzable, and therefore controllable nature that would yield all its secrets to human inquiry and human labor. Unlike the Roman desire for
a little holiday relief topped off with political satire, this new view of
nature was characterized by the urge to begin again, to get back to
roots, and to dispense with all that burdened the human race in the
name of history and society.

From the first, then, the Enlightenment belief in progress is undermined or complemented by an often equally strong commitment to
primitivism.[7] In fact, little of this skepticism about progress and technology, along with allied stories of the power of the primitive perspective, is unprecedented. Mary Shelley's *Frankenstein* may have helped
begin the attack against the misuses of the new knowledge. But the tale
of a visitor to our world whose innocent clarity of vision mocks an over-
sophisticated society—shall we call him *Starman* or *E.T.*?—has been a
device of satire for centuries. Other visitors from the realms of nature,
like the mermaid who has been stranded on land through love, or the
boy who has grown up with animals, have been paying calls since the
Middle Ages and before. The more intriguing question is how such old
stories either are reinterpreted to deal with a new world, or else become
of only historical interest, no longer open to adaptations that might satisfy the concerns of a new audience.

By now, some two centuries later, any wholehearted belief in the in-
exhaustible exploitability of the natural world is, to say the least, problematic: we question technology, we question the machine, and we
question the power of science to define reality. The Enlightenment-
based myths of our culture, especially those linked to scientific progress
and the benevolence of established power, are not compelling anymore.
Instead, audiences look to more ancient myths to provide less tainted
explanations to hold together the world. The immensely popular Bill
Moyers shows with Joseph Campbell; the many books about matriarchy,
goddesses, and the Gaia theory of the earth; Robert Bly's use of the
Grimm fairy tale "Iron John" to sponsor a renovation of masculinity;
the search for the "inner child" to purify an adult nature corrupted by
a dysfunctional family—all embody an urge to get back to the origin,
purge the dross and rust of history, and—in a kind of secular millenari-
anism—begin again.

These dark murmurings may also be more apparent in popular forms because their artistic premises emphasize familiarity and repetition even as they search for new beginnings. During the 1940s and 1950s, horror films were often preoccupied with a fear of a primitive world erupting into ordered social space. Nature had an often anthropological inflection that barely veiled a social fear that "darker" races would blight daytime and well-lit America. Such films were often filled with tribal rituals (usually voodoo) and animal familiars that still intrigue such English and Australian directors as Peter Weir (*The Last Wave*, 1977), John Boorman (*The Emerald Forest*, 1985), and Alan Parker (*Angel Heart*, 1987).[8] In the United States, though, the uncertain line between the human and the primitive that marks films like Jacques Tourneur and Val Lewton's *Cat People* (1942) and *I Walked with a Zombie* (1943) gloomily contrasts with the optimistic urge to conquer and civilize nature that is celebrated in postwar epics of South Sea mercantilism like *Wake of the Red Witch* (1948) and *His Majesty O'Keefe* (1953). This close linking of the primitive to the unconscious or at least to repressed passion is reflected as well in the way a whole genre of forties and fifties film, film noir, emphasized the destructive sexual forces that lay beneath the veneer of urban order and postwar prosperity.

From the moment of its explosion over Hiroshima, the nuclear bomb has been a symbol of the human desire and inability to control nature. In the shadow of the Bomb, the science fiction and horror films of the 1950s made discomfort with scientific progress even more explicit. Crucial to fifties science fiction was the question of whether knowledge was to be controlled by military or civilian power. The moral of *The Thing* (1951) was that pure scientists have too much intellectual tunnel vision and ignore real dangers. *The Day the Earth Stood Still*, its liberal doppelgänger of the same year, implied that the individualist scientist has the moral answer because his concerns *aren't* directly political or military.

*   *   *

There are important differences between the earlier questionings of knowledge and technology and those implicit in science fiction films now, including the near-abandonment of the old anticommunist political agenda. It has clearly not been enough merely to reassert a romantic view that a restored connection with nature can be a corrective for the ills of society. Under the pressure of ever-expanding technological and communications revolutions, we are forced to wonder what kind of stories will survive and which stories may even be enhanced. The interest in Campbell's efforts to find a Jungian monomyth underlying the variety of human social forms, as well as the feminist and ecological interest in myths of the earth, somewhat obscure the way in which science and technology themselves have been mythologized. Jerome Bruner has remarked that nature as a category has moved from the world of science to the world of story. Perhaps we are telling ourselves new stories about nature because the stories science tells no longer seem compelling—unless they are told by a Stephen Hawking, himself a marvel of nature and technology.[9]

Even during the Cold War there was an optimism about the search for ever more data to accumulate: knowledge was power, knowledge was control. By the 1980s and 1990s, it is not the accumulation and control of scientific facts that are at issue but the possibility that no one really has any idea what to do with all the information that is available. Now knowledge itself has become suspect. The plots of fifties science fiction films, like those of thirties detective novels, emphasized the search for the crucial detail that would crack the case, transforming confusion into rational order. Now, the plot is more likely to emphasize the ambiguity of factual detail, the detective or scientist's inability to decide what is relevant and what isn't. Either the solution, if there is one, appears from a mystical or instinctual source, or else, as in *Terminator 2* (1992), the story clearly asserts that certain discoveries would perhaps be better left unmade.

Works of recent popular culture therefore accuse science and technology of inadequate and corrupt storytelling, of a moral inability to distinguish what is crucial from what is not, what is a human order from what is an inhuman one. *Elephant Man* (1980), *Quest for Fire* (1981), *Never Cry Wolf* (1983), *Greystoke* (1984), *Splash* (1984), *Iceman* (1984), *Emerald Forest* (1985), *The Mission* (1986), *Predator* (1987), *Project X* (1987), *Gorillas in the Mist* (1991), and many others feature almost infinite variations on the conflict between, on one side, the primitive and the natural and, on the other, technological, scientific, or social progress. Sometimes primitive innocence and purity win out; sometimes they are obliterated, depending on the degree of utopian optimism or apocalyptic pessimism in the script. But the same concerns cut across a wide variety of otherwise very different-looking works: medieval and science fantasy hybrids such as *Dragonslayer* (1981) and *Conan the Barbarian* (1982); threatened farmers in *The River, Places in the Heart,* and *Country* (all 1984); the Rambo series with its stripped-to-the-waist indomitable hero; comical or malevolent films about creatures bent on human destruction such as *Gremlins* (1984), *Arachnophobia* (1990), and *Tremors* (1991); along with the many films (and novels) preoccupied with cyborgs and robots—beings created by a technology that blurs the line between the human and the inhuman body: *Alien* (1979), *Blade Runner* (1982), *Terminator* (1984), *Aliens* (1986), *Robocop* (1987), and their descendants.

The difference between *Star Wars* (1977) and its sequels is a barometer of the shifting cultural atmosphere in the early years of this nature genre. *Star Wars* is almost entirely oriented toward technology: the combat is between a fascist militarist civilization (complete with uniforms and ugly robots) and a feudal-individualist group of misfit heroes (complete with its own set of cute robots). *The Empire Strikes Back* (1980) and *Return of the Jedi* (1983) make the technology versus nature contrast even more acute: the natural world of the cuddly Ewoks is to be destroyed by the Death Star (which resembles the techno-sculpture of the Italian artist Arnoldo Pomodori). Before he can help the Ewoks battle the evil Empire, Luke Skywalker, the young hero, must lose his hand (prosthetically replaced) and be trained in heroic virtue by the swamp-dwelling ancient Yoda: true power comes from plunging into the murk and coming out whole. The Ewoks themselves are primitive Pooh creatures, with a clear vision of who's good and who isn't, and a fierce loyalty. The mystic powers learned by the young from the very old, combined with the indomitable innocence of a bow-and-arrow civilization of teddy bears, thereupon defeat the forces of technologically sophisticated totalitarianism.

Oddly or appropriately, the Death Star is most closely equivalent to George Lucas's production company and the technological finesse that went into the making of the films themselves. Loaded with innovative special effects, these productions reveal the nostalgia of a generation of techno-brats for an undespoiled nature.[10] Perhaps only with such an obvious mea culpa can they successfully defeat the armored mercenary father, Darth Vader, who has betrayed the past, and justify the good father, Obi-wan Kenobi, who has retained its values. As in the *Godfather* films, the family tries to assert itself as a center of feeling and justice otherwise missing in "the real world." In these more realistic urban epics, however, the family slowly becomes tainted by the lust for power that suffuses the society around it. In the *Star Wars* films, with their fantastic setting, power loses out constantly to camaraderie and friendship. The evil family may invariably try to break up or corrupt the good family, but the good family needs more than its purity to defend itself.

Luke Skywalker (Mark Hamill). *The Empire Strikes Back*, George Lucas.
© Twentieth Century Fox/Lucasfilm, 1980.

It needs to maintain its relation to nature rather than to society or technology or politics.

The conception of nature underlying many early versions of the nature story has two prime aspects: nature as a physical place and nature
as an ideal human setting. Often these two aspects conflict. Nature as
place stresses the eternity of the natural and animal realm, compared to
the smallness, frailty, or insignificance of the human—a contrast later
pushed to an extreme in *Jurassic Park* (1993). Nature as an ideal setting
accents the harmony with nature of particular "natural" peoples: Native
Americans facing an encroaching European frontier; or more contemporary embattled ethnic families, their traditional values threatened by
urban variety and assimilation.

In all, however, it is the "normal" structure of civilization that is
in question. Unlike the "giant carrot" in *The Thing*, the thawed-out
Neanderthal in *Iceman* (1984)—or in its comic version *Encino Man*

(1992)—is not a blood-drinking monster spaceman; he is an imposed-upon innocent, a caveman bewildered by the modern world that seeks to study him. Other recent films play more or less realistic variations on the same elements. *At Play in the Fields of the Lord* (1992) and *Medicine Man* (1992) are set in the South American rain forests and preoccupied with indigenous peoples and lost natural secrets. Within every film there are small betrayals. But the largest betrayal is always the promise of a natural paradise to the people who will live in it. And for that overriding sense of loss, nature is also the emblematic compensation. The conclusion of *Grand Canyon* (1992) resolves its urban melodrama by taking its embattled Angeleno survivors to the overwhelming wonder evoked by the movie's title, so as to put their (and the country's) problems in a natural perspective.

Movies—especially genre movies—and culture—especially popular culture—are always in search of story. As movies developed in America, they consistently projected large national social and cultural issues into personal stories that were resolved (usually by love), while the more general problems remained. This may be a necessary ambivalence in any popular form that seeks to engage the emotions of its audience and to continue to engage them. If all the dragons are defeated, the film closes in on itself and remains an experience separated from the real, unresolved life of the audience. But when the resolution of the personal problem and the irresolution of the social or cultural problem coexist most obviously and uneasily, then other truths may be hinted at.[11] Thus, in *Never Cry Wolf* (1983), the ability of the single man to renew himself in contact with nature is joyously confirmed, even while the entrepreneurs of ecological disaster are clearly on the march. In *Emerald Forest* (1985), we are given two endings: in one, the dam that would destroy the forest is itself destroyed; in the other, the tribe whose world the dam's destruction would have inundated still preserves its primitive paradise of magic and free sexuality.

Such double or ambivalent endings imply that neither resolution—revenge against machine technology or retreat to a world elsewhere—is enough to resolve the story in its own terms. Unlike artistic forms that seek to stand apart from more immediate conflicts, popular stories in both film and literature gather energy from their dynamic ability to represent unresolved conflicts in national consciousness. When the issues have been transformed (although not necessarily resolved) and are no longer so emotionally pressing, the stories lose that energy and become mere historical data.[12]

As the critically despised phenomenon of sequels makes clear, the basic urge of popular culture is to discover how to be new in spite of history and how to reconcile innovation with tradition. In nineteenth-century England, industrial culture tried to validate itself by inventing a whole series of political and social traditions, from the Scottish kilt to the cozy British royal family.[13] In the United States, we had ready-made mythic material in the sharp contrast between the Europe-facing cities of the East and the open spaces of the West. Frederick Jackson Turner's 1893 meditation on the end of the frontier was just the signal for the western novel and film to break out of the corral.

The western is a prime forerunner for the nature film's renovation of tradition because hankering for the past is one of its central themes. From the 1920s to the 1960s, the western frequently was set at the origins of social institutions and principles—the law, justice, religion, and the community. Its stories usually focused on the conflicts over what these institutions should be and what values they should embody. Like the British invention of parliamentary and royal rituals to symbolize a continuity that stretched back before history, the makers and consumers of westerns engaged in a mutual ritual of getting back to the beginning. The town with one banker, one storekeeper, one teacher, one boardinghouse keeper, one prostitute, one sheriff, one bartender, one blacksmith, one doctor—and a shifting population of the good and the bad—allowed the audience to see how it all had started and meditate on how it might be renewed.

After a number of revisionist westerns in the 1970s, by directors such as Don Siegel, Robert Altman, Robert Aldrich, Clint Eastwood, and Arthur Penn, the western as a self-contained genre had almost vanished. Its revival in the 1990s, I would argue, occurs because the nostalgic motifs and preoccupations of the genre of nature gave the western a revived symbolic charge. Appropriately for a series fascinated with changing the past to ensure the present, *Back to the Future III* (1990) looks for Marty McFly's roots not in the Revolutionary War but in a parodied Old West. Even the great recent successes of purer (more generically consistent) westerns like *Lonesome Dove* on television and, in film, *Dances with Wolves* or *Unforgiven* are individual exceptions rather than genre revivals. *Lonesome Dove* ends at the dusty town where it begins, with all its life and energy drained away, whereas *Dances* is less about the western issues of social origins than about the effort to strip them away entirely and, in the spirit of a return to nature, to discover the Native American world so often distorted or ignored in the classical western.[14] The 1993

Best Picture award to *Unforgiven* conveys the same double message, paying belated tribute both to the western genre and to Clint Eastwood's career, while celebrating a film that is itself unsentimentally and savagely critical about the myths of western male honor and violence that animated the form.[15]

*   *   *

No matter how flexible its definitions, genre criticism has rarely shaken the prescriptive tone that seeks to specify what elements allow us to say that this is one genre and not another.[16] But the genre of nature combines those categorical aspects of genre with a more general atmospheric collection of traits that might be called a mode. The way it has inflected preexisting forms such as the western, the horror film, and the science fiction film indicates something of its transgeneric nature and aligns it less with the traditional, self-contained forms than with what I might call the transformative genres (such as melodrama and satire), a great part of whose power comes from the ease with which they can permeate seemingly more settled genres.[17]

Nevertheless, some elements of a nature genre per se—short of an inventory—might be specified. The heroes and heroines of many of these films are often primitives: Neanderthals, aborigines, animals, or a wide array of psychics or natural wonders who draw upon superhuman resources for their power. Even when they come from another planet and a presumably more technologically advanced civilization, they retain an indomitable innocence. In a way that usually undermines whatever partisan political message the director or scriptwriters may intend to get across, established society—*any* established society—is hostile to these powerful but simple adults and children. With rare exceptions, evil wears the guise of official, paternal power, and its villainy is defined by insisting that heaven-sent natural gifts have to be made useful, in other words, politicized. *Close Encounters of the Third Kind* (1977), for example, seems to fall into the pattern of *The Day the Earth Stood Still:* the wise aliens find their true affinity with the good earth people, not the government. But politics has been drained almost entirely from *Close Encounters.* The nearest character to a government representative is played by François Truffaut, and the human-alien affinity is based on wordless harmonies of music and art rather than articulated knowledge.

The nature-culture continuum has a major thematic and structural force in the films, especially in terms of tensions between civilization (technology, urbanism) and primitivism (magic, the context of a rural or pastoral or undeveloped world). As the double ending of *Emerald Forest* exemplifies, there is also often a syntactic disjuncture at the point of narrative closure in which the discourses of real (dystopian civilization) and ideal (natural community) clash. Such endings may specifically invoke the motifs of another genre, preferring in that way to leave the door of closure somewhat ajar, instead of slamming it shut.

Part of the tone of these films is an elegy for an epic martial world that can no longer exist, an attack on a world of corporate and individualist greed that should not exist, and a satire of a world of invidious political, social, economic, and national distinctions that must transform itself before the spectacle of nature. The old theme of the werewolf—the human who involuntarily gets transformed into an animal—gets turned around in films like *Iceman* and *Wolf* (1994). The animal self is the energetic, vital, positive side, and the human is the weak, corrupt, and negative side. Underlining the linkage between nature stories and horror stories, the images of the hero's emergence from earth and water suggest that a baptism in the primitive promises an exemption from death far more definitive than does any successful combat with the monster.

Thus, within the body of a nature film, there are often clashes of language and discourse—cold science versus emotional empathy, primitivism versus progress, commercialism versus humanitarianism. These clashes, not invariably so binary as I have listed them, usually feature a resounding rebuke from the representative of nature: "You do with Mogwai [the gremlin they had called Gizmo] what your society has done to all of nature's gifts. You do not understand," says the wise Chinese seller of curios to the hero and his inept inventor father in *Gremlins* (1984). "You never learned my language," says the Caribbean tribesman to Columbus in *1492: The Invasion of Paradise* (1992).

Animals and children are often the incantatory familiars of this commitment to nature, and their fluidity is expressed by a visual preoccupation with rivers, streams, oceans, islands, rain, and dam-bursting waters. Water in particular stands in for the repressed values of nature that must be acknowledged before heroism can be achieved and culture renovated. Heroes like Rambo or Kevin Costner's Robin Hood take their energy from the water or the earth or the trees, from which they so frequently emerge, to defeat an evil defined by its relation to organized political power. By tying their prowess more tightly to nature, the stories of such heroes emphasize their distance from the moral structures of organized Judeo-Christian religion and assert a more pagan, even oddly classical, heroism. This heroism also has a feminine aspect that sometimes plays a crucial role. In *Jaws* (1975), the paradigmatic early film of the nature cycle, three men set out to do battle with the shark: the misogynist shark expert is swallowed up by the beast itself; the impassioned but fact-obsessed ichthyologist seems to have drowned, although he emerges after the climactic battle; and only the common-sensical but psychologically more confused sheriff (whose marriage is in trouble) can find the resources to defeat the threat from the sea.

As the genre of nature has developed in the past two decades, two modal attitudes have become pervasive, inflecting earlier conceptions of nature as physical place or ideal setting. In one, the natural world is still potentially benevolent and transfiguring if we know where and how to look. This sort of film is connected to the long history of urban idealization of natural renewal. *The Little Mermaid* (1991), as befits an animated cartoon, offers a benevolent version of the basic Ondine myth by bringing the mermaid back to land for a happy ending. In the more satiric *Splash* (1984), the part human and part animal mermaid also sees a kindred spirit in the water and follows him onto the land. But its ending gives the myth a reverse ecological twist: the mermaid takes her earthbound lover back to the sea with her, where it turns out he can breathe, as Ondine could not on the corrupted land.

The second sort of nature film, now perhaps the dominant mode, develops the melancholic and apocalyptic view of nature that in the past was primarily represented by horror films and science fiction extravaganzas. But the visionary possibilities of much of the science fiction of the past—which could exist even in the Cold War 1950s—has now disappeared almost entirely. In what is by now an almost exclusively gloomy view, the natural world has become irredeemably corrupted. Human nature is either forced into monster shapes (*Alien*) or needs techno-monsterizing itself to be truly effective against its enemies (*Aliens, Robocop, Terminator 2*).[18]

Both of these possibilities mark a peculiarly twentieth-century romanticism about nature, energized by a sense of imminent world destruction that results not from war but from the fatal by-products of human progress and success—the apocalypse of trash. The 1890s artistically were a time of increased refinement and artistic self-consciousness summarized in the arch phrase *fin de siècle*: history would be a process of increasing sophistication. But the 1990s seem more attached to the assumption that only an untouched and perhaps impossible freshness will allow a new beginning.

Through the mediations worked by the nature genre, the western locale, with its potential for growth and choice, has thus been replaced either by images of unnatural futurity in science fiction or by images of the natural lushness of the precivilized world—outer space or primitive space. In political life, this division corresponds to a shift in national priorities. The old teleology of "Where are we going and how do we get there?" has given way to a nervous "How can we stop from going where we don't want to go?" Fundamentalisms of all sorts have arisen here and abroad to reject change and innovation as sacrilege. But even in the mainstream, national purpose has ceased to be a question of right choices (the mode of the western) and has concentrated instead on a need to retain older values that are eroding or vanishing (the mode of nature). The inner meaning of such stories similarly sprawls across the political spectrum. In the classic western, individualism could be either left-wing or right-wing in its political implications, and so in the audience of the nature film might be found environmentalist prochoicers along with antiabortionist advocates of the death penalty.

What is conspicuously left out and even actively ignored is the existence of almost any kind of history outside the self. To the extent that history does appear, it is understood almost entirely as technological advance, celebrated, as in *Star Wars*, or mocked, as in *Iceman*. To the extent that social groups exist at all, they are rarely couples, more often groups of friends. Virtue, as in the western, is essentially freelance. Even sympathetic scientists are as bound by their own manacled habits of thought as by bureaucratic rules and regulations. *Forrest Gump* (1994) does an intriguing take on some of these themes. The retarded hero's adventures mock the expectation that knowledge is needed to deal with the late-twentieth-century environment. Gump moves through the catastrophic public history of the last thirty or so years, experiencing "important" events but responding primarily to his own friends and feelings. All his boldest acts have something directly to do with a natural setting, including the most bizarre: running back and forth across America. But it is exactly this sense of the sweep and beauty of American nature that remains the only enduring value.

The same transformation of the western's primary concerns into utopian or apocalyptic preoccupations with nature has been accompanied and perhaps intensified by the disappearance for the vast majority of Americans of open space of the kind that filled the western screen. At nearly the same time that outer space was being trumpeted as a "new frontier" unforeseen by Frederick Jackson Turner, Rachel Carson's *Si-*

lent Spring (1962) sounded an early tocsin about earthly self-poisoning that grew throughout the Vietnam War and the recurrent energy crises of the 1970s. Even in the 1980s, when personal winning was encouraged and general losing ignored, these nature films were finding their stories (as in the *Alien* series) in the inability of the big bad corporation, let alone single individuals, to control nature. The unalloyed vision of endless earthly expansiveness was over, the human race was itself a potentially endangered species, and the turn toward nature in these films— their cultural work—was part of an effort to refound lost values.

Any twenty-year-old in 1997 can now reminisce as fervently as did a seventy-year-old in 1957 about the changes that have occurred since he or she was young. The filling up and tarring over of vacant lots and all but officially designated chunks of urban greenery, the expansion of shopping malls and strips into suburbia and exurbia, the dreadful ambiguity that infects the word *park*—have created an America characterized by an ersatz continuity of visual texture: fast food drive-ins, chain grocery stores, and postmodern pastels across the country. As a result, the experience of nature has become not an everyday event but a special occasion—ski trip, hiking trip, or scenic trip—in which the consumer seeks to experience a more intense, more "natural nature" that is no longer part of daily life. All that is left in the contemporary American West, as the line from *Urban Cowboy* (1980) to *Thelma and Louise* (1991) demonstrates, is a fallen world of male corruption and inadequacy, which can be escaped only in a stylized heroic death.

The lost natural innocence celebrated by the romantic poets as a reproach to industrial society has thus metamorphosed into a late-twentieth-century dream of renewing that innocence and thereby evading the twin nightmares of being swallowed up by either an unappreciated past or an unknown future. In this view, nature is the truth under appearances, the substantial, unalienable reality beneath the technological appliances. In the positive versions of the story, salvation comes out of the lower world like Rambo arising from underwater or Yoda coming out of the swamp. But the hand that pulls us back into the grave comes from the underworld as well.

We enter a nature film, as we enter a horror film, with the general expectation that what is warped or ignored in the "normal" world will return to exact its price. The horror film's fascination with the revenge taken on the present by a forgotten and ignored past, and its energetic preoccupation with the clash of the normal and the abnormal, accords well with the theme of a nature run amok because it has been obliterated and repressed. Jung's formulation seems particularly relevant here, since he uses *nature* to refer to the lowest level of our collective affinity—whatever links human beings in ways that replace or circumvent political and social connections. This irreducible, basic nature cannot be depended upon to correspond to anyone's particular desires; it designates all that cannot be controlled or manipulated, and in Jung's system is akin to the unconscious: "The unconscious was like nature, and like nature it could either help man or destroy him." [19]

On the level of popular culture, this Jekyll-and-Hyde view of nature is reflected in the symbiotic connection both to the western and to the horror films that, since the late 1960s (*Night of the Living Dead*, 1968) and early 1970s (*Texas Chainsaw Massacre*, 1974), have resurrected aspects of a genre that had seemed forever buried by Abbott and Costello's comic versions in the 1950s.[20] But horror at the moment does not seem as interesting a form as it was in the great days of early George Romero and Tobe Hooper. Although David Cronenberg and Wes Craven still maintain their originality, the importance of the horror film seems to be petering out culturally, especially in its generic impulse to trace virtually every moral lapse to a sexual origin. The fascination with the dead and the burden of a forgotten or despoiled past has become instead a preoccupation with saving that past in its purity as an emblem of what has been lost and should be restored. Horror films are notoriously susceptible to sequels, because the evil they represent can never really be defeated. In one aspect, nature films promise a renewal that need not be dramatized, or perhaps cannot be, because a closeness to nature implies that death itself is part of the cycle. But of course it is death that dramatizes the actual difference between the individual human life and the renewing natural cycle.

Two contrasting versions of this concern are Stephen King's novel and the film version of *Pet Sematary* (1989), and James Cameron's film *The Abyss* (1989). In *Pet Sematary* the message seems to be that the dead should be left alone. When they return resurrected, they are not as they were: something vital is missing. But then why did the ancient Micmac tribe of Maine have this magical power to raise the dead? Perhaps only when there was a vital relation to nature could natural magic be effective and death defeated. In our world, it produces only horror. In *The Abyss*, with its greater commitment to the benevolent side of technology, both hero and heroine must briefly drown, dying out of one life into a more fruitful one. *The Abyss* also contains another version of double ending. As so often happens at the end of utopian science fiction films, the imagined paradise, the goal of all understanding, is visually unconvincing. Here the alien spaceship that emerges triumphantly from the depths seems markedly artificial. A failure of production design perhaps. But on another level, this is also a trope of visual inadequacy: what image of utopia would be convincing? The truly utopian, the truly transcendent, cannot really be appreciated by the unenlightened vision of the audience, which has witnessed the story but has not yet experienced the grandeur.

*   *   *

The world of politics and public debate may seem very different from the world of myth and story that structures popular culture. But in this last decade of the twentieth century, the question of nature gives a freshly energizing force to both the perennial American distrust of politics and the nostalgia for an unconditioned, unalloyed past. In the history of American culture, that distrust has often been cast as an opposition between the political and the natural, empowering an assumption that politics is unnatural, self-seeking, pseudorational, and already tainted. The concept of nature therefore comes ready to hand as a standard by which to judge and a hammer to smash the unnatural impositions on the individual by social and political power.

Profoundly divided and even contradictory themes of nature as power and nature as victim permeate the films briefly surveyed here. When so many warring factions in a society each claim the sanction of nature as central to their political and imaginative concerns, it is clear that underlying their differences is a common sense of loss. So bereft, it thus makes practical sense to search for ceremonies of innocence that can restore the natural core of belief, in the world, in the country, and in the self. Oliver Sacks has written of the way in which individuals who have suffered the loss of brain functions renarrativize that absence, that lack, into a regenerated sense of self. As we near the end of the century, perhaps something similar has been occurring on the level of culture. In the imaginative life of the nation, whether that life is expressed in political activity or on movie screens, the ceremonies of innocence are constantly staged and restaged. Are we in control of science and technology, or are they in control of us? If the fundamental clash is between technology and nature, there's little difference between the debates over abortion, artificial life-support systems, or the use of steroids to enhance athletic performance. When similar questions were raised in the 1950s, one answer was rooted in the secular optimism that there was an innate benevolence in scientific progress, whereas another derived from the religious optimism that God would step in and right the balance if things were really to go wrong. But by the end of the century, these questions of authority and control are not open to such confident answers.

But technology in the service of industrial progress is much easier to justify than is technology in the service of creating what some consider an unnatural human body. In the 1960s, the body and nature were both seen positively; as in the drug culture, any experimentation was potentially life-affirming and expansive. The 1970s saw the growth in popularity of physical culture and "body work," jogging, dieting, and other efforts to control the body's potential excesses. But by the 1980s, despite the increase in health-food restaurants and gyms, the overriding metaphor was consumption rather than growth, an all-encompassing greed rather than a path. The preoccupation with the body became darker; the relation between the human and the natural became more vexed. Instead of intensifying and liberating, technology, especially as it applied to the body, was seen as organizing and repressive. The suspicion across the political spectrum, the suspicion that so many of these films draw upon, was that technology is neither art nor science—only a morally vacant urge to greater profits and power.

To what extent, say, does medical technology enhance life and to what extent does it illegitimately warp or distort life processes? We retain a residual Enlightenment belief that technology and science can save an otherwise attacked and debilitated nature. Through organ transplants or surrogate mothering or cryogenics, medicine promises a resurrection or an extension of the body unknown to the past. But in that promise also lies the nightmare. In the gloomier film versions of this preoccupation (*Robocop, Aliens,* and *Terminator*) the entire body threatens to become a kind of prosthesis, the only way to survive in a world of violence and death. The potential for abuse in the modification of the natural body has thus engendered cinematic images of the robot and the replicant, envisioning a future in which our frail flesh will be preserved only by an indestructible carapace (*Robocop, Aliens*) or by artificial human beings who do our dirty work for us (*Terminator, Terminator 2*). Nature, which was to be our salvation, seems unable to help us. Or perhaps it is that we have crippled her too much for any help to be forthcoming. One pervasive image is that of Karen Quinlan, kept alive by IV-drips and a respirator; another is Robocop, the melancholic cyborg, with only a dim memory of his formerly human nature.

Along with these expanded medical and scientific possibilities comes

The Terminator, James Cameron. © Orion, 1984.

the inescapable question of whether such refined powers of resurrection are desirable. Many contemporary horror films, inflected by the genre of nature, supplant the vitality and renewal of nature with images of its decay, mess, and rottenness. Like living wills, such films are a response to a medicine that now has the power to keep the body alive long past the death of any recognizable self—all in the name of scientific progress. By romanticizing the afterlife, by exploring the limbo between life and death, other films try to purge the pervasive cultural fear of being put into a situation in which you may not know whether you're dead or alive. The optimism of *Ghost* or even *Flatliners*, as well as the many films in which angels make an appearance, transforms the boundary between life and death into an area of exploration, a place where magical, scientific, or spiritual knowledge may lead to more rather than less control. Like genetic engineering, they promise the chance to rebegin ourselves, as a race if not as individuals.

The frailty of the body and what to do about it also underlies legal, moral, and emotional attitudes toward child abuse. Because of the continuing debates over the evidence offered by the children, parents, and psychological experts on both sides, it is hard to say to what extent the

The Terminator (Arnold Schwarzenegger). *Terminator 2: Judgment Day*, James Cameron. © Guild, 1991.

preoccupation with child abuse that peaked in the late 1980s is an instance of a society waking up to a real problem, and to what extent it is rooted in cultural myths of a polluted nature and a corrupted innocence. But the language of the accusations is certainly suffused by a sense of an innocence molested and polluted, often in tandem with a postulation that in everyone's past is a dysfunctional family from which the "inner child" must be rescued. Such language draws so powerfully on cultural myths that many cases seem to be tried on the principle that the charges of abuse *ought* to be true, and that it is the defendants who must prove otherwise.

Metaphors of molestation and corruption are a common language by which partisans defend whatever they suspect is in danger of corruption. These metaphors become pervasive when suspicions about power are extended to all forms of authority. Reaganism was successful in the 1980s partly because it tapped into a fear across the political spectrum of the many ways the innocent individual could be molested by evil paternalistic forces. This was as much an issue for the Right (for example, bearing arms) as for the Left (for example, choice in abortion). Reagan's rhetorical claim to have removed the effects of government intervention by neofederalist politics implied that at least the malignant forms of paternalism had been defeated. Yet, at the same time, he and Interior Secretary James Watt fully supported business intervention in the environment, and were roundly opposed by environmentalists, who were protecting *their* innocent world.

In the cinematic subtexts of these controversies, the assumption that adults naturally have the best interests of children at heart has failed utterly. The child in *The Fury* (1978), for example, is pursued by a secret CIA-like group who wants to subject its powers to scientific experiment, corrupting them into tools of political domination, and the mermaid in *Splash* must escape from a covey of scientists and government agents. Similarly, in *Firestarter* (1984), the good father is characterized as a gently ineffectual child of the sixties, whereas the evil father is a Vietnam vet Native American who wants to kill the little girl so that he can absorb her power. This essentially brutal character typically remains somewhat sympathetic because he wants the child's secret for his own magical uses, scorning the government effort to turn it into a scientific weapon.

Uniting the partisan political arguments about these issues is the perception that the modern world is filled with forces that rob the individual of a natural innocence identified with personal freedom. The conflicting definitions of that innocence proposed by the Right and the Left are directly tied to their different definitions of will. For the prolife groups, will is a principle of limit, equivalent to self-control and subordination to proper authority. For the prochoice groups, will is a principle of expansiveness, equivalent to self-expression and self-determination.[21] The moral arguments for both prolife and prochoice may differ in their definition of human nature, particularly in the prolife emphasis on self-sacrifice, and the prochoice emphasis on self-realization. But both feel that the moral sense that used to unite nature and science has been lost. They thus disagree in their opinions but agree in the emotional language by which they frame their central questions. A crucial issue for both sides is what behavior is assigned to the order of individual rights, what to the order of governmental-societal action, and what to the order of spiritual imperative.[22] AIDS, for instance, is often perceived by the Right not as a disease or a social problem, but either as an indication that nature has betrayed the human race or that homosexuals are unnatural and therefore deserve nature's punishment. In such a climate, it is no wonder that defenses of homosexuality must also take the "natural" route, arguing that it is genetically determined or, in recent findings, traceable to physical structures in the brain.

Once again, the films of nature offer an alternative way of comprehending these cultural antagonisms, through imagery and stories paradoxically far more precise and self-aware than they are in their more overtly political and social guises. The indomitable barrier to salvation in many of the films of nature is not science itself but a misguided effort (of which science is only the most obvious example) to investigate and analyze the entire universe in order to discover a saving secret. Perhaps, goes the false assumption of the misguided scientists and bureaucrats, some new phenomenon, some new process, some new piece of equipment will point the way to the truth. But as these films indicate so clearly, the phenomenon that science and technology fruitlessly seek to control is innocence, which can never open its secrets, because *telling* isn't what it does. Innocence just *is*. You either have it or you don't.

*　　*　　*

Vital questions in the life of a society or culture rarely vanish entirely. When no one cares about them with the old emotional intensity, they go underground, only to emerge, sometimes decades later, in different forms. The analytic media—along with interpretation of all types—enjoin us to pay strict attention to certain issues and winnow their truths by argument and reason—or at least by reasons. But the media of the imagination have a very different agenda. The films of nature surveyed here suggest in particular that beneath immediate political conflicts we share common imagery and preoccupations; in Edward Hall's terminology, low-context (seemingly more rational and explicit) politics subsists on an aquifer of high-context (more intuitive and implicit) popular culture.

Imaginative works, even those in popular culture, can take the measure of cultural issues with perhaps more insight than do journalists or politicians. But they rarely resolve, on the level of reason, action, or political program, the conflicts they have mythically resolved on the level of story and character. The age-old questions they raise change and mutate, as the awareness of the audience changes. The mermaid in *Splash*, like the innocent Chauncey Gardener in *Being There*, learns language from television, but perhaps like Caliban, only to curse. Whether this shared context also implies shared values is doubtful. Communications may not have broken down, but coherence has, and the global village has succeeded only in making everyone feel more isolated. Within the groups who read and interpret as a matter of training and profession, this skepticism about language corresponds to the difficulty of knowing whether you have read the right things or the anxiety over taping shows you never get a chance to see, because you ought to see them.

The process I am suggesting is neither Aristotelian purgation nor fin de siècle boredom but a seepage between the audience's public life and its imaginative life. Consciousness is rarely altered as much by unambiguous exhortation as by a persuasive retelling of stories.

As the end of this century approaches, two thousand years or so after a revelation of innocence that undergirds and sponsors the religious beliefs of a good portion of the world, we still face the difficulty of deciding what innocence is—and what people or acts embody it. In part, our difficulty comes from another half-articulated assumption about innocence. In the Christian view, the intricacies (and ambiguities) of words are a result of the Fall, which disrupted the natural innocence of language (God speaking the world into being; Adam naming the animals). To convey the difference between language in Eden and language after the Fall, John Milton in *Paradise Lost* invokes the analogy between English words and their Latin roots. Thus, for example, the "Word" that in the Gospel of St. John creates the word he calls "infant," Latin for *unspeaking*.

But after the Fall, innocence has become essentially mute and cannot—perhaps ought not—argue for itself. From one point of view, then, the work to establish meaning has come into the world along with other forms of labor. But from another, the difficulties of making meaning are ignored entirely: Why learn about complicated issues, why consider the points of view of others, if only the naturally innocent response is valuable? In *Clan of the Cave Bear*, the Cro-Magnon heroine at first assumes that verbal ability means complexity and humanness, and that the almost nonexistent spoken language of the Neanderthal tribe that has taken her in is evidence of their barbarism. But she gradually acquires the nonverbal knowledge that her own tribe's movement into language has obliterated—the group consciousness of the tribe and the connection with natural magic of her adoptive mother.[23]

The postulation of an unreadable innocence that can only be appreciated but never explained is a reflection of the acute problem American culture now faces of knowing what to read and how to read it. The best legacy of the 1960s, in the mainstream as much as the counterculture, was to break down in a salutary way the assumption that there is only one hierarchy and one way of looking at things. But our reward thus far has been not variety and fruitfulness so much as confusion and a retreat to paranoid visions of singularity. In so many political arguments these days, it is more important to be sincere than to be right. In fact, it is assumed that to be sincere *is* to be right. There is no need to persuade anyone else, no assumption that argument and consensus and even politics itself has a point, only the desire to stand out as a beacon in one's natural sincerity and innocence.

With widely differing political goals, groups and individuals have for the last decade and more looked into nature and seen an innocence that needs protection. But they rarely see a complex power in both the language and reality of nature that needs understanding in its diversity and contradiction. Much of 1960s polemic argued that the political should be infused with the personal. But this insight has now become a rallying cry for purists in all parts of the political spectrum, who assume that there is no difference between the personal and the political, no vital reciprocity between individual desires and group goals. The great combat of our age is not between differing political and economic theories so much as it is between those who think that the opposite of purity is impurity and those who think that the opposite of variety is rigidity. To identify nature with innocence and purity is to create a particularly suffocating fiction. Difficult as it is for Americans to believe because we are conditioned to give a moral interpretation to everything, nature is both other and us, part of the web, neither moralistic nor moralizable.

Looking at the range of films about nature, it isn't hard to appreciate how so many partisans on opposing sides of political issues all insensibly feel the need for a return to basics. The problem with most of their approaches, as the films of nature make clear, is that they rarely understand how their quests are reflected in the quests of others, who otherwise seem unlike them—and how those "basics" are themselves the product of historical attitudes and cultural urges. These issues have a particular immediacy now because much of the current preoccupation with nature and innocence focuses on the effort to begin again, to restart time. Even though the Cold War is over, Americans, as a nation and as individuals, still cling to the habit of being defined solely by our enemies. But is the only choice between a debilitating individualism on the one hand and a patriarchal ineptness on the other, with criminality evenly distributed on all sides?

Every day, we watch the erosion of the eighteenth-century idea that nature could be controlled to man's benefit. But nature's other face has always been the unmediated and undefinable—both beyond and superior to human control. These films of nature constitute not a clearly delineated genre with a catalogue of recognizable motifs and themes so much as a metagenre that seeks to transcend generic confines in order to seek salvation in realms far away from the rational and orderly, realms that have more in common with the energetic and form-questioning role of both the primitive and the innovative in popular culture itself. The urge to nature as a response to moral and cultural disarray has a long history, and the resurrection of primitive forms often characterizes periods in which elite answers and their languages are perceived as worn out. With their dystopian gloom or utopian optimism, these films similarly assert the need for a reconnection to what is vital in nature in order that we might escape from the dilemmas history has forced upon us. Whether their settings are the primitive world of the past, the natural world of the present, or the unexplored world of the future, their common impulse is to begin again, to have a second chance at creation.

Notes

This article is an expanded and revised version of "Ceremonies of Innocence," which was first published in *Raritan* 13, no. 4 (1994).

1. This approach contrasts sharply with those critics who would see in genre film a continual restatement of a certain number of fixed formal characteristics

whose social implications are necessarily conservative. Thomas Sobchack, for example, takes the Aristotelian view that genre presents "the experience of an ordered world" with "general conclusions that have stood the test of time" and thereby constitute a "ritual of reaffirmation of group values"; Sobchack, "Genre Film: A Classical Experience," *Film Genre Reader*, ed. Barry Keith Grant (1975; Austin: University of Texas Press, 1986), 102, 103, 109. Judith Hess Wright similarly argues that genre films have been successful "because they temporarily relieved the fears aroused by a recognition of social and political conflicts . . . [and] helped to discourage any action"; Wright, "Genre Films and the Status Quo" [1974], in Grant, *Film Genre Reader*, 41.

The cataloguing of formula and the emphasis on intertextual repetition has been a characteristic of genre criticism since the classical rhetoricians. But as Alastair Fowler points out, "the character of genres is that they change. Only variations or modifications of convention have literary [or any critical] significance. . . . When we try to decide the genre of a work . . . our aim is to discover its meaning"; Fowler, *Kinds of Literature: An Introduction to the Theory of Genres and Modes* (Cambridge: Harvard University Press, 1982), 18, 38. As I argue, meaning resides not only in the classificatory history of the genre but also in its emphasis on the rooting of genre in ideological contradictions. Robin Wood's "Ideology, Genre, Auteur" (1977) (also included in Grant, *Film Genre Reader*) represents another strain in genre criticism, to which my approach is more allied.

2. For a work long on the statistics of how Hollywood came to dominate the world market but short on why (while it assumes that how equals why), see Kristin Thompson, *Exporting Entertainment: America in the World Film Market, 1907–1934* (London: BFI, 1985). It's clear enough that *choice* or *freedom* is the wrong term when in fact there is little alternative. But when did such absolute freedom or choice ever exist? Non-English speaking immigrants in urban areas placed moviegoing among their priorities along with sports and other similarly inexpensive leisure activities. Theorists such as Theodor Adorno who emphasize the top-down "administration" of popular culture by hidden agendas in smoke-filled rooms, ignore the extent to which audience choice actually functions in the long-run life of stories. Stuart Hall's commentaries on Gramsci are one important effort to perceive how much of cultural reality is ignored by the assumption that hegemony is exclusively monolithic and top-down. See, for example, "Gramsci's Relevance for the Study of Race and Ethnicity," *Journal of Communication Inquiry* 10, no. 2 (1986): 5–27.

3. "While a linguistic code can be analyzed on some levels independent of context . . . *in real life the code, the context, and the meaning can only be seen as different aspects of a single event.* . . . A high-context (HC) communication or message is one in which most of the information is either in the physical context or internalized in the person, while little is in the coded, explicit, transmitted part of the message. A low-context (LC) communication is just the opposite; i.e., the mass of information is vested in the explicit code." Edward T. Hall, *Beyond Culture* (New York: Doubleday, 1976), 79.

4. As I suggest here, Hall's high context versus low context polarity needs at the very least a more dynamic third term to account for the many ways cultures actually impinge on each other. Where do we draw the line between one cul-

ture's imperialism and another's co-optation? Economic dependence clearly has a crucial role to play. But, like children who prefer the boxes to the presents they contain, cultures also take what they want from the worlds outside them. Whatever their professed or hidden motives, they are still in great part members of each other's audiences. For an intriguing case study of this process that criticizes, among others, Jean Baudrillard's view of American cultural imperialism, see Mary Yoko Brannen, "'Bwana Mickey': Constructing Cultural Consumption at Tokyo Disneyland," in *Re-Made in Japan: Everyday Life and Consumer Taste in a Changing Society,* ed. Joseph J. Tobin (New Haven: Yale University Press, 1992).

5. Bakhtin's concept of heteroglossia is obviously relevant here, although he rarely considers the constructive (rather than the dialogic or disruptive) aspect of his texts. M. M. Bakhtin, *The Dialogic Imagination,* ed. Michael Holquist, trans. Caryl Emerson and Michael Holquist (Austin: University of Texas Press, 1981). See also Rick Altman's attack on the way theory has too often disenfranchised "parallel," paradigmatic, and often unresolved structures in favor of narrative linearity and closure, "Dickens, Griffith and Film Theory Today," *South Atlantic Quarterly* 88 (spring 1989): 321–59.

6. Arthur O. Lovejoy, "'Nature' as Aesthetic Norm," in *Essays in the History of Ideas* (Oxford: Oxford University Press, 1948), 69–77. The sociobiologist Edward O. Wilson has argued that the human desire to connect with the rest of the natural world is genetically based and becomes increasingly fragile with the rise of urbanism. See Wilson, *Biophilia* (Cambridge: Harvard University Press, 1984), and Stephen R. Kellert and Edward O. Wilson, eds., *The Biophilia Hypothesis* (Washington, DC: Island, 1993).

7. In *The Secular Scripture: A Study of the Structure of Romance* (Cambridge: Harvard University Press, 1977), Northrop Frye rejects the exclusive association of *primitive* with *early* or *before* and argues that it is "a quality in literature which emerges recurrently as an aspect of the popular and as indicating also that certain conventions have been exhausted" (29). In his usual way, Frye makes the literary manifestation not just primary but virtually exclusive: "In Homeric conditions of life—that is, the conditions assumed in the literary conventions adopted by the Homeric poems" (69). But a reading more attentive to the vagaries of cultural history also seems possible.

8. An intriguing allusion to this tradition appears in the dreadlocks of the monster alien in *Predator* (1987) and may explain the strange metamorphosis by which the setting of *Predator 2* (1991) has changed from the jungle to the city, and the hero from the muscled commando Arnold Schwarzenegger to the harassed black cop Danny Glover.

9. Jerome Bruner, *Actual Minds, Possible Worlds* (Cambridge: Harvard University Press, 1986). *A Brief History of Time* (1992), the documentary about Hawking directed by Errol Morris, is a good example of this mythologization process. Hawking's own speculations test the boundaries between science and theology, and his theological views were reportedly one of the causes of the breakup of his marriage, an aspect of his life repressed by the film, just as it represses his subsequent relationship with the wife of the man who devised his computerized speaking system. Compare also the effort to link science, especially astronomy, with a kind of spiritual awe in Carl Sagan's *Cosmos* series.

10. George Lucas has frequently referred to his indebtedness to Joseph Campbell's writings on myth and was the host at his Skywalker Ranch to the Moyers-Campbell interviews.

11. It would be interesting to establish a genre continuum in terms of the relative uneasiness with which the audience accepts the "separate peace" of the characters. Musicals may be at the less disruptive end, with their generic commitment to the belief that everything can be resolved on-stage (wonderfully parodied in Lubitsch's *To Be or Not To Be*, 1942). Film noir would be close by because it so often sees the social world entirely as a personal projection. The more history a western tries to include, however, the more its resolutions are obviously only personal. And, at the other extreme of the continuum, horror foregrounds the contrast sharply: you may think you're safe, but how do you know the monster is dead? The sequelization of monster films in the 1930s made this obvious to fans, but it is only with the 1970s and 1980s that the monster's return itself becomes part of the original film, especially in the hand-from-the-grave trope of films like *Carrie* (1976).

12. Theorists such as Fredric Jameson have claimed that national consciousness has been superseded by international economic and media structures. But the genre of nature, even as it may appeal to groups of many different national origins, has a high degree of national specificity in its engagement with issues, images, and language that have been present in the discourse of America for centuries. To the extent, say, that European opinion has lagged behind American in its sensitivity to issues such as environmentalism, some of these films could be "portable" into a European context. The metaphor of innocence, however, may still remain a particularly American take on the inner meaning of these issues. In an analysis more attuned to contradictions, Thomas Schatz emphasizes that "cultural specificity . . . is actually vital to any mythic structure" and cites Lévi-Strauss's invocation of "the common conceptual world" within which "contrasts and correlations" are manipulated; Schatz, "New Directions in Film Genre Study: The Structural Influence," in Grant, *Film Genre Reader*, 97.

13. See Eric Hobsbawm and Terence Ranger, eds., *The Invention of Tradition* (New York: Cambridge University Press, 1983).

14. The western's relation to real history has always been problematic, and in the heat or ignorance of polemic it's easy to forget the number of films that don't fit the stereotype or that play against it. Reviewers trumpeted the newfound "homoerotic" side of the relationship between Doc Holliday and Wyatt Earp in *Tombstone*, as if no one had ever seen *My Darling Clementine* (1946) or the intriguingly displaced *Warlock* (1959), where Henry Fonda is once again the object of affection.

15. To the extent that the western still had vitality in the 1980s, it was often in Australian films, where the national experience retained the animating spirit of an older, purer, freer community, like nineteenth-century America. I break my purposefully nonauteurist orientation in this essay for a moment to mention the interesting example of Fred Schepisi, who made *The Chant of Jimmy Blacksmith* (1978), an Australian analogue to *Tell Them Willie Boy Is Here* (1969), and later directed *Iceman* (1984) and *Black Robe* (1991). His submergence in the primitive is an intriguing complement to both George Miller's *Mad Max* series, which sets the primitive world not at the beginning of history but at the end and

defines it not as innocence but as ultimate corruption, as well as to Peter Weir's preoccupation in films such as *Picnic at Hanging Rock* (1975) and *The Last Wave* (1977) with the eruptive natural world just below the everyday surface.

It remains to be seen whether the effort to recreate a western genre, rather than a handful of films, will succeed despite the box-office failures of *Wyatt Earp, Bad Girls, Posse,* and so on.

16. A classic effort to bring together the internal view of genre with its re-curring elements and the external view of their mutation and evolution is Rick Altman's "A Semantic/Syntactic Approach to Film Genre," in Grant, *Film Genre Reader,* 26–40, whose terminology derives from a linguistic model, even though Altman concludes that syntax and semantics meet in the spectator. Alt-man has more recently turned away from his earlier "film as language" emphasis to expand upon an audience-centered definition of genre. See "Dickens, Griffith and Film Theory Today," 321–59, as well as his essay in this volume.

17. Alastair Fowler points out that "[s]atire is the most problematic mode to the taxonomist, since it appears never to have corresponded to any one kind" (*Kinds of Literature,* 110). Kinds, he argues, tend to be nouns, while modes are adjectival. Kind has "a distinctive *representational aspect* . . . characterized by an *external structure*" (60) with specific elements, whereas mode employs only "an incomplete repertoire" (108). But mode, although painted with broader strokes, is still inflected by history: "even modes are subject to mutability and become obsolete when the values they enshrine, or the hometowns they evoke, grow alien" (111).

18. Donna J. Haraway has attempted to turn some of these polarities on their heads by arguing for a renewal of nature through technology. See *Simians, Cy-borgs, and Women: The Reinvention of Nature* (New York: Routledge, 1991), es-pecially "A Cyborg Manifesto: Science, Technology, and Socialist-Feminism in the Late Twentieth Century," 149–182. John E. Mack points out in *Abduction: Human Encounters with Aliens* (New York: Scribner's, 1994) that, aside from their sexual interest in earthlings, many of the alleged aliens who have visited Earth are most concerned to lecture their captive audiences on environmental-ism. But in films thus far, these elements seem less compatible. The abrupt ap-pearance of a lush natural landscape through which Deckard (Harrison Ford) and Rachael (Sean Young) drive in the final scene of *Blade Runner* is almost comically out of place after the dystopian world of the rest of the film. As Paul M. Sammon points out, this scene was shot after preview audiences were confused about Ridley Scott's original ending—in which elevator doors close on the couple—restored in the "Director's Cut." See Sammon, "Do Androids Dream of Unicorns?: The 7 Faces of *Blade Runner,*" *Video Watchdog* 20 (November-December 1993): 32–59. Sammon also adds the appealing information that some of the footage consists of aerial shots discarded from *The Shining.*

19. Aniela Jaffe, *From the Life and Work of C. G. Jung,* trans. R. F. C. Hull (New York: Harper, 1971), 21.

20. Nature as mode in the horror film has strong precedents in the 1950s, when technological and scientific tinkering with nature releases monsters in such different forms as *The Creature from the Black Lagoon, Them!,* and *God-zilla* (all 1954). Later transformations, with an increasingly realistic setting—and an inclination to blame the monstering on more than just the Bomb—

include *Frogs* (1972), *Swamp Thing* (1982), *Arachnophobia* (1990), and *Tremors* (1991).

21. The prochoice position, originally more traditionally liberal and looking to the state for intervention (when abortion was illegal), now more consistently argues that *no* outside force should determine a woman's choice of what to do with her body. The other political attitudes of the prolife forces are characterized by a resistance against all forms of government, summed up in the right to bear arms against the potential enemy (including an illegitimate government itself). Nevertheless, in the arguments over abortion, prolifers expect the state to reinforce the will of the father or husband as protector of the fetus and prime arbiter of woman's choice.

22. See, for example, the argument in Ronald M. Dworkin, *Life's Dominion: An Argument about Abortion, Euthanasia, and Individual Freedom* (New York: Knopf, 1993). It may make sense to say that, if one is prolife, one should also be in favor of welfare and an easy availability of contraceptives. But that logic is dependent on valuing relationships within a society and perceiving the connections between a group of socially pressing issues. Instead, partisans invoke a quasi-theological argument about what constitutes true obedience to nature. In this combat of purity and impurity, any appeal to the social realm of relative rather than absolute truths is by definition immoral.

23. Speaking specifically of melodramatic elements in nineteenth-century fiction, Peter Brooks in *The Melodramatic Imagination: Balzac, Henry James, Melodrama, and the Mode of Excess* (New Haven: Yale University Press, 1976) explores the concept of a "text of muteness" as a way of understanding the narrative situation in which virtue and innocence must be revealed without speaking for themselves. His comments have a particular saliency for the ordeals of innocence staged so frequently in American silent films. This theme of beset innocence certainly does ally the films of nature with melodrama, to the extent that we see nature itself in these films as the beset and inarticulate victim, for whom the films have to fashion a voice. Once again, Jung's desire to reserve an area within the self and the world that resists articulation is more intriguing here than Freud or Lacan's view that even the unconscious resembles a language that must feel the impact of culture. For Jung, once the unconscious speaks, it is no longer the unconscious—a formulation that usefully corresponds to the way the nature film so frequently foregrounds the inarticulateness of the innocence it interrogates.

Notes on Contributors

Rick Altman is Professor of French and Communication Studies at the University of Iowa. His early semiotics-inspired work spawned a number of influential semiotics-inspired genre-study dissertations (Tom Schatz, Jane Feuer, Jim Collins) and two of his own books: *Genre: The Musical* and *The American Film Musical*. Currently, he is working on a book entitled *Doing Things with Genre*, which develops a discursive, reception-oriented genre theory.

Leo Braudy is Bing Professor of English at the University of Southern California. He is the author most recently of *The Frenzy of Renown: Fame and Its History* and *Native Informant: Essays on Film, Fiction, and Popular Culture*. His other books include *Narrative Form in History and Fiction: Hume, Fielding, and Gibbon*; *Jean Renoir: The World of His Films*; and *The World in a Frame: What We See in Films*. He has edited anthologies dealing with Norman Mailer and François Truffaut, was the coeditor with Morris Dickstein of *Great Film Directors*, and with Marshall Cohen coedited the fourth edition of *Film Theory and Criticism*.

Nick Browne is Professor of Film and Television Studies at UCLA. He is the author of *The Rhetoric of Filmic Narration*, and *Film Theory: An Historical and Critical Perspective* (in Chinese) and is editor of *The Politics of Representation: Perspectives from Cahiers du Cinema, American Television: History and Theory*, and coeditor of *New Chinese Cinemas: Forms, Identities, Politics*. He served as convener of the seminar.

Carol J. Clover is Professor in the Departments of Scandinavian and Rhetoric at the University of California, Berkeley. She is the author of *Men, Women, and Chain Saws: Gender in the Modern Horror Film* and *Old Norse-Icelandic Literature: A Critical Guide*, as well as numerous other books and journal articles.

George Lipsitz is Professor of Ethnic Studies at the University of California, San Diego. He is the author of *Rainbow at Midnight: Labor and Culture in the 1940s, Dangerous Crossroads: Popular Music, Postmodernism and the Poetics of Place, The Sidewalks of St. Louis, Time Passages: Collective Memory and American Popular Culture,* and *A Life in the Struggle: Ivory Perry and the Culture of Opposition.*

Michael Rogin teaches political science at the University of California, Berkeley. His most recent books are *Subversive Genealogy: The Politics and Art of Herman Melville,* and *Ronald Reagan, the Movie and Other Episodes in Political Demonology.* The present essay forms part of his recently published book from the University of California Press, *Blackface, White Noise: Jewish Immigrants in the Hollywood Melting Pot.*

David J. Russell was a Ph.D. student in film studies at UCLA. He recently completed his dissertation on the modern horror movie genre, "Parts of Darkness: A Rescue of the Modern Horror Film Genre through a Classification of Its Monster Characters," and is teaching film history at the University of Southern California.

Thomas Schatz is Professor in the Department of Radio-Television-Film at the University of Texas, Austin. His publications include *The Genius of the System: Hollywood Filmmaking in the Studio Era* and *Hollywood Genres: Formulas, Filmmaking, and the Studio System.*

Vivian Sobchack is Professor of Critical Studies in the Department of Film and Television at UCLA. She is the author of *Screening Space: The American Science Fiction Film* and *The Address of the Eye: A Phenomenology of Film Experience,* as well as of numerous articles on film and visual culture that have appeared in journals such as *camera obscura, Representations,* and *Artforum.*

Linda Williams is Professor of Film Studies at the University of California, Irvine. Her most recent publications include *Hard Core: Power, Pleasure, and the Frenzy of the Visible* and *Viewing Positions: Ways of Seeing Film.*

Index

Compositor: G & S Typesetters, Inc.
Text: Galliard
Display: Galliard
Printer and Binder: Malloy